The Heirloom Tomato

THE *Heirloom* TOMATO

From Garden to Table

RECIPES, PORTRAITS, AND HISTORY
OF THE WORLD'S MOST BEAUTIFUL FRUIT

Amy Goldman

PHOTOGRAPHS BY Victor Schrager

BLOOMSBURY

For my family

Contents

preface

BY CARY FOWLER, PH.D.

EXECUTIVE DIRECTOR, GLOBAL CROP DIVERSITY TRUST

With the possible exception of the apple, there is no food crop in North America or Europe more evocative, more capable of stirring passions and memories, than the tomato. This is odd in a sense, because the tomato has a relatively short history on both continents.

Wild forms are found in a narrow band along the western coast of South America. Unlike most cultivated crops, however, the tomato was not domesticated where its wild botanical relatives are endemic, but instead was most likely first "tamed" in the Vera Cruz–Puebla area of Mexico. Tomatoes made their first journey to Europe in the early 1500s, as part of what historians call the Columbian Exchange, wherein the crops of the New World (corn, potato, beans, cacao) sailed eastward, while crops from Europe, Africa, the Near East, and Asia (wheat, barley, oats, sorghum, banana, onion) headed west. Later, before the Revolutionary War, the tomato made a return voyage and slowly became established as a food crop in the United States.

Hundreds of years of cultivation in distinct environments around the world gave rise to thousands of distinct tomato varieties, varieties selected, bred, and conserved by many generations of our ancestors—and by contemporaries such as the author of this book. In *The Heirloom Tomato*, Goldman picks up and enriches a scientific and literary tradition of varietal descriptions, interrupted for the better part of a century as fascination with "modern" varieties displaced interest in the many wonderful heirloom varieties grown by stubborn and discerning gardeners and farmers.

Goldman's collaboration with Victor Schrager, who contributes hundreds of exquisite photographs, is a treasure. One doesn't have to be a gardening nerd or agricultural historian to appreciate their accomplishment. One simply has to thumb through *The Heirloom Tomato* to discover its bounty. And the varieties listed here still exist!

The diversity in *The Heirloom Tomato* is important in many ways. At the most basic level, diversity is the biological foundation for the directed evolution of a crop. It is a genetic resource used by farmers and by scientists engaged in the development of new tomato varieties, creating plants that are better adapted to new climates or to pests or diseases that have mutated and thus acquired the ability to mount a better attack. Diversity provides evolutionary options. Without it, the crop is at the end of its noose.

We can appreciate the utility of diversity, whether we are farmers, consumers, scientists, or businesspeople. But there are so many additional ways to value it—for its beauty, for the spice it adds to life, for its contribution to the culinary traditions of a broad range of cultures, for the important role it has played in history, art, and economic life. Our appreciation may be at a distance, or it might be through cultivating the heirloom varieties ourselves.

As a board member at the New York Botanical Garden and chair of the board of the Seed Savers Exchange (www.seedsavers.org), the largest organization of such devotees in the world, Amy Goldman works tirelessly to preserve that diversity. And her engagement with tomatoes goes far beyond just writing about

Big Ben (page ii); Aunt Ruby's German Green (opposite)

them—as well it must if the varieties so lovingly portrayed in this book are to be around for future generations to use and enjoy.

Crop diversity is threatened from all directions. It can be lost when a farming or gardening family "breaks the chain" by giving up the practice of selecting, saving, and replanting seeds of a unique variety. Changing tastes and replacement of older varieties by newer ones can lead to the loss of distinct varieties and the knowledge associated with them. And in gene banks, mismanagement, equipment failures, natural disasters, and funding shortages take their toll.

How, then, can we ensure that these wonderful varieties do not go the way of the dinosaurs and the dodo? In a world of changes—climatic and otherwise—our own survival and well-being could easily come to depend on whether we can answer this question. Fortunately, a plan is taking shape. In the same year as the publication of this book, the Svalbard Global Seed Vault opens its doors. Located at 78 degrees north, far above mainland Norway, the Seed Vault aims to provide an ultimate safety net for gene banks conserving different crop varieties. Three vault rooms, with a total capacity of 4.5 million samples (averaging 500 seeds each), have been fashioned inside a mountain, down a 125-yard tunnel chiseled out of solid stone. Naturally cold already, the Seed Vault is further cooled to below -2 degrees Fahrenheit. At this temperature, seeds can be stored safely for decades. The Seed Vault thus holds out the promise that together with other elements of a global conservation system, we might put an end to the extinction of crop varieties and associated loss of genetic diversity.

Thanks in part to Amy Goldman's book, hundreds of heirloom tomato varieties may also now be grown by an increasing number of gardeners and farmers. Seeds of these varieties can, for the most part, be found in the Seed Savers Exchange's seed bank in Iowa (and through its network of gardeners), as well as in some government collections. The Seed Savers Exchange will deposit seeds of these varieties in the Svalbard Global Seed Vault. Through these efforts, virtually all the varieties in this book can look forward to a long, long life. Many other varieties, equally interesting and valuable, may not be so lucky, unless we act now to ensure their continued survival. We are in the midst of a mass extinction event in agriculture, at precisely a moment in history when diversity for further adaptation is most needed. The very traits that a species will need tomorrow to survive and thrive could be lost today. Their future is in our hands; as Sir Otto Frankel, one of the early pioneers of conservation, once put it, "we have acquired evolutionary responsibility." A humbling thought.

In the end, *The Heirloom Tomato*—a great reference work, a valuable history, a useful guide, and an inspiring and beautiful tribute—serves as a wake-up call for what might be lost if we fail to meet our responsibilities, and what will be gained if we do. It is not too late.

specimen days

BY VICTOR SCHRAGER

Amy Goldman wants to feed the world. But before she attends to the issues of seed saving, biodiversity, and Third World agro-independence, she wants to beguile you with the beauty, taste, and fascinating histories of the plants to which she is so passionately devoted.

I, on the other hand, tend to think more locally, and for thirty years have concerned myself mainly with the making of still-life photographs. I continue to be intrigued and fulfilled by the range of pictures that can be pulled out of the small parcel of space in front of my camera. The results of positioning objects in this space, playing sharp edges against soft, and organizing planes and clouds of color mean the world to me.

Amy first contacted me in the spring of 2000, calling up to ask if I would be interested in collaborating with her on a book of a hundred varieties of heirloom melons. After some thought, I went to visit her at her Rhinebeck farm with a pile of dog-eared books of medieval illuminated manuscripts, Dutch flower paintings, still lifes by the Peale brothers, and nineteenth-century theorems. I also brought along photographs by Charles Jones, Karl Blossfeldt, Edward Weston, and Irving Penn, and glossaries of fruits and vegetables from *Martha Stewart Living*. If we were to take on a 1,500-year tradition of botanical art and illustration, we would want to acknowledge all these beloved antecedents, then bring our own modern sensibilities to bear.

Amy, characteristically, took all this in and gave a big-picture answer: Yes, this is what we should do; these references animate this world we love. (Then she showed me her own stockpile of inspiration—a stack of books and prints that was astonishingly similar to mine.)

So we began. I put a board across two sawhorses in a barn 50 yards from the garden, set up my wooden Deardorff view camera, and started to work. It was the first day of what turned out to be an eight-year field trip, photographing and responding to the voluptuous and delicious particularities of more than nine hundred varieties of melons, squashes, and now tomatoes.

On August and September days, when the fruit was coming in ripe, I would come to our studio by the garden. Amy would harvest the specimens and use a kitchen knife (or machete!) to see what delights were inside. We would taste them and pronounce them fabulous or fit only for the local pigs, and I would go inside and, again and again, try to come up with a collaboration of shapes and colors that both described them and celebrated them. If the specimens looked their best, were true to form, and would be informative to plant scientists and growers, Amy would say, "Fine."

With melons, there was a wonderful interplay between the outer surfaces and the glorious, often unexpected, color inside. The squashes were more consistent inside (and usually in need of cooking), so I concentrated on the varied outside surfaces and markings, warts and all. And the tomatoes, ranging in size from pearl to softball, were smooth and striped, some taut like balloons, some like corrugated hearts, all expressing in flavor, color, or other dimensions the diversity of their genes.

These days were long and deeply satisfying. Working alongside Amy, so quietly, unhurriedly immersed in this ancient enterprise, was for me a unique and extravagant pleasure.

Red Cup

introduction

Tomatoes and I go way back. You might even say they're in my blood. When I was a teenager, my parents bought a home on the North Shore of Long Island. Off in a forgotten corner of the property was a drafty old greenhouse (minus half of its glass), a mysterious relic that no one but me cared much about—until I started producing tomato plants there. The structure stood on a rise, steps away from an abandoned garden. Later, I would plant an orchard on one side and grapes on the other, reclaiming the land and building. As a girl, though, I was captivated by the greenhouse just the way it was: the spooky coal room and furnace, the nifty trapdoor, and the floor-to-ceiling stacks of vintage unglazed terra-cotta pots. These empty vessels—embodiments of gardens past—seemed as if they were just waiting for me to fill them with new life.

That first spring, after buying some books on vegetable gardening and seeking some words of advice from an experienced neighbor, I filled wooden flats with a mix of potting soil and vermiculite and planted my first tomato seeds. After the seedlings had acquired their first set of true leaves, I transferred them to those terra-cotta pots. My peroxided hair stuffed under a straw hat, I transplanted my seedlings into the garden. Later, on summer weekends, my father, Sol, would park himself in an Adirondack chair between the greenhouse and the garden to read the newspapers. He managed to keep a watchful eye on the harvest, as if he were still manning the cash register in Goldman's Italian-American, his family's Brooklyn grocery store, where he'd helped out since he was five. When I walked by with a basket of tomatoes, he took a childlike glee in the vegetables I produced; I can still see him holding one of my tomatoes, sniffing it, squeezing it. Nothing made him happier than the fruits of the earth. My mother, Lillian, was also appreciative: She did wonders with my tomatoes in the kitchen. Her specialties were Hungarian goulash and stuffed peppers with tomato sauce, and I swear they tasted better with my homegrown tomatoes. Both my parents were, in their way, tomato experts. Long before I was born, they began importing *pelati* (whole peeled tomatoes in a can) from Italy for their grocery store. (Sixty years later, I named a tomato for the store, in honor of my parents; see page 130.) I'm convinced that we had pasta with marinara sauce every single day of my childhood.

But that's not my only family connection to tomatoes. Cousin Myrtle "Tillie" Lewis (née Ehrlich), who was related to both of my parents, was a giantess in the world food industry, the woman destined to be the "Queen of the Pear-Shaped Tomatoes." Tillie amazes me: Jewish girl makes good by introducing the San Marzano tomato (see page 137) as a successful commercial crop in the United States. Despite skepticism from agricultural experts, she succeeded in canning *pelati* and *concentrati* that rivaled Italy's best. Tillie earned her stripes in the food business by working with her first husband, Louis Weisberg, a wholesale grocer in Brooklyn. Weisberg was in partnership with Tillie's sister Bea and her husband, Samuel Hochheiser. Tillie was no farmer, but she knew a good thing when she ate it: *pomodori pelati*, imported from the fertile farmland near Naples. She became a purchasing agent for the business and made frequent trips to Italy.

On one of those trips, she met Florindo Del Gaizo, head of the Del Gaizo Distributing Company, the sales subsidiary of the largest canner in Italy. It was a family firm, and quite a family at that: Florindo's father, Senatore Luigi Del Gaizo, was president of the company, director of the Italian branch of the Bank of America, and head of Il Duce's Italian corporate state. Here's the official version of what happened next: Tillie and Florindo hatched a plan to raise and pack the San Marzano in the San Joaquin Valley of California. This filled a niche created when the United States slapped prohibitive duties on imported Italian canned tomatoes in 1934. The new company was named Flotill Products—the "Flo" for "Florindo" and the "Till" for "Tillie." A cannery was built and opened for business in 1935. It boasted state-of-the-art equipment such as Anderson-Barngrover continuous, atmospheric, agitating cookers and coolers, closing machines, and a repatriated Fred H. Knapp labeler. This was the start of something big: Flotill eventually became one of the world's largest canners. It produced not only tomatoes—some unpeeled during World War II, when there weren't enough hands on deck to skin the fruit—but also dozens of other products, such as halved peaches, whole apricots, fancy prunes, all-white asparagus spears, soups, meats, and innovative low-calorie foods.

There was more to the story, of course. Finally, my mother told me what the *Brooklyn Eagle*, *Reader's Digest*, and the *Stockton Record* never did: Tillie and Florindo had fallen madly in love. Mom led me to believe that Flo and Till had divorced their respective spouses and married each other, but that seems to be a whitewash. The pair were lovers for more than ten years, until Flo's death in 1937. The San Marzano is their love apple.

During the course of my tomato researches at the San Joaquin County Historical Society and Museum, after both my parents had died, I located ninety-year-old Arthur Heiser (formerly Hochheiser), Tillie's nephew and the long-serving president of Flotill; Arthur's daughter Barbara; and family friend and "Tillyophile" Kyle Tobin-Williams. They shared their pictures and stories with me and confirmed what I already knew. The photographs from the family album of Tillie and Florindo aboard transoceanic liners and relaxing in Monopoli, Italy, are images that I hold dear. One black-and-white photograph taken in 1926 is so endearing that I've made it my computer screen saver: Florindo and Tillie leaning against a marble balustrade near a lamppost, resting after an uphill climb, with the city of Florence in the background. They're fashionably dressed, he in a three-piece suit with bow tie and fedora, she in basic black with a cloche hat. They are obviously happy to be where they are. And their smiles light up the Italian landscape.

Every time I turn on my computer, I see the two of them smiling at me. Their happiness is contagious. I'm delighted to make their acquaintance and grateful to tomatoes for bringing us together. Tomatoes, in fact, have allowed me to take my place in a community of gardeners, seed savers, breeders, scholars, and seedsmen who care about tomatoes with a zeal that reminds me of my father's. My "friends across the miles" live all over the world: France, Italy, England, Australia, and down-home America. We usually communicate by e-mail, but it's fun to pick up the phone and chat. Their camaraderie and generous sharing of knowledge and seeds have enriched my life, my garden, and this book. My fellow tomatophiles—from Dorothy Beiswenger of Minnesota, seed saver extraordinaire, to Cary Fowler, guardian of the world's plant genetic resources—have inspired me to put into words what can be learned from the past in hopes of creating a more bountiful future.

In the pages that follow, you'll find everything you need to know to grow your own heirloom tomatoes and fifty-five recipes to make the most of your harvest. At the heart of the book are portraits in words and photographs of two hundred tomatoes grown in my garden during the past five years. These beautiful photographs, and all the other art in the book (except the photo of me on the facing page, by Sandi Fellman), are by the incomparable Victor Schrager.

The beauty of these tomatoes is more than skin deep. My thirty-five years of experience as a gardener, coupled with considerable book learning, have taught me that heirlooms, ripened on the vine in full sun, are the most delicious tomatoes of all. People long for more natural beauty, more flavor, and better nutrition on their dinner plates. Tomatoes have never been more popular, yet tomato land in America is dominated by commercial F_1 hybrids with only their unyielding flesh to recommend them to the consumer. These hybrid tomatoes, bred to be grown in high plant densities and harvested mechanically, are a tool of industry and the market economy. Hybrids reduce biodiversity and prevent farmers and gardeners from saving harvested seed to regrow. Heirloom tomatoes are the natural alternative: capable of breeding true from seed (unlike F_1 hybrids) and designed to be homegrown. Many are living legacies: old-time handed-down tomatoes, valued by generations of gardeners. Tomatoes feed your soul as well as satisfying your more corporeal appetites. Seedsman and pollination expert Jeff McCormack captured an essential truth about growing heirloom tomatoes: "The world is a large garden and there is room enough for everybody to cultivate a piece of happiness."

growing

It's the last week in April, cold and raining in the Hudson Valley of New York. Tulips and fruit trees flower; robins nest on windowsills. I've been eating homegrown asparagus for a week but homegrown tomatoes are a distant pleasure. It's still hard to believe that winter is over, that a new spring has sprung—and not just in my head, where a garden is always brewing. In order to begin "seedwork," some reorganizing is called for in the potting shed, adjacent to the greenhouse. Once supplies are laid in, and the stainless-steel countertop is gleaming, I bring my creature comforts—thermal mug of coffee, stack of CDs—and take possession.

By the time the robins on my windowsills flex their wings and fly, my tomato fledglings will be ready to be conveyed to the garden. Tomatoes have a longer infancy than melons and squashes, but it doesn't have to be as long as the six to eight weeks generally recommended. If you can speed germination by cranking up the soil temperature to 90 degrees Fahrenheit, four to five weeks is enough. And there's no need for a greenhouse or for elaborate germination chambers if you're growing things on a small scale: A uniform, radiant bottom heat can be achieved with an electric seed-propagation mat, a heated rubber mat contained within a wire cage upon which trays or seed flats are placed. The top of a water heater works, too, but don't use heating pads; they're unsafe! Start your tomato plants about five weeks in advance of the safe-planting-out date—the point after which frost is unlikely—and your transplants will be sturdy and stocky and not overgrown or root-bound. Don't agonize if you're late getting started, even as much as two weeks; tomato plants have a remarkable ability to catch up with the season.

If your gardening season is short—fewer than 120 frost-free days—direct sowing of seeds in the cold, cold ground is not a viable option. Those gardeners with longer growing seasons can give direct seeding a whirl (particularly with sub-arctic types), but even on fertile ground, temperature and soil moisture fluctuate, and the direct route isn't as foolproof as growing containerized transplants. Tomato seeds germinate best when given a measured supply of water, cover of darkness, and plenty of heat. I find that insulated seed trays with water reservoirs and capillary matting (which wicks moisture) make the best seed beds; ordinary seed trays are fine, but they tend to dry out more quickly. Fill your seed bed with a sterile artificial soil mix (containing materials such as peat moss, vermiculite, and perlite) and water until thoroughly wetted; allow it to drain.

After your seed trays have been readied, set the stage for sowing by organizing your seeds and preparing plant labels. I cut four-inch plastic labels short (to three inches) or use plastic collar stays so that they don't overshadow emerging seedlings, and I write names or numbers on the labels with a permanent marker. It's helpful to label each tray with the start date, and to make a master list of varieties by date sown; that way you can keep track of germination rates and percentages, if you're so inclined. A well-lit workspace with a sink and sink sprayer will make seedwork a snap; in the absence of a sprayer, use a watering can with a removable "rose" for gentle spraying. A big fat sponge will come in handy to wipe up *schmutz*.

The smart home gardener is discriminating. If you want to grow quality plants, select for the most plump, regular-shaped, and hairy seeds (commercial ones are often "defuzzed") and reject the weirdos—a dictum that applies to the whole process. Seed sowing requires meticulous care. Using a seed tweezers to place seeds with precision can help prevent mix-ups and make thinning less necessary later on. Space five or six seeds equidistant on top of the moistened soil in each seed cell (sow old seed more generously), and label as you go. Then dust a quarter-inch layer of potting mix on top and tamp down the mix to ensure good soil-seed contact. Seeds and seedlings abhor cold water, so always use lukewarm; and to avoid damping-

(a) Costoluto Genovese, (b) Green Doctors, (c) Sara's Galapagos, (d) Plum Lemon, (e) Victory, (f) Red Pear, (g) Wonderberry, (h) Green Zebra, (i) Black Cherry, (j) Czech's Excellent Yellow

off disease (sudden death), don't overwater. Spray the surface carefully until thoroughly moistened, and fill the reservoirs, if you're using them. Then set covered trays aside in a warm place such as a propagator or atop a propagating mat and cage. I've found that the optimum soil temperature for germination is 85 to 90 degrees Fahrenheit, but 75 to 85 degrees is effective, too. A soil thermometer will help you monitor the situation. If you see running rivulets inside the covered trays, open them a crack to improve ventilation.

The early-bird tomatoes will emerge within three days, announcing their presence with a little loop (stem) above the soil surface. A week or ten days after sowing and the application of heat, a majority of the seeds will have germinated. It's time to move the trays to cooler climes. The newbies will look sallow, blanched, and desperate for light. Give it to them by removing the tray cover after the emergence of even a handful of seedlings per tray. (Keep trays of late starters warm with covers slightly ajar, until you see some action.) Place the whole kit and caboodle under fluorescent grow lights rigged with a timer to provide sixteen hours of light daily. The lights should be elevated as the seedlings grow; maintain them at a respectful distance of three inches above the tomato tops. The room temperature should be about 70 degrees Fahrenheit.

Attending to tomato seedlings is a daily job. I flit over them like a mama bird, plucking off an occasional recalcitrant seed coat to allow the embryonic leaves to emerge. You'll need to select the healthiest-looking seedling in each cell and thin the rest; I do this as early as one week after germination, or when seedlings crowd the cells. After gently pulling the weaklings and leggy (overly elongated) sprouts, use a Rumford seedling tool to prick the chosen one out; center it in the same cell and plant it a bit deeper. The root can be quite long at this stage—or nearly nonexistent. If there's a barren cell, move a plant in, and continue until all accommodations have been filled and labeled. Spray the trays with lukewarm water and return them to their station under the lights. Remove any latecomers that emerge in the coming days.

After the first set of true leaves appears (as opposed to the pair of seedling or cotyledonary leaves that the plant was born with),

give the plantlets a half-strength dose of water-soluble chemical fertilizer. I go organic *except* when it comes to seedlings, which need more umph. The first true leaves show their true colors and shapes: It's fascinating to see the miniature rugose, angora, potato leaf, and regular leaflets so early in the tomato's life. Cull or discard the abnormal, sickly, stunted, and "blind" (without a stem) plants. This is no time for empathy: if you're ruthless about roguing them out, then you'll be left with plants of higher quality.

Within a few days the tomatoes will outgrow their cells. When that happens "pot them up": Transfer the plants to individual three- or four-inch plastic pots filled with soil mix, then water well. I place my pots in clear plastic bins (23 inches long by 16 inches wide by 6 inches high) for ease of handling and watering. (These bins are also useful for carrying transplants to the garden, and for collecting tomatoes at harvest time.) Plants grow stockier if you brush the tops lightly with your hand every day. So-called mechanical conditioning (MC) reduces stem elongation and leaf expansion, resulting in more compact plants; root growth is also reduced and plants can acquire a darker green color because of increased chlorophyll. They'll put on substantial biomass before plant-out begins—which will be near the frost-free date, when the outside soil temperature has reached 70 degrees—but prune off any early flowers that form.

As tomato seedlings grow and develop, prepare the garden to receive them. The greatest gift you can offer your plants is a plot situated in full sun. First runner-up is well-drained, fertile, crumbly, warm soil. If your soil doesn't pass muster, you can improve the quality and structure by adding organic matter. This goes for soils with varying compositions, "from a gumbo prairie, a black marsh muck, a stiff, tenacious clay, to one of light drifting sand," Will W. Tracy said in 1919. One of the tricks of the trade is to plant a soil-building cover crop such as hairy vetch and rye in the fall, then plow it in to feed the tomatoes in spring.

The level of soil acidity is also critical to plant health. The optimal pH for growing tomato plants is 6.5, but tomatoes will do well at pH 6.0 to 7.5. Cornell University's Professor Thomas A. Zitter,

Peters Seed & Research
407 Maranatha Lane
Myrtle Creek, OR 97457
(503) 863-3693

ELBERTA GIRL
Dusty Miller foliage, distinctly striped
fruits. Unique, no other tomato is like
it. An *Angora* type plant, but much
furrier and whiter. The fruit is of the
Tigerella type, but much more
pronounced in its stripes. Good acidic
tomato flavor. Yields are about half
that of *Tigerella*. Fruit size averages
2½ - 3 oz. Short vines.
Origin: Tom Wagner, independent
breeder.

coauthor of the *Compendium of Tomato Diseases*—and the go-to man for questions about diagnosis and treatment of tomato pathology (www.vegetablemdonline.ppath.cornell.edu/Home.htm)—told me that this range "will keep nutrients available to the plants and is a good environment for helpful bacteria and fungi in the soil. Too acid or low a pH (5.5) will encourage soil-borne diseases like Fusarium wilt and foliar pathogens like Botrytis gray mold. Too alkaline or high a pH (8.0) will favor Verticillium wilt. When pH is either too high or too low, nutritional disorders are invited, and plants will certainly be less productive. In general, if your soil is too acid you will need to add lime. If it's too alkaline, you must add sulfur." Do yourself a favor and test the soil with a kit that can be purchased from Cornell Cooperative Extension or state land-grant universities; follow recommendations for adjusting the pH and amending the soil as needed.

There is no single right way to grow tomatoes, but I'd recommend that you consider installing black plastic mulch or ground cloth. The added expense and labor pay off. Mulches will reduce the need for weeding and watering, warm the soil, conserve moisture, and decrease the incidence of soil-borne diseases. My new favorite thing is ground cloth, a durable fabric mulch that comes in 12-foot-by-300-foot rolls. I like the nonglare surface, weed suppression, softness underfoot, and good drainage. I lay out the cloth, with help from my assistant, Ken Marshall, over tilled and raked soil; then we secure it with earth staples.

I also recommend that you stake your plants rather than letting them sprawl on the ground. Sure, it's easy to let tomatoes loll where they're planted, and the fruits will crack less because they're not as exposed to wind and sun. But there the benefits end. Providing upright supports for tomato plants—whether they be stakes, wire cages, teepees, or spirals—will increase air circulation and sun exposure, prevent disease and insect damage, produce earlier and higher yields, and facilitate harvesting. So once the mulch is stapled down in my garden, the metal tomato cages go up: five feet between cages in a row, seven feet between rows. They're supported by two pine furring strips (slats of wood that measure 1 inch by 2 inches by 5 feet); these are driven into the ground and secured to the cage. Later, I'll write plant names on the furring strips at eye level. If using black plastic mulch, cut out a circular piece of mulch about two feet in diameter (before or after erecting the cages) to reveal the soil, in anticipation of planting. When ground cloth is used, cut an X in the fabric, using the four spikes of the cage as a guide, and fold the pieces underneath; the planting hole will be about a foot in diameter.

"Harden off" your tomato seedlings a few days before planting in the garden by placing them outside in a sheltered spot such as a cold frame, thus reducing the possibility of transplant shock. Some gardeners also cut back on water and fertilizer, especially if the tomatoes are overgrown. In my garden on planting day, the show hits the road: Flats of moistened seedlings are loaded into the flatbed of my motorized "mule" or pickup truck. I motor slowly down the driveway to the garden. If the plants sense my excitement, they don't show it. After unloading, I make my way along the rows on bended knee, digging the dirt, tucking in plants just a little lower than they were in their pots (not trenched sideways as some gardeners do), and giving them a deep drink of water. The rhythm of planting comes easy.

With a good start in life and favorable weather—bright sunny days in the eighties and nights in the sixties—transplants are primed to produce fruit, some in as few as forty-five days after being set in the ground. But if the weather is unsettled or days and nights are cold, you should delay planting until conditions improve to prevent setbacks. Protect standing plants from cold temperatures with Wall O' Waters, cloches, or other mechanical barriers. I water with a hose when rainfall is lacking; and, with a garden feeder attached to the hose, I deliver a gallon of water-soluble fertilizer to the plants once or twice each season (usually at transplant time and again after first flowers form). Over-fertilizing can lead to blossom drop and lower yields. Pruning is my only other major intervention: it produces earlier, larger, and more high-quality fruit. In early July, I plop down, splay my legs, and straddle the tomato plants, with scissors in a gloved hand. I snip away at the ground suckers—thereby earning the nickname that Ken gave me, "Amy Scissorhands." Feeling my way up with my fingers (the foliage is often too dense to see through), I denude the plant of the axillary shoots also known as suckers, shoots, and leaves to a height of six to twelve inches. (Only prune ground suckers from dwarf plants.) Be careful not to cut your fingers in the process. The plant will acquire a bonsai-like appearance; no boughs touch the soil. It's a good idea to set a bed of straw underneath the plant to protect it from soil-borne pathogens that might splash back onto leaves after rain or watering. Take one precaution to avoid transmitting disease between plants: Get yourself some germicidal spray or germicidal wipes with a 1:10 concentration of bleach to water. A simple spray or wipe of your pruning scissors or knife, and you're set to go on to the next plant.

My garden isn't troubled much by tomato diseases. Once I learned what a tomato wants—fertile soil, brilliant sun, and lots of room to breathe—I had the key to primary prevention. Infectious diseases thrive in dank, dark, airless, and overcrowded places. So let the sun and air in! I'm religious about crop rotation, mulching, staking, pruning, wide spacing, and good field sanitation. Non-infectious diseases and insects don't pester me much, either. But chipmunks are a scourge: They steal my newly planted seedlings and signal to me by hanging the plant carcasses out of the rock walls in which they live. Seasoned seed saver Gary Staley had an even more bizarre experience: Squirrels in his backyard in Florida picked Czech's Excellent Yellow tomatoes (see page 85) off the vine, carried them in their mouths into a large oak tree, ate them, then tossed the skins into Gary's bird bath. You *could* call that seed dispersal.

Even if the critters don't decimate your crop, you have your work cut out for you. Within a month after plants are set out, flowers begin to form (that's late June in my garden). It's the fertilized flowers, of course, that later give rise to fruits, and the fruits that give rise to seeds. One of the beauties of heirloom tomatoes is that they're capable of reproducing themselves true-to-type from seed (F_1 hybrids don't breed true). They pollenize themselves, thus keeping the genetic stock pure—*but* insects can bring in foreign pollen. If you wish to save your own pure garden-grown seed, you must prevent natural cross-pollination by sweat bees and honeybees. One excellent strategy involves isolating a variety by planting it far from other varieties with which it could cross. But there's a lot of misinformation on the subject; recommended minimum distances are often insufficient. Isolation distances vary as a function of flower structure: Tomatoes with longer styles are more easily crossed. To preserve a cultivated variety (*Lycopersicon esculentum* [*Solanum lycopersicum* L.]) in its purest form, isolate it by 100 feet from other cultivated varieties; the currant tomato (*Lycopersicon pimpinellifolium* [*Solanum pimpinellifolium*]), as well as the potato-leafed varieties, should be isolated by at least 175 feet. For more on the subject, visit www.savingourseeds.org.

But if you don't have room in your garden for this kind of separation, and you're growing many cultivated tomato varieties in close proximity, erecting a mechanical barrier early in the season between flowers and insects is a practical solution. Wrap a piece of spun polyester cloth carefully around each unopened flower cluster, and secure it with a twist tie or twine so insects are excluded and the bag stays in place. (Drawstring spice bags or other weather-resistant bags can be substituted.) Remove the covering once tiny tomatoes have formed, and tie surveyor's tape to the stem to mark the new fruit for seed saving after they ripen later in the season. Or you can cover entire plants with pollination cages: Mine are constructed of 1-inch-by-2-inch pine furring strips with standard mesh fiberglass screening, and they are big enough (5 feet high by 3 feet wide by 3 feet deep) to place over tomato cages. Once fruits have set, I remove the cage and tag the trusses.

With the exception of plants grown in pots on the patio or in hanging baskets—which require almost daily watering and more frequent fertilizing than field-grown plants—tomatoes don't need too much coddling in midsummer, so your pace can slacken. By this time, plants should be growing vigorously and forming fruits. Most heirloom tomatoes have an indeterminate growth habit, a trait allied to fruit quality: They grow large and produce fruit over

an extended period. Not only do heirlooms have "personality," as we shall soon see, but the larger photosynthetic surface per unit of fruit weight (that is, their higher leaf-to-fruit ratio) makes them a magnet for sucrose and flavor. Determinate and dwarf plants are smaller and produce an early and concentrated fruit set; their fruit isn't nearly as good.

Even when your tomatoes are in their glory, be on the lookout for signs of trouble. Plum tomatoes are prone to blossom-end rot, which is black moldy lesions promoted by fluctuations in the water supply; just remove the bad ones. Ditto for ugly cat-faced beefsteaks, with their corky brown lines, holes, and blemishes; cold weather early in the season grossly deforms and scars them for life. To promote growth and prepare plants for the heavy fruit load to come, adjust plants in their cages so they grow upright, reposition fruits if jammed or cramped, tie trailing vines to stakes, remove new ground suckers, and do a little weeding. Just make sure that tomatoes in the "mature green" stage (at about 80 percent of their final size) and "breaker" stage (starting to change color at the blossom end) have good foliage cover; sudden sun exposure and fruit temperatures over 100 degrees can lead to sunscald, marked by white necrotic tissue surrounded with a yellow halo. If *you're* too hot and bothered, take a well-deserved hour's nap on the ground in the shade of a tomato plant. And don't forget to hydrate yourself!

By the third week in July—before the deluge—the first cherry and currant tomatoes are trickling in. They're not as delicious now as they will be in August, when days are longer and the sugar is high. For the moment, I'm picking blueberries, early peaches, and figs. Melons form, cabbages "head up," and beans twine. Ten days later, I go prospecting for a ripe beefsteak and find one of my favorites: African Queen (see page 97). I take my friend Larry Condon's advice and bring a linen napkin, a pocketknife, and a shaker of salt. I feast on one pink meaty slice, followed by another, sprinkled with salt. Delicately, I wipe away the juices seeping from the corners of my mouth—but I am tempted to slather the rest all over my face.

Many such pleasures await you in tomato time—a plentiful spell that can last as long as two months, depending upon your growing season and whether you've planted late-maturing varieties. All you need do at this point is start bringing in the harvest. It's simple to tell when a full-sized tomato is ripe: At least 90 percent of the surface has changed from uniform green to a telltale color—and it's not always red! The fruit softens too, and acquires its characteristic flavor and aroma. If in doubt about readiness, take a whiff and a bite. Some gardeners prefer to harvest their tomatoes at the "pink" stage (up to 60 percent of the surface is colored) or when "light red" (up to 90 percent colored), and ripen them at room temperature. (This can be a boon with black tomatoes, beefsteaks, and other softies that turn mealy and mushy at full maturity.) Grow fine-flavored varieties, like many profiled in this book, and you'll be doubly fortunate.

Bring to the task of reaping some clippers, plastic bins or flats (wicker baskets are lovely but, unless lined, they'll puncture the fruit), perhaps some resealable plastic bags for cherry and currant tomatoes, and a little muscle for hauling the precious cargo home. Some tomatoes are easily plucked: those with a "jointless" smooth stem, which remains on the plant, a relative rarity in the heirloom garden; and the tomatoes with a "jointed" stem—or an "arthritic knuckle" that rips, leaving a small bit of stem on the fruit—a charming indicator of "homegrown-ness." A goodly number of heirloom tomatoes have obstinate and persistent stems and will need to be cut from the vine. Place tomatoes carefully in the bins or flats, and mind the stems to avoid injuring adjacent fruits. Don't squish tomatoes by piling them on too thickly.

The tomato tide will continue to rise as the main-crop varieties mature. In my garden, August 15 seems to be the high-water mark. What to do with the bounty is a matter of personal preference, but if you're looking for ways and means, I've got lots of ideas for you in the recipe section (see page 179). Or share the wealth with friends: A gift of sun-ripened heirlooms is not soon forgotten. I buy as many wicker baskets as I can find, line them with straw or linen towels, select and arrange the tastiest and most beautiful tomatoes, and deliver. Ripe tomatoes are perishable and can only be kept a week or two (if stored at 50 degrees with 90 percent relative humidity). I know that even brief refrigeration reduces tomato fruit quality, but I'm easy—as long as chilled tomatoes are not too far gone, some use can be made of them in cookery.

Not all tomatoes are for eating. Those that were isolated, bagged, or caged earlier in the summer are ripening and ready to process for seed. I've saved seeds many times from tomatoes whose pollination wasn't controlled, but it's an iffy proposition—a gamble with seed purity. Use fully ripe disease-free tomatoes for seed processing. Seeds can be saved casually by, for example, squeezing them out on a paper napkin (I've done that scores of times in restaurants or when traveling) and air-drying them. Fermentation is the better route, though, because it removes germination inhibitors and the gelatinous sheath, and it may treat some seed-borne diseases. (See Vegetable MD Online at http://vegetablemdonline. ppath.cornell.edu for more options.) This is how it's done: Cut tomatoes open—one variety at a time—and squeeze the pulp, juice, and seeds into a glass or plastic container. You may need to work the cavities with your fingers to liberate all the seeds. Cherry and currant tomatoes can, instead, be pulverized whole in the blender. Fill the container halfway, but never add water as a substitute for tomato juice; water slows fermentation. Label and set the containers aside for 96 hours at a temperature not exceeding 70 degrees. Two or three times daily, stir the fermenting juices to submerge the floating pomace (pulpy material). Mold may form, fruit flies may hover, and one thing is certain: It'll stink to high heaven.

After four days, go to the sink and fill the container with water, stir, and pour off the pulpy water—but *not* the seeds, which accumulate in the bottom. Repeat two or three times. Dump the seeds into a fine-mesh sieve and, under running water, use your fingers to drive any remaining pulp through the strainer and remove the fruit jelly that adheres to the seed. Once the seed is clean, knock the strainer against the sink to remove excess water, and wipe the strainer bottom with an absorbent paper towel. Quickly flip the strainer over, smacking it on a waiting paper plate, and deposit the seeds. (Practice helps to improve your aim.) Spread the seeds out on the plate, gently pour off drops of water, and label the plate with the variety name and date. Allow the seeds to dry for three to four weeks in a well-ventilated place at room temperature. Then put them in labeled paper packets; place these in an airtight container and store it in a dark, dry place. (If refrigerated, tomato seeds can last for twenty years.)

Around Labor Day, the law of diminishing returns begins to apply to fruit quality and quantity. Cooler nights, shorter days, and sometimes seam-splitting rains hasten the plants' decline. The first maple leaves start yellowing in the Hudson Valley, and fires are lit in the kitchen hearth. As the end of the season approaches, the harvest can be extended by picking "mature green," "breaker," and "turning" tomatoes—full-sized but less than 30 percent colored-up—and ripening them slowly inside at temperatures between 54 and 68 degrees. Longkeeper tomatoes, with extended shelf lives of up to six months, should be harvested now, too. Even whole plants loaded with mature-green fruit, such as King Humbert (see page 134), can be cut and hung up to ripen. But—just so you don't get your hopes up too high—these will never have that sun-kissed quality.

At the end of September, about two months after the appearance of the first vine-ripened homegrown tomato of summer, the time has come to dismantle the garden before the cover crop is sown. Frost is coming: fermentation and decay are in the air. Plants have fallen down, top heavy, and many tomatoes look like sad sacks, flaccid and drained. It's time to head home and inspect my dining room table and every other horizontal surface, which are covered with paper plates of seeds, slowly drying, the makings of next year's crop.

Clockwise from top left: Tiny Tim, Lime Green Salad, Amber-Colored, Goldman's Italian American, Silvery Fir Tree

ABOUT THE tomatoes

It's the second week in July, and my tomato plants are growing like crazy; I can see them as I proudly circumnavigate the one-acre garden in my motorized "mule." This year, the rusty chicken-wire fence is gone, replaced by sturdy aluminum panels and fieldstone pillars. This structure, built to bear a summer's worth of heavy fruit loads, defines the borders of my world. As if I were entering a temple—or my own living room—I leave my clogs at the garden gate and step inside onto the welcoming ground cloth. No hard physical labor today. I finished the first round of pruning last week, and my back has finally begun to unbend. It's time to write the first field notes of the season.

One thousand plants, two each of five hundred tomato varieties, is a lot of territory to cover; it'll take me two or three days. Making my rounds, notebook and pen in hand, I am amazed by the contrasts in plant habit, foliage, and fruiting bodies. It's "flower city" out here: Tomatoes are forming with abandon, and disease hasn't yet reared its ugly head. Next week, the first cherries and currants will ripen. Elberta Girl has a bluish cast; she wins the prize for most fuzzy. A thought for my notebook: "What's the story behind Stump of the World? Is it the same as Big Ben?" Around the corner, Livingston's Honor Bright signals to me with its "lutescent" white flowers and pale foliage. And look at White Beauty: a well-filled shrub with tomatoes coyly hiding underneath. I write, "Excuse me, ma'am, may I lift your petticoats and take a peek?" Then: "Sara's Galapagos, at garden's edge, is the most vigorous of all. May you continue to live and thrive." These tomatoes are almost human.

I'd known that writing and illustrating a tomato book would be a huge undertaking—if only because there are more than five thousand cultivated varieties to choose from! (Nearly all the tomatoes in this book are "cultivated" types belonging to the species *Lycopersicon esculentum* [*Solanum lycopersicum* L.]; a handful of "currant" types belong to the closely related species *Lycopersicon pimpinellifolium* [*Solanum pimpinellifolium*].) Over the course of five summers, I trialed more than a thousand tomatoes, starting with my favorites and letting the tribe increase until I reached capacity.

The leading candidates were grown at least twice so that I had good "test-retest reliability"; those that didn't strike my fancy got chucked. In the process, a dozen notebooks filled with field observations and taste-test results; from these, I generated voluminous card files.

Victor Schrager and I worked closely to capture the tomatoes on film. Together we hit upon a formula for the portrait photography that is slightly historic, slightly domestic, with little eccentricities and faded antique milk glass as backdrops. These photos, accompanied by my "pen portraits"—which were inspired by the work of the late U. P. Hedrick, author or coauthor of numerous books about the fruits and vegetables of New York—give you a representative sample of the most beautiful, delicious, celebrated, and unusual tomatoes in my garden—and in the world.

Now down to the nitty-gritty details. Here's the key to understanding the tomato descriptors:

SIZE AND WEIGHT

Soon after harvest, average specimens were measured for length (polar diameter) and broadest width (equatorial diameter), and also were weighed. The smallest tomatoes, lighter than a feather, were measured in grams; all others were measured in ounces and pounds.

SHAPE

For this book, tomatoes have been classified into eight horticultural groups based on the shape and size of the fruit. Those that defy description are labeled "eccentric."

CURRANT: These are the minuscule red round two-locular (two-celled) tomatoes of the plant called *Lycopersicon pimpinellifolium*, also known as *Solanum pimpinellifolium*. (Locules are the cavities or cells that contain seeds and jelly; the locular tissue is higher in acid than the wall tissue.) Fruits are no bigger than 1/2 inch in diameter, about the size of a garden pea; they weigh in at less than 2 grams. They boast higher total acidity and Brix readings than many cultivated tomatoes.

CHERRY: These small spherical two-celled tomatoes are often referred to as *L. esculentum* var. *cerasiforme*. They include the "currant crosses" or "mini-cherries," which are ½ inch to 1 inch in diameter and have very high sugar content. Larger cherries range in size from 1 to 2 inches in width. Cherries come in many colors.

ROUND, RIBBED: Typically medium to large tomatoes, round in shape and more or less grooved, furrowed, segmented, or ribbed. Squatty and broad. Multilocular (meaning that most sorts have more than two locules) but generally less fleshy than smooth rounds. Can be hollow or puffy. Good for making sauce.

ROUND, SMOOTH: These tomatoes are smooth and regular, more or less round, multilocular, and medium to large in size. They include all the smoother roundish sorts greater in size than Currant and Cherry. The larger smooth rounds tend to be more oblate (that is, flattened). A refinement over ribbed rounds. Nowadays the smooth globe is the norm. A tomato that comes in many colors.

BEEFSTEAK: Large to huge multiloculed tomatoes good for eating fresh. Usually distinctly wider than long. The bigger they get, the more they deviate from roundness and become flattened. Beefsteaks are typically more misshapen or "cat-faced" than other tomatoes. At the extreme end of the range are the eccentric types: convoluted, doubled-over, and even "coxcomb" beefsteaks. Irregularities such as these minimize usable flesh. The more regular and round sorts are characteristically meaty and dense, juicy, with few seeds and a bland-to-sweet flavor.

PEAR AND PLUM: More or less uniformly elongated tomatoes (the polar diameter exceeds the equatorial diameter), with two or more cells. Generally smooth, or with slight grooved depressions over the locule walls. There are three general types:

• *Pear:* Asymmetrically elongated. Fruits have a distinct bottle neck and are very much contracted at the stem end. These are small: 1½ inches or less in diameter. Typified by Red Pear and Yellow Pear.

• *Fig:* Sensibly, these are shaped more like a fig and less like a pear; tapered but less contracted at the stem end. Asymmetrical and obovoid (bottom-heavy), with a wider blossom end that is sunken, rounded, or blunted but not pointy. Can be small (less than 2 inches long) or large. Ribbed or smooth. Firm-textured; some are meaty with good flavor. These come in various colors.

• *Plum:* More uniformly elongated than pear or fig; not all are bilaterally symmetrical. Rarely do they have constricted necks. Most of the variability in plum tomatoes is at the fruit's blossom end, which can be sunken, blunted, tapered, pointed, or even crooked. Fruit shapes in this group can be described as elliptical, cylindrical, oblong, mini-plum, roma, square, sausage, giant plum, torpedo, carrot, candle, or banana pepper. Plums are smooth, obscurely angled, or slightly grooved. Fruits generally have thick, firm walls; some have puffy or hollowish interiors. Dry firm-fruited tomatoes like these are ideal for canning and processing.

BELL PEPPER: These are "superpuff" tomatoes, hollow to the core. Blocky or like a bell pepper in shape, squarish or rectangular, they are many-lobed and variously furrowed, usually with three to five locules. As broad as long. Mostly nearly regular at the stem end. Generally used for stuffing.

OXHEART: Shaped much like its namesake, or like an inverted fig: blocky at the stem end and tapered to a blossom end that is more or less blunted or pointed. Multiloculed, and usually 1 pound or more in weight. This group includes conical tomatoes that can be short or long, and roundish or more or less broadly wedged. Fruit quality is generally excellent: flesh is meaty and well flavored.

COLOR

Tomatoes come in an almost unbelievable array of colors. Red may be the norm, but—*vive la différence!*—there's also black, brown, green, purple, pink, orange, and yellow. In order to identify specific colors, and to provide accurate descriptors that would enable us to "think in color," I relied upon Kornerup and Wanscher's classic *Methuen Handbook of Colour*. By comparing the tomatoes (both peels and flesh) with standard samples in the color dictionary, I was able to find the closest matches. For example, nearly all of my red tomatoes fall in the "primary red family," with the exception

of a dozen reds that belong to the closely related "scarlet family," more toward the orange side of the spectrum. So-called "white" tomatoes are actually light or pale yellow; "black" tomatoes are brownish violet, and so on.

It's often difficult to discriminate between so-called "pink" or "purple" tomatoes and the red ones without peeling the tomatoes to examine the skin. Pink tomatoes have a colorless epidermis, whereas red tomatoes have a yellow epidermis; flesh color in both is usually red but can be pink or mixed. With the exception of two "outliers" (Ramillete de Mallorca and Thai Pink, see pages 65 and 146), all the pinks that I grew belong in the "carmine or crimson family," which is on the purple side of the red spectrum. Their color names are dark red, madder red, carmine, crimson, fraise, and geranium red. To avoid confusion with the true reds (primary reds and scarlet reds), I've dubbed these "pinks by other names": tomato pink.

SOLUBLE SOLIDS

Tomatoes vary in sugar content, an important component of flavor. I provided an objective index of tomato sweetness by averaging Brix readings (a measure of the ratio of dissolved sucrose to water in a liquid) of raw expressed tomato juice, taken with a handheld refractometer, on at least two separate occasions, often in separate years. A Brix reading of at least 5 degrees is nearly always a prerequisite for good fruit quality. Indeterminate plants, which have more foliage than determinate plants, produce fruits with higher soluble solids. Cherry and currant types can attain readings of 10 degrees Brix or better.

FLAVOR

Most of the variation in flavor between tomato varieties is accounted for by differences in sugar and acid content, but flavor is a complicated chemical construct and a lot depends on how the tomatoes are grown. Harold McGee says, "Tomatoes that are allowed to ripen fully on the vine accumulate more sugar, acid, and aroma compounds, and have the fullest flavor." My subjective rating system for flavor, based on sugar content and perceived acidity (tongue-tingling, mouthwatering), is derived from the work of horticultural scientist M. M. Peet, at North Carolina State University. There are four general categories of fruit quality:

POOR: Includes the tasteless (low acid, low sugar) and tart (high acid, low sugar). These tomatoes are of the lowest quality. They may have one or more of what are called grave faults, or fatal flaws such as severe cracking that make them not worth planting.

FAIR: Includes the bland and sub-acid (low acid, high sugar) tomatoes. Mildly pleasing and refreshing at best. Many of these cultivars are tolerant to cold, drought, and adverse conditions; some tend to be highly productive and early ripening.

GOOD: Good tomatoes are sweet and tart (high sugar, high acid), sugary and brisk or sprightly. Finely balanced, with a pleasant mingling of sweet and sour. High- or well-flavored. Delicious and juicy, with no fatal flaws. Ought to be grown.

EXCELLENT: Scarcely equaled in texture of flesh and richness of flavor. Distinctive, delicious, deep and complex, with luscious, rich flavor. Savory, mouth-filling, and juicy. No grave faults. Finely balanced sugar-acid ratio yet endowed with intense flavor. Extremely desirable.

TEXTURE

Descriptors of flesh quality include *meaty*, *beefy*, *fleshy*; *mealy* or *coarse-grained*; *dry*, *juicy*; *puffy* or *hollow*; *corky* or *hard-cored*. I used the "press test" (that is, I gave 'em a squeeze) to determine the degree of firmness:

SOFT: Ripe fruits are strictly garden-to-table; fragile; damaged by rough handling. Can have a melting and juicy quality. Mainly for the home gardener.

REASONABLY FIRM: Ripe fruits are firm but tender. Agreeable mouthfeel. May be distinctly marked after mild or moderate pressure by fingers, but not damaged. Mainly for the home and market gardener.

FIRM AND EXTRA-FIRM: Ripe fruits are hard to extra-hard. Described as crunchy or hardball (a texture preferred by many Europeans). Least susceptible to bruising. The firm store-bought tomatoes are bred to withstand mechanical harvesting and the perils of transport; they are slow-ripening and have an extended shelf life.

BEST USES

Any red tomato can be used to make Bloody Marys—even I wouldn't care about fruit quality after the fifth drink—but some cultivars are better suited than others. Likewise with other purposes. Recommended uses of tomatoes by variety include: fresh eating; cooking; multipurpose; ornamental or decorative; exhibition; and novelty.

PLANT HABIT

Tomatoes are viny herbs that are erect initially and later procumbent (lying along the ground). The wild types or currants have spreading habits; they grow out into a weedy "tangle of herbage" (though one well worth the garden space). The majority of heirlooms are indeterminate. Indeterminate types are not quite as unwieldy as currants but require staking; seemingly immortal, they grow large (having three nodes between each flower cluster), and produce continuous crops until felled by frost. The determinate sorts have a more compact, bushy growth habit with fewer nodes between inflorescences (clusters of blossoms). Their flowering and fruiting period is restricted, producing an early concentrated fruit set. The stems give rise to a terminal inflorescence after which no more fruits are formed and the plant stops growing. These can benefit from staking. Dwarf plant types stand less than 2 feet high with very short internodes and rugose leaves. Many have an erect carriage and heavy, somewhat self-supporting stems (use short staking). Dwarf and short determinate tomatoes can be easily grown in pots.

LEAF TYPE

Botanists describe tomato leaves as "interrupted imparipinnate." This means that the leaf is compound; it has lateral leaflets, both large and small, along the main axis, with a lone leaflet at the terminus. Small leaflets or folioles may be scattered among the others. Most gardeners distinguish between several types of leaflets, textures, and color:

REGULAR LEAF: Leaf margins are dentate (toothed) or crenate (scalloped), more or less deeply divided or cut (dissected).

POTATO LEAF: A simple leaf-form. Leaf margins are entire or uncut; leaf size is large.

RUGOSA (OR RUGOSE): Crinkly or wrinkled dark-green leaves; associated with dwarf growth habit.

Less common are the droopy-leafed tomatoes; the leaf margins are serrated and their "attitude" is drooping. These tend to be cultivars with elongated or oxheart fruit. Angora foliage is fuzzy and often has a bluish or silvery cast. Variegated refers to a rare tricolor leaf. Currant tomato leaflets are small and have margins that are entire (uncut) or only slightly crenate (scalloped).

YIELD

I've rated the fruitfulness over the lifespan for tomatoes, based upon plant size, as: Low, Fair, Good, and High.

MATURITY

Maturity was defined as number of days from transplant to appearance of the first ripe fruit. The categories are:

Very Early Crop (45 to 50 days)
Early Crop (51 to 65 days)
Main Crop (66 to 80 days)
Late Crop (80 to 95 days)
Very Late Crop (more than 95 days)

ORIGIN

Includes date and place of origin; originator, introducer, or breeder; pedigrees; seed sources; and other pertinent information related to parentage and provenance. Uncovering the origin of my tomatoes—doing the detective work—was half the fun of writing this book. Facts were found in old seed catalogs, scholarly works in three languages, annual yearbooks from the Seed Savers Exchange, and in the fine print in many obscure places. Oftentimes, the answers were found simply by picking up the telephone and asking the right person the right question.

SYNONYMS

Tomato names can be confusing. Many tomatoes have more than one name; on the other hand, dissimilar varieties sometimes share the same name. Old varieties are constantly being renamed, too; the older the variety, the more synonyms, or names that can be attached to a particular fruit. I've listed everything that could be verified as synonymous.

NY

"NY" is the official acronym for the William and Lynda Steere Herbarium at the New York Botanical Garden. The Steere Herbarium is the largest herbarium in the Western Hemisphere, with a collection totaling more than seven million preserved plant specimens. Michael Nee, curator of NYBG's Institute of Systematic Botany, along with some of his students, collected tomato plant specimens from my garden in 2005 and 2006 and added them to the herbarium collection. Michael generated collection numbers for each sample in his sequence; these IDs, which I've provided, reflect the name of the collector and the grower. Visit www.nybg.org to learn about how to use the herbarium and access the collections digitally or in person.

SEED SOURCING

Seeds for a majority of the cultivars featured in this book are available from commercial sources in the United States and Canada, though many varieties are available only through membership in the Seed Savers Exchange—a good reason to join! Each variety has an abbreviated seed source code (some have more than one), and these are matched to full names, addresses, and contact information for the sources on pages 249 to 253.

Herbarium specimens from the New York Botanical Garden (clockwise from top left): Plum Lemon, Novogogoshary, Brown Derby Mix, Red Cherry Large, Bonny Best

Currant & Cherry

(a) Wild Sweetie, (b) Red Pear, (c) Sara's Galapagos, (d, m) Galina's, (e, s) Gardener's Delight, (f) Green Doctors ,
(g) Matt's Wild Cherry, (h) Dr. Carolyn, (i) Yellow Pear, (j) Blondköpfchen, (k) Broad Ripple Yellow Currant, (l) Large Red Cherry,
(n) Black Cherry, (o) Bicolor Cherry, (p) Dr. Carolyn Pink, (q) Yellow Pygmy, (r) Elfin

BLACK CHERRY *page 4, fig. 1i; page 25, fig. 6n; page 173, fig 120e*

SIZE: *1¼" long by 1⅜" wide*

WEIGHT: *22.19 grams*

SHAPE: *Cherry*

EXTERIOR COLOR(S): *Maroon*

FLESH COLOR(S): *Wine red*

SOLUBLE SOLIDS: *9 degrees Brix*

FLAVOR: *Excellent; fruity and well-balanced. CR Lawn of Fedco Seeds gives this one the nod: "Yum!"*

TEXTURE: *Firm; juicy*

BEST USE(S): *Fresh eating; garnish*

PLANT HABIT, LEAF TYPE, AND YIELD: *Indeterminate habit; regular leaf; high yield*

MATURITY: *Very early crop*

ORIGIN: *Developed from a "natural occurrence" by the late Vincent Sapp of Tomato Growers Supply Company and released in 2003*

SYNONYMS: *Similar to Burpee's Black Pearl Hybrid and possibly Black Sweet Cherry. Not the same as Brown Berry, which is brownish red.*

SEED SOURCES: *Ba8, Fe5, Ga22, Go8, Ha26, Ki4, Ma18, Se17, So25, Te4, To1, To9, To10, Und, Vi4*

If one of the greatest services a man can render his country is to add a useful plant to its agriculture, then Vincent Sapp deserves a Medal of Honor. Black Cherry is a joy to behold—and then to eat. This tomato tastes like plum-stone fruit without the stone; it bests any bigger black plum or beefsteak. A must for Cherry Tomato Focaccia (see page 215).

AMBER-COLORED *page 15, fig. 4b*

SIZE: *1¾" long by 2" wide (sometimes larger)*

WEIGHT: *3 ounces*

SHAPE: *Cherry*

EXTERIOR COLOR(S): *Golden yellow*

FLESH COLOR(S): *Light yellow*

SOLUBLE SOLIDS: *5½ degrees Brix*

FLAVOR: *Poor; tart, forgettable*

TEXTURE: *Reasonably firm*

BEST USE(S): *When well-watered, flourishes in pots on patios*

PLANT HABIT, LEAF TYPE, AND YIELD: *Dwarf habit; rugosa leaves; high yield*

MATURITY: *Very early crop*

ORIGIN: *Russian in origin. Introduced in 1995 by Seed Savers International as part of the Russian Collection.*

SYNONYMS: *Amber-Coloured*

SEED SOURCES: *To9*

This variety wins no prizes for flavor, but when you need a little tomato in your life, Amber-Colored is adorable in containers—and the yield is impressive for a tiny tom. Dwarf tomatoes, with their husky stems and dark-green rugose foliage, are generally self-supporting until they bear fruit. Be sure to stake the plants since a full load of ripe fruit will topple them.

GARDENER'S DELIGHT *page 25, fig. 6e, s*

SIZE: *1½" long by 1½" wide*

WEIGHT: *1 ounce*

SHAPE: *Cherry*

EXTERIOR COLOR(S): *Blood red*

FLESH COLOR(S): *Blood red*

SOLUBLE SOLIDS: *5½ degrees Brix*

FLAVOR: *Fair; high acid; deep, serious, old-fashioned flavor according to fans*

TEXTURE: *Reasonably firm*

BEST USE(S): *Multipurpose*

PLANT HABIT, LEAF TYPE, AND YIELD: *Indeterminate habit; regular leaf; high yield*

MATURITY: *Early crop*

ORIGIN: *Popular in England, although not of English origin as is commonly believed. Introduced in 1950–1951 by Ernst Benary Samenzucht GmbH (formerly of Erfurt, East Germany; now Hann Muenden, Germany). Bred by Paul Tellhelm and given the name "Benary's Gartenfreude, Hochzucht." Cataloged in 1960 as "Jung's Sugar Lump" by Jung Quality Seed, Randolph, Wisconsin.*

SYNONYMS: *Benary's Gartenfreude, Hochzucht; Délice du Jardinier; Delight; Jung's Sugar Lump; Sugar Lump; Tomato Gartenfreude. Not the same as Gardener VF.*

NY: *Nee & Goldman 53404 and Nee & Goldman 53444 (as Sugar Lump)*

SEED SOURCES: *Bo17, Bou, Bu2, Coo, Ers, Fe5, Ga1, Ga7, Ga22, He8, Pe2, Pin, Pr3, Ra6, Re8, Sa5, Se26, Shu, Sk2, St18, Tho, To1, To3, To9, Up2, We19*

Despite its dulcet synonym Sugar Lump, this tomato is too sour for my taste. Nonetheless, it has a loyal following, particularly in England; Gardener's Delight was the most popular cherry tomato until Sweet 100 F₁—with Gardener's Delight as a parent—set a new standard.

YELLOW PYGMY *page 25, fig. 6q*

SIZE: *1⅛" long by 1¼" wide (size varies)*

WEIGHT: *15.67 grams*

SHAPE: *Cherry*

EXTERIOR COLOR(S): *Yolk yellow*

FLESH COLOR(S): *Amber yellow*

SOLUBLE SOLIDS: *8 degrees Brix*

FLAVOR: *Poor; sour*

TEXTURE: *Firm*

BEST USE(S): *Ornamental container plant; a pet tomato*

PLANT HABIT, LEAF TYPE, AND YIELD: *Dwarf habit; rugose foliage; good yield*

MATURITY: *Early crop*

ORIGIN: *Introduced as Golden Pygmy circa 1987 by Le Marché Seeds International. Reintroduced as Yellow Pigmy in 1989 by Glecklers Seedmen.*

SYNONYMS: *Golden Pygmy; Yellow Pigmy. Sometimes described as the yellow version of Tiny Tim (see page 28). Not related to (red) Pigmy or Pygmy from Nigeria.*

SEED SOURCES: *Sk2*

Yellow Pygmy looks cute, but no one has ever accused it of being palatable.

GALINA'S page 25, fig. 6d, m; page 161, fig. a, n

SIZE: *1½" long by 1⅛" wide*

WEIGHT: *1 ounce*

SHAPE: *Cherry*

EXTERIOR COLOR(S): *Orange yellow*

FLESH COLOR(S): *Deep yellow*

SOLUBLE SOLIDS: *5½ degrees Brix*

FLAVOR: *Fair; bland*

TEXTURE: *Reasonably firm*

BEST USE(S): *Multipurpose*

PLANT HABIT, LEAF TYPE, AND YIELD: *Indeterminate habit; potato leaf; high yield*

MATURITY: *Very early crop*

ORIGIN: *Original stock from Siberia. Cataloged circa 1991 by High Altitude Gardens, Ketchum, Idaho.*

SYNONYMS: *Galina; Galina's Cherry; Galina Siberian Cherry*

NY: *Nee & Goldman 53388*

SEED SOURCES: *Hig, Ma18, Sa5, Se17, To1, To9*

This hardscrabble fruit is well adapted to cold mountain climates. "Frustratingly impure from generation to generation," reported Steve Draper, the man who named the (far superior) ivory mutant of Galina's (see Dr. Carolyn, page 43).

BROAD RIPPLE YELLOW CURRANT fig. 7c; page 25, fig. 6k

SIZE: *¾" long by ¾" wide*

WEIGHT: *3.91 grams*

SHAPE: *Cherry*

EXTERIOR COLOR(S): *Yolk yellow*

FLESH COLOR(S): *Banana*

SOLUBLE SOLIDS: *8½ degrees Brix*

FLAVOR: *Good; mildly sweet, with a pleasant aftertaste*

TEXTURE: *Firm; seedy, juicy*

BEST USE(S): *Fresh eating; salads, garnish*

PLANT HABIT, LEAF TYPE, AND YIELD: *Indeterminate habit; regular leaf; high yield*

MATURITY: *Very early crop*

ORIGIN: *Initially listed by John M. Hartman of Indianapolis, Indiana, in the 1984 Seed Savers Exchange yearbook. As John wrote, Broad Ripple was "found growing as an escape in cracks in the street at 56th and College in Indianapolis; obviously hardy, yellow marble-sized fruits." Commercialized in 1999 in the Seed Savers Exchange public catalog.*

SYNONYMS: *Broad Ripple Yellow*

SEED SOURCES: *Co32, Se16, Yu2*

An imposter: not a true currant at all, but rather a small cherry with a sneaky name. Tastes great nonetheless when roasted with a sprinkling of olive oil and salt.

(a) Yellow Pear, (b) Sara's Galapagos, (c) Broad Ripple Yellow Currant, (d) Wild Sweetie, (e) Red Currant

TINY TIM *page 15, fig. 3*

SIZE: *1" long by 1¼" wide*

WEIGHT: *16.88 grams*

SHAPE: *Cherry, irregular sizes and shapes*

EXTERIOR COLOR(S): *Crayfish red*

FLESH COLOR(S): *Grayish red*

SOLUBLE SOLIDS: *4½ degrees Brix*

FLAVOR: *Poor; sour*

TEXTURE: *Reasonably firm*

BEST USE(S): *Container growing (short staking required)*

PLANT HABIT, LEAF TYPE, AND YIELD: *Dwarf habit; rugosa; good yield*

MATURITY: *Early crop*

ORIGIN: *A dwarf tree-like plant adapted to pot culture in the North. According to Dr. Brent Loy, "Tiny Tim was released in 1949. It was developed from a cross of Window Box [Redskin x Dwarf Champion] x Red Currant, followed by selfing and selection for determinate growth habit, dwarfness, and tiny fruit. It is difficult to know who made the selections, but the breeding program was directed and carried out by Professor Albert F. Yeager, a breeder and head of the Department of Horticulture at the University of New Hampshire at Durham." Introduced by the Hepler Seed Company.*

Dwarf tomato plants were noted in Europe as early as the late sixteenth century. Matthias de l'Obel wrote in Flemish in 1581, "Another kind of Poma amoris which comes forth from Spanish seed sown in our gardens has erect stalke, one cubit in height [17 to 22 inches] and is similar in appearance to the aforementioned [furrowed red and yellow tomatoes on indeterminate vines], but is smaller" (McCue, 1952).

Almost three hundred years later, Fearing Burr Jr. described a similar sort known as "Tree Tomato," "New Upright," or "Tomate de Laye": "A new variety, raised from seed by Grenier, gardener to M. [le comte] de Fleurieux, at a place in France called Château de Laye (whence the name), and introduced by M. Vilmorin of Paris. It is distinct from all others; rising quite erect to the height of two feet or upwards, with a stem of remarkable size and strength. The branches are not numerous, and comparatively short, usually eight or ten inches in length, thus requiring no heading-in; leaves not abundant, rather curled, much wrinkled, very firm, closely placed on the sturdy branches, and of a remarkably deep, shining-green color; fruit bright-red, of large size, comparatively smooth, and well filled to the centre … From the peculiar, tree-like character of the plants, the variety is remarkably well adapted for cultivation in pots."

In 1870, seedsman James J. H. Gregory of Marblehead, Massachusetts, cataloged "Tomato de Laye" and two other dwarf tomatoes, "Early York" and "Dwarf Scotch"; in 1875, he added "Early Dwarf Red" (a French variety) and "Wonder," which he described as "remarkably dwarf; vines very stalky; shy bearer; allied to De Laye."

The still extant pink-fruited "Dwarf Champion," a part of Tiny Tim's lineage, cataloged by W. A. Burpee in 1889, shares the "HR" traits of Tomate de Laye—heavy stems and rugose foliage. Burpee wrote that the new Dwarf Champion "is dwarf and compact in growth, the plants growing stiff and upright, with thick-jointed stems and foliage unlike any other Tomato, of an unusually dark-green color, thick and corrugated."

SYNONYMS: *Resembles Tomate de Laye and Dwarf Champion in plant habit.*

SEED SOURCES: *All, Bo19, Com, Ear, He8, Pe6, Ra6, Re8, So25, Sto, To1, To3, To10, Up2, Ves, Vi4*

Ever since the days of l'Obel, the trend for tomato plant size has been downward. Half a cubit high, Tiny Tim is what Alex Caron, cofounder of Seeds of Diversity Canada, might call "a sitting duck for soil-borne diseases." "Dead ducks" might describe some of the newer extreme dwarf or "bird's nest" types of tomato, which are no taller than a mushroom or form ground-hugging mounds. In order to grow any dwarf successfully, primary prevention is key: I'd recommend pot culture with sterile potting soil and mulch. It also helps to trim the ground suckers.

SWEET PEA CURRANT *fig. 8*

SIZE: *¼" long by ½" wide*

WEIGHT: *1.54 grams*

SHAPE: *Currant*

EXTERIOR COLOR(S): *Brownish red*

FLESH COLOR(S): *Brownish red*

SOLUBLE SOLIDS: *8 degrees Brix*

FLAVOR: *Fair to good; like wine*

TEXTURE: *Firm; juicy and seedy*

BEST USE(S): *Fresh eating; decorative fruit and plant*

PLANT HABIT, LEAF TYPE, AND YIELD: *Spreading habit; currant-like leaflets; high yield*

MATURITY: *Very early crop*

ORIGIN: *Introduced in the 2004 Seed Savers Exchange public catalog. Described as "the best red currant tomato we can offer to gardeners … Hundreds of fruits per plant. Excellent clean flavor. Fruits borne in trusses of 10–12 and do not drop off the vine." Has many of the hallmarks of a true currant (L. pimpinellifolium or S. pimpinellifolium). Cornell plant breeder George Moriarty told me that bees love currants—you can even see their "footprints" on the flowers four to five hours after pollination. Exerted styles (flower stigmas in "outie" position) and more UV light attract insects and account for the high fruit set.*

NY: *Nee & Goldman 54569*

SEED SOURCES: *Se16, To1*

A stupendously spreading plant— at times reaching more than twelve feet in diameter—with the smallest nonshattering tomato fruits I've seen! I wrote the following in my garden journal, dated August 6, 2006: "This plant is on the march—headstrong across the garden. It's alarming how weedy it is." And Sweet Pea Currant produces a superabundance of fruit, borne on very long trusses. Leonard C. Luckwill (1943) said, "Although not much used as a food plant, the Currant Tomato is sometimes grown in greenhouses for the decorative effects of its long pendent infructescences. In wild plants these rarely exceed 10 cm. in length, but under greenhouse conditions the truss continues to elongate indefinitely, often attaining a length of 120 cm. or more during a single season, and bearing up to 150 fruits." Luckwill's glasshouses at the University of Aberdeen, Scotland, must have been immense to accommodate such specimens: One Sweet Pea Currant plant would probably smother everything in my fifteen-by-thirty-foot greenhouse. But, still, I'm tempted to grow the currant under glass so I can witness those long trusses.

WILD SWEETIE *fig. 9; page 25, fig. 6a; page 27, fig. 7d*

SIZE: *⅝" long by ¾" wide*

WEIGHT: *3.27 grams*

SHAPE: *Currant type*

EXTERIOR COLOR(S): *Brownish red*

FLESH COLOR(S): *Brownish red*

SOLUBLE SOLIDS: *10 degrees Brix*

FLAVOR: *Excellent; super-sweet*

TEXTURE: *Firm*

BEST USE(S): *Fresh eating; makes a wonderful dessert course*

PLANT HABIT, LEAF TYPE, AND YIELD: *Spreading habit; regular leaf; high yield*

MATURITY: *Very early*

ORIGIN: *Cataloged by the Digger's Club of Australia as "A flavour sensation in a currant-size tomato." Described by botanist Michael Nee as* Lycopersicon esculentum *var.* esculentum.

SYNONYMS: *Similar to Red Currant. Not the same as Sweetie.*

NY: *Nee & Goldman 53502*

Tastes like candy; kids go wild for it.

RED CURRANT *fig. 10; page 27, fig. 7e*

SIZE: *⅝" long by ⅝" wide*

WEIGHT: *1.92 grams*

SHAPE: *Currant*

EXTERIOR COLOR(S): *Blood red*

FLESH COLOR(S): *Blood red*

SOLUBLE SOLIDS: *9 degrees Brix*

FLAVOR: *Good; well balanced*

TEXTURE: *Firm; seedy and juicy; plant has a distinctive aroma*

BEST USE(S): *Fresh eating; decorative fruit and plant*

PLANT HABIT, LEAF TYPE, AND YIELD: *Spreading habit; round-ovate, obtuse, entire; high yield*

MATURITY: *Early crop*

ORIGIN: *The currants (*Lycopersicon pimpinellifolium *or* Solanum pimpinellifolium*) may be the smallest edible-fruited red tomatoes. They are native to coastal areas of Chile, Peru, and Ecuador and are closely allied to the cultivated tomato (*L. esculentum *or* S. lycopersicum L.*); the two types cross freely. May be the same as the wild* Lycopersicum Pimpinella *depicted by Feuillée in 1725. The currant tomato was described by Linnaeus in 1763 (Morrison, 1938).*

Fearing Burr wrote in 1863: "This variety, or more properly species, differs essentially in the character of its foliage and manner of fructification, from the Garden Tomato. The leaves are much smoother, thinner in texture, and have little of the musky odor peculiar to the Common Tomato-plant. The fruit is nearly globular, quite small, about half an inch in diameter, of a bright-scarlet color, and produced in leafless, simple, or compound clusters, six or eight inches in length, containing from twenty to sixty berries, or tomatoes; the whole having an appearance not unlike a large cluster, or bunch of currants."

Liberty Hyde Bailey wrote in 1887: "It has probably not been long in cultivation … The species has not yet been modified by domestication. The fruits are clear, bright red, somewhat larger than a very large currant, and are borne on long-two-ranked clusters. The plant is very ornamental. Trained upon a trellis, near a window, it would make one of the most attractive screens. The whole aspect of the plant is delicate."

A hundred years later, plant breeder Rob Johnston Jr. of Johnny's Selected Seeds wrote, "Until recently, these 'currant tomatoes,' little changed from the wild, were known only to botanists and breeders, who crossed them to cherry tomatoes to provide the remarkable sweetness and long-trussed fruit habit of varieties such as Sun Cherry, Sun Gold, and Sweet 100 … The species is naturally resistant to many diseases including Fusarium wilt, late blight, bacterial canker, bacterial wilt, and spotted wilt virus."

SYNONYMS: *Cluster Tomato; Crimson Currant; Currant (Holds Fruit); Currant Type B; Currant Tomato; German Raisin; Grape Tomato; Johannisbeer Tomate; Microtomate groseille; Small Red Currant; Red Currant Non-Shattering; Red Current; Rothe Johannisbeerfruchten; Tomato-Grape; Tomate groseille*

SEED SOURCES: *Abu, Bo19, Coo, Go8, Ha26, Hi13, Jo1, Ki4, Mi12, Ni1, Pin, Pr3, Ra6, Re8, Ri2, Sa9, Se7, So1, Sw9, So25, Te4, Ter, To1, To3, To9, Twi, We19, Yu2*

Red Currant is the icing on the cake of every tomato basket I create for family and friends: They look like cabochon rubies dangling from graceful stems. The variety can be grown in containers but, if given free rein in the garden, will form a bushy tangle with thousands of sweet tidbits. Seedswoman Jan Blum once said, in her singular way, that the currant tomato is "what the cherry tomato tried to be. You can pop these pea-size fruits in your mouth, and they won't squirt all over."

ALBERTO SHATTERS *fig. 11*

SIZE: *Teeny; ½" long by ⅜" wide*

WEIGHT: *1.30 grams*

SHAPE: *Currant*

EXTERIOR COLOR(S): *Blood red*

FLESH COLOR(S): *Blood red*

SOLUBLE SOLIDS: *7 degrees Brix*

FLAVOR: *Good; acidic; for lack of a better word, tomatoey*

TEXTURE: *Very firm; tough skin; seedy and crunchy*

BEST USE(S): *Fresh eating; tomato marmalade; decorative plant and fruit. Can be grown in a topsy-turvy (upside-down) planter, with a basket for collection positioned underneath.*

PLANT HABIT, LEAF TYPE, AND YIELD: *Spreading habit; heart-shaped, entire (explained in intro); high yield*

MATURITY: *Early maturity*

ORIGIN: *Initially listed in the 1980 Seed Savers Exchange yearbook by Alberto W. Vasquez of Free Union, Virginia. Alberto obtained the seed from a research botanist circa 1970. Here's how he described his currant tomato (technically classed as* Lycopersicon pimpinellifolium *or* Solanum pimpinellifolium*): "long trusses of pea-sized tomatoes, sprawling sub-shrub, tends to shatter off the vine." (In 1981, he listed a nonshattering red currant in the SSE yearbook; he renamed it a year later "Currant Tomato Holds Fruit" [see Red Currant, page 30] and wrote "berries don't shatter off as badly.") Alberto continued in 1982, "I sent Ben Quisenberry [see Big Ben, page 94] about 2 oz. of currant tomato seed about 10 years ago, and my wife sent a jar of tomato marmalade out of the same with the whole little tomatoes visible in the transparent gel. Really freaked the old*

boy out. That started the correspondence and resulted in our being sent all sorts of tomato seed. I believe that as long as the currant tomato seed held out, he sent free packs of ten seeds each to all his customers as a premium."

Commercialized in 1985 by Ken Ettlinger of Long Island Seed and Plant Company; and by Jan Blum of Seeds Blüm in 1986–1987. Ken Ettlinger, now of the Long Island Seed Project, writes on his Web site (www.liseed. org), "The world's tiniest tomato has to be Alberto's Shattering Currant! It's the size of a garden pea. The species is often considered different than the conventional garden tomato ... but they easily cross with one another and are functionally variations of the same species." Alberto traded seeds of his shattering currant tomato for Ken's rat-tail radish seed; Ken sold seeds of both of Alberto's "holds" and "drops" types of currant for many years. Ken writes, "Why, people ask me, would you want a currant tomato that drops its fruit? Why indeed! The labor involved with picking currant tomatoes for market is considerable. We developed a technique, though, of planting the shattering currant tomatoes on mounds with landscape cloth sloping downward from the base of the plants. Shake the bushes every couple of days and scoop up tomatoes that roll down to the base of the cloth. So simple."

SYNONYMS: *Alberto's Currant; Alberto's Shattering Currant; Currant; Currant Drops; Currant (Drops); Currant Tomato (Drops Fruit); Currant Type A; Red Currant; Red Currant–Shatters; Shattering Red Currant*

Alberto Shatters is the smallest tomato I've ever seen; it freaks the old girl out! And I love its shattering ways, spreading habit, and pleasing aroma. The variety is primitive, but I wouldn't change a thing about it.

I didn't know from "shattering" until I read a book by Cary Fowler and Pat Mooney entitled *Shattering: Food, Politics, and the Loss of Genetic Diversity*. They wrote, "It has been a long time since women first learned to control the shattering of seeds. Early grains 'shattered.' The seeds did not cling to the plant but were easily dispersed. But in those stands of wild grains some plants were different. As a result of minor genetic differences, some held on to their seeds. Normally this was dysfunctional for the plant. But to the early 'farmer' it was a boon, enabling her to collect seed more easily. Harvesting and subsequently sowing seeds that remained on the stalk encouraged the non-shattering trait and meant that less seed shattered and fell to the ground before harvest. Harvesting and sowing non-shattering seeds led to the domestication of our food crops." Cary and Pat would agree that we can't forget to preserve shattering and wild types, too, because they contain vital genetic resources that breeders can use to transfer disease resistance, drought tolerance, and other fine traits into modern cultivated forms.

a

b

MATT'S WILD CHERRY *fig. 12b; page 25, fig. 6g*

SIZE: *⅜" long by ⅜" wide*

WEIGHT: *2.94 grams*

SHAPE: *Currant type; ellipsoidal*

EXTERIOR COLOR(S): *Cardinal red*

FLESH COLOR(S): *Cardinal red*

SOLUBLE SOLIDS: *11½ degrees Brix*

FLAVOR: *Excellent*

TEXTURE: *Firm; juicy, seedy*

BEST USE(S): *Fresh eating; salsa; garnish. Ornamental plant.*

PLANT HABIT, LEAF TYPE, AND YIELD: *Spreading habit; deeper green and more dentate or "toothed" than Sara's Galapagos; high yield*

MATURITY: *Very early crop*

ORIGIN: *Introduced in 1996 by Johnny's Selected Seeds. Rob Johnston Jr., founder and chairman of Johnny's, wrote in the catalog:* "The wild tomato with luscious taste. Like, wow! *These small cherry tomatoes are packed with more taste than you can believe … Teresa Arellanos de Mena, a friend of U. of Maine ag faculty [members] Drs. Laura Merrick and Matt Liebman, brought seeds to Maine from her family's home state of Hidalgo in Eastern Mexico; it's the region of domestication of tomatoes, and where these grow wild. We were given seeds by Matt."*

Rob Johnston wrote to me, "I had visited Matt and he gave me a small bag of the tomatoes to take home and eat but, after eating one, I kept the seeds from all the others so Johnny's could produce and market the seeds. I named it Matt's Wild Cherry, which has a nice sound even though it's also perfectly literal."

Matt Liebman, now in the Department of Agronomy at Iowa State University in Des Moines, wrote to me: "My relationship with the plant is one of affection for its weediness—I work on weed ecology and management—and enjoyment of its flavor. It's still the best, though most laborious, salsa tomato we raise. Actually, it raises itself every year as a volunteer. I just move a few plants around the garden, set up some concrete reinforcing wire cages, and turn 'em loose."

SYNONYMS: *Tomatillo; Wild Cherry. Resembles Sara's Galapagos (see next entry).*

NY: *Nee & Goldman 53491*

SEED SOURCES: *Go8, He8, Hi6, Jo1, Ma18, Mi12, Se7, So1, Te4, To10*

The color of Matt's Wild Cherry is so intense that the fruit looks poisonous—but not to worry. This tomato is savory, fruity, juicy, and completely edible. Matt and his wife, Laura, recently put me in touch with Teresa Arellanos. Here is her account of the tomato: "I got those 'tomatillo' seeds from the Huasteca Polosina, around my hometown of Tamazunchale, but they grow wild everywhere, including Hidalgo and Veracruz. I took a bunch of the seeds back to Maine in 1992 … Later on, I planted the seeds at the community garden in Orono, Maine. And I gave that tomatillo seed to Matt. Tomatillos are used in so many ways. They can be boiled with water, roasted, or even used fresh to make different types of salsa with peppers like serrano and jalapeño. The best salsa made with these tomatillos is the one with piquin peppers, which grow wild in the same area. The peppers and tomatillos are roasted and blended with garlic, water, and salt to taste."

Teresa uses the word *tomatillo* to describe a small tomato, but it can also refer to the husk tomato, including the Mexican green version (*Physalis philadelphica* Lam.) well known to lovers of Mexican food. As Michael Nee says, "*P. philadelphica* Lam. is the ubiquitous 'tomate' of Mexico. It is found in the green sauces on virtually every table in every house and restaurant in the country, and that is scarcely an overstatement."

SARA'S GALAPAGOS *fig. 12a; fig. 13; page 4, fig. 1c; page 25, fig. 6c*

SIZE: *½" long by ½" wide*

WEIGHT: *2.81 grams*

SHAPE: *Currant type; "off-round" or ellipsoidal*

EXTERIOR COLOR(S): *Blood red*

FLESH COLOR(S): *Blood red*

SOLUBLE SOLIDS: *10 degrees Brix*

FLAVOR: *Excellent; sweet; lots of flavor in a little package. Smells of the leaf.*

TEXTURE: *Firm; seedy and juicy*

BEST USE(S): *Fresh eating; garnish. Ornamental plant.*

PLANT HABIT, LEAF TYPE, AND YIELD: *Spreading habit; small body parts and currant-type foliage; high yield*

MATURITY: *Very early crop*

ORIGIN: *I initially listed this tomato in the 2004 Seed Savers Exchange yearbook. The entry in the 2007 yearbook reads,* "One of the best tasting, most prolific red currant tomatoes I know, collected in the wild [in 2002] on a trip to the Galápagos [Santa Cruz Island] with my daughter, Sara."

SYNONYMS: *Not the same as the Galapagos Wild tomato listed in the 2007 Seed Savers Exchange yearbook by John F. Swenson (*"vigorous vine, correct name Solanum cheesmaniae *per Galápagos botanist Sarah Darwin [a great-great-granddaughter of Charles], golden cherry; the red fruited one is not this species but an introduced one from the mainland."*) Resembles Matt's Wild Cherry (see previous entry), but Sara's is smaller and less red.*

NY: *Nee & Goldman 53431 and 53432*

SEED SOURCES: *Sa9*

Call it coincidental: Sara's Galapagos usually sets its first ripe fruits on my daughter Sara's birthday, July 26. It's a sad day when, toward the end of September, the time comes to dismantle the plants—especially since Sara's namesake variety can still be found creating currant tomatoes by the thousands. I think this variety might be the most vigorous, crack-resistant, and prolific tomato in my garden. Brava, Sara!

13

(a) Sara's Galapagos, (b) Matt's Wild Cherry

WHITE CURRANT *fig. 15*

SIZE: *¾ " long by ⅞" wide*

WEIGHT: *5.15 grams*

SHAPE: *Currant cross; ellipsoidal*

EXTERIOR COLOR(S): *Light yellow*

FLESH COLOR(S): *Pale yellow*

SOLUBLE SOLIDS: *8½ degrees Brix*

FLAVOR: *Good; grapelike clusters and flavor*

TEXTURE: *Firm; seedy and juicy*

BEST USE(S): *Multipurpose*

PLANT HABIT, LEAF TYPE, AND YIELD: *Spreading habit; regular leaf; high yield*

MATURITY: *Very early crop*

ORIGIN: *Listed in the 1997 Seed Savers Exchange yearbook; the original seed source was Craig LeHouillier. Cataloged in 2005 by Territorial Seed Company; they described White Currant as "one of the most unique and sweetest tasting tomato varieties known. The tiny fruit are half the size of a cherry tomato and grow in nice heavy clusters." In 2006, Baker Creek Heirloom Seeds cataloged it as a new favorite with superb flavor and high sugar.*

SYNONYMS: *Currant White; White Currant Grape. Appears to be similar to Coyote. Not the same as Snow White and Super Snow White.*

NY: *Nee & Goldman 54633*

SEED SOURCES: *Ba8, Te4, Ter, Ra6*

A "near currant" experience: White Currant will fill your needs for fruity mini cherries until frost. Enjoy these dainty fruits baked into savory breads, in mixed peeled tomato salads, and as a substitute for table grapes.

BLONDKÖPFCHEN *fig. 14; page 25, fig. 6j; page 161, fig. 114m, o*

SIZE: *1" long by ⅞" wide*

WEIGHT: *7.40 grams*

SHAPE: *Baby plum, beaked*

EXTERIOR COLOR(S): *Yolk yellow*

FLESH COLOR(S): *Yolk yellow*

SOLUBLE SOLIDS: *7 degrees Brix*

FLAVOR: *Excellent*

TEXTURE: *Reasonably firm*

BEST USE(S): *Multipurpose; for bouquets*

PLANT HABIT, LEAF TYPE, AND YIELD: *Indeterminate habit; regular leaf; high yield*

MATURITY: *Early crop*

ORIGIN: *Obtained by Seed Savers Exchange from Gatersleben Seed Bank in Germany. Commercialized by Grandview Farms Tomato Seeds of Sebastopol, California, circa 1998. J. W. MacArthur, a Professor of Genetics at the University of Toronto, described and illustrated a similar tomato in 1947 (MacArthur's Beaked Plum).*

SYNONYMS: *Same as or resembles Dattelweintomate Gelbe, Gelbe Dattelweintomate, Ildi, Lemon Drop F₁, Little Blonde Girl, MacArthur's Beaked Plum, Mirabell, and Yellow Butterfly*

NY: *Nee & Goldman 53472*

SEED SOURCES: *He8, Ma18, Ra6, Se16, Sk2, So25, To9, To10, Up2*

This yellow tomato is incomparable. I'm overwhelmed every time I see Blondköpfchen's cascading flower trusses. They promise an impressive number of choice golden nuggets; use the sprays in floral arrangements or serve the miniature plums in Spicy Tomato Salsa (see page 219).

GOLD NUGGET *fig. 16*

SIZE: *1⅛" long by 1⅛" wide*

WEIGHT: *12.61 grams*

SHAPE: *Cherry; round to slightly ovate*

EXTERIOR COLOR(S): *Golden yellow*

FLESH COLOR(S): *Maize yellow*

SOLUBLE SOLIDS: *4 degrees Brix*

FLAVOR: *Fair; acidic*

TEXTURE: *Firm; juicy*

BEST USE(S): *Fresh eating; a sprinkle of salt or sugar can do wonders*

PLANT HABIT, LEAF TYPE, AND YIELD: *Compact determinate habit; regular leaf; high yield*

MATURITY: *Very early*

ORIGIN: *Bred by Dr. James R. Baggett of Oregon State University, Corvallis, Oregon, and released in 1983. "An early maturing golden cherry tomato with a strong tendency for seedless fruit and a compact semi-dwarf growth habit," Baggett wrote. "'Gold Nugget' should be useful where fruits resembling 'Yellow Plum' and 'Yellow Pear' [see page 144] in flavor and color are desired, but where* these indeterminate varieties are too late in maturity. 'Gold Nugget' resulted from bulking plants from an F₆ line, T58-2-2-2-7, which derived golden yellow color from an immediate parent, 'Yellow Plum.' Determinate plant habit and parthenocarpic [seedless] fruiting tendency came from a red fruited cherry tomato, OSU T19. In the pedigree, T5-4-2 is one of two sublines making up a released breeding line, Oregon T5-4; and T6-13-5 is a line from the same cross as 'Oregon Cherry.'"*

SYNONYMS: *Not the same as Sutton's Golden Nugget; or the Golden Nugget ground cherry* (Physalis pruinosa).

SEED SOURCES: *Abu, Bo19, Ers, Ga1, Hig, Hum, Jo1, La1, Ni1, Pe2, Pin, Ra6, Re8, Roh, Se26, Sk2, So25, Ter, Tho, To1, To3, Up2, We19*

Worth growing for its earliness and fecundity.

HARTMAN'S YELLOW GOOSEBERRY *fig. 17*

SIZE: *1½" long by 1½" wide*

WEIGHT: *1 ounce*

SHAPE: *Cherry*

EXTERIOR COLOR(S): *Yolk yellow*

FLESH COLOR(S): *Amber yellow*

SOLUBLE SOLIDS: *5 degrees Brix*

FLAVOR: *Poor; tasteless*

TEXTURE: *Reasonably firm*

BEST USE(S): *Fearing Burr's (1863) opinion of yellow cherry tomatoes applies to Hartman's: "Quite showy, but of little value for culinary purposes." Vilmorin Andrieux (1885) was in complete accord; yellow-fruited tomatoes were disdained in France.*

PLANT HABIT, LEAF TYPE, AND YIELD: *Indeterminate habit; regular leaf; high yield*

MATURITY: *Early crop*

ORIGIN: *A very old sort. Illustrated in Johann Wilhelm Weinmann's* Phytanthoza Iconographia *(1734–1745), as* Poma amoris fructu luteo minore; Pomme d'Or, *and* Gold Apffel *(Plate N. 935). This yellow cherry tomato was named by John M. Hartman of J. M. Hartman and Daughters Seed Company, Indianapolis, Indiana.*

SYNONYMS: *Cerise Jaune; Cherry-formed Yellow; Kirschförmige gelbe; Tomate Jaune Petite; Tomate Jaune Ronde Petite; Yellow Cherry; Yellow-Cherry Tomato*

SEED SOURCES: *Lan, To9, To10*

Hartman's is tempting to the eye—more like a pretty little Mirabelle plum than a gooseberry—but not half as sweet as some of the smaller yellow tomatoes in commerce these days (see Gold Rush Currant, page 41). Still, it can happily be the stuff of refrigerator preserves when peeled and simmered in simple syrup with cinnamon, cloves, and sliced lemons.

a

b

18

GREEN GRAPE *fig. 18b*

SIZE: *1½" long by 1½" wide*

WEIGHT: *1 ounce*

SHAPE: *Cherry*

EXTERIOR COLOR(S): *Olive yellow*

FLESH COLOR(S): *Spring green*

SOLUBLE SOLIDS: *7½ degrees Brix*

FLAVOR: *Good; sweet and fruity*

TEXTURE: *Firm; juicy*

BEST USE(S): *Fresh eating*

PLANT HABIT, LEAF TYPE, AND YIELD: *Determinate habit; regular leaf; fair yield*

MATURITY: *Early crop*

ORIGIN: *Green Grape was bred by Thomas P. Wagner and introduced in his 1983 Tater Mater Seeds catalog under the heading "P-2," a "green when ripe fruit with the appearance of Thompson seedless grapes. Very sweet, oblong, cherry-sized fruit grows in large clusters and many are seedless. Only 10% of the seed of other cherry tomatoes. Large indeterminate vine." Tom named the variety Thompson Seedless Grape Tomato in 1985. Four heirloom types are in the parentage, including Evergreen (see page 174). Cataloged in 1997, in determinate form, as Green Grape by Thompson and Morgan and by Totally Tomatoes.*
Tomato breeder and seedsman Ken Ettlinger wrote in his Long Island Seed and Plant Company catalog: "Tom Wagner has to be one of the most noteworthy of tomato collectors and prolific hybridizers of all time. His Tater Mater Seeds in the early 80's made really neat breeding lines of tomatoes and potatoes available to gardeners looking to share in some of the excitement of his breeding experiments. He collected some very unusual material and made available some exciting crosses. The tomatoes were mind expanding."

SYNONYMS: *Thompson Seedless Grape (Tomato); Thompson Seedless Green Grape. Beyond Verde Claro is said to be one of Tom's unreleased improved selections of Thompson Seedless Grape—with a clear epidermis.*

SEED SOURCES: *Ag7, Ba8, Bo19, Bou, Co32, He8, La1, Lan, Ma18, Na6, Ra6, Re8, Roh, Sa9, Se16, Se17, Shu, So1, So25, Sw9, Te4, Tho, To1, To3, To9, To10, Up2*

Will the original Green Grape please stand up? Let's give Green Doctors (see page 43) a run for its money! Thompson Seedless Grape was the first green cherry tomato available to gardeners; it's too bad that an apparently inferior stock—Green Grape—is now circulating. Tom Wagner wrote me, "Thompson Seedless Grape Tomato is the original name of the ubiquitous Green Grape moniker. However, some of the segregating seed which I sent out in the early 1980s tended to be re-selected as a rather determinate line. My Thompson Seedless Grape is indeterminate, is virtually seedless, and has better flavor and yield."

19

GOLD RUSH CURRANT *fig. 19; page 164, fig. 115h*

SIZE: *⅝" long by ¾" wide*

WEIGHT: *17.70 grams*

SHAPE: *Currant cross*

EXTERIOR COLOR(S): *Orange*

FLESH COLOR(S): *Golden yellow*

SOLUBLE SOLIDS: *8½ degrees Brix*

FLAVOR: *Excellent; high acid and high sugar*

TEXTURE: *Firm; seedy*

BEST USE(S): *Fresh eating; decorative*

PLANT HABIT, LEAF TYPE, AND YIELD: *Spreading habit; currant-like leaflets; high yield*

MATURITY: *Very early crop*

ORIGIN: *Introduced in the 2004 Seed Savers Exchange public catalog: "This strain was a selection by a Dutch seedsman, chosen for its manageable growth habit and excellent set of ¼" fruits borne in trusses of 10–12. Does not drop fruit." (True currants come only in red and are much smaller, so this yellow currant, like others of its kind, is a currant cross.)*

Yellow currants date back to as early as 1934, when Herbst Brothers of New York carried Sakata's Yellow Currant. Gold Rush is classified as Lycopersicon esculentum var. esculentum by Dr. Michael Nee.

NY: *Nee & Goldman 54562*

SEED SOURCES: *Pr3, Se16*

A great color contribution to the currant universe, though the plant is not exactly "manageable." Don't even think about staking or caging this free spirit. Squatting astride the plant to gather fruits makes you feel like Godzilla stomping Tokyo. Like any early currant or cherry tomato, the Gold Rush Currant improves in flavor as the season progresses if given lots of sunshine.

(a) Green Doctors, (b) Green Grape

DR. CAROLYN *fig. 20b; page 25, fig. 6h*

SIZE: *1¼" long by 1¼" wide*

WEIGHT: *16.69 grams*

SHAPE: *Cherry*

EXTERIOR COLOR(S): *Wax yellow*

FLESH COLOR(S): *Pastel yellow*

SOLUBLE SOLIDS: *8 degrees Brix*

FLAVOR: *Good; like Concord grapes*

TEXTURE: *Reasonably firm*

BEST USE(S): *Fresh eating*

PLANT HABIT, LEAF TYPE, AND YIELD: *Indeterminate habit; regular leaf; good yield*

MATURITY: *Early crop*

ORIGIN: *First listed in the Seed Savers Exchange 1996 yearbook by Steve Draper, Midvale, Utah. Carried by Southern Exposure Seed Exchange in 1997.*

SYNONYMS: *Dr. Caroline; Galina Ivory Mutant*

SEED SOURCES: *Ap6, Ba8, Ga21, Go8, Ha26, La1, Ma18, Sa5, So1, So25, To1, To9, Up2*

A fine-quality pale yellow sport of Galina's. Named by Steve Draper in honor of his tomato comrade Dr. Carolyn Male, author of *100 Heirloom Tomatoes for the American Garden* and former co-editor of *Off the Vine* tomato newsletter.

DR. CAROLYN PINK *fig. 20a; page 25, fig. 6p; page 176, fig. 122i*

SIZE: *1¼" long by 1⅛" wide*

WEIGHT: *Ranges from 15.11 grams*

SHAPE: *Cherry*

EXTERIOR COLOR(S): *Tomato pink*

FLESH COLOR(S): *Tomato pink*

SOLUBLE SOLIDS: *8 degrees Brix*

FLAVOR: *Good*

TEXTURE: *Reasonably firm*

BEST USE(S): *Fresh eating*

PLANT HABIT, LEAF TYPE, AND YIELD: *Indeterminate habit; regular leaf; good yield*

MATURITY: *Main crop*

ORIGIN: *First listed by Dr. Carolyn Male in the Seed Savers Exchange 2002 yearbook*

NY: *Nee & Goldman 53500*

SEED SOURCES: *Ma18*

A pink sport of Dr. Carolyn discovered by Robert Martin in 1999. Fruits vary widely in size and shape. Appears to be genetically unstable.

GREEN DOCTORS *fig. 20c; page 4, fig. 1b; page 25, fig. 6f; page 40, fig. 18a*

SIZE: *1¼" long by 1¼" wide*

WEIGHT: *19.25 grams*

SHAPE: *Cherry*

EXTERIOR COLOR(S): *Olive yellow*

FLESH COLOR(S): *Spring green*

SOLUBLE SOLIDS: *9½ degrees Brix*

FLAVOR: *Excellent; sweet and tart*

TEXTURE: *Reasonably firm*

BEST USE(S): *Fresh eating*

PLANT HABIT, LEAF TYPE, AND YIELD: *Indeterminate habit; regular leaf; good yield*

MATURITY: *Early crop*

ORIGIN: *A green cherry sport of Dr. Carolyn, which I discovered in my 2002 garden; named by Victor Schrager after a trout fly and in honor of Drs. Amy Goldman and Carolyn Male. I initially listed it in the 2007 Seed Savers Exchange yearbook.*

NY: *Nee & Goldman 53499*

SEED SOURCES: *Sa9*

If you like Green Grape (see page 41), then you'll love Green Doctors—and I don't say that *just* because I'm the proud parent. This handsome little tomato is like the Green Grape but smaller, sweeter, and borne on longer trusses. Tomato aficionado Neil Lockhart of Oblong, Illinois, who maintains a collection of more than 800 varieties, fell for it, too: "It's absolutely fabulous. There's no other green cherry that compares with it for flavor."

LARGE RED CHERRY *fig. 21; page 25, fig. 61*

SIZE: *1½" long by 1½" wide*

WEIGHT: *1 ounce*

SHAPE: *Cherry*

EXTERIOR COLOR(S): *Cherry red*

FLESH COLOR(S): *Vivid red*

SOLUBLE SOLIDS: *6 degrees Brix*

FLAVOR: *Fair; high acid*

TEXTURE: *Firm; juicy and seedy*

BEST USE(S): *Salad; traditionally used for preserves and pickles*

PLANT HABIT, LEAF TYPE, AND YIELD: *Indeterminate habit; regular leaf; high yield*

MATURITY: *Very early crop*

ORIGIN: *Grown in Europe as early as the eighteenth century. Illustrated in Johann Wilhelm Weinmann's* Phytanthoza Iconographia *(1734–1745) as* Solanum pomiferum fructu rubro minore. *Fearing Burr Jr. described two red cherry tomatoes in America in 1863: a larger one, Round Red ("A small, round, red variety, measuring about an inch in diameter. It is one of the earliest of all the cultivated sorts, but of little value except for pickling or preserving.") and a smaller one, Red Cherry ("A small, red Tomato, nearly spherical, and about half an inch in diameter. The fruit is produced in great profusion, in large bunches, or clusters; but is comparatively of little value, on account of its small size. It is sometimes used as a preserve, and by some is esteemed for pickling.").*

SYNONYMS: *Cerise rouge; Cherry; Cherry-formed Red; Cherry Large Red; Kirschförmige rothe; Kirsch rothe; Love Apple Cherry; Old Fashioned Red Cherry; Red Cherry; Red Cherry Large; Round Red; Solanum pomiferum, fructu rubro minore.*

NY: *Nee & Goldman 53402 and 53420*

SEED SOURCES: *Bu3, But, Com, Ers, He8, He17, Jor, La1, Mo13, Or10, Ra6, Re8, Roh, Se16, Se26, Sh9, Shu, Sk2, To1, To3, Wi2*

The Red Cherry tomato is a seedy character, but its seediness gives it great survival value. Liberty Hyde Bailey echoed the sentiments of Fearing Burr Jr. when he said, in 1887, that cherries are "entirely unprofitable on account of the small size of the individual fruits." Yet if one measured profitability in terms of seed production per pound of fruit, cherry tomatoes would be the most lucrative of all. Bailey weighed and measured more than two dozen varieties and found that the red cherry tomatoes had the greatest number of seeds per pound: 7,312 for the Red Cherry and 4,830 for the Kirsch rothe from Prussia. The closest competitor was Improved Large Yellow, with 2,250 seeds a pound; most others weighed in at about half that. On the downside, there also appeared to be an inverse relationship between fruit quality and seed density: the most flavorful tomatoes tended to have lower seed counts.

BROWN BERRY *fig. 22*

SIZE: *1¼" long by 1½" wide*

WEIGHT: *22.10 grams*

SHAPE: *Cherry*

EXTERIOR COLOR(S): *Brownish red*

FLESH COLOR(S): *Brownish red*

SOLUBLE SOLIDS: *5½ degrees Brix*

FLAVOR: *Fair; bland*

TEXTURE: *Reasonably firm*

BEST USE(S): *Multipurpose; novelty; garnish*

PLANT HABIT, LEAF TYPE, AND YIELD: *Indeterminate; regular leaf; high yield*

MATURITY: *Very early crop*

ORIGIN: *Original stock from Sahin Seeds in Holland who also offer Red Berry, Orange Berry, Yellow Berry, and Snow Berry. Introduced by Totally Tomatoes in 2004.*

SYNONYMS: *Brownberry; Chocodel. Not the same as Black Cherry (see page 26), which is violet brown and far superior in fruit quality.*

NY: *Nee & Goldman 54615*

SEED SOURCES: *He8, Hi13, Ra6, Sa5, Sa9, Se16, Se17, To3, Up2, Vi5*

The first brownish-red cherry tomato available to gardeners and cooks. The taste doesn't amaze me, though the color does. Brown Berry is a swell addition to Tomato and Shelly Bean Salad (see page 233) or anything else that calls for a colorful accent. Raymond Blanc, chef-patron of Le Manoir aux Quat' Saisons in Oxfordshire, England, says this tomato reminds him of "bacon, eggs, and sausages with a hint of sage." I'd call that wishful thinking.

RIESENTRAUBE *fig. 23*

SIZE: *1¼" long by 1" wide*

WEIGHT: *18.85 grams*

SHAPE: *Miniature plum, beaked*

EXTERIOR COLOR(S): *Blood red*

FLESH COLOR(S): *Crayfish red*

SOLUBLE SOLIDS: *6½ degrees Brix*

FLAVOR: *Fair; sometimes lemony*

TEXTURE: *Firm; tough skin*

BEST USE(S): *Floral arrangement*

PLANT HABIT, LEAF TYPE, AND YIELD: *Indeterminate habit; regular leaf; high yield*

MATURITY: *Main crop*

ORIGIN: *Named evocatively as "a giant bunch of grapes," Riesentraube was one of eleven rare tomato varieties entrusted to seed saver Curtis D. Choplin of North Augusta, South Carolina, by Professor Jurgen Klapprott of Germany. Choplin spread the wealth in 1992 via the Seed Savers Exchange yearbook. Southern Exposure Seed Exchange was the first to catalog Riesentraube, in 1994. The earliest historical precedent I've found for a red-fruited multiflora type is the extant Semper Fructifera (now known as Britain's Breakfast), a bright red, pear-shaped tomato borne in immense sprays, often having as many as sixty little fruits in each cluster. In 1901, George Nicholson, curator at the Royal Gardens at Kew, England, pronounced the tomato suitable only for dessert. Apparently, in those days, the glorious full English breakfast—scrambled eggs with bacon, black pudding, sausages, mushrooms, beans, cold toast, and grilled tomatoes—was not commonplace.*

SYNONYMS: *Riesentraube; Riesentraube Cherry*

SEED SOURCES: *Abu, Ap6, Ba8, Co32, Ers, He8, He17, Lan, Ma18, Ra6, Sa9, Se16, Sk2, So25, Te4, To1, To3, To9, To10, Und, Up2, Yu2*

I love to watch Riesentraube bloom and grow: It sets fruit on large sprays bearing as many as three hundred flowers and buds, although only 10 to 20 percent of the blossoms bear fruit. The display may not be as spectacular as that of the Kiku—the chrysanthemums that have been artfully trained in Japan for hundreds of years, with up to a thousand blooms—but growing Riesentraube is effortless and rewarding.

Ribbed

(a) Costoluto Genovese, (b) Yellow Ruffled, (c) Purple Calabash, (d) Zapotec

COSTOLUTO GENOVESE *fig. 25; page 4, fig. 1a; page 47, fig. 24a*

SIZE: *3" long by 4½" wide*

WEIGHT: *10 ounces*

SHAPE: *Round, ribbed*

EXTERIOR COLOR(S): *Cherry red*

FLESH COLOR(S): *Cherry red*

SOLUBLE SOLIDS: *5 degrees Brix*

FLAVOR: *Fair to good; acidic*

TEXTURE: *Reasonably firm; meaty*

BEST USE(S): *Cooking; traditionally the tomato of choice for "conserve" or tomato purée in Italy*

PLANT HABIT, LEAF TYPE, AND YIELD: *Indeterminate habit; regular leaf; high yield*

MATURITY: *Very early crop*

ORIGIN: *One of the first kinds of tomato to be introduced in Europe, initially in Spain, and then in Italy and France. Costoluto Genovese (Costoluto means ribbed) looks like the conspicuously ribbed red tomato of Oellinger (1553), the Poma amoris fructu rubro of Besler (1613), the common Large Red (Burr, 1863), and the Rouge Grosse of Vilmorin (1869). It was introduced in the United States circa 1985 via Le Marché Seeds International and Redwood City Seed Company.*

SYNONYMS: *Costoluto di Parma; Grossa Rossa Costoluta; Italian Costoluto Genovese; Large Red Italian; Parmesan Tomato; Pomodoro Genovese; Pomodoro Nizzardo; Pomodoro Rosso Grosso; Quaratine Piatto; Quarantine Rosso; Red Calabash; Red Ruffled; Ribbed Genova; Rouge Grosse; Ruffled Red*

NY: *Nee & Goldman 53395 and 53498*

SEED SOURCES: *Ap6, Coo, Ga1, Ha26, He8, Ki4, Ma18, Na6, Ra6, Re8, Sa5, Se7, Se17, Se24, Se28, So1, Sw9, Te4, Ter, Th3, To1, To3, To9*

By the nineteenth century, the tomato—whether fresh or prepared in pastes, purées, and juices—had become indispensable for cooks and homemakers in Italy, and was grown in virtually every garden. The Pomodoro rosso grosso, synonymous with Costoluto Genovese, was the local favorite, familiarly known as *nostrale* or *commune*. But the Italians have had an intimate relationship with ribbed tomatoes for five hundred years. The *pomodori costoluti* are the tomatoes of choice for *conserve* or tomato purées and concentrates, including *conserva nera*—cakes of dense blackish paste which were the first semi-industrial (and less than sanitary) tomato product on the Italian market, circa 1840 (Amadei and others, 1990). I adopted this tomato in 1989 and have made it mine, too. I put the precious scalloped slices on everything from sandwiches (see Pan Bagnat, page 222) to pizza (see Pizza Margherita, page 207), knowing I'm eating a bit of history.

PURPLE CALABASH

page 47, fig. 24c; page 173, fig. 120d

SIZE: *2¾" long by 3⅜" wide*

WEIGHT: *9½ ounces*

SHAPE: *Round, ribbed*

EXTERIOR COLOR(S): *Violet brown*

FLESH COLOR(S): *Raspberry red*

SOLUBLE SOLIDS: *6½ degrees Brix*

FLAVOR: *Poor; very tart; tastes under-ripe—Glenn Drowns generously calls it "assertive"*

TEXTURE: *Firm; seedy and juicy*

BEST USE(S): *Novelty; decorative. Most people think this tomato is worthless, but Suzanne Ashworth found its highest and best use in 1988: as a base for meat stock. (There's also tomato vinegar …)*

PLANT HABIT, LEAF TYPE, AND YIELD: *Indeterminate habit; regular leaf; good yield*

MATURITY: *Early crop*

ORIGIN: *First brought to attention in the 1985 Seed Savers Exchange yearbook by Gary Staley of Brandon, Florida, who was as obsessed as any SSE member in the early days with finding a "true purple" tomato. The tomato originated in Texas; Gary, along with Will Bonsall of Maine, obtained the variety from the USDA (PI 290857). Purple Calabash was commercially introduced by several seed companies (including Seeds Blüm, Glecklers Seedmen, and Peace Seeds) in 1987. Red Calabash, a sport of Purple Calabash, was introduced several years later by Peace Seeds.*

SYNONYMS: *Noire de Coseboeuf; Noire des Coseboeuf*

SEED SOURCES: *Ag7, Ba8, Co32, Go8, He8, Hi13, La1, Pla, Pr3, Sa9, Se17, Sk2, So25, Sw9, Te4, Ter, Th3, To1, To9, To10, Up2*

This is the tomato everyone—except me and Jeff Nekola—loves to bash. A representative sample of opinion from some well-known genetic preservationists:

"A grotesquely convoluted blob of flesh the color of a bad bruise."

"It looks like something you wouldn't want to step in."

"A contorted mass of tasteless flesh."

It's a mystery to me that these people don't appreciate the subtle beauty of the Purple Calabash's ribbing and color. To my eye, it glows like eighteenth-century mahogany.

YELLOW RUFFLED

page 47, fig. 24b; page 161, fig. 114c

SIZE: *2¼" long by 4" wide*

WEIGHT: *9½ ounces*

SHAPE: *From round and angular to coxcomb*

EXTERIOR COLOR(S): *Yolk yellow*

FLESH COLOR(S): *Corn*

SOLUBLE SOLIDS: *4½ degrees Brix*

FLAVOR: *Fair to poor*

TEXTURE: *Very firm; puffy (hollowish) and pithy (whitish core)*

BEST USE(S): *Decorative; can be stuffed; attractive garnish when sliced*

PLANT HABIT, LEAF TYPE, AND YIELD: *Indeterminate; regular leaf; high yield*

MATURITY: *Early crop*

ORIGIN: *This is the yellow version of Red Ruffled (see Costoluto Genovese, page 48). Introduced by Glecklers Seedmen as Ruffled in 1957 and reintroduced in 1976. Ken Ettlinger of Long Island Seed and Plant Company described it in 1990 as a novelty with ridges like the folds of a bellows—something between a true stuffer and a tomato with meaty, juicy flesh.*

SYNONYMS: *Grosse Gelbe; Jaune Grosse; Large Yellow; Persian Yellow; Poma amoris fructu luteo; Ruffled; Ruffled Golden; Ruffled Yellow; Yellow Accordion; and Yellow Ruffles*

SEED SOURCES: *Ma18, Sa9, To1*

A distinctive tomato with some history behind it, the Yellow Ruffled has been known in Europe for hundreds of years. It mimics the Poma amoris fructu luteo in Besler's *Hortus Eystettensis* (1613), and more than 250 years later, in 1879, its spitting image, Grosse Gelbe, could be found in Germany's *Album Benary*. That same year, Joseph Harris of Rochester, New York, cataloged a synonymous variety called Persian Yellow with the following copy: "At one time highly recommended, and still occasionally grown. But we have now so many better sorts that it is not worth while to grow this for general use. It is a large, rather coarse tomato, of a creamy yellow color."

I agree that there are far better tomatoes for fresh eating. But Yellow Ruffled is gladly received in my kitchen as a decorative element or for stuffing and baking.

ZAPOTEC

page 47, fig. 24d; page 176, fig. 122a

SIZE: *2½" long by 4½" wide*

WEIGHT: *12 ounces*

SHAPE: *Eccentric; heavily ribbed, pleated, or ruffled*

EXTERIOR COLOR(S): *Tomato pink*

FLESH COLOR(S): *Tomato pink*

SOLUBLE SOLIDS: *5½ degrees Brix*

FLAVOR: *Surprisingly good*

TEXTURE: *Very firm; nearly hollow*

BEST USE(S): *Stuffing*

PLANT HABIT, LEAF TYPE, AND YIELD: *Indeterminate habit; regular leaf; high yield*

MATURITY: *Early crop*

ORIGIN: *A high-altitude drought-tolerant tomato from Oaxaca, Mexico. Cataloged in 1987 as "Large Ribbed Pink Zapotec" by J. L. Hudson, Seedsman. In 1998 Hudson called it "Enrollado": "An old favorite of the Zapotecs ... Large, ribbed pink fruits." Hudson carried an extensive Zapotec collection for many years. Their catalog boasted of "vegetables, herbs, ornamental and medicinal plants collected deep in the Sierra Madre del Sur, in southern Oaxaca, Mexico. The population of this rugged, mountainous region is largely Zapotec, and many of these plants have been grown by this tribe since pre-history. Called 'People of the Clouds' by neighboring tribes, this aptly describes life at this high elevation. Fog, cold winds, and mist are frequent at the higher elevations: a few hours walk down the mountain, bananas and sugar cane can be grown. These seeds are collected from about 8000 feet down to 4000 feet elevation, so a great range of microclimates is represented. There are two great seasons—the 'time of water' and the 'time of wind' ... Planting dates and the time of burning for slash-and-burn agriculture are by season and are marked by fiestas ... people cannot afford to grow anything that is not hardy and productive. If a plant does not grow like a weed and produce abundantly without fertilizer, they say 'It doesn't give here.'*

"Most of these seeds are collected by the last herbal healer in this locality, and by his family. Conditions in this remote, roadless area are difficult. Some corn fields are so steep that the people joke about falling out of them, and this occasionally does happen. Crops are sometimes uncertain, and it is difficult to properly dry and store seed due to the humidity. Each parcel must be packed out over narrow mountain trails. It is hard to describe the human effort that has gone into bringing these seeds to you, and I hope you will bear with us if supplies are irregular."

SYNONYMS: *Enrollado; Large Pink Ruffled; Large Red Zapotec; Large Ribbed Pink Zapotec; Mexican Ribbed; Pink Accordion; Pink Ruffled; Zapotec Pink; Zapotec Pink Pleated; Zapotec Pink Ribbed; Zapotec Ribbed. Shares features with Gezahnte Tomate (see page 55).*

SEED SOURCES: *Hi13, Ma18, Na6, Pr3, Se7, To1, To9, To1*

After the Conquest of Mexico in 1521, tomatoes made their way to Europe. Some of the tomatoes illustrated in sixteenth-century European herbals were multilocular and heavily ribbed—similar in shape to Zapotec (Harlan, 1995; Daunay et al., 2007). The Mexican legacy is still clearly evident today in the "costoluto" or ribbed tomatoes of Italy (see Costoluto Genovese, page 48).

CEYLON *fig. 26*

SIZE: *1¼" long by 2½" wide*

WEIGHT: *4 ounces*

SHAPE: *Round, ribbed*

EXTERIOR COLOR(S): *Blood red*

FLESH COLOR(S): *Blood red*

SOLUBLE SOLIDS: *6 degrees Brix*

FLAVOR: *Excellent when cooked*

TEXTURE: *Reasonably firm; meaty, juicy, and seedy*

BEST USE(S): *Great on the stovetop, but by-pass the broiler; not for fresh eating, either*

PLANT HABIT, LEAF TYPE, AND YIELD: *Indeterminate habit; regular leaf; high yield*

MATURITY: *Very early crop*

ORIGIN: *Introduced in 1997 by Tom Stearns of High Mowing Organic Seed Farm. Tom's seed came from Bryan Connolly of Mansfield Center, Connecticut, who describes himself as a "botanist for hire, rare plant monitor, food co-op worker, seed saver, and chicken farmer."*

SYNONYMS: *Red Calabash. Resembles Red Star. Similar to many ribbed Italian sorts.*

NY: *Nee & Goldman 53401*

SEED SOURCES: *Hi6, Sa9, To1, To9, To10*

A traditional Italian ribbed tomato type, smaller and more primitive than Grossa Rossa Costoluto or Costoluto Genovese (see page 48). Though the Ceylon is popular in parts of Asia, some people in this part of the world are turned off by its knobbly looks and sour taste. I felt that way, too, until my friend Ethne Clarke, garden editor at *Traditional Home* magazine, used Ceylon to whip up a revelation: the best cooked tomato sauce, in moments. She sautéed the diced tomatoes in a little olive oil, with garlic, salt, pepper, and fresh basil, just the way her Florentine friends had taught her to make *la bella figura* of tomato sauce: "with none of that southern messing around with herbs, carrots, celery, and onions, or hours of simmering—understated and elegant, just like they are."

27

ROSSO SICILIAN *fig. 27*

SIZE: *1½" long by 2½" wide*

WEIGHT: *4 ounces*

SHAPE: *Round, ribbed*

EXTERIOR COLOR(S): *Crayfish red*

FLESH COLOR(S): *Coral red*

SOLUBLE SOLIDS: *4 degrees Brix*

FLAVOR: *Fair to good*

TEXTURE: *Very firm; thick walls; pithy, and puffy (with air spaces in locules)*

BEST USE(S): *Cooking; for* conserva di pomodoro *(tomato purée)*

PLANT HABIT, LEAF TYPE, AND YIELD: *Determinate habit; regular leaf; low to good yield*

MATURITY: *Main crop*

ORIGIN: *An Italian heirloom brought by a Sicilian man to the United States in 1987; given to Ann Fuller of Mitchell, Indiana, who said its slices look like red-petaled flowers (rosso means "red"); and perpetuated in the Seed Savers Exchange 1988 yearbook under the name "Russo Sicilian" ("russo" is another way of saying "rosso"). Commercialized by Marianna's Heirloom Seeds and by TomatoFest Homegrown Seeds circa 2004.*

SYNONYMS: *Red Sicilian; Russo Sicilian; Russo Sicilian Toggetta; and Togetta*

SEED SOURCES: *Ma18, To9*

An alluring plant that produces several sets of disproportionately large "costoluta" (ribbed) tomatoes. Rosso Sicilian is apparently the short form of Grossa Rossa Costoluta, one of the earliest varieties to be imported to Italy. It fits the description of Barr and Sugden's Large Red Italian, known as early as 1868, and conforms to Vilmorin-Andrieux's (1883) and Bailey's (1887) descriptions of Tomate Rouge Naine Hâtive (also known as Early Dwarf Red Tomato, Früheste rothe Zwerg-Tomate, and Roode vroege dwerg tomaat). It makes a tomato sauce that is *squisita* with Fresh Corn Polenta (see page 197).

REISETOMATE *fig. 28*

SIZE: *2" long by 3½" wide*

WEIGHT: *5 ounces*

SHAPE: *Eccentric: a mutant with unfused carpels*

EXTERIOR COLOR(S): *Blood red*

FLESH COLOR(S): *Cock's comb red*

SOLUBLE SOLIDS: *5½ degrees Brix*

FLAVOR: *Poor; very sour*

TEXTURE: *Soft; readily damaged by rough handling. Quite seedy. Fruits should be removed from the plant by cutting with a scissors.*

BEST USE(S): *Novelty; exhibition*

PLANT HABIT, LEAF TYPE, AND YIELD: *Indeterminate habit; regular leaf; high yield*

MATURITY: *Early crop*

ORIGIN: *The original stock came from Nancy Arrowsmith of Arche Noah in Schiltern, Austria, via Ulrike Paradine of England. Bärbel Schmidt, of the Institute for Plant Genetics and Crop Plant Research in Gatersleben, Germany, said in the Seed Savers 1996 Summer Edition: "The Indians of Central America include another unusual and very large type of tomato in their diet, one they refer to as a traveler tomato. The fruits are irregular and lobed and consist of many individual cavities that can be torn apart. The tomato can thus be easily divided up without the use of a knife."*

Reisetomate's bizarre appearance is due to a mutation at the fasciated locus associated with more and unfused carpels (Tanksley, 2004). Reminds me of the Turk's Cap (Turkenbund)—a tomato "crowned by a singular, irregular mass of protruded, fleshy cells"—documented as a curiosity by L. H. Bailey in 1887; also known as Tomato Orchids (Glecklers Seedmen, 1954).

SYNONYMS: *Pocketbook; Purse; Travel; Voyage (introduced by J. L. Hudson, seedsman, in 2007 and described as a "Siamese-twin-like bunch")*

NY: *Nee & Goldman 53495*

SEED SOURCES: *Hud, Sk2, So25*

A tomato gone haywire—or hemorrhoidal—Reisetomate looks like a bunch of small tomatoes randomly stuck together. The lobes can be easily removed and dispersed, a trait that appeals to hungry small and large. Assistant Professor Burkhard Schulz at Purdue University explained that the fruit is brilliantly utilitarian: It can be eaten one piece at a time and the rest can be saved for later by travelers on their merry way. I created a sensation on *The Martha Stewart Show* on TV by taking in a stalk of Reisetomates (also known as Pocketbook) as my purse on "handbag" day. The tomato may not be as classic as an Hermès, but it's nonetheless a priceless heirloom.

28

MR. BROWN *fig. 29; page 59, fig. 33g*

SIZE: *2¾" long by 3¾" wide*

WEIGHT: *10 ounces*

SHAPE: *Round, moderately ribbed*

EXTERIOR COLOR(S): *Reddish brown and cardinal red*

FLESH COLOR(S): *Cardinal red*

SOLUBLE SOLIDS: *4½ degrees Brix*

FLAVOR: *Poor; low acid, low sugar*

TEXTURE: *Reasonably firm; mealy*

BEST USE(S): *Decorative*

PLANT HABIT, LEAF TYPE, AND YIELD: *Indeterminate habit; regular leaf; good yield*

MATURITY: *Main crop*

ORIGIN: *Listed in the Seed Savers Exchange 2003 yearbook by Jeff Dawson of Napa, California. Mr. Brown appeared in Jeff's garden as a sport of Brown Flesh (see page 150), a Tom Wagner variety.*

SYNONYMS: *Not the same as Mr. Brown's (a large pink tomato from Pennsylvania)*

NY: *Nee & Goldman 53473*

SEED SOURCES: *Ma18, To9*

Definitely one for the camera, with a patina that begs to be reproduced in bronze. Who needs it to be palatable when it's so beauteous?

29

GEZAHNTE TOMATE *fig. 30*

SIZE: *3½" long by 4" wide*

WEIGHT: *8 ounces*

SHAPE: *Eccentric. Ribbed hollow stuffer in a range of shapes*

EXTERIOR COLOR(S): *Tomato pink*

FLESH COLOR(S): *Tomato pink*

SOLUBLE SOLIDS: *6 degrees Brix*

FLAVOR: *Fair*

TEXTURE: *Very firm; thick walls, hollow, mealy and dry*

BEST USE(S): *Novelty, ornament, stuffing*

PLANT HABIT, LEAF TYPE, AND YIELD: *Indeterminate habit; regular leaf, high yield*

MATURITY: *Main crop*

ORIGIN: *Frau Isabella Bührer-Keel, of Basel, Switzerland, donated Gezahnte to ProSpecieRara, Aarau, Switzerland; her seed had come from an Italian man whose mother had grown it in Naples since his childhood. Sylvia Davatz, of Hartland, Vermont, obtained the seed from ProSpecieRara and listed it in the 2002 Seed Savers Exchange yearbook.*

SYNONYMS: *Dentelée de Buhrer-Keel; Gezahnte Tomate Bührer-Keel*

Gezahnte's deeply pleated corrugations defy belief. It shares certain features with Zapotec but shows more panache. Makes a dazzling centerpiece or unusual side dish when filled with tabbouleh, couscous, or rice salad.

RED CUP *page x*

SIZE: *3" long by 5" wide*

WEIGHT: *1 pound, 3 ounces*

SHAPE: *Eccentric. Pleated.*

EXTERIOR COLOR(S): *Tomato pink*

FLESH COLOR(S): *Tomato pink*

SOLUBLE SOLIDS: *4½ degrees Brix*

FLAVOR: *Fair*

TEXTURE: *Firm*

BEST USE(S): *A stuffing tomato; semi-hollow*

PLANT HABIT, LEAF TYPE, AND YIELD: *Indeterminate habit; regular leaf; good yield*

MATURITY: *Late crop*

ORIGIN: *This variety was given to tomato seedsman Ben Quisenberry by his friend and employee Don Hubbard, who called it "Tomango." Ben preferred the name "Red Cup," and he cataloged it as such in 1976 (Big Tomato Gardens, Syracuse, Ohio). He wrote: "This unique hollow variety is ideal for stuffing foods, like sweet peppers are used." The right size, he said, was "as large as 3 to 4 inches across and 2 to 3 inches deep."*

SYNONYMS: *Stuffing; Tomango. (The Tomango I know, smaller and not as ruffled, isn't synonymous with Red Cup.) Red Cup became quite popular circa 1990, by which point a yellow version, Yellow Cup (see Yellow Stuffer, page 150), was also circulating.*

NY: *Nee & Goldman 54579*

SEED SOURCES: *Ag7, Ma18, To1*

Don Hubbard now sells tomatoes for a living from his commercial greenhouse in Syracuse, Ohio. He doesn't remember where he got the Tomango or Red Cup—"I came up with it somewhere"—but he'll never forget Ben Quisenberry, who was like a father to him. In 1950, when Don was in the eighth grade, he began working in Ben's stamping business, Safety Tag Company, stamping name plates for dog collars. (Roy Rogers was one of their clients.) At times, they set up shop at local dog trials and made tags on the spot. Don later helped Ben haul mail after school, and he worked in Ben's printing business, among other enterprises. "I learned more from Ben Quisenberry than from anyone else: how to manage money, how to live, and never to smoke a cigarette."

31

SUPERMARMANDE *fig. 31*

SIZE: *2¼" long by 4" wide*

WEIGHT: *11 ounces*

SHAPE: *Round, ribbed*

EXTERIOR COLOR(S): *Cherry red*

FLESH COLOR(S): *Cherry red*

SOLUBLE SOLIDS: *4 degrees Brix*

FLAVOR: *Fair to good*

TEXTURE: *Firm*

BEST USE(S): *The French seedhouse Vilmorin-Andrieux says, "ideal for cooking and for salads," but I'd say use it for cooking; in salads it's bland.*

PLANT HABIT, LEAF TYPE, AND YIELD: *Indeterminate habit; regular leaf; high yield*

MATURITY: *Early crop*

ORIGIN: *Marmande is a traditional variety from the South of France according to Marie-Christine Daunay of INRA (Unité de Génétique et Amélioration des Fruits et Légumes) in Avignon, France. Her retired colleague, tomato specialist Henri Laterrot, says that very little is known of Marmande's origins, although it bears the same name as a French town. In the 1950s, Marmande was widely cultivated in France, particularly in the Southeast; today it's cultivated by home gardeners but not by commercial growers.*

The earliest mention I've found of Marmande is in Baldoni's Il Pomodoro *in 1940: "Through experimenta-*tion it was found that, in better soil, this variety is the most productive of all in absolute terms as well as for yielding extract. It does not, however, have good organoleptic and industrial processing qualities." Vilmorin wrote in 1946: "Beautiful fruits, bright scarlet, smooth, lightly ribbed, firm fleshed; vigorous and early; disease resistant." In the United States, Supermarmande was described as novel in the February 1980 issue of* Flower and Garden*: "Comes from France where it's been a favorite. Large, early, flavorful and prodigiously produced, it has gourmet quality; will be offered by Epicure Seeds Ltd."*

SYNONYMS: *Marmalade Super; Marmande Super. Resembles Marmande and its many variants (including De Marmande, Marmande Ancienne, Marmande Extra, and Marmande VF) but is supposedly* earlier and more disease resistant. Similar to Ugly (see page 57) and UglyRipe. Strongly resembles the Perdrigeon featured in Zago (1913), a tomato once popular in the Parma region of Italy.

SEED SOURCES: *Bou, Sa9, Se7, Syn, Tho, To9*

Supermarmande is not as "groovy" as the old Large Red or Pomodoro Rosso Grosso (see Costoluto Genovese, page 48), from which it is evidently descended, but it's excellent in French cookery. In 1828, Descourtilz gave a description of the uses of tomato in the Continental kitchen: "Cultivated in America and in Europe, particularly in Portugal, in Spain, and in the central part of France. The resources which it offers to the culinary art in the preparation of ragouts and 'coulis' have given it admittance to all the vegetable gardens in the vicinity of Paris. Its paste is conserved for the winter, by means of drying; then, when the vegetable resources are limited, in the middle of the winter, the tomato sauce appears on our tables in a thousand ways—to serve in beef or mutton soups, to be associated with codfish and many other varieties of fish" (McCue, 1952).

32

UGLY *fig. 32*

SIZE: *2½" long by 4½" wide*

WEIGHT: *14 ounces*

SHAPE: *Round, ribbed*

EXTERIOR COLOR(S): *Cherry red*

FLESH COLOR(S): *Cherry red*

SOLUBLE SOLIDS: *6 degrees Brix*

FLAVOR: *Good*

TEXTURE: *Reasonably firm; meaty*

BEST USE(S): *Cooking; purée and sauce*

PLANT HABIT, LEAF TYPE, AND YIELD: *Indeterminate habit; regular leaf; high yield*

MATURITY: *Early crop*

ORIGIN: *Ugly strongly resembles the common red tomato grown in Europe for hundreds of years. Cataloged by Tomato Growers Supply Company in 2004. Resembles the large ribbed bronze tomato found by Professor Jules Janick of Purdue University on the door of the cathedral in Pisa, Italy, dated 1601.*

SYNONYMS: *Similar to Costoluto Genovese (see page 48) and many other ribbed or angled tomatoes such as Pomodoro rosso grosso, Rouge grosse, and the old Large Red. Not the same as the "heirloom type" UglyRipe, a hybrid tomato developed by Joseph Procacci, CEO of Procacci Brothers Sales Corporation and owner of Santa Sweets, Inc., at a reported expenditure of three million dollars and over twenty years' time. Not the same as Mr. Ugly, a hybrid tomato cataloged by the D. Palmer Seed Company. (Mr. Ugly is also the name of a muskmelon from Italy with deep ribs and big warts, cataloged by Glecklers in 1977.)*

NY: *Nee & Goldman 53414*

"Ugly" is in the eye of the beholder. This one is beautiful to me.

Globe

(a) Aunt Ruby's German Green, (b) Rutgers Improved, (c) Manyel, (d) White Beauty,
(e) Aunt Gertie's Gold, (f) Burpee's Globe, (g) Mr. Brown, (h) Eva Purple Ball, (i) Peach Blow Sutton

WHITE BEAUTY *fig. 34; page 59, fig. 33d; page 87, fig. 59a*

SIZE: *2" long by 3¾" wide*

WEIGHT: *8 ounces*

SHAPE: *Ranges from smooth and round to slightly ribbed beefsteak*

EXTERIOR COLOR(S): *Pale yellow*

FLESH COLOR(S): *Pale yellow*

SOLUBLE SOLIDS: *5 degrees Brix*

FLAVOR: *Excellent*

TEXTURE: *Soft; meaty*

BEST USE(S): *Fresh eating*

PLANT HABIT, LEAF TYPE, AND YIELD: *Indeterminate habit; regular leaf; high yield*

MATURITY: *Main crop*

ORIGIN: *Cataloged as early as 1926 by Harris Seeds. Touted by Burgess Seed and Plant Company since circa 1929 as "the Anti-Acid tomato," sweet and low in acid. Adopted by nonagenarian Ben Quisenberry and cataloged in 1981 by his Big Tomato Gardens with the legend "White inside, and out. Sweet!"*

SYNONYMS: *Albino; Beauté Blanche; Crystal White; Frew's Snowball; New White Beauty; and Snowball. Not the same as the smaller (1- to 1½-inch-diameter), generally spherical, yellowish-white tomatoes: White Apple, New White Apple, Nellis' Snowball, Apfelweisser, Green Gage, or Ivory Ball.*

NY: *Nee & Goldman 53427*

SEED SOURCES: *Ba8, Co32, Roh, Se26, To1, To10*

I'm crazy about this superexcellent, whitest of white tomatoes, with long, eyelash-like calyces. White Beauty has compared favorably with the best reds for over eighty years: "Remarkably sweet" (Harris Seeds, 1926); "absolutely the best white tomato to be had" (House of Gurney, 1929); "tastes red—close your eyes—can you tell by tasting?" (Seeds Blüm, 1982 and 1984).

White (pale yellow) tomatoes have been known and grown in Europe for hundreds of years, but they haven't won many popularity contests. Most nineteenth-century American tomato commentators dismissed whites as watery and unpalatable or met them only with astonishment. A notable exception was Benjamin K. Bliss, seedsman and florist in Springfield, Massachusetts; Bliss cataloged the New White as fine-flavored in 1866 and four years later described it as productive, with fruit nearly white, but not widely grown.

Fearing Burr noted in 1863 that if the white tomato is screened by foliage or grown in the shade, then the fruit will be almost clear white; otherwise it assumes a yellowish tinge. Part of the beauty of White Beauty is the sheer mass of foliage, which does a great job of blanching. Be prepared to claw your way in.

BURPEE'S GLOBE *page 59, fig. 33f*

SIZE: *2½" long by 3" wide*

WEIGHT: *6½ ounces*

SHAPE: *Round, smooth*

EXTERIOR COLOR(S): *Tomato pink*

FLESH COLOR(S): *Tomato pink*

SOLUBLE SOLIDS: *6 degrees Brix*

FLAVOR: *Excellent; honey sweet*

TEXTURE: *Firm; meaty, somewhat grainy*

BEST USE(S): *Multipurpose*

PLANT HABIT, LEAF TYPE, AND YIELD: *Indeterminate habit; regular leaf; good yield*

MATURITY: *Main crop*

ORIGIN: *Introduced in 1935 by W. Atlee Burpee Company. Parentage unknown. Winner of the All-America Selections Silver Medal in 1936.*

SYNONYMS: *Similar to Livingston's Globe (1905)*

SEED SOURCES: *Vi4*

What can I say? This is a perfect globe. Burpee's Globe made its commercial debut in Burpee's 1935 *Annual Garden Book*—and was so highly regarded that it appeared on the back cover of at least three Burpee annuals. As Burpee observed, "We have great pleasure in introducing to our friends this season a decidedly new and distinct Tomato of superior merit … This tomato contains little or no acid and can be classed as a sweet, pinkish-red Marglobe. It abounds in vitamins A, B and C. It is a shy seeder, the seed cavities being full of solid meat … Excellent for both home and market garden … and for forcing in the greenhouse." Plus the flavor. This tomato tastes so good, you'll plotz.

AUNT GERTIE'S GOLD *page 59, fig. 33e*

SIZE: *3" long by 4" wide*

WEIGHT: *15 ounces*

SHAPE: *Oblate globe, smooth; shape and size vary*

EXTERIOR COLOR(S): *Tangerine*

FLESH COLOR(S): *Deep orange*

SOLUBLE SOLIDS: *6 degrees Brix*

FLAVOR: *Excellent; sumptuous, rich flavor*

TEXTURE: *Firm; tender and meaty*

BEST USE(S): *Fresh eating*

PLANT HABIT, LEAF TYPE, AND YIELD: *Indeterminate habit; potato leaf; good yield*

MATURITY: *Early crop*

ORIGIN: *Introduced circa 2004 by Heirloom Tomatoes of Rosedale, Maryland. The original seed was given to the late proprietor Chuck Wyatt by a friend in Virginia.*

NY: *Nee & Goldman 53486*

SEED SOURCES: *Ma18, To1, To9*

Six degrees of Brix makes for a delicious tomato, and Aunt Gertie's Gold qualifies as one of the greats. Reminds me of persimmon—without the pucker.

MANVEL *page 59, fig. 33c; page 161, fig. 114h*

SIZE: *3" long by 3¼" wide*

WEIGHT: *12 ounces*

SHAPE: *Round, smooth*

EXTERIOR COLOR(S): *Yolk yellow*

FLESH COLOR(S): *Butter yellow*

SOLUBLE SOLIDS: *6 degrees Brix*

FLAVOR: *Good; sweet and tart; some describe it as lemony*

TEXTURE: *Soft; meaty and juicy*

BEST USE(S): *Fresh eating*

PLANT HABIT, LEAF TYPE, AND YIELD: *Determinate and indeterminate types; regular leaf; high yield*

MATURITY: *Main crop*

ORIGIN: *Original seed source was Joseph J. Bratka of Elmwood Park, New Jersey, in 1992. The variety, as well as the name, Manvel or Many Moons, is reportedly of recent American Indian origin. Cataloged by Sand Hill Preservation Center and by Southern Exposure Seed Exchange in 1995.*

SYNONYMS: *Manvel-Moons; Many Moons*

SEED SOURCES: *Ma18, Go8, Sa9, So1, So25, To1, To3, To9*

A bright, sunshiny yellow, Manvel produces perfectly uniform globes.

FORDHOOK FIRST *fig. 35*

SIZE: *3" long by 3¼" wide*

WEIGHT: *8 ounces*

SHAPE: *Round, smooth*

EXTERIOR COLOR(S): *Tomato pink*

FLESH COLOR(S): *Tomato pink*

SOLUBLE SOLIDS: *5½ degrees Brix*

FLAVOR: *Good to excellent; nice acid; aromatic*

TEXTURE: *Firm to very firm; meaty and juicy*

BEST USE(S): *Multipurpose*

PLANT HABIT, LEAF TYPE, AND YIELD: *Indeterminate habit; regular leaf; good yield*

MATURITY: *Early crop*

ORIGIN: *Introduced in 1894 by W. Atlee Burpee and Company*

SYNONYMS: *Early Fordhook First; and Fordhook. Not the same as Fordhook Fancy (which is a ruby-red-fruited dwarf rugose tomato). Fordhook First is similar to the Trucker's Favorite, as noted by Craig LeHouillier, the North Carolina seed saver who liberated these and many other commercial heirlooms from the USDA.*

NY: *Nee & Goldman 53473a*

SEED SOURCES: *Vi4*

Fordhook First is a treasure—a perfectly lovely, firm pink slicer that's consistently among the first earlies, as precocious today as it was when Burpee introduced it back in 1894. The variety originated with market gardeners S. D. Woodruff and Sons of New Haven, Connecticut. The Woodruffs sold their entire crop of first-class selected seed of the new tomato to Burpee "with the exclusive privilege of its introduction." "Your selection of a name is most happy," the vendor wrote, "as this has been **THE FIRST** TOMATO to appear in our local markets for the past three or four seasons." The *Rural New-Yorker* also found Fordhook First to be as early as any they had trialed.

Fordhook First is *the* tomato to eat with Iceberg lettuce—one of the sweetest and firmest of head lettuces, yet much maligned for lack of flavor; the two vegetables were illustrated together in color in the 1894 *Burpee's Farm Annual*. Fordhook and Iceberg, cut in wedges and drenched in blue cheese and buttermilk dressing, is a mainstay of my summer diet. Whatever it may lack in snob appeal, it makes up for in sheer deliciousness. Pull down the blinds and try it!

VICTORY *fig. 36; page 4, fig. 1e*

SIZE: *2" long by 2½" wide*

WEIGHT: *3½ ounces*

SHAPE: *Round, smooth*

EXTERIOR COLOR(S): *Blood red*

FLESH COLOR(S): *Blood red*

SOLUBLE SOLIDS: *6 degrees Brix*

FLAVOR: *Good to excellent*

TEXTURE: *Very thin-skinned and soft; meaty and juicy*

BEST USE(S): *Multipurpose*

PLANT HABIT, LEAF TYPE, AND YIELD: *Indeterminate habit; regular leaf; high yield*

MATURITY: *Early crop*

ORIGIN: *Victory is an English commercial heirloom maintained by Garden Organic, the working name for the Henry Doubleday Research Association (HDRA) in Coventry, England. It was reportedly introduced by Clibran's of Altrincham in 1918. Mary Eastwood, an HDRA seed guardian who worked for Clibran's as a seed cleaner in 1945, wrote, "I can well remember the wonderful thick, red flesh with few seeds and very thin skins. This made them of little use for commercial grading machines and probably caused its demise."*

SYNONYMS: *This is not the same as the Victory tomato from Sakhalin Island or the Victory tomato (John Baer x Greater Baltimore) created in America during World War I by John Baer and cataloged by J. Bolgiano and Son in 1920; it had been introduced by Bolgiano as Baltimore Baer in 1919 and was renamed a year later. Renowned hybridizer Baer is now remembered mostly for the John Baer tomato (synonymous with Bonny Best; see page 77). According to the Bolgiano catalog, Baer, with his only boy off fighting in France, "labored unceasingly during the four long years of the Great World War" to produce Victory.*

NY: *Nee & Goldman 53503*

This is a nice tomato—if only it had thicker skin.

35

MANITOBA *fig. 37*

SIZE: *3" long by 3¼" wide*

WEIGHT: *10 ounces*

SHAPE: *Round, smooth*

EXTERIOR COLOR(S): *Blood red*

FLESH COLOR(S): *Blood red*

SOLUBLE SOLIDS: *5¼ degrees Brix*

FLAVOR: *Excellent; well-balanced, winey*

TEXTURE: *Firm; skin is tough to cut but easy to peel; seedy and juicy*

BEST USE(S): *Fresh eating and canning*

PLANT HABIT, LEAF TYPE, AND YIELD: *Determinate habit; regular leaf; high yield*

MATURITY: *Early crop*

ORIGIN: *An early variety, bred for the prairie provinces by Dr. Charles Walkof at the Morden Experiment Station, Morden, Manitoba. Released in 1956. Derives from a cross of Morden BB3 (a selection from Marglobe x Bounty) and Redskin.*

SYNONYMS: *Manitoba Bush; Manitoba Improved. Resembles Bounty. Similar to Bush Beefsteak but slightly earlier and smoother.*

NY: *Nee & Goldman 53452*

SEED SOURCES: *Ear, Ers, Ga1, He8, He17, Pr3, Re8, Sa5, Sa9, So25, Te4, Ter, To1, To3, To9, Up2*

Like Admiral Peary, this tomato helped open up the Great White North. Before its introduction, growing commercial canning tomatoes in Manitoba was impossible. The variety is also good for fresh market and is widely adapted. In Dutchess County, New York, Manitoba brightens my life in early August, when, tomato-starved, I just can't stop eating it straight from the vine. The late cookbook author Lee Bailey might have described Manitoba as "reward food," something you could continue eating after you are finished eating. It's a striking exception to the general rule that tomatoes for northern gardens don't travel south.

37

CANABEC ROSE *fig. 38*

SIZE: *2½" long by 2¾" wide*

WEIGHT: *6 ounces*

SHAPE: *Round, smooth*

EXTERIOR COLOR(S): *Tomato pink*

FLESH COLOR(S): *Tomato pink*

SOLUBLE SOLIDS: *4 degrees Brix*

FLAVOR: *Fair to good*

TEXTURE: *Reasonably firm; juicy*

BEST USE(S): *Multipurpose; bred for Canadian climes*

PLANT HABIT, LEAF TYPE, AND YIELD: *Determinate habit; regular leaf; good yield*

MATURITY: *Early crop*

ORIGIN: *Bred by Roger Doucet of the Station Provinciale de Recherches Agricoles, Saint-Hyacinthe, Québec, Canada; released in 1976. Pedigree includes PI 263726—a Puerto Rican tomato collected by the late Dr. Charles Rick.*

SEED SOURCES: *Pr3, Sa9*

Québecois love pink tomatoes, especially this one. Canabec Rose is one of a dozen cultivars with the suffix *-bec*—for Québec—bred by Roger Doucet in the 1960s and '70s: Canabec, Précocibec (Québec Early Market), Maskabec, Ilabec, Usabec, Yorkbec, Canabec Super, Rosabec, Canabec Rose, Superbec, Ultrabec, and Petitebec.

All of the "Becs" perform admirably under cool growing conditions that are marginal for most varieties. My garden was beautifully enriched by seeds sent by Jim Ternier, former president of Seeds of Diversity (SoDC), Canada's Heritage Seed Program. Canabec Rose is one of a hundred tomatoes, bred in or adapted to Canada, that are marked for salvation in SoDC's Canadian Tomato Project.

38

RAMILLETE DE MALLORCA *fig. 39*

SIZE: *2¼" long by 2⅞" wide*

WEIGHT: *6 ounces*

SHAPE: *Round, smooth*

EXTERIOR COLOR(S): *Grayish red stippled with minute white specks*

FLESH COLOR(S): *Cock's comb red*

SOLUBLE SOLIDS: *5½ degrees Brix*

FLAVOR: *Poor; sour like a lemon*

TEXTURE: *Very firm; rocklike*

BEST USE(S): *Longkeeper; decorative; popular in Majorca, where it's grown without irrigation and hung up in clusters to store for the winter.*

PLANT HABIT, LEAF TYPE, AND YIELD: *Determinate habit; regular leaf; good yield*

MATURITY: *Late crop*

ORIGIN: *Collected by Ulrike Paradine of Hythe, Kent, England, on the island of Majorca in 1999. Initially listed in the 2001 Seed Savers Exchange yearbook by Jeff Nekola and William Woys Weaver.*

SYNONYMS: *Mallorquin; Ramillete; Tomatiga de Penjar; and Tomatiga de Ramellet*

A dazzling tomato. I've devoted one row in my garden to strange ducks, and Ramillete de Mallorca has pride of place. Majorcans make a snack by rubbing the tomato pulp and garlic on toasted country bread, topping it with olive oil, and sprinkling it with salt—in a preparation similar to my Spanish Tomato Bread (see page 212).

RED ROSE *fig. 40*

SIZE: *2¾" long by 3½" wide*

WEIGHT: *11 ounces*

SHAPE: *Round, smooth*

EXTERIOR COLOR(S): *Tomato pink*

FLESH COLOR(S): *Tomato pink*

SOLUBLE SOLIDS: *7 degrees Brix*

FLAVOR: *Excellent; very sweet and rich*

TEXTURE: *Reasonably firm*

BEST USE(S): *Multipurpose*

PLANT HABIT, LEAF TYPE, AND YIELD: *Indeterminate habit (has a trunk like a tree); regular leaf; high yield*

MATURITY: *Early crop*

ORIGIN: *Red Rose was first brought to notice by Lloyd Duggins of Mauckport, Indiana, in the Seed Savers Exchange 1988 yearbook. Duggins was not the breeder, as is sometimes reported; rather,* he obtained the tomato from a local family who said they'd had it for many years, and who told him Red Rose was a cross of Sudduth's Brandywine and Rutgers (see pages 108 and 67). Commercialized by Totally Tomatoes and two other firms, circa 1994.

NY: *Nee & Goldman 53397*

SEED SOURCES: *Ga21, Sa9, To1 Und*

Red Rose is as good as a tomato gets. It's a perfect globe that embodies the best qualities of its putative parents. Just right for sandwiches: Try it on Pita Sandwich with Tomatoes and Falafel (see page 224).

MARGLOBE *fig. 41*

SIZE: *2½" long by 3" wide*

WEIGHT: *7½ ounces*

SHAPE: *Round, smooth*

EXTERIOR COLOR(S): *Vivid red*

FLESH COLOR(S): *Cock's comb red; as noted by Boswell (1933), Marglobe's flesh can have a little yellow.*

SOLUBLE SOLIDS: *5 degrees Brix*

FLAVOR: *Good; pleasantly acidic*

TEXTURE: *Firm; meaty, very thick inner and outer walls*

BEST USE(S): *Multipurpose; splendid for canning. Ken Ettlinger reports: "This was the all-purpose tomato my mom used to put up in jars in the 1950s and the first tomato I ever ate fresh and warm from the garden when I was five or six years old."*

PLANT HABIT, LEAF TYPE, AND YIELD: *Indeterminate habit; regular leaf; good yield*

MATURITY: *Main crop*

ORIGIN: *Developed (from a cross of Marvel and Globe) by Frederick J. Pritchard and William S. Porte of the USDA, in cooperation with the Florida Agricultural Experiment Station. Released by the USDA in 1925. First offered commercially by Francis C. Stokes and Company, Philadelphia, in 1926 along with a Super-Standard Strain for greenhouse forcing. Other Pritchard tomatoes with Marvel or Marglobe (or both) in their parentage include: Marvana and Marvelosa (1924); Break o' Day (1931); Pritchard (1932), which was introduced as Scarlet Topper but renamed after Frederick Pritchard's death in 1931; and Glovel (1935), a "pink sister" or a sport of Marglobe. The many descendants of Marglobe also include Livingston's Marvelous (1937), a wilt-resistant pink Marglobe; and Rutgers (see page 67).*

SYNONYMS: *Mar Globe. There are many "new and improved" variants of Marglobe (for example, Improved Marglobe, Marglobe VF, and Master Marglobe); most are quite similar in type. Some are reportedly more compact in habit or more resistant to disease; others have bigger, more rounded, or more uniform fruits.*

NY: *Nee & Goldman 54635*

SEED SOURCES: *Bu8, Ha26, He8, Hi13, La1, Mo13, Roh, Sa9, Se24, Sh9, So1, To1, Up2, Vi4, Wi2*

41

Marglobe was developed in response to the need for a high-quality and disease-resistant shipping tomato. According to Boswell, the tomato was released by the USDA in 1925 "… just in time to save the Florida tomato-shipping industry from virtual extinction through the ravages of nailhead [rust] and [Fusarium] wilt." Francis C. Stokes, who led the commercial introduction of Marglobe in 1926, and who had seen the devastation firsthand in Florida in 1924, thought Marglobe was "one of the greatest triumphs recorded to the credit of the plant breeder" (Stokes, 1928).

Pritchard began his efforts to improve disease resistance in 1915 and eventually produced many notable tomato varieties. But his most famous work was with Marvel. He developed Marvel by selection from the French heirloom Merveille des Marchés (synonym: Tomate Austain) or Marvel of the Market, a red tomato introduced by Vilmorin-Andrieux and Company, Seed-Growers, of Paris, in 1899 or 1900. Marvel of the Market was noted for its resistance to cracking, wilt, and rust, as well as for its keeping and shipping qualities. In 1917 or 1918, Pritchard crossed Marvel with Livingston's Globe (a pink shipper, resistant to wilt but not nailhead, and reportedly selected from a cross of Stone and Ponderosa). The perfected variety was named Marglobe.

The year after Frederick Pritchard died, in 1931, Stokes wrote in his catalog: "The remarkable varieties developed through his hybridization and selection, especially of tomatoes, will bring wealth and a sense of well-being to generations yet unborn—yet he said he had only begun his work. His modest, kindly spirit will be remembered by all who knew him. His consecrated life will be an inspiration to his fellows. We salute the memory of a great and good man."

Marglobe certainly contributes to my well-being. If not still the most important variety of tomato in the United States and in the world, then it is admirably suited for the home and market gardener. I find no fatal flaws or imperfections (such as the tendency to star crack like other commercial heirlooms of the same era) and much to recommend it—especially for making ketchup (see page 235).

RUTGERS IMPROVED *fig. 42; page 59, fig. 33b*

SIZE: *2½" long by 3⅛" wide*

WEIGHT: *9 ounces*

SHAPE: *Round, smooth*

EXTERIOR COLOR(S): *Cherry red*

FLESH COLOR(S): *Cherry red*

SOLUBLE SOLIDS: *5 degrees Brix*

FLAVOR: *Fair to good*

TEXTURE: *Reasonably firm; meaty*

BEST USE(S): *Multipurpose; juice*

PLANT HABIT, LEAF TYPE, AND YIELD: *Determinate habit; regular leaf; good yield*

MATURITY: *Early crop*

ORIGIN: *The story, in brief, according to Gordon Morrison (1938): "Rutgers is the result of selection following a cross made in 1928 between Marglobe [see page 66] and J. T. D. by the Campbell Soup Company and later fixed in type by [Professor Lyman G.] Schermerhorn of the New Jersey Experiment Station." Dr. Dick Robinson told me that Rutgers was bred to ripen from the inside to ensure good color for processing, as well as for flavorful juice.*

Rutgers was introduced in 1935. Its forebear the J. T. D. was developed fifteen years earlier by Campbell breeder Dr. Harry F. Hall, a former president of the American Vegetable Growers Association. Hall named the variety in honor of Dr. John Thompson Dorrance, the nephew of one of Joseph Campbell's partners, and a chemist with a taste for the finer things in life. Dorrance was an innovator in the mass production of quality condensed soups (Smith, 2000).

The longer story of Rutgers, according to the American Tomato Yearbook (1951): "Each season for 6 years workers at the New Jersey station carefully studied selections from a cross made in 1928 between the Marglobe and J. T. D. varieties. Selections were made for earliness, vigor of foliage, freedom of the fruit from cracks and disease, smoothness, productiveness, and uniformity of type. The next year some 75 among the best plants were selected, and then followed extensive field tests to reduce further those considered worthy of introduction to the vegetable industry ... By 1933 the number had been reduced to 25, and these harbingers of a new tomato were sent out to a number of growers in New Jersey. Here for the first time the selections were subject to the close scrutiny of those whose livelihood depended upon serving the market with a quality product. A year later four selections emerged as worthy of a rigid trial at 75 farms in the tomato-growing region of the State of

New Jersey. At harvesttime, after a season of searching examination, number '500' emerged from anonymity, and on September 19, 1934, this superior selection was given the name 'Rutgers' ... One phase of the story remains yet to be told. Even when a superior variety is established, the work is still not complete. Variability remains a factor that may deteriorate a superior stock from year to year if record-keeping comparisons and culling are not maintained. Workers at the New Jersey station have exercised rigid control over the seed they have certified ... Through such painstaking research at this station, the Rutgers tomato was given to industry and to the home gardener, and its quality at the same time maintained."

SYNONYMS: *"Rutgers" was not the original name of this tomato. Lyman G. Schermerhorn said in November 1950, upon introducing a new tomato named "Queens," that "'Queens' tomato takes its name from the fact that Rutgers was originally named 'Queens College.'" Queens is an early Rutgers type "developed from a cross made in the fall of 1941 between the Valiant and Rutgers varieties." Improved versions of Rutgers include Early Rutgers; Improved Rutgers; New Rutgers; Rutgers VF; Rutgers VFA; Rutgers Improved VF; Rutgers PS (Rutgers PS-R); Rutgers Select (Rutgers S); and Select Rutgers 8828. Other off-spring of Rutgers include Ace, Caro-Red, Jubilee, Purdue 1361, and Ontario.*

NY: *Nee & Goldman 53406*

SEED SOURCES: *Bou, Bu2, Com, Ers, Fe5, Ha26, Hi13, Jor, Or10, Roh, Se26, Shu, So1, To1, To3, To10, Tu6, Vi4*

Countless breeders have been 'improving' Rutgers since 1928. Nowadays, there are two basic forms: the original indeterminate version, which was described by seedsmen and breeders in the 1930s and '40s as too strongly vegetative, and the more compact determinate version. The fruit quality of each is similar, at least in my garden, and I can't get too excited about either one—except when I think of those Rutgers California Supreme seeds famously blasted into space in 1984; they orbited the earth in a satellite for six years (Cutler, 1997). No "killer tomatoes" resulted from the NASA seeds later planted on terra firma, much to the disappointment of millions of children.

43

BURBANK *fig. 43*

SIZE: *2¼" long by 2¾" wide*

WEIGHT: *7 ounces*

SHAPE: *Round, smooth*

EXTERIOR COLOR(S): *Blood red*

FLESH COLOR(S): *Blood red*

SOLUBLE SOLIDS: *5 degrees Brix*

FLAVOR: *Good*

TEXTURE: *Firm; juicy*

BEST USE(S): *Multipurpose*

PLANT HABIT, LEAF TYPE, AND YIELD: *Determinate habit; regular leaf; high yield*

MATURITY: *Early crop*

ORIGIN: *Introduced in 1914 by the Luther Burbank Company, San Francisco, California. The original Burbank as described by the master in his seed catalogs was indeterminate in growth habit, whereas the Burbank of today is determinate or self-pruning. Coincidentally, the first self-pruning or "self-topping" tomato was a chance seedling discovered by Bert Croft in Florida the same year the Burbank was introduced. The variety derived from that single plant selection was introduced circa 1923 as the Cooper Special by C. D. Cooper, a farmer near Fort Lauderdale, Florida. Burpee's Self-Pruning, introduced in 1924, is considered synonymous with Cooper's Special.*

SYNONYMS: *Burbank Red Slicing; Burbank Self-Pruning and Early; (New) Burbank Early. Not the same as Burbank Preserving (a "unique cross of the currant and tree tomato").*

NY: *Nee & Goldman 54621*

SEED SOURCES: *Co32, Se7, So9, Te4, Ter, To9, Up2*

Breeder Luther Burbank (1849–1926) had this to say about the new Burbank in 1914: "The earliest, smoothest, largest and most productive of all early tomatoes. It is of a bright red, the flesh being firm and of superior quality. The plants resist disease in an unusual manner, and unlike most early tomatoes, it produces heavily all summer. A fine home or market tomato, as it is a fine keeper and shipper." Burbank made further improvements in 1919 and 1924—but I scratch my head wondering how.

Burbank himself wasn't this variety's only fan; it has met with receptive audiences, both domestic and foreign. Melvin A. Pellett (junior author of *Practical Tomato Culture* [1930]) found the Burbank very satisfactory on warm, sandy soils (but disappointing on heavy soils). Burbank became popular in Australia as a first-class tomato of the Earliana type. And in Dutchess County, New York, where it flourishes in my garden, Burbank is juicy and appetizing and holds well for a week at room temperature.

In recognition of its fine qualities and historical import, Slow Food USA boarded the Burbank tomato onto its Ark of Taste in 2006.

44

EVA PURPLE BALL *fig. 44; page 59, fig. 33h; page 176, fig. 122j*

SIZE: *2½" long by 3¼" wide*

WEIGHT: *9 ounces*

SHAPE: *Round, smooth*

EXTERIOR COLOR(S): *Tomato pink*

FLESH COLOR(S): *Cherry red*

SOLUBLE SOLIDS: *5 degrees Brix*

FLAVOR: *Good*

TEXTURE: *Reasonably firm*

BEST USE(S): *Multipurpose*

PLANT HABIT, LEAF TYPE, AND YIELD: *Indeterminate habit; regular leaf; good yield*

MATURITY: *Main crop*

ORIGIN: *Evidently brought from Germany in the late 1800s by the family of Joseph J. Bratka of Elmwood Park, New Jersey. Introduced in 1994 by Southern Exposure Seed Exchange.*

SYNONYMS: *Eva's Purple Ball*

SEED SOURCES: *Ap6, Ba8, Co32, Ga21, He8, Jo1, Ma18, Pr3, Ra6, Re8, Sa9, Se17, Sk2, So1, So25, To1, To9, To10, Vi4*

Eva Purple Ball is so perfectly shaped that it could pass for a hybrid. It reminds me, in fact, of Momotaro (a hybrid from Takii Seed Company in Japan) except it's not as firm. Good in salads and salsas and on sandwiches.

AILSA CRAIG *fig. 45a*

SIZE: *1¾" long by 2¼" wide*

WEIGHT: *3½ ounces*

SHAPE: *Round, smooth*

EXTERIOR COLOR(S): *Blood red*

FLESH COLOR(S): *Cherry red*

SOLUBLE SOLIDS: *4½ degrees Brix*

FLAVOR: *Poor; high acid*

TEXTURE: *Reasonably firm; seedy, juicy, prone to cracking*

BEST USE(S): *Mainly of historical interest*

PLANT HABIT, LEAF TYPE, AND YIELD: *Indeterminate habit; regular leaf; high yield*

MATURITY: *Early crop*

ORIGIN: *Introduced in 1912 by Alexander and Brown, the Scottish Seedhouse, Perth, Scotland. Bred by Alan Balch.*

SYNONYMS: *Ailsa Craig, Great Britain; Ailsa Craig, Scotland. Similar to Fillbasket. A parent of Michigan State Forcing (Marglobe X Ailsa Craig); Tiger Tom or Tigerella (see page 169); and many others. See Yellow Ailsa Craig (this page).*

SEED SOURCES: *Bou, Sa9, Te4, Up2*

A popular English heritage tomato for forcing or greenhouse culture. Alan Balch bred it a hundred years ago by crossing Fillbasket (another Balch tomato) and Sunrise; he named the new variety for a craggy isle in the Firth of Clyde. Alexander and Brown, seed merchants of Perth, proclaimed upon their introduction of Ailsa Craig in 1912: "…for shape, quality, flavor, and cropping powers it cannot be beaten; the shape is perfection, hardly an irregular fruit to be seen, whilst bearing an enormous crop."

While I agree that Ailsa Craig produces a huge crop, it's best suited for greenhouse growing and is consistently disappointing in my open fields. I wish it were a champ like the onion of the same name.

YELLOW AILSA CRAIG *fig. 45b*

SIZE: *1⅞" long by 2¼" wide*

WEIGHT: *3 ounces*

SHAPE: *Round, smooth*

EXTERIOR COLOR(S): *Golden yellow*

FLESH COLOR(S): *Corn*

SOLUBLE SOLIDS: *4 degrees Brix*

FLAVOR: *Fair*

TEXTURE: *Reasonably firm; juicy*

BEST USE(S): *Multipurpose*

PLANT HABIT, LEAF TYPE, AND YIELD: *Indeterminate habit; regular leaf; high yield*

MATURITY: *Early crop*

ORIGIN: *Obtained by the USDA from Hungary in 1963; identified as PI 289301*

SYNONYMS: *Ailsa Craig, Yellow. May be the same as Scotland Yellow.*

SEED SOURCES: *Vi4*

Yellow Ailsa Craig is the most prolific and continuous bearer in its class. Unfortunately, that means too much of a bland, uniform thing. Neither the date of origin nor the parentage of this tomato is known. The originators of Ailsa Craig—Alexander and Brown of Perth, Scotland—had nothing to do with it.

POTENTATE *fig. 46a*

SIZE: *2¼" long by 2½" wide*

WEIGHT: *5 ounces*

SHAPE: *Round, smooth*

EXTERIOR COLOR(S): *Crayfish red*

FLESH COLOR(S): *Cherry red*

SOLUBLE SOLIDS: *4½ degrees Brix*

FLAVOR: *Poor to fair; mild at best*

TEXTURE: *Firm; meaty hardballs*

BEST USE(S): *Multipurpose; greenhouse culture and open field*

PLANT HABIT, LEAF TYPE, AND YIELD: *Indeterminate habit; regular leaf; high yield*

MATURITY: *Main crop*

ORIGIN: *Introduced circa 1940 by Sutton's Seeds of Reading, England. Potentate appears in the Yates' Annual of 1941 (of Australia): identified as an English cluster variety that had already proven very successful, apparently on trial from Sutton's, with some Sydney market growers. Colin Randel of Thompson and Morgan (England) believes Potentate was developed from Sutton's Best of All, which was introduced in 1895 by Sutton's and Sons, Seed Growers and Merchants, and remained popular for nearly 100 years.*

SYNONYMS: *Improved Potentate (cataloged by Sutton's in 1952); Potentate, Harrison's English Strain. Resembles Sutton's Best of All, Bonny Best (see page 77), and Moneymaker (see next entry).*

SEED SOURCES: *Sa9*

Potentate: a grandiose name for a pipsqueak of a tomato. In the same league as Bonny Best and Moneymaker, old-time commercial favorites once extensively grown for forcing or greenhouse culture in England, Australia, and New Zealand. There's still a place in the world for these old reliables—for greenhouse culture, cool and wet conditions, and for the show bench. Potentate is an English "cluster variety" which, like Sutton's Best of All, Prosperity, and Woodward's Sensation, bears an immense early crop of small to medium, perfect red globes.

MONEYMAKER *fig. 46b*

SIZE: *2¼" long by 2½" wide*

WEIGHT: *3½ ounces*

SHAPE: *Round, smooth*

EXTERIOR COLOR(S): *Blood red*

FLESH COLOR(S): *Cherry red*

SOLUBLE SOLIDS: *4 degrees Brix*

FLAVOR: *Fair; subacid, subsugar, subpar*

TEXTURE: *Firm*

BEST USE(S): *Multipurpose; greenhouse and field culture; exhibition. When Bob Sherman, director of gardens and gardening at Garden Organic (also known as Henry Doubleday Research Association) in Coventry, England, first started gardening in the 1970s, Moneymaker "was still a commercial favorite and much derided by foodies and home growers as being tough enough to bounce off a wall." I acquired Moneymaker in New Zealand twenty years ago, and I still love to poke fun at it.*

PLANT HABIT, LEAF TYPE, AND YIELD: *Indeterminate habit; regular leaf; high yield*

MATURITY: *Main crop*

ORIGIN: *Introduced in 1954 by Stonors in England. There was a spate of "improved Moneymaker" breeding and selection during the 1960s, according to Colin Randel at Thompson and Morgan: Alicante was released in 1966; Moneymaker F_1 in 1966; and Moneycross F_1 in 1968.*

SYNONYMS: *Money Maker; Stonor('s) Money Maker. Not the same as the Money Maker (an early, flattened red tomato borne on silvery-leafed plants) cataloged by D. Landreth and Sons of Philadelphia, Pennsylvania, in 1894, or the Money Maker (a first-early purple, also known as Tomato No. 105) introduced in 1897 by Johnson and Stokes of Philadelphia, Pennsylvania. Similar to Potentate.*

SEED SOURCES: *Ba8, Bo19, Bou, Co32, Ga22, Ha26, Ra6, Se7, Se26, Sk2, Te4, Tho, To3, To10, Up2, Vi4, We19*

If you could coin money the way this plant puts out tomatoes—or just sell them for a good price—then you'd be very wealthy indeed. The money-making mortgage-lifters emerged in the mid-nineteenth century as tomatoes became more popular on both sides of the Atlantic, and cultivation spread from small garden plots to farms, fields, and finally to industry. The Johnson and Stokes Money Maker (1897) was one of the first get-rich-quick

tomatoes. The name had been suggested by an enthusiastic market gardener who believed the tomato would "prove a money maker for every market man who grows it, as he can distance all competition."

The Wealthy tomato, introduced circa 1903 by Bolgiano and Son in Baltimore, Maryland, was also filled with great promise: "In [this tomato], Mother Earth pays us a thousand-fold for our efforts. In Springtime, those who have the means are only too glad to spend it freely if in return they can get the first fruits of the season. Then the fancy prices are realized; and if you trust the Wealthy Tomato, it will put you in a position to get your share and also the share of the man who takes two years to find out a money-maker." If only it were as delicious as it is prolific.

PINK PEACH *fig. 47c*

SIZE: *1¾" long by 2" wide*

WEIGHT: *2½ ounces*

SHAPE: *Round, smooth*

EXTERIOR COLOR(S): *Tomato pink*

FLESH COLOR(S): *Tomato pink*

SOLUBLE SOLIDS: *5 degrees Brix*

FLAVOR: *Peachy keen*

TEXTURE: *Very soft; pubescent skin; juicy; tends to "puff"*

BEST USE(S): *Fresh eating; fruit tart; nectar. Ken Ettlinger of Long Island Seed and Plant Company suggests that the fruit be served chilled, whole, or as a snack.*

PLANT HABIT, LEAF TYPE, AND YIELD: *Indeterminate habit; regular leaf; good yield*

MATURITY: *Early crop*

ORIGIN: *The downy Pink Peach doesn't seem to have entered the seed trade until 1885, although Burpee's noted in 1889 that "many years ago we were familiar with this Tomato, but in some way or other the stock seems to have been lost." D. Landreth and Sons of Philadelphia wrote in their 1894 catalog: "Peach (Second Early)—introduced by us in 1885, and in appearance almost identical with some forms of Peaches both in shape and color." L. H. Bailey provided a fuller description in 1887 of Landreth's Peach: "Plants producing many upright branches when allowed to fall upon the ground; foliage fine; fruit small and spherical (one and one-half to two inches in diameter), very regular and uniform, indistinctly mottled with purple and red purple, the surface roughish, often two-celled, the juice very dark colored. A singular sort."*

In 1902, seventy-one North American seedsmen listed the Pink Peach. James J. H. Gregory of Marblehead, Massachusetts, was enchanted by Peach's fuzz: in 1889 he called it "The Wonderful Peach." In 1891, he listed the tomato as a "Vegetable Novelty of 1890": "The looks of the tomato will sell it, for never did one fruit look so much like another as this does like a peach in form, size, and color. Rather soft for marketing purposes." Vaughan's Seed Store gushed about the novelty in 1889: "This is the most delicious and handsomest Tomato ever introduced, having an appetizing fruity flavor not met with in any other … deep rose and orange amber beautifully blended and covered with a delicate bloom or furze like a peach … The skin is very thin and can be peeled off like that of a peach."

SYNONYMS: *Fuzzy; Landreth's Peach; New Peach; Peach; Purple Peach; Rose Peach; Red Peach; Tennessee Peach Fuzz; The Wonderful Peach. Companion to Yellow Peach (see next entry). Similar to Pêche and Peach Blow Sutton (see page 74) but smaller and more regular. Same goes for Livingston's Large Rose Peach, introduced in 1893: "This sort originated with us and has all the general characteristics belonging to this singular and distinct class of Tomatoes, but is much larger than any peach variety yet brought out."*

NY: *Nee & Goldman 53478 (Fuzzy)*

SEED SOURCES: *To9*

Pink Peach is a velveteen tomato: plush on the outside, sweet and juicy on the inside. Unlike such tough guys as Landreth's Red Rock, it may be defenseless against a drop from a six-story window (indeed, even from a height of six inches), but it is self-protective. Many experienced growers, including James J. H. Gregory, have noted Pink Peach's rot resistance on damp ground, which seems to stem from its velvet cloak. According to Young and MacArthur (1947), three kinds of epidermal hairs give Pink Peach its "furze" or peachy bloom: lots of pointed, septate, and hyaline hairs 180 to 360 microns long; a small amount of hairs 700 to 1000 microns long; and four-celled brown capitate glandular hairs with short hyaline basal cells. But you knew that.

YELLOW PEACH *fig. 47b; page 161, fig. 114d*

SIZE: *1⅞" long by 2¼" wide*

WEIGHT: *2½ ounces*

SHAPE: *Round, smooth*

EXTERIOR COLOR(S): *Yellow*

FLESH COLOR(S): *Light yellow*

SOLUBLE SOLIDS: *7 degrees Brix*

FLAVOR: *Excellent; well balanced*

TEXTURE: *Very soft; pubescent skin; juicy; puffy*

BEST USE(S): *Multipurpose; Galette of White Peaches and Tomatoes (see page 241)*

PLANT HABIT, LEAF TYPE, AND YIELD: *Indeterminate habit; regular leaf; high yield*

MATURITY: *Early crop*

ORIGIN: *White Peach originated with Elbert S. Carman, plant breeder, editor, and owner of the* Rural New-Yorker, *in 1890. Cataloged in 1893 as New Golden Peach Tomato and in 1894 as New Yellow Peach Tomato by A. W. Livingston's Sons. Livingston wrote: "Differs from [New Peach Tomato; see Pink Peach, this page] in color only, being of a rich golden color and having the bloom or furze of a peach upon its surface." By 1902, fifteen North American seedsmen cataloged Yellow Peach. A British firm, James Veitch and Sons Limited of Chelsea, England, listed a synonymous variety in 1905 named Chiswick Peach, which earned a first-class certificate from the Royal Horticultural Society: "In colour a soft lemon-yellow, it is unusually distinct, the attractiveness of its appearance being greatly enhanced by a beautiful peach-like bloom. Of delicious flavour, it is unequalled for dessert purposes. It is very prolific and sets freely, the bunches numbering from six to ten perfectly round solid fruits. It is specially adapted for pot culture."*

SYNONYMS: *Chiswick Peach; Garden Peach [pubescent type]; Garden Peach Fuzzy; (New) Golden Peach; New Yellow Peach; Pêche blanche; Pêche jaune; Wapsipinicon Peach; White Peach. Similar to Ghost Cherry but larger. Companion to Pink Peach (see previous entry). Not the same as the longkeeper "peach" tomatoes.*

NY: *Nee & Goldman 53476 (White Peach); Nee & Goldman 53470 (Pêche blanche); and Nee & Goldman 53464 (Wapsipinicon Peach)*

SEED SOURCES: *Ap6, Co32, Coo, Fe5, Ga1, Ha26, He8, He17, Hi13, Ma18, Pe2, Ra6, Roh, Se7, Se16, So25, Te4, To1, To3, To10, Tu6, Und, Vi4*

There are two types of "peach" tomatoes, which, although vastly different, are often confounded. In one category are the sweet and juicy "fuzzy softies," like our Yellow Peach, with rot resistance and a storage life measured in weeks. In the other are the hard, smooth (glabrous), tasteless "longkeepers," with shelf lives up to six months, such as Garden Peach (Blum's), Peach–Long Storage Type (Long Island Seed and Plant's), Longkeeper (Burpee's), Reverend Morrow's Peach (first listed in the 1978 annual Seed Savers Exchange yearbook), and Thorburn's Long-Keeper (1893). The longkeeper peaches don't ripen uniformly; in storage they turn a blotchy yellowish on the outside and salmon or capsicum red on the inside.

Longkeeper peach tomatoes will see you through the cold months, but I prefer to wait for summer and the return of my Yellow Peaches: so soft, so luscious, so pleasing to the touch and eye. Raw or cooked, they're tops in my taste tests. No less a personage than Barbara Melera, the new proprietor of D. Landreth Seed Company (the oldest seed house in America, which introduced Landreth's Peach back in 1885), describes Yellow Peach as the very best. I'm inclined to agree.

(a) Peach Blow Sutton,
(b) Yellow Peach, (c) Pink Peach

PEACH BLOW SUTTON *page 59, fig. 33i; page 72, fig. 47a; page 176, fig. 122c*

SIZE: *2¾" long by 2¾" wide*

WEIGHT: *6 ounces*

SHAPE: *Round, smooth, sometimes "boxy"*

EXTERIOR COLOR(S): *Tomato pink*

FLESH COLOR(S): *Tomato pink*

SOLUBLE SOLIDS: *5 degrees Brix*

FLAVOR: *Excellent; cool and refreshing "tomato lite" flavor*

TEXTURE: *Very soft; pubescent skin; juicy, subject to "puffing"*

BEST USE(S): *Fresh eating; to have and to hold*

PLANT HABIT, LEAF TYPE, AND YIELD: *Indeterminate habit; regular leaf; good yield*

MATURITY: *Main crop*

ORIGIN: *Introduced in 1897 as "Sutton's Peachblow" by Sutton and Sons Seed Growers and Merchants of Reading, England. Sutton wrote: "Most of our customers have become acquainted with 'The Peach' Tomato, which was introduced from America several years ago. We were amongst the first to recognize the distinct and ornamental character of this variety, but it ripened so late and was so shy in cropping that it never became popular. We at once perceived that a hybrid between The Peach Tomato and some first-class scarlet variety might result in an entirely new and free-bearing race of great beauty. The Pomegranate and Tender and True were both obtained by crossing Sutton's Perfection with The Peach. Our Peachblow had a different origin. All three possess the downy skin which is the special characteristic of The Peach, but in other respects they are a very marked advance on that variety, being superior in productiveness, in appearance, and especially in flavour. The distinction in appearance is most apparent when quite ripe." Both Sutton's Pomegranate (named for the tint of the Pomegranate flower) and Sutton's Tender and True were described as medium-size and deep red in color. Sutton's Peachblow was cataloged as follows: "Although this variety partakes distinctly of The Peach character, it is a perfectly distinct Tomato, the fruit being very much larger, produced in astonishing profusion, and the flavour will gratify the most fastidious palate."*

SYNONYMS: *Peachblow; Sutton's Peachblow; Sutton's Peach Blow. (In the late nineteenth century, the term "peach blow" was commonly used to describe an American art glass form with subtle "peachy" gradations of color.) Similar to Pink Peach (see page 73). Resembles Livingston's Large Rose Peach Tomato (1893). Not the same as the fuzzy orange Thorburn's Terra Cotta (1893).*

SEED SOURCES: *Pin, Sa9*

Peach Blow Suttons are irresistibly downy and delicate; I love to rub them across my cheek before biting into them. The sweet flesh dissolves in the mouth like a fig. All pubescent "peach" tomatoes are similar in flavor and texture, but Peach Blow Sutton is larger and more angular, and it has a woodier and persistent stem. Peach Blow is remarkable in a red peach tomato galette; just substitute red peaches (or plums) for white in my recipe (see page 241).

PÊCHE *fig. 48*

SIZE: *2" long by 2½" wide*

WEIGHT: *4 ounces*

SHAPE: *Round, smooth*

EXTERIOR COLOR(S): *Tomato pink*

FLESH COLOR(S): *Tomato pink*

SOLUBLE SOLIDS: *5¼ degrees Brix*

FLAVOR: *Good; mildly sweet and refreshing*

TEXTURE: *Very soft; pubescent skin; juicy and melting; "puffy" (air pockets)*

BEST USE(S): *Fresh eating; dessert course; table ornament*

PLANT HABIT, LEAF TYPE, AND YIELD: *Indeterminate habit; regular leaf; good yield*

MATURITY: *Main crop*

ORIGIN: *It's commonly believed that the red or pink "peach tomato" (with a pubescent skin) is a French import, but I've found no evidence of that. Au contraire, this tomato seems to have originated in the United States. In 1897, Sutton and Sons Seed Growers and Merchants of Reading, England, called the peach an American tomato (see Peach Blow Sutton, this page). And Vilmorin-Andrieux, the well-known French seed house of Paris, France, didn't catalog the peach tomato until 1891, six years after Landreth's Peach was introduced in Philadelphia (see Pink Peach, page 73). Furthermore, Vilmorin named the tomato "T. peach" [Tomate peach]—and not "T. pêche," as would be expected if it had been French (they kept the American name until at least 1925). Vilmorin (1891) wrote: "Large plant, sufficiently hardy, extremely distinctive, characterized by bluish metallic foliage. Small fruits, perfectly round, the size of a medium Reine-Claude plum, of an uncommon pink color and produced in clusters of ten or twelve. Vilmorin commented in 1946: "excellent variety, little known. The red fruits are covered with light pubescence which gives the fruits an unusual appearance."*

SYNONYMS: *Pêche Vilmorin-Andrieux; T. pêche; Tomate pêche. Strongly resembles Peach Blow Sutton (see previous entry) and Pink Peach (see page 73) but intermediate in size. Also resembles Khaborovsky in fruit but not plant characters (dwarf rugosa). Not the same as the glabrous (smooth) long-storage hard "peach" tomatoes like Carry On, Carry On and Livingston's Stone.*

NY: *Nee & Goldman 53477*

SEED SOURCES: *Go8, Ra6*

The antithesis of the industrial Red Rock tomato, Pêche is a rare treat so fragile that it's strictly garden-to-table. It should inspire everyone to become a home gardener!

BONNY BEST *fig. 49*

SIZE: *2¼" long by 2¾" wide*

WEIGHT: *5½ ounces*

SHAPE: *Round, smooth*

EXTERIOR COLOR(S): *Cherry red*

FLESH COLOR(S): *Primary red*

SOLUBLE SOLIDS: *5 degrees Brix*

FLAVOR: *Fair; not well endowed with flavor*

TEXTURE: *Reasonably firm; mealy*

BEST USE(S): *Multipurpose; of historical interest*

PLANT HABIT, LEAF TYPE, AND YIELD: *Indeterminate habit; regular leaf; good yield*

MATURITY: *Main crop*

ORIGIN: *Introduced in 1908 by Walter P. Stokes of Stokes' Standard Seeds, Philadelphia, Pennsylvania. Bonny Best came from a chance seedling found by George W. Middletown of Jeffersonville, Pennsylvania, in a field of Chalk's Early Jewel. Chalk's Early Jewel was boarded onto Slow Food USA's Ark of Taste in 2007.*

SYNONYMS: *Bonny Best Early; Bolgiano's Capital; Chalk('s) Early Jewel; Clark's Early; Jewel; John Baer; Red Bird; Redhead; Stokes' Bonny Best; Stokes' Bonny Best Early; and dozens more*

NY: *Nee & Goldman 53450*

SEED SOURCES: *All, Co32, Ers, Fe5, Ga1, Ga22, Ha26, He8, He17, La1, Pr3, Ra6, Sa9, Sk2, Te4, To1, To3, Up2*

Amid all the beauties in my garden, this seems like a tomato only a hornworm could love—yet Bonny Best was once considered the finest of all early red varieties, desirable for greenhouse culture and canning. Some still quibble and attempt to draw fine lines of distinction between Bonny Best and John Baer's eponymous tomato. Horticulturist Victor Boswell (along with a distinguished group that included Oscar H. Pearson and Paul Work) set the record straight in 1933: "The supposed difference in plant characters is so slight and so indefinite that it cannot be described or demonstrated satisfactorily and is therefore considered negligible."

50

JOHN BAER *fig. 50*

SIZE: *2½" long by 2¾" wide*

WEIGHT: *5 ounces*

SHAPE: *Round, smooth*

EXTERIOR COLOR(S): *Cherry red*

FLESH COLOR(S): *Vivid red*

SOLUBLE SOLIDS: *4½ degrees Brix*

FLAVOR: *Fair*

TEXTURE: *Reasonably firm*

BEST USE(S): *Multipurpose*

PLANT HABIT, LEAF TYPE, AND YIELD: *Indeterminate habit; regular leaf; high yield*

MATURITY: *Main crop*

ORIGIN: *Introduced in 1914 by J. Bolgiano and Son of Baltimore. Gordon Morrison said in 1938: "John Baer is the leading canning variety in New York, Michigan, and southeastern Wisconsin, where it consistently outyields other varieties. It is identical with Bonny Best." Not the same as J. Bolgiano's Baltimore Baer (1919), an apparent cross of John Baer and Greater Baltimore. Greater Baltimore was a 1905 J. Bolgiano introduction, "reported to have been developed from a single plant selection made about 1900 by John Baer, of Baltimore, in a field of tomatoes grown from seed obtained under the name of Stone" (Boswell et al., 1933).*

SYNONYMS: *Bonny Best (see previous entry)*

SEED SOURCES: *Jun*

The 1914 Bolgiano catalog cover depicts a brilliant red John Baer—the "Earliest Tomato on Earth"—on a snow field in the company of two polar bears. Bolgiano made fifteen distinct claims about its quality, each more exuberant than the last. Here's Number 13: "'John Bear' [sic!] Tomato Seed was saved only by John Baer, the originator, who personally selected and picked every Tomato from which he saved this seed, selecting only the most beautiful perfect fruit of the early Stem Set Clusters." Number 14: "'John Baer' Tomato is the offspring of two marvelous Tomatoes—One Great Specialist having devoted 10 years in selecting and improving one parent and Another Expert devoted five years in selecting and improving the other parent." And 15: "As a Packing Tomato, 'John Baer' is a miracle, they all pack Fancy, no seconds, and all pack whole. Peelers can prepare three bushels of 'John Baer' Tomatoes to one bushel of any other Tomato." The John Baer tomato was the subject of a similarly effusive 1915 Bolgiano pamphlet (*What Tomato Growers Are Saying About 'John Baer' Tomato*), which contained eight pages of testimonials from happy customers. This variety reappeared on the cover of the catalog in 1916.

OREGON SPRING *fig. 51*

SIZE: *2⅜" long by 3½" wide*

WEIGHT: *10 ounces*

SHAPE: *Comes in a range of sizes and shapes; most are oblate*

EXTERIOR COLOR(S): *Blood red*

FLESH COLOR(S): *Blood red*

SOLUBLE SOLIDS: *5½ degrees Brix*

FLAVOR: *Good; well balanced*

TEXTURE: *Reasonably firm; meaty, juicy*

BEST USE(S): *Fresh eating; makes lovely solid wedges for salads. A cold-tolerant tomato with parthenocarpic fruit set that does well in cold and hot climates.*

PLANT HABIT, LEAF TYPE, AND YIELD: *Determinate habit; regular leaf; good yield*

MATURITY: *Very early crop*

ORIGIN: *Bred by Dr. James R. Baggett of Oregon State University, Corvallis, Oregon, and released in 1984. When he released it, Baggett described Oregon Spring as "an early maturing, Verticillium wilt–resistant tomato with a compact growth habit and large fruit which are mostly seedless. It should be especially useful in cool summer areas where its seedlessness and relative earliness will be maximized." Two years later he said, "'Oregon Spring' is a bulk of 3 F_7 sister*

lines from an F_6 line (OSU T65-5-1–14-9) … developed by pedigree breeding from the cross 'Severianin' x 'Starshot.' 'Severianin' is an early parthenocarpic cultivar developed in Russia. 'Starshot' is a commercial cultivar of about 'Fireball' maturity."*

Dr. Jim Myers told me, "About thirteen lines have been released by Oregon State University over the years, mainly by my predecessors, Jim Baggett and Tex Frazier. OSU tomatoes have been bred for home garden production in the cool Pacific Northwest environments and are able to set fruit under conditions that are suboptimal for most other varieties. They are determinate, which is associated with earliness, and parthenocarpic (seedless), which allows fruit set when it's too cold for fertilization."

SYNONYMS: *Similar to Santiam, a sister line (developed from the same cross) released in tandem with Oregon Spring; and Siletz (Oregon Spring x Pikred), released in 1994.*

SEED SOURCES: *Abu, Bou, Com, Ear, Fe5, Ga1, Goo, He8, He17, Hi13, Hig, Hum, Jo1, Me7, Ni1, Pin, Pr3, Ra6, Re8, Se7, Se25, Se26, Se28, Ter, To1, To3, To9, Up2, Vi4, We19*

If you're starved for good early tomatoes—and for space—grow the compact Oregon Spring. It's a reliable tomato for the home gardener, in the Northeast and elsewhere. Rose Marie Nichols McGee of Nichols Garden Nursery wrote in 1996, "Since we introduced Oregon Spring in 1986 we have been hearing raves about it from gardeners in every part of the United States, especially where pollination is a problem. Because it sets fruit on every blossom (seedless if cool or hot), Oregon Spring has extended the season for tomatoes in hot summer areas where setting fails because of hot nights. For very short growing season areas it may be the only tomato with ripe fruit. In parts of the country with long cool springs, setting starts out very early and protecting with hotcaps has produced fruit as much as 4 to 6 weeks before other early tomatoes."

RUSSIAN BLACK *fig. 52*

SIZE: *2½" long by 3" wide*

WEIGHT: *7 ounces*

SHAPE: *Round, smooth*

EXTERIOR COLOR(S): *Garnet brown with violet brown shoulders*

FLESH COLOR(S): *Brownish violet*

SOLUBLE SOLIDS: *5 degrees Brix*

FLAVOR: *Excellent; earthy*

TEXTURE: *Soft*

BEST USE(S): *Fresh eating*

PLANT HABIT, LEAF TYPE, AND YIELD: *Indeterminate habit; regular leaf; good yield*

MATURITY: *Early crop*

ORIGIN: *Introduced in 2000 by the Seed Savers Exchange. SSE's stock seed came from Clive Blazey of the Digger's Club in Dromana, Victoria, Australia. The seed was donated by Digger's beekeeper from Gippsland in 1992 or 1993.*

SYNONYMS: *Black Russian*

NY: *Nee & Goldman 54648*

SEED SOURCES: *Go8, He8, Hi13, Ki4, La1, Ma18, Pr3, Ra6, Re8, Se28, Syn, Tho*

Clive Blazey describes this tomato as "rich and sweet as a Fabergé jewel, though not as good looking." I'd agree with that assessment.

53

NEW YORKER *fig. 53*

SIZE: *2½" long by 2⅜" wide*

WEIGHT: *4 ounces*

SHAPE: *Round, smooth*

EXTERIOR COLOR(S): *Vivid red*

FLESH COLOR(S): *Vivid red*

SOLUBLE SOLIDS: *5 degrees Brix*

FLAVOR: *Good; well balanced*

TEXTURE: *Reasonably firm; solid, well-nourished, wall-to-wall flesh*

BEST USE(S): *Best for processing but also used for fresh eating*

PLANT HABIT, LEAF TYPE, AND YIELD: *Determinate habit; regular leaf; high yield*

MATURITY: *Early crop*

ORIGIN: *Bred by Richard W. Robinson at the New York State Agricultural Experiment Station in Geneva, New York, and released in 1965. Parents: (Geneva 11 x Rhode Island Early) x Fireball. Commercialized by the Harris Seed Company. Dr. Robinson, now emeritus professor in the Department of Horticultural Sciences at Cornell University in Geneva, New York, and a part-time breeder, wrote me: "I came to this Experiment Station in 1961 and was given the responsibility for breeding canning tomatoes for New York. At that time, New York tomato growers were at a competitive disadvantage since they were growing only disease-susceptible*

varieties, while California growers had varieties resistant to the soilborne disease of Verticillium wilt, which cannot be economically controlled by any means other than resistant varieties. The resistant varieties being grown in California were too late in maturity for the shorter season of New York. New Yorker is slightly earlier than Fireball, the early but susceptible variety it replaced. New Yorker is resistant to race 0 of late blight as well as to Verticillium wilt, but it is susceptible to the race of late blight that has been such a problem in recent years.

"Although I've been given the credit for breeding New Yorker, much of that credit should be attributed to Bill Tapley and Jerry Marx, my predecessors as tomato breeder at Geneva. Professor Tapley, as you know, was co-author of The Vegetables of New York, *the 1937 classical treatise. He bred Geneva 11, the first Verticillium wilt-resistant tomato variety for New York, but its internal color made it unsuitable for commercial processing.*

"Dr. Jerry Marx, who is most noted for his breeding and genetic research with peas, crossed Fireball with a breeding line that Tapley developed from Geneva 11 x Rhode Island Early. My contribution was quite modest. I simply evaluated and selected a few generations the progeny of that cross. In 1963, an F₅ line from this cross grown in plot 790 appeared out-

standing in my trials and was determined to be resistant to Verticillium wilt and late blight. Because of the dire need of New York tomato growers for a disease-resistant tomato variety, I wanted to release this line for seed production as soon as possible, but I also wanted to make further selection for type and uniformity before introducing it as a variety. This dilemma was overcome by the Harris Seed Company, then at Rochester, New York, producing seed and selling it to our growers as NY 790 in 1964 and 1965, then replacing it with the improved selection released as New Yorker in 1965."

SYNONYMS: *NY 790. Maritimer (1967), also known as Maritime Chow, is a very closely related variety; resembles Fireball (1952), one of its parents. Not the same as Nystate, New York Market, or (Thorburn's) New York. Offspring include Usabec and Nova (from a cross of New Yorker with Roma VF).*

SEED SOURCES: *Ers, Hi13, Ra6, Sk2, Syn, To1, To3*

You don't have to be a New Yorker to love Dick Robinson's New Yorker tomato: it's early, compact, and a heavy yielder, in more states than one. Forty years after it was introduced, seed of the New Yorker

is still commercially available, but now it's grown primarily by home gardeners. I've been a fan of Dr. Robinson for more than ten years; his *Cucurbits* (1997) is my melon and squash bible. If I could haul myself away from the garden, I'd head to Geneva and park myself in Dick's classroom in Hedrick Hall. Cornell's Geneva campus is particularly devoted to fruit and vegetable research and extension and is perhaps most noted for fruit breeding. And the U.S. Department of Agriculture has one of four Plant Introduction Stations located on the campus, where they grow, evaluate, and increase seed that they provide free of charge to researchers. The Geneva Station maintains the collection of *Cucurbita maxima* (a species of squash) and also has responsibility for tomato and its wild relatives.

BISON *fig. 54b*

SIZE: *1⅞" long by 2½" wide*

WEIGHT: *4 ounces*

SHAPE: *Round, oblate, with ribbed shoulders*

EXTERIOR COLOR(S): *Blood red*

FLESH COLOR(S): *Cherry red*

SOLUBLE SOLIDS: *3¼ degrees Brix*

FLAVOR: *Poor; low acid and low sugar*

TEXTURE: *Very firm; waxy feel; juicy*

BEST USE(S): *A tomato for northern gardens. Not recommended for areas where standard garden varieties with better fruit quality may be grown.*

PLANT HABIT, LEAF TYPE, AND YIELD: *Determinate habit; regular leaf; high yield*

MATURITY: *Very early crop*

ORIGIN: *Developed in 1929 at the North Dakota Agricultural Experiment Station by the same man who brought us the Buttercup Squash: prolific breeder, heirloom advocate, and president of the American Society for Horticultural Science Albert F. Yeager (1892–1961). Bison originated from a cross between Red River (derived from Carter's Sunrise) and Cooper's Special (Burpee's Self Pruning). Introduced in 1931 by Oscar H. Will and Company of Bismarck, North Dakota, the faithful purveyor of the good professor's works, which include the Golden Bison (see page 81).*

SYNONYMS: *Extra Early Bison; said to resemble Danmark but not as smooth*

SEED SOURCES: *Sa9*

Bison is adapted to the northern Great Plains with their extreme temperatures, desiccating winds, and short growing season. One of the beauties of this variety is the self-topping or self-pruning (determinate) habit: The short main stems end in flower trusses that expose fruits to maximum sunshine. Oscar H. Will and Company knew the value of this trait, which was a novelty in the 1920s; they cataloged the tomato in 1933 as a Golden Anniversary Specialty: "In place of wasting its vitality in continuous branching, as do practically all other Tomatoes, Bison grows a compact plant and puts all its energies into producing and ripening a heavy and extra early crop." Indeed, this plant is so eager that it's already in full bloom at transplant time. Only self-pruning allowed.

GOLDEN BISON *fig. 54a*

SIZE: *2¼" long by 2¾" wide*

WEIGHT: *6 ounces*

SHAPE: *Round, with ribbed shoulders*

EXTERIOR COLOR(S): *Golden yellow*

FLESH COLOR(S): *Maize yellow*

SOLUBLE SOLIDS: *4½ degrees Brix*

FLAVOR: *Poor; sour*

TEXTURE: *Very firm; waxy feel, mealy*

BEST USE(S): *An early and compact tomato for the Far North*

PLANT HABIT, LEAF TYPE, AND YIELD: *Determinate habit; regular leaf; high yield*

MATURITY: *Very early crop*

ORIGIN: *Documented in the 1933 North Dakota Agricultural Experiment Station Bulletin. Developed from a cross (Bison x Golden Queen) made by Dr. Albert F. Yeager, breeder of many early-maturing and hardy cultivars of fruits, vegetables, and ornamentals. Introduced in 1934 by Oscar H. Will and Company of Bismarck, North Dakota, who thought it a fine addition to the Bison family. Some of Yeager's other tomato introductions for the Far North include Red River, Bison, Fargo Yellow Pear, Farthest North, Early Jumbo, and Pink Heart.*

SEED SOURCES: *To10, Vi4*

Golden Bison is a pretty tomato, regular in its irregularity and identical to Bison (see page 80) in all respects except color. Choose Golden Bison if your growing season is short with wide extremes of temperature and you want buckets of yellow tomatoes *right now;* otherwise you can do much better. I'm not knocking Albert Yeager, the breeder, or his Golden Bison. As pointed out by the USDA's Victor R. Boswell in 1937, Yeager was a public benefactor who bent his efforts toward developing varieties for conditions decidedly unfavorable for tomatoes. "The very characters that enable them to succeed in North Dakota appear valueless, for example, in Virginia ... They serve the purpose for which they were bred, and that is enough."

55

LIVINGSTON'S HONOR BRIGHT *fig. 55*

SIZE: *2½" long by 3⅞" wide*

WEIGHT: *10 ounces*

SHAPE: *Variable shapes and sizes*

EXTERIOR COLOR(S): *Cherry red*

FLESH COLOR(S): *Cherry red*

SOLUBLE SOLIDS: *5 degrees Brix*

FLAVOR: *Fair to poor*

TEXTURE: *Firm; waxy skin; juicy; can keep for weeks, but not a longkeeper like Livingston's Stone, which stays pert for up to six months*

BEST USE(S): *For collectors and plant breeders*

PLANT HABIT, LEAF TYPE, AND YIELD: *Indeterminate habit; lutescent (yellowish) leaves and white-petaled flowers; good yield*

MATURITY: *Early crop*

ORIGIN: *Introduced in 1897 by A. W. Livingston's Sons of Columbus, Ohio. C. E. Myers said in 1914 that Honor Bright was selected by E. C. Green and then introduced by Livingston (Morrison, 1938).*

SYNONYMS: *Honor Bright; Lutescent; Livingston's Honor Bright. C. E. Myers reported in 1914 that "Grandus, in trial in 1903, appeared to be a purple-fruited form otherwise similar to Honor Bright. Royal Colors, also in trial in 1903, appeared to be a dwarf, potato-leaved, purple-fruited variety with foliage like Honor Bright" (Morrison, 1938). Will Bonsall noted in the 1988 Seed Savers Exchange yearbook that Lutescent, which he'd retrieved from the USDA, resembled little Transparent cooking apples. Our Lutescent does not appear to be the same as the Transparent tomato noted by Glenn Drowns.*

SEED SOURCES: *To10, Vi4*

In their 1897 *Annual of True Blue Seeds*, Livingston described this as: "A Peculiar Bright Red Variety, which first appeared in the form of a single 'sport' plant in a large field of Livingston's Stone Tomato in 1894. Its Chief Peculiarities Are its Solidity, Changes of Color The Fruit Undergoes During Development, Long-Keeping Qualities After Being Picked, And Its Light Green Foliage. It Differs From Every Other Tomato ... The Color of the Fruit, when fully ripe, is a Rich, Bright Red, but before reaching this state it undergoes several interesting changes. First it is light green, then an attractive waxy white, then lemon, changing to red ... It can be shipped in barrels, like apples, if picked in the early stage of ripening, and will keep from one to four weeks if stored in a cool place. The skin seems to be crack-proof." Livingston's Honor Bright is fascinating—I enjoy watching the foliage and fruit go through the changes—but if it's sustenance you're after, seek further.

FLAMME *fig. 56*

SIZE: *2¼" long by 2⅜" wide*

WEIGHT: *4 ounces*

SHAPE: *Round, smooth*

EXTERIOR COLOR(S): *Tangerine*

FLESH COLOR(S): *Tangerine with a blush of crayfish red*

SOLUBLE SOLIDS: *6 degrees Brix*

FLAVOR: *Excellent; perfect blend of sweet and tart; fruity*

TEXTURE: *Soft; juicy*

BEST USE(S): *Multipurpose; author Barbara Kingsolver roasts them in a slow oven with salt and thyme, and freezes them by the hundreds in plastic bags, to be used for panini and pizzas.*

PLANT HABIT, LEAF TYPE, AND YIELD: *Indeterminate habit; regular leaf; high yield*

MATURITY: *Early crop*

ORIGIN: *Flamme originated with Norbert Perreira of Helliner, France. Commercialized in 1997 by Tomato Growers Supply Company.*

SYNONYMS: *Flame, Flammé(e), Flamme Jaune, Jaune Flamme, Jaune Flammé*

SEED SOURCES: *Co32, Ers, Ga22, Go8, He8, Hud, Ma18, Ra6, Sa9, Se16, Se17, So25, To1, To3, To9*

This tomato can do no wrong. Use it for anything: eating out of hand, on an open-face sandwich, grilled with eggs for breakfast—you name it. Strong out of the starting gate (with 100 percent germination in six days), Flamme delivers an early crop of outstanding little tomatoes on elongated trusses. Unsurpassed in flavor and appearance; looks like Tangella (see page 166) and Mini Orange (see page 166) without the red blush. I could fill a whole tomato garden with nothing but Flammes.

57

VARIEGATED *fig. 57*

SIZE: *2" long by 2¼" wide*

WEIGHT: *4 ounces*

SHAPE: *Round, smooth*

EXTERIOR COLOR(S): *Blood red*

FLESH COLOR(S): *Blood red, washed out*

SOLUBLE SOLIDS: *6 degrees Brix*

FLAVOR: *Poor; anemic and unappetizing, with no perceptible sweetness*

TEXTURE: *Very firm; pithy*

BEST USE(S): *Ornamental plant; the foliage looks similar to that of the Fish Pepper (Capsicum annuum), but the mix of dark green, grayish green, and pale yellow is ephemeral (more common in the juvenile stage), and the pigments are not widely distributed. Stems, too, can be "splashed with cream."*

PLANT HABIT, LEAF TYPE, AND YIELD: *Indeterminate habit; variegated foliage; good yield*

MATURITY: *Late crop*

ORIGIN: *This variety seems to have originated in Europe, possibly Ireland. Introduced in 2005 by Seed Savers Exchange.*

SYNONYMS: *Splash of Cream; and Variegata*

NY: *Nee & Goldman 53434*

SEED SOURCES: *Hud, Pe6, Ra6, Sa9, Se16, To1, To3, Vi4*

Variegated is distinctive. Camouflage patterning—with dark green, grayish green, and pale yellow pigments—can occur on every part of the leaflet, in small islands or isolated strips, or, sometimes, not at all.

Tomato breeder Dr. Richard W. Robinson offered me some fascinating insights about variegation:

"Tomato plants with variegated foliage are often due to a chimera, with some cells having the genotype for normal green leaves, and other cells of the same plant for chlorophyll deficiency. These plants most often do not breed true but usually produce only normal progeny. If the germ cells include the gene for chlorophyll deficiency, then the chlorophyll deficiency can be transmitted to the progeny; but all the progeny of a variegated plant would be chlorophyll deficient, not variegated, which is not the case here.

"The late Dr. Charley Rick, who was my professor at the University of California at Davis and inspired me to be a tomato breeder, found several single genes for variegated leaves but normal red fruit. Each bred true for variegation when self-pollinated, and segregated for variegation in the F_2 generation when used as either male or female parent. This may well be the case with Variegated."

ELBERTA GIRL *fig. 58a*

SIZE: *2¼" long by 2¼" wide*

WEIGHT: *4 ounces*

SHAPE: *Round, smooth*

EXTERIOR COLOR(S): *Cherry red with carrot-red striping*

FLESH COLOR(S): *Cock's comb red*

SOLUBLE SOLIDS: *4½ degrees Brix*

FLAVOR: *Poor; low acid and low sugar*

TEXTURE: *A juicy hardball. Though some call it fuzzy, I find the skin waxy.*

BEST USE(S): *Novelty; ornamental plant and fruit. David Cavagnaro described the plant in 1989 as "a showy addition to any edible landscape."*

PLANT HABIT, LEAF TYPE, AND YIELD: *Indeterminate habit; regular leaf; low yield*

MATURITY: *Main crop*

ORIGIN: *Bred by Thomas P. Wagner and introduced in his 1983 Tater Mater Seeds catalog under the heading of "T-3" with this legend: "Red and yellow striped fruit with light peach fuzz. The rest of the plant has a dusty miller look with grayish-white fuzz all over it." Tom listed the tomato by name in 1985 and added that the interior of the fruit is "bright red."*

SYNONYMS: *Elberta Peach. Different from Angora. Not the same as Tom Wagner's Wax Striper, which is reportedly a "softball."*

SEED SOURCES: *Pr3, Sa9*

Bypass the striped fruit of Elberta Girl—unless you want a hood ornament—and go directly to the plant. The foliage is much more "angora" than Angora's (see next entry).

ANGORA *fig. 58b*

SIZE: *2⅞" long by 2⅜" wide*

WEIGHT: *3½ ounces*

SHAPE: *Round, smooth*

EXTERIOR COLOR(S): *Crayfish red*

FLESH COLOR(S): *Grayish red; can have a red star in the middle, like Flamme (see page 83)*

SOLUBLE SOLIDS: *3½ degrees Brix*

FLAVOR: *Poor; tasteless*

TEXTURE: *Very firm; mealy*

BEST USE(S): *Ornamental "dusty miller" plant; the fruit is for the birds*

PLANT HABIT, LEAF TYPE, AND YIELD: *Indeterminate habit; angora foliage; fair yield*

MATURITY: *Late crop*

ORIGIN: *Named by the codeveloper of Marglobe (see page 66), William S. Porte, of the United States Department of Agriculture. The unusual horticultural characters of Angora were described by Young and MacArthur in 1947.*

SEED SOURCES: *Ra6, Sa9, Te4*

Call it what you will—canescent, pubescent, tomentose, or hirsute—Angora's hoarfrosted blue-green foliage is ravishing. Even the tiniest seedlings are woolly (though regular-leafed plants will appear; toss them). There seems to be an inverse relationship between the novelty of foliage and the quality of fruit (see, for example, Elberta Girl). I've heard rumors of more palatable variants, but my Angora's fruit is like a rock and a hard place.

Merlin W. Gleckler plastered Angora's image on the cover of his 1954 seed catalog of wonders (Glecklers Seedmen, Metamora, Ohio), and proclaimed it the most beautiful plant in the vegetable garden. When a customer remarked that Angora was never bothered by tomato hornworms, Gleckler famously replied that encroaching hornworms were tickled to death: "They can't stand being tickled by the woolly fuzz while chewing away." Although my Angoras seem immune to hornworms, the more wily aphids have learned to get around the fuzz factor by feasting on the leaves' undersides.

LIME GREEN SALAD *page 15, fig. 4a*

SIZE: *2" long by 3¼" wide*

WEIGHT: *7 ounces*

SHAPE: *Round, smooth to rough; variable sizes*

EXTERIOR COLOR(S): *Olive yellow*

FLESH COLOR(S): *Olive yellow (with yellowish green gel)*

SOLUBLE SOLIDS: *4½ degrees Brix*

FLAVOR: *Poor; high acid and low sugar*

TEXTURE: *Reasonably firm; mealy*

BEST USE(S): *Ornamental container growing*

PLANT HABIT, LEAF TYPE, AND YIELD: *Dwarf habit; rugosa foliage; high yield*

MATURITY: *Early crop*

ORIGIN: *Bred by Thomas P. Wagner and introduced in his 1983 Tater Mater Seeds catalog under the heading of "P-5": "green-when-ripe fruit on a dwarf plant for window boxes and gardens. Salad-sized fruits add unique variations to lettuce and tomato salads." In 1985, Tom named the variety "Green Elf" because of its "elfish" or dwarfed vine. Tim Peters of Peters Seed and Research later gave it the name Lime Green Salad.*

SYNONYMS: *Green Elf; Lime Green. Same as the Golden Green (Gold 'N Green or Green 'N Gold) carried by Ken Ettlinger as early as 1985 in his Long Island Seed*

and Plant Company catalog. Ken told me, "It was labeled as an F₅ 'Dwarf Green Salad Type' when I obtained it from Tom through Tater Mater in a heat-sealed plastic envelope. There has always been a bit of variation in it, from somewhat flattened to a more roundish shape and even little beefsteak variations." Not the same as Dorothy Beiswenger's Garden Lime, which is indeterminate and regular-leafed.

SEED SOURCES: *Ba8, Sa9, So25, Te4, To1, To9, Vi4*

I was never one of those kids who could suck on sour balls or, like my younger sister Jane did, drink caper juice. So it's no surprise that I pucker when presented with high-acid tomatoes. I grow Lime Green Salad for amusement rather than for salad: The knee-high plant bears a profusion of blossoms and more fruit than foliage. I shiver to think of the "delectable acid bite" of Tom Wagner's Sour Boy, which is even higher in citric acid.

CZECH'S EXCELLENT YELLOW *page 4, fig. 1j*

SIZE: *2½" long by 2½" wide*

WEIGHT: *4 ounces*

SHAPE: *Round, smooth*

EXTERIOR COLOR(S): *Cadmium orange*

FLESH COLOR(S): *Light orange*

SOLUBLE SOLIDS: *5 degrees Brix*

FLAVOR: *Fair; low acid*

TEXTURE: *Soft; juicy and seedy*

BEST USE(S): *I find this variety very ordinary, but seedsman Ben Quisenberry, whose advice was always sound, said it was excellent for making preserves. Squirrels love it.*

PLANT HABIT, LEAF TYPE, AND YIELD: *Indeterminate habit; regular leaf; good yield*

MATURITY: *Early crop*

ORIGIN: *Ben Quisenberry of Big Tomato Gardens, Syracuse, Ohio, cataloged this variety in 1976. The "Czech" was probably Milan Sodomka, from whom Ben obtained Czech's Bush, Tiger Tom (see page 169), and other tomatoes. Reintroduced in 1993 by Synergy Seeds of Orleans, California.*

SYNONYMS: *Czeck's Excel Yellow, Czech's Yellow*

NY: *Nee & Goldman 53422*

SEED SOURCES: *Se16, St18, SynVi4*

When Bernard Kravitz of Woodland Hills, California, ordered seed of Czeck's Excel Yellow from Ben Quisenberry in 1976, Ben offered him a few words of advice, scribbled on the Tomato Seed List: "I have been growing tomatoes organically for 80 years, started at age 8 with my dad in Kentucky. Organic growing means no 'hot shot' fertilizers; use all natural plant food. Turn under cover crops. Make compost from waste. We ship lots of tomato seed to California so they must have good success in your locality. Sincerely, B. Quisenberry, grower. P.S. Have you read the Organic Magazine?—it would help you."

SILVERY FIR TREE *page 15, fig. 5*

SIZE: *2⅛" long by 3" wide*

WEIGHT: *6½ ounces*

SHAPE: *Round, more or less smooth*

EXTERIOR COLOR(S): *Blood red*

FLESH COLOR(S): *Blood red*

SOLUBLE SOLIDS: *3 degrees Brix*

FLAVOR: *Poor; tart*

TEXTURE: *Reasonably firm; very juicy and seedy*

BEST USE(S): *Ornamental edible landscaping; containers*

PLANT HABIT, LEAF TYPE, AND YIELD: *Determinate habit; finely dissected, carrot-like foliage; high yield*

MATURITY: *Very early crop*

ORIGIN: *Introduced in 1995 by Seed Savers International, Silvery Fir Tree is one of hundreds of traditional Russian varieties obtained by Kent Whealy from Moscow seedswoman Marina Danilenko*

SYNONYMS: *Carrot-Like; Carrot Top Tomato; Silvery Fir*

SEED SOURCES: *Abu, Co32, Ga22, Go8, He8, Hig, La1, Pe6, Pr3, Ra6, Sa5, Se7, Se16, Te4, To1, To3, Up2, Yu2*

An unusual and delicate little plant that can easily be grown in containers on your patio. Produces a tremendous crop of disproportionately large fruits—if you let it. Don't.

Beefsteak

(a) White Beauty, (b) Black Krim, (c) Yellow Jumbo, (d) Pruden's Purple, (e) Ananas Noire, (f) Ugly

a

b

c

d

e

f

PRUDEN'S PURPLE *page 87, fig. 59d*

SIZE: *5" long by 5¾" wide*

WEIGHT: *1 pound, 12 ounces*

SHAPE: *Beefsteak*

EXTERIOR COLOR(S): *Tomato pink*

FLESH COLOR(S): *Cock's comb red*

SOLUBLE SOLIDS: *6½ degrees Brix*

FLAVOR: *Excellent; luscious, savory, and sweet*

TEXTURE: *Soft; meaty and juicy*

BEST USE(S): *Fresh eating; does well in short-season areas such as Ontario, where Brandywine doesn't stand a chance of maturing*

PLANT HABIT, LEAF TYPE, AND YIELD: *Indeterminate habit; potato leaf (regular leaf seedlings should be culled); good yield*

MATURITY: *Early crop*

ORIGIN: *Introduced circa 1990 by Dick Meiners of Pinetree Garden Seeds. His seed originated with Garrett H. Pittenger of Ontario in the mid-1980s. Pittenger's seed, in turn, came from Alex Caron of King City, Ontario (founder of Seeds of Diversity Canada).*

SYNONYMS: *Peruvian Black; Potato Top; Pruden Purple; Prudence; Prudence Pink; Prudence Purple; Pruden's Purple True Variety; Purple Potato Top. Similar to Brandywine, Sudduth's (or Quisenberry Strain).*

NY: *Nee & Goldman 53440*

SEED SOURCES: *Ba8, Co32, Fe5, Ga1, Go8, Ha26, He8, He17, Hi6, Jo1, Ma18, Na6, Ni1, Pe2, Pin, Sa5, So25, Sw9, Syn, Te4, To1, To3, To9, To10, Up2, Vi4*

Pruden's Purple is an old handed-down pink potato-leafed tomato—the kind legends are made of. It compares favorably to Brandywine in flavor but is an earlier and heavier cropper. Rumor has it that Pruden's is, variously, the work of a Mrs. Pruden of eastern Kentucky; a West Virginia family heirloom; or even the last in a long-lost line of French violet-hued tomatoes. Little has been found to verify any of these beliefs.

If not French in origin, Pruden's is French at least in color: it's *fraise*, which is tomato speak for pink. Early members of Seed Savers Exchange worked themselves into a frenzy trying to find a Pruden's Purple—one "so purple it looked black, about the color of the Black Beauty eggplant," fantasized Milan Rafayko of New Haven, Kentucky, in the 1981 yearbook. Alas, such a creature never materialized. Rare cultivated tomatoes, it turns out, don't normally contain the purple pigment anthocyanin—although some of their wild relatives do. (Professor Jim Myers and his graduate students at Oregon State University have recently bred a purple tomato—as close to that mythic Pruden's as we're likely to get—by incorporating genetic materials from wild tomatoes.)

The search for Pruden's Purple came to a halt in the mid-1980s when the tomato, in all its pink glory, was finally listed by Seed Savers Exchange members in the annual yearbook. Most of these members had gotten their seed from an ad in a National Gardening Association publication called *Gardens for All*. The first two members to possess Pruden's Purple, in 1984, were Alex Caron and Richard L. Arnold of Lone Grove, Oklahoma (although Arnold's seed, from a woman in West Virginia, was impure). George McLaughlin (now of Tahlequah, Oklahoma) was in on the ground floor, too, one year later (1985). His seed came "from an old gent in Charleston, Illinois, who spelled it Prudence Purple"—a spelling he keeps alive out of respect for that old gent.

Landscape architect Garrett H. Pittenger is credited as the original source of "the true variety," although the seed came from his friend Alex Caron, who also worked for the Canadian Ministry of Natural Resources at the time. "It's the best tomato I've ever had," Garrett recently told me. He likes to pick them slightly green for salads but uses the fully ripe fruits for sauce. Alex Caron finds Pruden's Purple something of a letdown: "I gave Garrett what was reputed to be the true variety, but it was certainly not purple." I think Alex still believes in the existence of a "true" Pruden's Purple, deep in color as an aubergine.

BLACK KRIM *page 87, fig. 59b*

SIZE: *4" long by 5½" wide*

WEIGHT: *1 pound, 4 ounces*

SHAPE: *Round, smooth; beefsteak forms*

EXTERIOR COLOR(S): *Violet brown*

FLESH COLOR(S): *Violet brown and raspberry red*

SOLUBLE SOLIDS: *5 degrees Brix*

FLAVOR: *Excellent. CR Lawn of Fedco Seeds advocates harvesting Krims as soon as they're half-green and still firm but before they "disintegrate like a chunk of road kill."*

TEXTURE: *Soft; meaty and juicy; can be corky*

BEST USE(S): *Fresh eating*

PLANT HABIT, LEAF TYPE, AND YIELD: *Indeterminate habit; regular leaf; high yield*

MATURITY: *Early crop*

ORIGIN: *From Krim, Russia, in 1990, via Lars Olov Rosenstrom of Bromma, Sweden, who could grow the blackest Krim in his heated greenhouse*

SYNONYMS: *Black Crimea, Black Crimean, Noire de Crimée, Noire de Krimée*

NY: *Nee & Goldman 53424*

SEED SOURCES: *Ap6, Ba8, Bo17, Bo19, Bou, Bu2, Co32, Coo, Ers, Fe5, Go8, He8, He17, Hi13, Hud, Ma18, Na6, Pr3, Ra6, Sa5, Sa9, Se16, Se28, Shu, Sk2, So25, Sw9, Syn, Te4, To1, To3, To9, To10, Tu6, Und, Up2, Vi4, Vi5, We19*

Black Krim should be welcome in every garden. I was sold even before I bit into it: The violet brown and raspberry red are amazing technicolors. The flavor is exotic and musky; the fruit acid hits me in the roof of my mouth and tickles my tongue. Others describe Krim as "very intense," "smoky," "salty," or even like downing "a good single malt scotch"—and that, I assume, is before fermenting it for seed-saving purposes!

ANANAS NOIRE *page 87, fig. 59e*

SIZE: *4" long by 5" wide*

WEIGHT: *1 pound, 12 ounces*

SHAPE: *Beefsteak*

EXTERIOR COLOR(S): *Olive yellow with cherry red at the blossom end*

FLESH COLOR(S): *Olive yellow and yellowish green, with flecks of cherry red*

SOLUBLE SOLIDS: *5 degrees Brix*

FLAVOR: *Fair; bland; some describe it as smoky or citrusy*

TEXTURE: *Soft*

BEST USE(S): *Novelty*

PLANT HABIT, LEAF TYPE, AND YIELD: *Indeterminate habit; regular leaf; good yield*

MATURITY: *Early crop*

ORIGIN: *Introduced to Seed Savers Exchange by Luc Fichot of Falisolle, Belgium. Ananas Noire originated as a sport (a spontaneous mutation) in a field of Pineapple tomatoes and was further developed by horticulturist Pascal Moreau. It still appears to be genetically unstable; saved seeds don't breed true.*

SYNONYMS: *Black Pineapple*

NY: *Nee & Goldman 53465*

SEED SOURCES: *Ba8, Hi13, Ma18, Se17, So25, Ter, To1, To10, Und*

Ananas Noire—beautiful, but almost too weird to be real—comes in a range of color combinations, all of them startling. I prefer the green-when-ripe with cherry-red splashes: it looks like a Big Rainbow (see page 112), but in green. I find Ananas Noire tasteless but, with such spectacular looks, the flavor is almost irrelevant.

GREEN GIANT *fig. 60*

SIZE: *3¼" long by 4¾" wide*

WEIGHT: *1 pound*

SHAPE: *Beefsteak*

EXTERIOR COLOR(S): *Yellowish green*

FLESH COLOR(S): *Yellowish green*

SOLUBLE SOLIDS: *5½ degrees Brix*

FLAVOR: *Excellent; this is the best-tasting green-when-ripe beefsteak*

TEXTURE: *Soft; meaty and juicy*

BEST USE(S): *Fresh eating; try thick slices of Green Giant with a dash of extra-virgin olive oil and basil*

PLANT HABIT, LEAF TYPE, AND YIELD: *Indeterminate habit; potato leaf; high yield*

MATURITY: *Early crop*

ORIGIN: *An apparent sport of an unidentified regular-leafed green-when-ripe tomato, brought to notice by Reinhard Kraft of Neukirchen, Germany, in 2004. Commercialized in the United States in 2007. Initially listed in the 2005 Seed Savers Exchange yearbook by Neil Lockhart.*

SEED SOURCES: *Hi13, La1, To1, To9, Vi4*

A superlative tomato that ought to be more widely disseminated. The humongous potato-leaved plants bear bountiful harvests of the greenest, cleanest beefsteaks, with a lovely hue and no grave faults in sight. Green Giant is richly flavored, sweet and sprightly—even better than the standard of excellence, Aunt Ruby's German Green (see page 174)—though I feel like a traitor to Ruby Arnold when I say that. Michelle Baity, a fourteen-year-old homeschooler from High Point, North Carolina, knows a good thing, too. She wrote to me after I showed off this tomato (and some others) on *The Martha Stewart Show*: "I was really excited to hear you mention the Green Giant. I grew that variety this year. The 'tree' is amazing! It is tied to the chimney. I have to use a ladder to pick the tomatoes. Their taste is awesome."

YELLOW JUMBO

page 87, fig. 59c; page 164, fig. 115d

SIZE: *3¼" long by 4⅝" wide*

WEIGHT: *1 pound, 3 ounces*

SHAPE: *Beefsteak*

EXTERIOR COLOR(S): *Orange*

FLESH COLOR(S): *Orange yellow*

SOLUBLE SOLIDS: *5¼ degrees Brix*

FLAVOR: *Fair*

TEXTURE: *Soft; meaty*

BEST USE(S): *Multipurpose*

PLANT HABIT, LEAF TYPE, AND YIELD: *Indeterminate habit; regular leaf; good yield*

MATURITY: *Main crop*

ORIGIN: *First brought to attention by Benny Michitti of Carrollton, Virginia, in the Seed Savers Exchange's 1984 yearbook. Said to be a Kirby family heirloom from West Virginia that dates to circa 1900.*

SYNONYMS: *Yellow Jumbo Heirloom; may be the same as Large Yellow Heirloom.*

Doesn't thrill me.

PURPLE SMUDGE, ORANGE FLESHED *fig. 61*

SIZE: *2½" long by 4⅛" wide*

WEIGHT: *14½ ounces*

SHAPE: *Beefsteak*

EXTERIOR COLOR(S): *Tangerine with dark violet shoulders*

FLESH COLOR(S): *Orange*

SOLUBLE SOLIDS: *6½ degrees Brix*

FLAVOR: *Fair; low acid, mildly sweet*

TEXTURE: *Soft; very juicy*

BEST USE(S): *Multipurpose; novelty*

PLANT HABIT, LEAF TYPE, AND YIELD: *Indeterminate habit; regular leaf; high yield*

MATURITY: *Early crop*

ORIGIN: *An orange-fleshed sport of the red-fleshed Purple Smudge, which Richard Rahn of Bay City, Michigan, erroneously thought he might have caused by grafting; reported in the 1994 Seed Savers Exchange yearbook. The original (red) Purple Smudge was obtained from the USDA (PI 290858) by Gary Staley and Will Bonsall; Gary listed it in the 1985 Seed Savers yearbook.*

SYNONYMS: *Purple Smudge, Orange Flesh*

The purple patch at the top crowns this tomato king. Dr. Jim Myers at Oregon State University analyzed fruits I'd sent him and confirmed that the purple smudge is due to anthocyanin in the shoulder region. The anthocyanin is located in the pericarp just below the inner epidermis layer. This color pigment is rare in ripe cultivated tomato fruits but common in tomato's wild relatives. The trait may have been introduced from a wild species or else it was a spontaneous mutation. Whatever the source of Purple Smudge's smudge, the tomato is truly a thing to behold: I delay eating it as long as possible. "Has a beautiful green taste, not sweet, so special," according to Slow Foodies who sampled it *chez moi* one summer.

AUNT GINNY'S PURPLE *fig. 62*

SIZE: *3½" long by 6½" wide*

WEIGHT: *2 pounds, 3 ounces*

SHAPE: *Beefsteak*

EXTERIOR COLOR(S): *Tomato pink*

FLESH COLOR(S): *Tomato pink*

SOLUBLE SOLIDS: *5 degrees Brix*

FLAVOR: *Excellent; rich flavor*

TEXTURE: *Soft; meaty, juicy, and well-marbled*

BEST USE(S): *Fresh eating*

PLANT HABIT, LEAF TYPE, AND YIELD: *Indeterminate habit; potato leaf; high yield*

MATURITY: *Main crop*

ORIGIN: *First listed in the 1991 Seed Savers Exchange yearbook by Rick Burkhart of Indianapolis, Indiana. The variety is of German extraction. It has been grown for exceptional flavor and texture by Burkhart's family since the late 1960s.*

SEED SOURCES: *Ap6, Ma18, Sa9, So25, Sw9, To1, To9*

This big beautiful pink mama cuts and tastes like filet mignon. Even in bad years—such as 2004, which had rampant viruses and a late season—Aunt Ginny's Purple produces a heavy crop of two-pounders in my garden that are the essence of vine-ripened tomato. And unlike many other beefsteaks, which become bloated after a thunderstorm, Aunt Ginny hardly cracks an inch.

62

AMANA ORANGE *fig. 63*

SIZE: *3¼" long by 5⅛" wide*

WEIGHT: *1 pound, 8 ounces*

SHAPE: *Beefsteak*

EXTERIOR COLOR(S): *Cadmium orange*

FLESH COLOR(S): *Orange*

SOLUBLE SOLIDS: *5½ degrees Brix*

FLAVOR: *Fair to good; mildly pleasing*

TEXTURE: *Soft; meaty*

BEST USE(S): *Fresh eating*

PLANT HABIT, LEAF TYPE, AND YIELD: *Indeterminate habit; regular leaf; good yield*

MATURITY: *Late crop*

ORIGIN: *Introduced to Seed Savers Exchange in 1985 by Gary Staley of Brandon, Florida, who named it for the Amana Corporation (where he worked as a customer service manager) and not for the Amana Colonies, as is sometimes reported. Cataloged as "a tomato of a different color" in 1995 by Tomato Growers Supply Company, and by seven additional seed houses in 1998.*

SEED SOURCES: *Ba8, Co32, Ga1, Go8, He17, Pe2, Ra6, Re8, Sa9, Se7, Se28, So25, To1, To3, To9, To10*

Gary Staley, a Seed Savers Exchange mainstay, hates orange tomatoes the same way that I hate yellow daffodils: passionately. Yet he'll probably be best remembered for a handsome orange sport—a "happy accident" or, in this case, an unhappy accident— in his all-red-and-pink tomato patch. Amana Orange may not be as tasty as Yellow Brandywine (see page 109), but it fills a gap in my tomato procession, providing me with juicy, unblemished beefsteaks when all the rest have petered out.

63

GOLDEN JUBILEE *fig. 64*

SIZE: *3¾″ long by 4¼″ wide*

WEIGHT: *1 pound*

SHAPE: *Round, smooth*

EXTERIOR COLOR(S): *Cadmium orange*

FLESH COLOR(S): *Orange yellow*

SOLUBLE SOLIDS: *6 degrees Brix*

FLAVOR: *Good; sprightly and richly flavored*

TEXTURE: *Firm; solid, meaty, and juicy*

BEST USE(S): *Multipurpose; made for juicing; easy to peel*

PLANT HABIT, LEAF TYPE, AND YIELD: *Indeterminate habit; regular leaf; good yield*

MATURITY: *Main crop*

ORIGIN: *Introduced as "Burpee's Jubilee" by W. Atlee Burpee Company in 1943. A sixth-generation selection from a cross of Tangerine (Burpee, 1931) and Rutgers (see page 67). Not the same as "Veitch's Golden Jubilee" (a yellow tomato veined with red, introduced by James Veitch and Sons, Middlesex, England, in 1898); or "Golden Jubilee Climbing" (a red tomato introduced by Farmer Seed and Nursery Company of Faribault, Minnesota, in their golden jubilee year, 1938).*

SYNONYMS: *Burpee's Golden Jubilee; Burpee's Jubilee; Golden Sunray; Jubilee; Orange Jubilee; Sunray; Yellow Jubilee. Burpee's Sunray (1950) is an improved Jubilee with Fusarium wilt resistance.*

According to Glecklers Seedmen (1954), Sunray was developed by Dr. William S. Porte; it was the result of a cross between Pan American and Jubilee.

SEED SOURCES: *Ba8, Bu8, Ear, Ers, Fe5, Ga1, Gr27, Ha5, Ha26, He8, He17, La1, Mo13, Pep, Ra6, Re8, Sh9, Shu, Sk2, So25, Te4, To1, To3, Up2, Vi4, Wi2*

What a beauty this one is! A first-class tomato, well deserving of its All America Selections (AAS) bronze medal in 1943. Seedsman Ben Quisenberry (1887–1986) adored it, too; he sold the variety under the name of Golden Sunray. "Looks like an orange," he wrote approvingly on one of his seed bottles. "I want you to cut that and see how nice it is inside," he told John and Helen Gorman during a taped interview in 1981. It has a distinctive flavor, too: Ben's friend and neighbor Mrs. Best served the Gormans a smashing Golden Sunray tomato juice that they've never forgotten.

MCCLINTOCK'S BIG PINK *fig. 65*

SIZE: *3¼″ long by 5⅛″ wide*

WEIGHT: *1 pound, 9 ounces*

SHAPE: *Beefsteak*

EXTERIOR COLOR(S): *Tomato pink with olive yellow shoulders*

FLESH COLOR(S): *Tomato pink*

SOLUBLE SOLIDS: *5½ degrees Brix*

FLAVOR: *Excellent; delicious rich flavor*

TEXTURE: *Soft; meaty and juicy*

BEST USE(S): *Fresh eating; juice*

PLANT HABIT, LEAF TYPE, AND YIELD: *Indeterminate habit; regular leaf; high yield*

MATURITY: *Early crop*

ORIGIN: *Listed in the 1998 Seed Savers Exchange yearbook by Will Bonsall of Industry, Maine, as "an heirloom collected by my parents from Mack and Emeline McClintock of Wellington, Maine, brought thence by them from Pennsylvania." When I asked Will to send me a few of his favorite tomatoes for trial, McClintock was tops on his list.*

SYNONYMS: *Not the same as the small red "McClintock."*

Those in the know prefer McClintock's Big Pink to Brandywine. It's comparable in flavor but far more productive.

BIG BEN *fig. 66, page ii*

SIZE: *4½" long by 5½" wide*

WEIGHT: *1 pound, 7 ounces*

SHAPE: *Beefsteak*

EXTERIOR COLOR(S): *Tomato pink*

FLESH COLOR(S): *Blood red*

SOLUBLE SOLIDS: *5 degrees Brix*

FLAVOR: *Excellent. A peach of a tomato —not as sweet as the Brandywines, but very rich.*

TEXTURE: *Soft to reasonably firm; meaty and juicy*

BEST USE(S): *Multipurpose. Slices of Big Ben do wonderful things for a nice fat juicy hamburger.*

PLANT HABIT, LEAF TYPE, AND YIELD: *Indeterminate; regular leaf foliage; good yield.*

MATURITY: *Main crop*

ORIGIN: *Cataloged by Benjamin Franklin Quisenberry (1887–1986) of Big Tomato Gardens, Syracuse, Ohio, in 1976. His catalog copy: "Our largest and smoothest pink. Delicious flavor, sub-acid, firm; few seeds. Averages 20 ounces each: some 2 pounds. Very prolific—heavy yield." The price was a bargain: "100 seeds for $1, postpaid, small gardeners may order less than 100. Get a gift packet of seed with each order." Ben later reported, "In 1967, an old acquaintance of mine at Boonesboro, Kentucky, Bob Dyke, now deceased,*

mailed the seed to me, it proved to be an excellent, large pink variety. I didn't like the name for a tomato"—it was then called Stump of the World—"so I list it as 'Big Ben.'" Dyke's tomato was probably named for the peach of the same name, described by U. P. Hedrick (1917) as melting, juicy, sparkling, and rich; it originated on the farm of Samuel Whitehead in Middlesex County, New Jersey, circa 1825.

SYNONYMS: *Stump of the World; Stump-of-the-World; Stump the World; Seed Savers Exchange Tomato No. 4. A couple of growers have reported a red-skinned version of Big Ben—which I think is an error. Big Ben's skin is very deep red (pink). There has also been some confusion about Big Ben's foliage: In the early 1980s, Ben Quisenberry offered Big Ben seed in a "Three Large Pinks" mixture with Brandywine and Mortgage Lifter. When Ken Ettlinger asked Ben how to figure out which was which, Ben told him that Brandywine was the only potato leaf type, so we can deduce that the real Big Ben is a regular leaf type.*

SEED SOURCES: *Ma18, To1, To9, To10*

Ben Quisenberry was the oldest active tomato seedsman in America when he retired, in 1981, at the age of ninety-four, after fifteen years in the business. He is perhaps best known for introducing Sudduth's Brandywine (see page 108), but that's just one high point in a lifetime of tomato triumphs. His lifelong love for tomatoes was fostered early on by his parents, Roger E. and Rose Quisenberry in Winchester, Kentucky. Their example took. As Ben's protégé Don Hubbard told me, "Ben always had a little tomato garden. Then he started raising novelties in 1956. By the late 1960s, he had his tomatoes advertised in magazines like *Progressive Farmer* and was selling seeds in every state."

Ben lived in and worked out of the cavernous old two-story white post office building he owned on Route 124 in Syracuse, Ohio. There was a small garden out back, a larger one three blocks away, and several other lots, scattered all over town, that he either owned or rented. He grew many crops in addition to tomatoes, including sweet potatoes, strawberries, Brussels sprouts, and asparagus. He processed his tomatoes by hand for seed and even printed his own Big Tomato Gardens price lists and seed packets. He hand-set the type on the same printing press that he used for poetry and gospel tracts; he always printed bits of wisdom on the back of his packets. One favorite included the words of Dorothy Frances Gurney:

The kiss of the sun for pardon
The song of the birds for mirth
One is nearer God's heart in a
    garden
Than anywhere else on earth

People adored "Big Ben" Quisenberry. "Ben made friends with everyone," Hubbard said. "He was a wonderful sweet person—a very godly man. He got me on right." Ben grew frail and thin as he aged, but he never stinted on giving his time and advice to others. He was often spotted driving friends and neighbors to church, the grocery store, and doctor's offices. And his largesse extended to his seeds; his customers frequently received more than they'd paid for. Ben's "friends across the miles"—his mail-order clients, and the members of Seed Savers Exchange—were able to return the favor on one notable occasion. When they learned that Ben had become ill and lost most of his tomato seed crop, during the summer of 1980, they replaced everything that had been claimed by the weeds.

In 1983, from a "haven of rest for old folks," ninety-five-year-old Ben gratefully wrote to Kent Whealy, who had led the seed rescue brigade: "[After] 15 years in the tomato seed business, I figure that gardeners are our most lovable people. I feel sure you are a most lovable man, how I would love to give you a big hug to prove my appreciation of you. I <u>love you</u>. I am completely <u>out</u> of the seed business. <u>I am sorry!</u>"

Ben's legacy begins in 1915, when his motorcycle broke down near Forest Run, Ohio; he was returning to an engineering job (building shells for war) at Westinghouse in Pittsburgh, after a vacation with his folks in Kentucky. Ben boarded the steamboat *Joe Fulton* to Pittsburgh, and on the boat he met and fell in love with a local, Miss Oa Baer, whose father owned the Peacock Coal Company. Ben and Oa married in 1916 and produced three accomplished sons: Joe Fulton (named for that steamy boat), Donald (who taught industrial arts with a specialty in printing), and my informant Roger C. Quisenberry (former chair of the Department of Engineering at Ohio University). Roger told me that Oa divorced his father years later and outlived all three of her husbands, before she died at a spry 106 years of age.

Ben was a most enterprising man: a licensed stationary engineer; proprietor for forty years of the Safety Tag Company (which manufactured tags for dog collars, cab drivers' caps, hunting horns, and golf bags); and twenty-five-year veteran of the postal service. He carried mail twice a day in his eighties, even in tomato season—and the women chased after him. To supplement his income and as a hobby, he built a greenhouse shortly after his marriage and raised flower and vegetable plants. And he still had time to raise canaries, paint signs, print pamphlets and envelopes, cobble shoes, and sell homegrown roasted peanuts and popcorn in nickel bags. According to Don Hubbard, Ben didn't stop until he dropped: "He'd be up at evenings working. I remember one hot day in July, when the plants were three and a half or four feet tall, Ben was a-hoeing along at age eighty-seven, and laid down in the shade of the plants. The emergency came, called by a neighbor who thought Ben had had a heart attack. 'No, I just took a nap,' he told them."

Just before Ben retired, he had special visitors, in September 1981, from Snook, Texas: longtime customer John Gorman, also known as "Mr. Tomato," and his wife, Helen. Ben said they took him to dinner and treated him like a king. The next day, Ben hosted a lunch for the Gormans with the help of his old friend Mrs. Best. After lunch, Ben gave John and Helen the garden tour, followed by a tutorial on seed saving—which John recorded for posterity. Helen spied some tomatoes in the garden, down low on one plant, which were so heavy they were breaking the vines. Ben said, "I didn't keep them tied up very good." Then he added, more proudly, "Isn't that a good size? That one took a notion to get natural size. That's Big Ben."

As the Gormans prepared to leave, Ben shared his philosophy of life: "I do marvel at myself sometime, the way I keep going. Indeed I do, indeed I do. I marvel at myself. I'm surprised sometimes the way I can keep going, from about seven o'clock till dark. And, you know, about dark, I'm like the chickens, I hunt my roost … To keep happy and to keep content, *do* something that's worthwhile. If you have a hobby and if you can make your hobby your business, you're just all the better off. You're setting good. But aging in rural America, the elderly man is very fortunate if he's in a rural district. Out in nature, out where he can work, out where he can fasten his hands onto the end of a hoe handle and make things grow—do things worthwhile. He's with nature, and when he's with nature, he's close to God. God is nature and nature is God. So you're in good company when you're in a rural district."

How I wish I'd had the chance to meet Ben Quisenberry. Ben's son Roger, employee Don Hubbard, and acolyte John Gorman have shared their memories, photographs, and yellowed newspaper clippings; the greatest joy in my research was tracking down eighty-year-old John Gorman at his cabin in the woods of Snook. With his daughter Lu Ann's help, John found what I'd been looking for, in an old shoe box hidden for twenty-six years in a back bedroom closet. Inside were the long-lost cassette tape of Ben talking with the Gormans; photographs, letters, and gospel tracts; and twelve of Ben's seed bottles, filled with part of the seed from his last harvest. These marvelous artifacts brought me as close to Ben as I could ever hope to be. John wrote, "Let me know if you're as excited as I was in finding this treasure. Ben was a remarkable gentleman. God bless the memory of this great gardener." Amen.

a

b

68

AFRICAN QUEEN *fig. 68a*

SIZE: *3¼" long by 5¾" wide*

WEIGHT: *2 pounds, 5 ounces*

SHAPE: *Beefsteak*

EXTERIOR COLOR(S): *Tomato pink*

FLESH COLOR(S): *Blood red*

SOLUBLE SOLIDS: *6 degrees Brix*

FLAVOR: *Excellent; well-balanced, like wine—a taste I wish could last forever*

TEXTURE: *Soft; meaty*

BEST USE(S): *Fresh eating; slices juice up before your eyes*

PLANT HABIT, LEAF TYPE, AND YIELD: *Indeterminate habit; potato leaf; high yield*

MATURITY: *Early crop*

ORIGIN: *African Queen is Jack Maderis' family heirloom from North Carolina. An unclaimed jewel, not available commercially.*

SYNONYMS: *Not the same as regular-leafed African Beefsteak*

While on a family trip to the idyllic Blackberry Farm in the Smoky Mountains of East Tennessee four years ago, I was fortunate enough to meet John Coykendall, an artist and seed collector who supplied the hotel with heirloom vegetables—and me with seeds of African Queen (as well as Miller's Cove, a pumpkin with the biggest blossoms in the world). Four tomato plants had been given to John in 1986 by an elderly gentleman, a friend of a neighbor's named Jack Maderis. Jack spoke in a Southern Mountain dialect—a remnant of early English—with Elizabethan pronunciation and words like *dreen* for "tiny stream," *nary* for "narrow," and *hit* for "it." But he reverted to plain English long enough to declare that "this'll make some big old pink tomatoes." They make some big old potato leaves, too, a funnel for sunshine and flavor.

Jack's family had cultivated African Queen for generations, with the aid of mules, on steep hillsides of western North Carolina—one of the richest areas in the United States for bean, tomato, and squash landraces (folk varieties). Since tomatoes had been cultivated in the Carolinas as early as the mid-eighteenth century, African Queen may have come directly to the Carolinas with British colonists or, more likely, with slaves from the Caribbean.

(a) African Queen, (b) Matt's Wild Cherry

69

BELIEVE IT OR NOT *fig. 69*

SIZE: *3½" long by 5½" wide*

WEIGHT: *1 pound, 13 ounces*

SHAPE: *Beefsteak*

EXTERIOR COLOR(S): *Blood red*

FLESH COLOR(S): *Cherry red*

SOLUBLE SOLIDS: *5¼ degrees Brix*

FLAVOR: *Excellent; perfectly balanced*

TEXTURE: *Soft; meaty*

BEST USE(S): *Fresh eating; sandwiches*

PLANT HABIT, LEAF TYPE, AND YIELD: *Indeterminate habit; regular leaf; high yield*

MATURITY: *Main crop*

ORIGIN: *First listed by Mrs. Ed (Dorothy) Beiswenger of Crookston, Minnesota, in the 1984 Seed Savers Exchange yearbook*

SYNONYMS: *Not the same as Super Big Believe It or Not (a cross with Big Boy)*

SEED SOURCES: *To1, To9, Up2*

Very hefty, red, and appetizing. Acquired by Dorothy Beiswenger of Crookston, Minnesota, from local nuns who also gave her the Froney, Jumbo, and Rockingham tomatoes. The nuns had christened the tomato Believe It or Not and had grown it for years because it gave them such pleasure: an impish cognomen but certainly not sinful behavior. According to taste physiologist Anthelme Brillat-Savarin, "Morally, it is an implicit obedience of the rules of the Creator, who, having ordered us to eat in order to live, invites us to do so with appetite, encourages us with flavor, and rewards us with pleasure."

Dorothy Beiswenger joined the Seed Savers Exchange in 1976 when there were only 141 members; for more than thirty years she has blessed thousands with her seeds, sent through the mail. I can envision her sitting at the farmhouse kitchen table, sorting stacks of letters with seed requests and seed offerings—including a small hill of beans sent by a woman because having so many different ones was driving her crazy. "I wondered what she was trying to do to me," Dorothy told me. I treasure Dorothy—who is saner than most—and her seed packets made from envelope corners and then Scotch-taped.

70

ILYA MUROMETS *fig. 70*

SIZE: *3" long by 4" wide*

WEIGHT: *14 ounces*

SHAPE: *Round, smooth*

EXTERIOR COLOR(S): *Deep orange*

FLESH COLOR(S): *Deep orange*

SOLUBLE SOLIDS: *6 degrees Brix*

FLAVOR: *Fair to good; low acid*

TEXTURE: *Reasonably firm; thick walls, meaty*

BEST USE(S): *Makes the deepest-orange juice*

PLANT HABIT, LEAF TYPE, AND YIELD: *Indeterminate habit; regular leaf; good yield*

MATURITY: *Main crop*

ORIGIN: *The variety was given to me several years ago by a friend, the architect Scott Newman, who gardens in upstate New York with even fewer frost-free days than I have. His seed came from Yana Blinova, whose mother brought it from Siberia.*
Listed in the 2007 Seed Savers Exchange yearbook by Tatiana Kouchnareva of Anmore, British Columbia, Canada, who wrote, "from Russian seedswoman Tamara Yaschenko of Byisk, Altai, Russia, 2006. Russian commercial variety, named after a Russian fairy tale hero, one of the three 'bogatyrs' (Alesha Popovitch, Ilya Muromets, and Dobrinya Nikitich)."

SYNONYMS: *Ilia Murometz; Ilya Murometz. Tamara believes that there are Russian tomatoes named after each of the three bogatyrs I know of a red one called Russian Bogatyr.*

Tomatoes named for heroes are usually forgettable: witness Mark Twain, Alice Roosevelt, Abe Lincoln, Paul Bunyan, and Paul Robeson. But I'll always have a soft spot in my heart for Ilya Muromets: It was the last tomato that Victor Schrager photographed for this book. Scott Newman and New York Botanical Garden president Gregory Long were there that day—August 31, 2007—to share our joy.

71

72

HUGH'S *fig. 71*

SIZE: *2¾" long by 3⅞" wide*

WEIGHT: *15 ounces*

SHAPE: *Beefsteak*

EXTERIOR COLOR(S): *Light yellow*

FLESH COLOR(S): *Light yellow*

SOLUBLE SOLIDS: *5½ degrees Brix*

FLAVOR: *Excellent; sweet and lemony. Seed-saving superman Neil Lockhart says Hugh's is one of his favorites for flavor.*

TEXTURE: *Reasonably firm*

BEST USE(S): *Fresh eating*

PLANT HABIT, LEAF TYPE, AND YIELD: *Indeterminate habit; regular leaf; good yield*

MATURITY: *Main crop*

ORIGIN: *An Indiana heirloom, brought to notice by Archie M. Hook of Alexandria, Indiana, in the 1986 Seed Savers Exchange yearbook. Introduced commercially in 1990 by Southern Exposure Seed Exchange.*

SEED SOURCES: *Ba8, Ma18, Sa9, So1, So25, To1, To9*

A sublime white beefsteak, second only to Great White. Archie M. Hook (the same man who brought us the Georgia Streak tomato) named this Indiana favorite, then in local circulation for fifty years, after the neighbor who had passed him the seed. Archie ended up raising plants for the entire community in his small greenhouse, and he reportedly exhibited Hugh's tomatoes weighing five pounds plus at the Indiana State Fair.

GREAT WHITE *fig. 72*

SIZE: *3½" long by 5⅝" wide*

WEIGHT: *1 pound, 6 ounces*

SHAPE: *Beefsteak*

EXTERIOR COLOR(S): *Light yellow*

FLESH COLOR(S): *Light yellow*

SOLUBLE SOLIDS: *6 degrees Brix*

FLAVOR: *Excellent; divinely sweet*

TEXTURE: *Soft; delicate, meaty, and juicy*

BEST USE(S): *Fresh eating*

PLANT HABIT, LEAF TYPE, AND YIELD: *Indeterminate habit; regular leaf; good yield*

MATURITY: *Main crop*

ORIGIN: *Introduced in 1991 by Glecklers Seedmen. Proprietor George Gleckler reported in 1995 that Great White was a single plant selection, derived from seeds for yellow and orange oxhearts sent to him by a customer some eight years earlier; however, it's unclear whether Great White was the result of chance variance from mutation, a natural outcrossing, or some sort of mix-up.*

SYNONYMS: *Great White Beefsteak; White Beefsteak; White Princess. Not the same as Big White. Strongly resembles Henderson's Crystal White (1941), described in their catalog as "a pure alabaster white as tempting and as delicious as it is beautiful."*

NY: *Nee & Goldman 54565*

SEED SOURCES: *Ba8, Go8, He17, Hi13, Jo1, La1, Ma18, Na6, Ra6, Re8, Se17, Se26, Sk2, So25, Tol, To3, To9, To10, Up2*

The name *Great White* understates the case: this white is the greatest. Unsurpassed in beauty and flavor—better than all other whites combined. It makes heavenly slices like angel food cake, and holds its own with great tomatoes of all colors.

73

KENTUCKY HEIRLOOM *fig. 73*

SIZE: *2⅝" long by 4¼" wide*

WEIGHT: *1 pound*

SHAPE: *Beefsteak*

EXTERIOR COLOR(S): *Light yellow*

FLESH COLOR(S): *Light yellow*

SOLUBLE SOLIDS: *5 degrees Brix*

FLAVOR: *Good*

TEXTURE: *Soft; meaty and juicy*

BEST USE(S): *Fresh eating*

PLANT HABIT, LEAF TYPE, AND YIELD: *Indeterminate habit; regular leaf; good yield*

MATURITY: *Early crop*

ORIGIN: *Harold R. Martin of Hopkinsville, Kentucky, was the initial lister of this variety in the 1985 Seed Savers Exchange yearbook. He found it "not particularly tasty," probably due to the low acid, but his seed donor and friend Mrs. Viva Lindsey treasured it; Kentucky Heirloom had apparently been given to her by her husband's great aunt in 1922.*

SYNONYMS: *With its occasional green shoulders or a hint of red at the distal end, this tomato is synonymous with Lenny and Gracie's Kentucky Heirloom, a family heirloom collected by Roger Wright of Hamilton, Ohio, in 1993, from Lenny and Gracie Adams of Kentucky, and named in their honor. Also synonymous with Kentucky Heirloom Viva; Mrs. Lindsey's Kentucky Heirloom; Yellow-White. Similar to Lillian's Yellow Heirloom (except not potato leafed). Not the same as Kentucky Beefsteak. There are many other heirloom tomatoes from Kentucky, including a red variant of Lenny and Gracie's.*

SEED SOURCES: *Ma18, To9*

A big, beautiful beefsteak, very juicy, sweet, and yummy, even when overripe. Kentucky Heirloom would make a crystal-clear Tomato Water (see page 245)—an end in itself or the starting point for refined cold tomato soups and aspic.

a

b

EARLY SANTA CLARA CANNER *fig. 74a*

SIZE: *2⅝" long by 3⅜" wide*

WEIGHT: *11 ounces*

SHAPE: *Beefsteak*

EXTERIOR COLOR(S): *Blood red*

FLESH COLOR(S): *Cock's comb red*

SOLUBLE SOLIDS: *4½ degrees Brix*

FLAVOR: *Good; acidic*

TEXTURE: *Reasonably firm, with meaty, thick walls*

BEST USE(S): *Canning. Adapted to climates too cool to ripen the regular Santa Clara Canner.*

PLANT HABIT, LEAF TYPE, AND YIELD: *Indeterminate habit; regular leaf; high yield*

MATURITY: *Early crop*

ORIGIN: *Early Santa Clara was released for trial circa 1928 by C. C. Morse and Company of San Francisco. It was used in cooler districts close to San Francisco Bay, on "late land" in other parts of the Santa Clara Valley and between the towns of Gilroy and Sargent. Five years later, according to trial records from the Ferry-Morse Seed Company (D. M. Ferry and C. C. Morse were consolidated in 1930), the tomato had "so completely replaced the regular strain that it is here described as the type of the variety."*

SYNONYMS: *Early Canner; Early Santa Clara; Santa Clara Canner, Early. Similar to Santa Clara Canner. Not the same as Diener (see page 125).*

Very similar in appearance to Santa Clara Canner, down to the blotchy ripening—which disappears, as noted by Young and MacArthur in 1947. It's a week earlier, but not as tasty as the original.

SANTA CLARA CANNER *fig. 74b*

SIZE: *2¾" long by 3½" wide*

WEIGHT: *13 ounces*

SHAPE: *Beefsteak*

EXTERIOR COLOR(S): *Blood red*

FLESH COLOR(S): *Cherry red*

SOLUBLE SOLIDS: *5 degrees Brix*

FLAVOR: *Excellent; well balanced*

TEXTURE: *Reasonably firm; meaty, weighty, and solid—this is no font of juice. Almost like a cross between a paste and a beefsteak.*

BEST USE(S): *Canning and sauce-making*

PLANT HABIT, LEAF TYPE, AND YIELD: *Indeterminate habit; regular leaf; high yield*

MATURITY: *Main crop*

ORIGIN: *The exact origin of Santa Clara Canner is a question mark; however, Morrison (1938) believed that "it probably came from Italy and was modified by the growers in the Santa Clara Valley before modern breeding work was undertaken. In 1918, this variety was fairly well stabilized as a very late, very large, flat, rough-fruited type with very large vines." If Morrison is correct, then the San Jose Canner—the "perfect California tomato" introduced and illustrated in 1914 by C. C. Morse and Company of San Francisco—may well have been the Santa Clara's inspiration. The San Jose Canner ("large-fruited … immense cropper … peculiarly solid and heavy") was named for Mr. J. F. Pyle, a prominent canner in San Jose, who "secured it originally, years ago, from a careful Italian market grower, but Mr. Pyle developed it by selection" (Morse, 1918). The photograph in the 1914 catalog looks indistinguishable from Santa Clara Canner.*

In 1923, a consortium of do-gooders (including C. C. Morse and Company, the Canners League of California, and the California Agricultural Experiment Station) set out to "smooth up" and hasten the maturity of the rough canning tomato. A committee of canners made the first single-plant selections and, three years later, F. A. Dixon named the variety "Santa Clara Canner" on behalf of the Canners League. Shortly thereafter, it was superseded by Early Santa Clara Canner

SYNONYMS: *Morse Canner, Late Santa Clara, and Medium Santa Clara. By 1933, the name "Santa Clara Canner" had been extended to all strains that resembled the Morse selections (Boswell et al., 1933). Similar to Cal(ifornia) 55 (1928); Canner (local Trophy); Jap(anese) Canner; San Jose Canner; San Jose Canner Medium Early; Santa Clara Canner Early; Strawberry. Not the same as Diener (see page 125) or "what seedsmen cataloged as Trophy or Improved Trophy" (Boswell et al., 1933).*

NY: *Nee & Goldman 54575 and 54608*

SEED SOURCES: *Sa9, To1, To9, To10*

Growing Santa Clara Canner has helped me think outside the box of "square" paste tomatoes like San Marzano (see page 137). It's simply not true, as some experts have said, that Santa Clara Canner is a poor choice for home gardeners east of the Rockies. It produces abundant crops in my garden, and it makes some of the most creamy and intense tomato sauce I've ever had. I skip the pasta and eat the sauce straight.

GERMAN PINK *fig. 75*

SIZE: *3½" long by 4½" wide*

WEIGHT: *1 pound, 2 ounces*

SHAPE: *Beefsteak*

EXTERIOR COLOR(S): *Tomato pink*

FLESH COLOR(S): *Cock's comb red*

SOLUBLE SOLIDS: *5½ degrees Brix*

FLAVOR: *Good; sweet*

TEXTURE: *Soft; meaty and juicy*

BEST USE(S): *Multipurpose*

PLANT HABIT, LEAF TYPE, AND YIELD: *Indeterminate habit; potato leaf; good yield*

MATURITY: *Early crop*

ORIGIN: *Brought from Bavaria by Michael Ott in 1883. Recently boarded onto Slow Food USA's Ark of Taste.*

SYNONYMS: *Lorraine Schrandt (Diane Ott Whealy's aunt), of Festina, Iowa, listed this as Deep Pink in the 1976–1977 True Seed Exchange (the forerunner of Seed Savers Exchange). "German" refers to place of origin but can also mean a noncommercial or home-started variety.*

NY: *Nee & Goldman 53426*

SEED SOURCES: *Coo, Co32, He8, Ki4, Ma18, Se16, Se28, To1*

German Pink is Diane Ott Whealy's family heirloom. Her paternal great-grandfather, Michael Ott, carried the seed with him from Bremen, Germany, on board the SS *Main*. He set foot on U.S. soil on November 3, 1883; three months later in West Union, Iowa, Ott filed an "Intention to become an American Citizen." One can suppose he planted saved seed that first Iowa spring, claiming American citizenship for the tomato now known as German Pink and for Grandpa Ott's Morning Glory—the two varieties with which Seed Savers Exchange was eventually founded. (He also brought a pole bean with him that has not been commercialized.)

I don't know what Michael Ott looked like, but anyone who has ever seen the photograph of his son Baptist John Ott (June 24, 1894–January 5, 1974) with his wife Helena Hackman Ott (April 16, 1897–December 29, 1982), taken near St. Lucas, Iowa, in 1972, can't fail to be moved. Still vital at the end of their long lives, gray-haired, bespectacled, and obviously happy in each other's company, Grandpa and Grandma Ott stand encircled by a wedding-like bower of purple morning glories bearing their name.

Baptist John Ott's ornery humor, vivid storytelling, and magic sparkle, as well as the spirit of Michael Ott, live on in the seeds passed down to granddaughter Diane and her then-husband, Kent. A year after Grandpa Ott's death, the Whealys founded Seed Savers Exchange, thus ensuring the survival of their own treasured seeds and those of thousands of other gardeners. German Pink became SSE's Tomato No. 1—out of a collection that now numbers 5,979 tomatoes. Diane's Dad, Dale Ott, still plants his German Pinks in Festina, Iowa, in the same way his parents did: with rusty old Folgers coffee cans (ends removed) placed around the plants for protection. And the Otts still love eating their tomatoes sprinkled with sugar.

RED BRANDYWINE *fig. 76; page 109, fig. 77a*

SIZE: *2⅞" long by 4½" wide*

WEIGHT: *1 pound, 2 ounces*

SHAPE: *Beefsteak*

EXTERIOR COLOR(S): *Blood red*

FLESH COLOR(S): *Blood red*

SOLUBLE SOLIDS: *7½ degrees Brix, with readings up to 9 degrees Brix*

FLAVOR: *Perfection; high sugar, high acid*

TEXTURE: *Reasonably firm; meaty*

BEST USE(S): *Multipurpose*

PLANT HABIT, LEAF TYPE, AND YIELD: *Indeterminate habit; regular leaf; good yield*

MATURITY: *Main crop*

ORIGIN: *Introduced as "The Brandywine, or No. 45 Tomato" in 1889 by Johnson and Stokes, Philadelphia, Pennsylvania, with these remarks: "Two years ago a customer in Ohio sent us a small package of tomato seed, requesting us to give it a fair test on our trial grounds. A few plants were set out along with forty-five other varieties we were testing, both new and old; this being the last on the list, was numbered 45. To our astonishment, it completely eclipsed, in great size and beauty, all other varieties we were testing, several specimens when ripe weighing over three pounds each, as smooth as an apple and remarkably solid. To still further test this tomato, we sent a few packets to tomato specialists, requesting them to report on its merits. The name given it was suggested by our friend, Thos. H. Brinton, of Chadd's Ford, Pa., who has probably grown and tested more varieties of tomatoes than any other person in the United States, who wrote September 25th, 1888: 'The more I see of the Tomato No. 45, the more I am pleased with it. It is certainly a magnificent new and distinct variety, and worthy of the name of 'Brandywine,' after that most beautiful of all streams, which flows near our Quaker village. It is also spoken of in the highest terms by all to whom I gave a few plants for trial.' We have not illustrated this new tomato, as had we given it a larger notice, we are afraid we would not have had half enough seed to go around."*

Brandywine was reintroduced one hundred years later–in 1989– as "Red Brandywine Tomato" by Thomas J. Hauch of Heirloom Seeds, West Elizabeth, Pennsylvania. Catalog copy: "We've found a great tomato for our customers in 1989. Judged BEST overall tomato at THE TERRIFIC TOMATO TASTE-OFF competition, HARVEST FAIR 88 held at Frick Nature Center, Pittsburgh, PA. An old Amish heirloom dating back to 1885. It's named after Brandywine Creek in Chester County, PA. Large indeterminate vines grow plenty of 8 oz. to 1 pound fruit. Tomatoes are deep red and very attractive. It has an excellent taste." Tom Hauch recently told me: "The seeds were from the Seed Savers Exchange yearbook, and for some reason, I think the person offering the seeds may have been from Ohio. The only other thing that may have happened is that I may have requested seeds from someone and they sent me Red Brandywine as an extra packet."

SYNONYMS: *Brandywine; Brandywine, Red; No. 45 Tomato; Red Brandywine Tomato; Red Brandywine, Regular Leaf; Red Brandywine, Regular-Leafed; The Brandywine. Red Brandywine is larger than the Landis Valley strain of Red Brandywine, which derives from Red Brandywine seed that Tom Hauch sent in 1989 to Steve Miller at Landis Valley Museum, Lancaster, Pennsylvania. Contrary to the beliefs of many tomato fanciers, the Brandywine has been red, not pink, from the beginning. In 1904 and 1906, Charles Johnson wrote that Brandywine was synonymous with Livingston's Favorite, Bell, Cardinal, Mayflower (1883), Optimus, Red Cross, and Scovill(e)'s Hybrid (and not synonymous with Turner Hybrid, 1,600 Dollar, Lorillard, Mikado, and Potato-Leaved). Twenty years earlier, Liberty Hyde Bailey equated the following red-fruited varieties, some of which Charles Johnson later found to be synonymous with Brandywine (Red Brandywine): Queen, Cardinal, New Cardinal, Prize Belle, Livingston's Favorite (1883), Market Champion, Champion, and Mill's Belle.*

Not the same as Red Brandywine, Potato Leaf or the potato-leafed OTV (Off the Vine) Brandywine. Also not the same as the F₁ hybrid Buck's County (Hybrid) from Burpee's.

Red Brandywine (Brandywine) was not introduced by Burpee's, and it was not introduced in 1885, as some believe. I have found no evidence that the tomato is an Amish heirloom, or that it is related to Turner Hybrid, or Mikado, as some have claimed.

SEED SOURCES: *He8, Hi13, Sa9, To1, To9, Vi4*

Eating a sweet and sprightly Red Brandywine can be a potent mood elevator. But, for me, unearthing new facts about this tomato is even more gratifying. I've discovered that the pink-fruited, potato-leafed Brandywine that we all know and love (see Sudduth's Brandywine, page 108), is *not*—as is commonly believed—the same as the original Brandywine, introduced in 1889, by Johnson and Stokes.

There's been a great deal of misinformation circulating, not only about Brandywine's horticultural characteristics, but about its origin, as well. If there had been a videotape—or even microfilm—I would've gone to it. Instead, I found something better: librarian Sherry Vance, standing by at Cornell's Ethel Zoe Bailey Horticultural Catalogue Collection in Ithaca, New York. "I want to get my hands on that 1889 catalog—and any other Johnson and Stokes catalogs you might have. Can you help?" I asked. Sherry replied, "I came across this information years ago, and have just been waiting for someone to ask me about it." I had hit the jackpot: Sherry miraculously was in possession of nearly every catalog published by Johnson and Stokes (or their successor, Johnson Seed Company) between 1883 and 1915.

The catalogs leave no doubt of the original appearance of Brandywine. The first color illustration, painted from nature on the back of the 1890 edition, is blood red, like today's Red Brandywine. No color was noted in the 1891 catalog, but on page 68, in "A Tomato Test of 1890," Brandywine is listed with the "Red Varieties" (which also include Livingston's Favorite, Lorillard, Cardinal), and not with the "Purple Varieties" (New Potato Leaf, Turner Hybrid, Mikado, and Livingston's Beauty, among others). In 1892, the introducers explicitly stated that Brandywine had "a beautiful bright red skin," and they never wavered in that description in subsequent years. Since all the illustrations of Brandywine show regular leaf foliage, and "potato leaf" was never uttered in the same breath as Brandywine, and since potato leaf was a novelty in those days, and something to write home about, I can confidently conclude that Brandywine was regular-leafed as well as red. It still is—only now we call it Red Brandywine.

SUDDUTH'S BRANDYWINE *fig. 77b*

SIZE: *3¼" long by 5½" wide*

WEIGHT: *1 pound, 10 ounces*

SHAPE: *Beefsteak*

EXTERIOR COLOR(S): *Tomato pink*

FLESH COLOR(S): *Tomato pink*

SOLUBLE SOLIDS: *6 degrees Brix*

FLAVOR: *Excellent; like a fine wine. I dare any hybrid to measure up.*

TEXTURE: *Soft; meaty and juicy*

BEST USE(S): *Fresh eating*

PLANT HABIT, LEAF TYPE, AND YIELD: *Indeterminate habit; potato leaf foliage; low yield*

MATURITY: *Main crop*

ORIGIN: *Introduced circa 1979 by nonagenarian Ben Quisenberry (see Big Ben, page 94) of Big Tomato Gardens in Syracuse, Ohio. Catalog copy from 1980: "Grown over 100 years, by the same family. Proof of excellence." Ben said in a 1981 interview, "I'm very fond of tomatoes … Brandywine, it has a kind of a sharp-like taste to it, you know. I believe it's my favorite, Brandywine. You know the lady that sent me the seed told me they had been in the family for over a hundred years!"*

Sudduth's or Quisenberry's Brandywine is now so ubiquitous that I can't imagine a tomato patch without it. In 1980, Dale Anderson of Anderson, Indiana, was the first Seed Savers Exchange member to list Brandywine in the annual yearbook. Word about this luscious tomato quickly spread through testimonials and over the garden fence. In 1984, Ken Ettlinger of Long Island Seed and Plant Company listed it: "Brandywine is a little-known heirloom beefsteak which we think has the finest old-fashioned flavor of any tomato we've tasted. Our selection was produced from seed originally sent to us by Ben Quisenberry." By 1986, the year Ben died, the Brandywine was being extolled by Jan Blum, of Seeds Blüm, as an "heirloom famous for its flavor." That same year, Jeff McCormack of Southern Exposure Seed Exchange said Brandywine was of "gourmet quality." Recently boarded on to Slow Food USA's Ark of Taste.

SYNONYMS: *Brandywine; Brandywine, Quisenberry Strain; Brandywine, Sudduth; Quisenberry's Brandywine; Brandywine (Sudduth's Strain); Pink Brandywine. Similar to Brandywine, Glick's Strain; Brandywine, Joyce's Strain, and Brandywine, Pawer's. Resembles many pink potato-leafed beefsteaks. Not the same as the regular-leafed red-fruited Brandywine, introduced in 1889, by Johnson and Stokes (see Red Brandywine, page 106). Not to be confused with Red Brandywine, Potato Leaf; OTV Brandywine; or Brandywine, Red (Landis Valley Strain). There are numerous offshoots or tomatoes with "Brandywine" in their name or background, including Black Brandywine, Brandy Stripe, Brandywine Cherry, Purple Brandywine (Marizol Bratka), and Yellow Brandywine (see page 109).*

SEED SOURCES: *Ag7, Ap6, Ba8, Coo, Fe5, Ga1, He8, Hi13, Hud, Jo1, La1, Ma18, Mo13, Pin, Ra6, Re8, Sa9, Se7, Se16, Se28, Shu, Sto, To1, To3, To9, To10, Tu6, Vi4*

Sudduth's Brandywine, commonly known as "Brandywine," is a family heirloom, lovingly tended and handed down from mother to daughter. Despite its flaws—low yield and poor adaptation to the North—Sudduth's Brandywine is a winner; according to seed saver Bill Runyan of Batavia, Iowa, it "brings raves from lucky eaters," including me.

There's been a great deal of speculation about the origins of Sudduth's Brandywine, most of it idle or inaccurate. It was widely known that Dorris Sudduth Hill had given the seeds to Ben Quisenberry, but mysteriously she had never been a focus of inquiry. Until, that is, one April evening (at 8:03, to be precise), I sent an e-mail to my friend Diana Gurieva: "Since you're a whiz on the Internet, and an expert on genealogy, please tell me how I might find out about Dorris Sudduth Hill." Sometime after one o'clock that morning, while I was off in tomato dreamland, Diana wrote back: "Unless you happen to be up now, I will call you in the morning. I think I may have found her, and she may still be alive."

Diana had found two very recent obituaries: one for Dorris's identical twin sister, Dorothy Sudduth of Murfreesboro, Tennessee; and the other for Dorris's husband of sixty-six years, James W. Hill Jr. of Woodbury, Tennessee. Dorris was noted among the survivors, as was her son, James W. Hill III. Two dozen phone calls later, I found ninety-three-year-old Dorris, living at home in Woodbury with her son and his wife, Sandra.

Dorris was in poor health and couldn't speak to me, but her son James, a retired engineer, was a kindly informant. James Hill told me: "My folks liked to grow lots of tomatoes. Especially my grandmother Julia Newsome Sudduth in Memphis. She had a rose bed, real fertile ground, and between the roses she put out tomatoes. As she lost rose bushes later in life, she ended with a complete bed of just tomatoes. The biggest tomato she'd slice up for dinner. She had a special dish for tomatoes, shaped like a saucer, so when the seeds dropped off, she could collect them. This way, the seeds wouldn't mix with the bean juice and gravy, and she could recover the seeds uncontaminated. Then she'd take them and dry them out on the windowsill. She used a sewing machine to make little pouches out of wax paper with tomato seeds in it. The next season, she'd put them into pots on trays, and slide them in front of the dining room and sunroom windows to get them growing."

Fig. 77 (a) Red Brandywine,
(b) Sudduth's Brandywine

77

78

YELLOW BRANDYWINE *fig. 78*

SIZE: *3½" long by 4¼" wide*

WEIGHT: *1 pound, 3 ounces*

SHAPE: *Beefsteak*

EXTERIOR COLOR(S): *Tangerine*

FLESH COLOR(S): *Deep orange*

SOLUBLE SOLIDS: *7 degrees Brix*

FLAVOR: *Excellent; high acid and high sugar. On everyone's list of favorites.*

TEXTURE: *Reasonably firm; meaty and juicy*

BEST USE(S): *Fresh eating*

PLANT HABIT, LEAF TYPE, AND YIELD: *Indeterminate habit; potato leaf foliage; good yield*

MATURITY: *Early crop*

ORIGIN: *First brought to notice by Barbara Ann Lund of Lynx, Ohio, in the 1991 Seed Savers Exchange yearbook. Barbara, now retired from her job as a ranger and naturalist with the National Park Service, told me, "I got the Yellow Brandywine in 1985 from Charlie Knoy while I was living in Bloomfield, Indiana. Charlie was quite elderly then. This man grew bedding plants to sell. It was a very low-tech operation; his plants were grown in cold frames under window sashes. He told me there were three kinds of Brandywine: yellow, pink, and red." Cataloged in 1993 by Seeds Blüm as "a famous flavor in a different shade" and by the Tomato Seed Company as "a yellow version of a famous old variety."*

SYNONYMS: *Brandywine Yellow. There are two strains of Yellow Brandywine which are reportedly more uniform: Yellow Brandywine (Platfoot Strain) and the regular-leafed Yellow Brandywine (Abundant Life). Strongly resembles Aunt Gertie's Gold (see page 61). May be the same as Apricot Brandywine. Offshoots (deliberate and chance crosses) include Bogeywine, OTV Brandywine, and Roughwood Golden Plum.*

SEED SOURCES: *Ag7, Ap6, Ba8, Bo19, Co32, Coo, Ers, Fe5, Go8, He8, He17, Hi6, Hi13, Jo1, Lan, Ma18, Or10, Pe2, Pin, Ra6, Roh, Sa9, Se26, Shu, So1, So9, So25, Sw9, Te4, Ter, To1, To3, To9, To10, Up2, Vi4, We19*

You could park Yellow Brandywine on my plate anytime. I'd eat it as an appetizer, soup, salad, entrée, or dessert. Yellow Brandywine looks like a miniature orange pumpkin, but the creamy texture and exquisite flavor are all tomato. It's even a shade bigger and better than that most esteemed and virtuous Aunt Gertie's Gold.

a

b

c

e

d

MARY ROBINSON'S GERMAN BICOLOR *fig. 79d*

SIZE: *3½" long by 5" wide*

WEIGHT: *1 pound, 8 ounces*

SHAPE: *Beefsteak*

EXTERIOR COLOR(S): *Orange yellow over-spread with tomato pink*

FLESH COLOR(S): *Buttercup yellow and cherry red*

SOLUBLE SOLIDS: *6 degrees Brix*

FLAVOR: *Good to excellent; fruity and sweet*

TEXTURE: *Soft; meaty and juicy*

BEST USE(S): *Fresh eating; juicing*

PLANT HABIT, LEAF TYPE, AND YIELD: *Indeterminate habit; regular leaf; high yield*

MATURITY: *Early crop*

ORIGIN: *Brought to notice by North Carolinian Craig LeHouillier, whose seed came from G. Fitzgerald of Virginia in 1994. Introduced by Pomodori di Marianna (now Marianna's Heirloom Seeds), circa 1998.*

SYNONYMS: *Similar to scores of other bicolor beefsteaks*

SEED SOURCES: *Ma18, So25*

Here's to you, Mary Robinson! This is the variety with which tomato collector Neil Lockhart weaned his father away from red tomatoes. Neil confessed to me: "I love Mary Robinson. It's so beautiful, and doesn't crack in Illinois"—a problem all bicolor beefsteak flesh is heir to. Try Mary on soft white bread with mayo, salt, and pepper; you'll be in seventh heaven.

BICOLOR MORTGAGE LIFTER *fig. 79b, c; page 119, fig 85f*

SIZE: *3" long by 5½" wide*

WEIGHT: *1 pound, 6 ounces*

SHAPE: *Beefsteak*

EXTERIOR COLOR(S): *Buttercup yellow and melon yellow with tomato pink at the distal end*

FLESH COLOR(S): *Buttercup yellow with smatterings of tomato pink*

SOLUBLE SOLIDS: *5½ degrees Brix*

FLAVOR: *Excellent*

TEXTURE: *Soft; beefy and juicy*

BEST USE(S): *Fresh eating; juice*

PLANT HABIT, LEAF TYPE, AND YIELD: *Indeterminate habit; regular leaf; good yield*

MATURITY: *Main crop*

ORIGIN: *Cataloged in 2000 by Tomato Growers Supply Company; and, about the same time, by TomatoFest Homegrown Seeds*

SYNONYMS: *Bicolour Mortgage Lifter; Bi-Color Mortgage Lifter; Mortgage Lifter, Bicolor Strain; Red and Yellow Mortgage Lifter (see page 123); Mortgage Lifter*

SEED SOURCES: *Sa5, To1, To9*

"Bicolor" doesn't jibe with my notion of a Mortgage Lifter—Mortgage Lifters are pink, of course—but this one is the nectar of the gods. Slurp it down, mainline; or make a select tangerine-colored juice.

MAMMOTH GERMAN GOLD *fig. 79a, e*

SIZE: *3" long by 5" wide*

WEIGHT: *1 pound, 5 ounces*

SHAPE: *Beefsteak*

EXTERIOR COLOR(S): *Orange yellow with tomato pink at the blossom end*

FLESH COLOR(S): *Orange yellow with tomato pink*

SOLUBLE SOLIDS: *6 degrees Brix*

FLAVOR: *Good; very sweet and delicious*

TEXTURE: *Soft; nectar runs out as you cut*

BEST USE(S): *Fresh eating; juicing*

PLANT HABIT, LEAF TYPE, AND YIELD: *Indeterminate habit; regular leaf; high yield*

MATURITY: *Main crop*

ORIGIN: *First listed in 1980 by the Reverend and Mrs. C. Frank Morrow of North St. Paul, Minnesota, in the Seed Savers Exchange yearbook: "Shaped like Big Boy, rich gold fruit, pink blush on blossom end when ripe." Cataloged in 1987 by the Tomato Seed Company, Metuchen, New Jersey.*

SYNONYMS: *German Gold; Mammoth German. Similar to dozens of other yellow and red or pink bicolor beefsteaks.*

SEED SOURCES: *Co32, Lan, Ma18, Roh, Se17, So25, To1, Up2*

Old-fashioned yellow beefsteaks veined with pink were rare in commerce thirty years ago and highly sought-after. In 1981, Shirley Ann Steiner of Atwater, Ohio, wrote to Kent Whealy, cofounder of SSE: "I want a two-toned pink and yellow tomato which was an old farmer's who lived in my neighborhood and died about ten years ago. His relatives will not share his seeds with anyone. *They were so good.*" Kent replied: "Ever think of making a midnight raid on a tomato patch?" A good way to get shot—although I, too, have larceny in my heart when people are less than neighborly about seeds.

(a, e) Mammoth German Gold,
(b, c) Bicolor Mortgage Lifter,
(d) Mary Robinson's German Bicolor

BIG RAINBOW *fig. 80*

SIZE: *3¾" long by 5¼" wide*

WEIGHT: *1 pound, 10 ounces*

SHAPE: *Beefsteak*

EXTERIOR COLOR(S): *Yellow with cock's comb red at the blossom end*

FLESH COLOR(S): *Yellow with markings of cock's comb red*

SOLUBLE SOLIDS: *5½ degrees Brix*

FLAVOR: *Good to excellent; melon-y, subtly pleasing*

TEXTURE: *Soft; meaty, juicy*

BEST USE(S): *Fresh eating*

PLANT HABIT, LEAF TYPE, AND YIELD: *Indeterminate habit; regular leaf; high yield*

MATURITY: *Early crop*

ORIGIN: *Strongly resembles Thorburn's Lemon Blush Tomato, developed by Elbert S. Carman, distinguished editor of the* Rural New-Yorker. *Introduced in 1893, and illustrated in color, by J. M. Thorburn and Company of New York. They wrote: "This is the nearest approach to a perfect Tomato that has been produced up to this time. The skin and flesh are a bright lemon-yellow, with a faint rose blush or light crimson tint diffused over a part of the surface opposite the stem. Its average size is larger than the 'Acme,' and in shape somewhat broader than deep—absolutely free of seams, lobes or irregularities. The seeds are notably small and few, the cell walls thick, tender, crystalline and melting—the quality being less acid than that of the red varieties, yet without the insipidity which characterizes the yellow kinds in general. The plant is a vigorous grower, ripening its fruit abundantly in mid-season." Big Rainbow first appeared in the Seed Savers Exchange 1983 yearbook, courtesy of Dorothy Beiswenger of Crookston, Minnesota. Commercialized in 1990 by Southern Exposure Seed Exchange.*

SYNONYMS: *Rainbow*

NY: *Nee & Goldman 53506*

SEED SOURCES: *Ba8, Bou, Bu2, Coo, Ers, Go8, He8, He17, Hi13, Ki4, La1, Ma18, Ra6, Sa9, So1, Te4, To1, To3, To9, Vi4*

Big Rainbow was my first bicolor. It's as breathtaking and dear to me today—even after sampling dozens of others—as it was nearly twenty years ago. When sliced and diced, the yellow flesh overspread with red reminds me of cut yellow peaches stained with red from the pit. Lloyd Duggins of Mauckport, Indiana, who was fond of offering old "No Name" (never-been-named or unidentified) favorite tomato varieties, gave many of them to Dorothy Beiswenger in the early 1980s.

Dorothy recalls, "When I grew this one, it surprised me so much that I named it Big Rainbow because of its beauty, and size, and hope. At that time, I was not familiar with tomato plants that were nontraditional, except for a small white one that I was given by a friend. Big Rainbow was such a delight, that I hoped for more such tomatoes. And so, in the years to come, I did get a lot of great tomatoes."

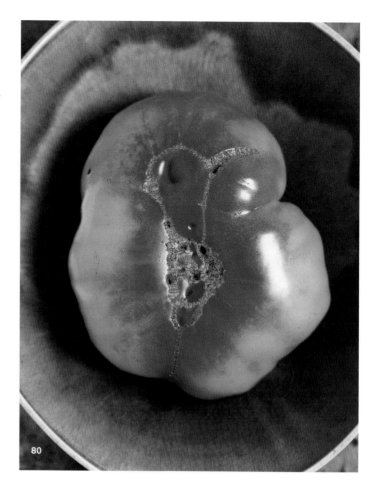

80

MARVEL STRIPED *fig. 81*

SIZE: *3" long by 5½" wide*

WEIGHT: *1 pound, 12 ounces*

SHAPE: *Beefsteak*

EXTERIOR COLOR(S): *Orange yellow with tomato pink at the blossom end*

FLESH COLOR(S): *Orange yellow and tomato pink*

SOLUBLE SOLIDS: *7 degrees Brix*

FLAVOR: *Excellent; sweet, one of the best bicolor beefsteaks*

TEXTURE: *Soft; meaty and juicy*

BEST USE(S): *Fresh eating; juicing*

PLANT HABIT, LEAF TYPE, AND YIELD: *Indeterminate habit; regular leaf; high yield*

MATURITY: *Early crop*

ORIGIN: *Collected in Oaxaca, Mexico, by Gabriel Howearth (director of the San Juan Pueblo Seed Project) of San Juan Pueblo, New Mexico, who grew tomatoes at 6,000 feet and irrigated with Rio Grande water. Introduced commercially circa 1987 by Alan Kapuler's Peace Seeds of Corvallis, Oregon, which was described in the* Garden Seed Inventory *(1988) as a planetary gene-pool resource where seeds were atoms and peace was grown.*

SYNONYMS: *Marvel Stripe. Synonymous with Georgia Streak, Gold Medal, Ruby Gold, and others. See one of its progeny, Copia, on page 169.*

SEED SOURCES: *Co32, Hi13, Ma18, Na6, Ra6, Se7, So25, To9*

I'm generally tolerant of those who don't share my love for beefsteaks. What floors me, though, is how anyone could dismiss a *bicolor* beefsteak just because it's bland. I once heard an auctioneer say at the end of a long night, while trying to wake a sleepy crowd and drum up some business, "Are you all unhappy?!" I, too, feel like banging a drum: Wake up and rejoice in the inherent beauty of these tomatoes. Marvel at what nature has provided. Then add a sprinkle of sugar or salt to slices and eat to your heart's content.

GOLD MEDAL *fig. 82, 83*

SIZE: *3¼" long by 5¼" wide*

WEIGHT: *1 pound, 9 ounces*

SHAPE: *Beefsteak*

EXTERIOR COLOR(S): *Orange yellow spread through with tomato pink*

FLESH COLOR(S): *Orange yellow with tomato pink markings*

SOLUBLE SOLIDS: *6½ degrees Brix*

FLAVOR: *Excellent. Well reviewed by tomato cognoscenti: "superbly delicious" (Darrell Merrell); "top rated in flavor" (Ken Ettlinger); "our finest bicolor" (Seed Savers Exchange).*

TEXTURE: *Soft; meaty and juicy*

BEST USE(S): *Fresh eating; juice*

PLANT HABIT, LEAF TYPE, AND YIELD: *Indeterminate habit; regular leaf; high yield*

MATURITY: *Main crop*

ORIGIN: *Gold Medal was cataloged in 1976 by Ben Quisenberry of Big Tomato Gardens in Syracuse, Ohio. His catalog copy: "The sweetest tomato you ever tasted. The yellow with streaks and blotches of red makes them very attractive and a gourmet's joy when sliced." Ben's seed came from Bob Barnitz of Bob's Market, Mason, West Virginia, in 1967. Bob told me: "I gave Ben several tomatoes [see Quisenberry's Mortgage Lifter, page 118]. This one I named Early Sunrise; it's a really good eating tomato. My in-laws from Nicholas County, West Virginia, gave me the seed."*

Ben changed the name of the tomato from Early Sunrise to Gold Medal, and then later, to Ruby Gold. Ruby Gold was introduced by John Lewis Childs of Floral Park, New York, in his 1921 catalog. Childs illustrated Ruby Gold on the back cover of his 1922 catalog, carried the tomato forward in 1923, and then dropped it from commercial production.

SYNONYMS: *Early Sunrise; Gold Metal; Ruby Gold. Similar to Georgia Streak and Marvel Striped (see page 112). Strongly resembles Thorburn's Lemon Blush Tomato (1893). Gold Medal Yellow (Gold Medal Yellow Sport) is a light yellow version of Gold Medal, with no splashes of color.*

NY: *Nee & Goldman 53421*

SEED SOURCES: *Ag7, Ba8, Go8, He8, Ra6, Se16, Ter, To9*

How great it is! Everything you read about it is true. The first description, in John Lewis Childs' 1921 catalog, is just as apt today: "It is a large luscious and superlatively beautiful fruit. Color outside ruby-red suffused marble and blended with gold. Inside a beautiful canary-yellow variegated with rich ruby … The fruit is very large, very smooth and of the richest flavor, lacking the rank acid of many tomatoes. Flesh also the most tender and melting of any tomato we ever tasted. For the home garden Ruby Gold is a gem."

Librarian extraordinaire Sherry Vance, of the Ethel Zoe Bailey Horticultural Catalogue Collection at Cornell University, helped me pinpoint Gold Medal's date of introduction and dug up the first descriptions and illustrations. She also handed me, quite by happenstance, on the same page (Childs, 1923) the earliest known photograph and listing of an oxheart tomato. That made my day, and hers: "This is why I tell people that the Bailey collection is so important. I'm convinced that it holds the key to many, many mysteries." For the proof that Sherry was right, see page 106 for my recounting of the hunt for the elusive Red Brandywine.

83

RADIATOR CHARLIE'S MORTGAGE LIFTER

fig. 84; page 119, fig. 85d; page 123, fig 89b; page 176, fig. 122e

SIZE: *4" long by 7" wide*

WEIGHT: *3 pounds, 8 ounces*

SHAPE: *Beefsteak, often two- or three-lobed*

EXTERIOR COLOR(S): *Tomato pink*

FLESH COLOR(S): *Cherry red*

SOLUBLE SOLIDS: *5 degrees Brix*

FLAVOR: *Excellent; well balanced*

TEXTURE: *Soft; meaty, marbled, and juicy*

BEST USE(S): *Fresh eating; casting in bronze. Mrs. Byles, wife of the originator, liked to can them; just four tomatoes, she said, would yield three quarts.*

PLANT HABIT, LEAF TYPE, AND YIELD: *Indeterminate habit; regular leaf; high yield*

MATURITY: *Main crop*

ORIGIN: *Marshall Cletis Byles, also known as M. C. Byles or Radiator Charlie, bred this tomato by crossing four beefsteak varieties while living in Logan, West Virginia, during the 1930s. The female parent was German Johnson and the pollen parents were Beefsteak, an unnamed English variety, and an unnamed Italian variety. Byles's breeding methods were unconventional. Dr. Jeff McCormack, the "storycatcher," obtained the story from Byles's grandson Ed Martin in the early 1980s, having serendipitously met Martin's wife in a computer shop. Martin told McCormack that "[German Johnson] was planted in the middle of a circle. Then, using a baby's ear syringe, [Byles] cross-pollinated the center plant with pollen from the circle of tomatoes. Next year he selected the best seedlings. He planted the best seedling in the center and the rest in a circle around it. The pollination and selection process was repeated six more years until he had a stable variety."*

William S. Estler also claimed to be the originator of the true mortgage lifter; he and M. C. Byles were contemporaries and neighbors—they lived a hundred miles apart (see Estler's Mortgage Lifter, page 118). There's been some jockeying for position between various factions, and even legal wrangling in recent years. The verdict is that no one has any legal claim to the name "mortgage lifter." Clearly, there's room for more than one mortgage lifter tomato in the world, and plenty of fame and fortune to go around.

Jeff McCormack, founder of Southern Exposure Seed Exchange, founder of Garden Medicinals and Culinaries, and breeder of Mortgage Lifter VFN (see page 121), introduced Radiator Charlie's Mortgage Lifter in 1986 as Mortgage Lifter–Pink or Railroad Tomato–Pink.

SYNONYMS: *Charlie's Pride and Joy; Halladay's Mortgage Lifter (see page 121); Mortgage Lifter; Mortgage Lifter–Generic Strain; Mortgage Lifter–Pink; Mortgage Raiser; Railroad Tomato–Pink; RCML. See Mullens' Mortgage Lifter (page 120), which may have been derived from RCML. Not the same as Charlie's Mortgage Lifter, which is teeny in comparison. Boarded onto Slow Food USA's Ark of Taste in 2007.*

NY: *Nee & Goldman 54636*

SEED SOURCES: *Ba8, Bu2, Co32, Ga21, Ha26, He8, He17, Hi13, La1, Ma18, Ni1, Ra6, Roh, Shu, Sk2, So1, Sw9, Ter, Th3, To1, To3, To9, Und, Ver, Vi4*

"Mortgage lifter" is a generic term that refers to a set of big old tomatoes, characteristically pink, from central Appalachia. Radiator Charlie's Mortgage Lifter is the best known—and weightiest—example, if not the first in existence (see Estler's Mortgage Lifter, page 118). Mortgage lifters tend to be subject to cracking and catfacing, corky, and cursed with stems that are difficult to remove. Aficionadas like me adore them anyway. Eating a thick juicy mortgage lifter slab, marbled with white—like fat—is like having a last steak supper before you die and go to tomato heaven.

My heart belongs to M. C. "Radiator Charlie" Byles—and his mortgage lifter. He got his start as a gardener—reluctantly—when, at the age of four, his mother instructed him to "come out from under there!" and go to work picking cotton, on their North Carolina farm. He eventually learned the virtue of manual labor, and developed a passion for big tomatoes.

Charlie Byles had a natural aptitude for mechanics. Without any schooling, he reportedly piloted small planes, delivered airmail, and invented a garden tiller. His skillful handling of radiator repairs earned him the nickname "Radiator Charlie." Byles's shop was located at the foot of a steep incline in Logan, where he waited for heavy coal and timber trucks with busted radiators to roll back down and land on his doorstep. To supplement his income in the 1940s, and help pay off the six-thousand-dollar mortgage on his home, Byles sold his tomatoes for a dollar a plant, and he paid off most of the loan within six years. Thus, Radiator Charlie's Mortgage Lifter.

M. C. Byles didn't invent the term; commodities that generate extra income for farmers, such as hogs, corn, or beans, have traditionally been labeled "mortgage lifters." As farmer Dorothy Beiswenger of Crookston, Minnesota, told me recently, in the old days, "farms were considerably smaller and more diversified, and if a farmer was having hard times and knew he had to come up with a payment, there were extra things on the farm to do to bring in money. Extra chickens, or a larger pumpkin patch, or tomatoes might just save the farmer from losing his property. Bankers were also known to have more than one or two shrewd characteristics, and would give out a mortgage that was rather impossible to meet, hoping to gain more for their bank. Hard-working farmers were often desperate, and with their many ways to make money, often got mortgages paid off.

"Farm wives were desperate for the well-being of their children, and pitched in or helped by baking or canning. Sewing, for other women, was common. When, of necessity, sewing was the only way to have clothes for the children, women sewed regardless of how the garments looked. The years of diversified farming were the very best years of farming for me. I loved the farm and all the animals, and especially the garden."

I love my garden, too, and thank goodness my mortgage has already been paid. On September 1, 2004, I picked the Radiator Charlie's Mortgage Lifter you see pictured here. It was destined for Victor Schrager's camera, and then the foundry the following day, where it was cast in bronze. I'd picked it too young, knowing it would never have survived the mold-making process if it had been riper. I'll never know what weight it might have attained if I'd left it to ripen on the vine. Still, a tomato three and a half pounds in weight and twenty-one inches in circumference is something to be proud of. One of the limited-edition bronze RCMLs sits on my desk—weighing in at ten pounds—where it will always remind me of Radiator Charlie and his tomato.

a

b

ESTLER'S MORTGAGE LIFTER *fig. 85b*

SIZE: *3¼" long by 5⅜" wide*

WEIGHT: *1 pound, 10 ounces*

SHAPE: *Beefsteak*

EXTERIOR COLOR(S): *Tomato pink*

FLESH COLOR(S): *Tomato pink*

SOLUBLE SOLIDS: *5¼ degrees Brix*

FLAVOR: *Good; acidic*

TEXTURE: *Soft; juicy and meaty*

BEST USE(S): *Fresh eating; salads, juice*

PLANT HABIT, LEAF TYPE, AND YIELD: *Indeterminate habit; regular leaf; good*

MATURITY: *Main crop*

ORIGIN: *An Estler family heirloom that seems to have originated in Barboursville, West Virginia, about 1922. In one version of the story, William S. Estler (1884–1968) discovered the sport or happy accident while strolling through the garden. In the other, the tomato was the result of a cross (either deliberate or not) between Ponderosa Pink and Prichard (Pritchard), circa 1922. Bill's son Bob speculated in 1994: "I think that it might have been a botanical accident, not a planned crossbreeding." Whatever the ancestry of Estler's might be, if the tomato was "discovered" in 1922, it couldn't have come from a cross with Pritchard, since that tomato was introduced later, in 1931, as Scarlet Topper, and renamed in 1932 (see Marglobe, page 66).*
Transplants have been sold by a number of West Virginia greenhouses for many years, starting with Archer's Flowers of Huntington in the 1930s. Cataloged by Appalachian Seeds, Flat Rock, North Carolina, and by Heirloom Tomatoes, Rosedale, Maryland, circa 2004.

SYNONYMS: *Mortgage Lifter. Resembles Carter's Mortgage Lifter (see page 122). Not the same as the smaller Australian Mortgage Lifter, which may be an offspring of Estler's.*

NY: *Nee & Goldman 54605*

The Estlers are deservedly proud of their mortgage lifter, a big old pink tomato that was handed down from patriarch Bill Estler. Bill supplied apples such as Ben Davis to company stores in coal fields, but the apple of his eye was this tomato. He grew it in isolation to preserve seed purity, kept a backup plot for added security, and carefully fermented his seeds when the time came.

When pesticides did in his 1930 crop, Estler decided not to chance losing his few remaining seeds, and called on friends at Archer's Flowers to help propagate the tomato in their greenhouse. A business arrangement ensued: "[Archer's] would raise the plants to sell to gardeners and provide Estler with a royalty for each one sold. There was enough money in it to keep everyone interested," according to John Marra, who wrote a 1994 story for *Goldenseal* entitled "The Mortgage Lifter: A Man and His Tomato." He added that greenhouse worker Shorty Meadows is credited with naming the tomato: Shorty presented Bill Estler with a tray of transplants and said, "I've brought you your mortgage lifters." Bill fell for the name and made it his own.

I don't know if the Estler strain of mortgage lifter is "the real McCoy" or predates Radiator Charlie's Mortgage Lifter (see page 116), but that's almost irrelevant. Fans rave. John Marra said in 1994: "No doubt, the [Estler's] Mortgage Lifter is a gardener's dream and a delightful addition to any summertime meal." Avid local gardener Jack Vannatter, who'd gotten seeds from Bill Estler and raised them for nearly forty years, concurred: "It's the tomato that can't be beat."

Of course, that's always a matter of opinion, and fruit quality varies as a function of locale. I've grown two dozen named or numbered mortgage lifters over the last five years in my upstate New York garden—and I've learned to play favorites. I'd give Estler's a solid "B." It would've earned an "A" were it not for the concentric ring cracking, and the acidity—a touch too much for my taste.

YELLOW MORTGAGE LIFTER *fig. 85j*

SIZE: *3¼" long by 5¼" wide*

WEIGHT: *1 pound, 6 ounces*

SHAPE: *Beefsteak*

EXTERIOR COLOR(S): *Cadmium orange*

FLESH COLOR(S): *Cadmium orange*

SOLUBLE SOLIDS: *5½ degrees Brix*

FLAVOR: *Excellent; sweet and sprightly*

TEXTURE: *Soft; glistening, meaty, and juicy*

BEST USE(S): *Multipurpose*

PLANT HABIT, LEAF TYPE, AND YIELD: *Indeterminate habit; regular leaf; high yield*

MATURITY: *Main crop*

ORIGIN: *Introduced as Mortgage Lifter–Yellow (or Railroad Tomato–Yellow)in 1984 by Southern Exposure Seed Exchange. A West Virginia heirloom sent to SESE founder Dr. Jeff McCormack by a woman who warned him that the seeds were so vigorous, he should plant them and stand back. Seeds of this tomato were apparently traded prior to 1940 and propagated by employees of the C & O Railroad. McCormack renamed the tomato Golden Ponderosa–Railroad Strain in 1986 because it appeared to be a variant of Golden Ponderosa (see Golden Ponderosa, page 162), rather than a variant of the pink Mortgage Lifter or Radiator Charlie's Mortgage Lifter (see page 116).*

SYNONYMS: *Golden Ponderosa, C & O (SESE select strain); Golden Ponderosa–Railroad Strain; Mortgage Lifter–Yellow; Railroad Tomato–Yellow; Seed Savers Tomato No. 387. Not the same as the potato-leafed Yellow Mortgage Lifter introduced in 2007 by Southern Exposure Seed Exchange. Not the same as Golden Ponderosa. Also not the same as Mortgage Lifter–Yellow introduced in 1998 by Underwood Gardens in Bensenville, Illinois, which was a sport of Mortgage Lifter in their gardens.*

SEED SOURCES: *To9*

An orange Mortgage Lifter gives me cognitive dissonance, and the synonymy is difficult to untangle. But who cares? Whatever its proper name or provenance, Yellow Mortgage Lifter is a tempting article of food.

QUISENBERRY'S MORTGAGE LIFTER
fig. 85a; page 94, fig. 67

SIZE: *2⅞" long by 5⅛" wide*

WEIGHT: *1 pound, 7 ounces*

SHAPE: *Beefsteak*

EXTERIOR COLOR(S): *Tomato pink*

FLESH COLOR(S): *Tomato pink*

SOLUBLE SOLIDS: *5 degrees Brix*

FLAVOR: *Good to excellent; well balanced*

TEXTURE: *Soft; meaty, juicy, no hard core or puff.*

BEST USE(S): *Fresh eating; juice*

PLANT HABIT, LEAF TYPE, AND YIELD: *Indeterminate habit; regular leaf; good yield*

MATURITY: *Main crop*

ORIGIN: *Cataloged as Mortgage Lifter in 1980 by Ben Quisenberry of Big Tomato Gardens, Syracuse, Ohio. Acquired by Seed Savers Exchange (Tomato No. 9); renamed and marketed as Quisenberry Mortgage Lifter in the SSE commercial seed catalog in 1999.*

SYNONYMS: *Mortgage Lifter. Same as the Mortgage Lifter carried by Ken Ettlinger of Long Island Seed and Plant, Riverhead, New York, in 1985.*

NY: *Nee & Goldman 54606*

One of the most beautiful and succulent of the Mortgage Lifters.

Descended from six plants that Ben Quisenberry bought in the 1960s or '70s from Bob Barnitz of Bob's Market in Mason, West Virginia. When I recently spoke to Bob, he recollected Ben as "an odd sort of fellow, inquisitive."

Here's how ninety-five-year-old Ben described this tomato during an interview: "Mine showed up pretty good. Rather rough but they're quite productive; they yield pretty heavy. They get quite that large, quite that large. They're a good size. Mortgage Lifter—that'd tell you they're a good size, wouldn't it?"

Shortly thereafter, Ben sent John Gorman some seeds for Mortgage Lifter—contained in a brown pill bottle, mixed with Big Ben and Sudduth's Brandywine seed (see pages 94 and 108)—and closed shop for the last time.

(a) Quisenberry's Mortgage Lifter, (b) Estler's Mortgage Lifter, (c) Halladay's Mortgage Lifter, (d) Radiator Charlie's Mortgage Lifter, (e) O'Driscoll's Mortgage Lifter, (f) Bicolor Mortgage Lifter, (g) German Mortgage Lifter, (h) Carter's Mortgage Lifter, (i) Watson's Mortgage Lifter, (j) Yellow Mortgage Lifter

WATSON'S MORTGAGE LIFTER *fig. 85i*

SIZE: *3⅛" long by 5" wide*

WEIGHT: *1 pound, 6 ounces*

SHAPE: *Beefsteak*

EXTERIOR COLOR(S): *Tomato pink*

FLESH COLOR(S): *Tomato pink*

SOLUBLE SOLIDS: *5 degrees Brix*

FLAVOR: *Good*

TEXTURE: *Soft; succulent and meaty but has too many fatal flaws: corky tissue, stem end cracking, and uneven ripening*

BEST USE(S): *None*

PLANT HABIT, LEAF TYPE, AND YIELD: *Indeterminate habit; regular leaf; good yield*

MATURITY: *Main crop*

ORIGIN: *First offered as Mortgage Lifter in the 1982 Seed Savers Exchange yearbook by Jerry A. Segler Sr. of Sparland, Illinois. His seed came from Thomas Watson of Charleston, Illinois. "Watson" was added to the name at the time of accession by SSE.*

SYNONYMS: *Mortgage Lifter; Mortgage Lifter, Watson; SSE Tomato No. 1684.*

See best uses.

O'DRISCOLL'S MORTGAGE LIFTER *fig. 85e*

SIZE: *2¾" long by 4⅛" wide*

WEIGHT: *1 pound*

SHAPE: *Beefsteak*

EXTERIOR COLOR(S): *Blood red*

FLESH COLOR(S): *Cherry red*

SOLUBLE SOLIDS: *5 degrees Brix*

FLAVOR: *Good to excellent*

TEXTURE: *Soft; very juicy and meaty; well-filled seed cavities*

BEST USE(S): *Fresh eating; juicing*

PLANT HABIT, LEAF TYPE, AND YIELD: *Indeterminate habit; regular leaf; good yield*

MATURITY: *Main crop*

ORIGIN: *First offered to Seed Savers Exchange members as Mortgage Lifter in 1981 by Robert P. O'Driscoll of Greenfield, Wisconsin. I renamed the tomato in honor of Robert.*

SYNONYMS: *Mortgage Lifter, Red; Seed Savers Tomato No. 1045. Smaller, rounder, and more regular than Mortgage Lifter VFN, also known as Mortgage Lifter Red (see page 121), developed by Jeff McCormack.*

NY: *Nee & Goldman 54622*

A magnificent, glossy red specimen, virtually unblemished, with no green shoulders and hardly any stem-end cracks—that's saying *a lot* for a mortgage lifter. Long-time seed savers Auburn and Clarice Cooper of Overland Park, Kansas, thought the world of O'Driscoll's: "fine taste, versatile, good fresh, cooked, in sauce and soup."

(a) Mullens' Mortgage Lifter, (b) Halladay's Mortgage Lifter, (c) Rieger's Mortgage Lifter, (d) Mortgage Lifter VFN, (e) McGarity's Mortgage Lifter

GERMAN MORTGAGE LIFTER *page 119, fig. 85g*

SIZE: *3" long by 4⅛" wide*

WEIGHT: *1 pound*

SHAPE: *Beefsteak*

EXTERIOR COLOR(S): *Tomato pink*

FLESH COLOR(S): *Tomato pink*

SOLUBLE SOLIDS: *5½ degrees Brix*

FLAVOR: *Good*

TEXTURE: *Soft; succulent and meaty*

BEST USE(S): *Fresh eating; juice*

PLANT HABIT, LEAF TYPE, AND YIELD: *Indeterminate habit; regular leaf; good yield*

MATURITY: *Main crop*

ORIGIN: *Donated to Seed Savers Exchange by Frederick L. Payne of Cincinnati, Ohio, but never offered in the annual yearbook. Said to have come from German immigrants circa 1900.*

SYNONYMS: *Seed Savers Tomato No. 2593. Similar to many other Mortgage Lifters and pink beefsteaks, including German Pink (see page 104).*

NY: *Nee & Goldman 54625*

Another admirable Mortgage Lifter, with a deep, seductive flavor. When I scrape my teeth across the whole expanse of German to get a representative sampling of juice and flesh, the old ditty pops into my head, "Sacramento, tomato, tomato, tomato juice," and inspires me to make juice.

MULLENS' MORTGAGE LIFTER *fig. 86a; page 123, fig. 89d*

SIZE: *3½" long by 5½" wide*

WEIGHT: *2 pounds, 8 ounces*

SHAPE: *Beefsteak*

EXTERIOR COLOR(S): *Tomato pink*

FLESH COLOR(S): *Tomato pink*

SOLUBLE SOLIDS: *5¼ degrees Brix*

FLAVOR: *Excellent*

TEXTURE: *Soft; meaty*

BEST USE(S): *Fresh eating; juice*

PLANT HABIT, LEAF TYPE, AND YIELD: *Indeterminate habit; regular leaf; high yield*

MATURITY: *Main crop*

ORIGIN: *Originated with Charlotte Mullens of West Virginia. Commercialized in 1995 by Southern Exposure Seed Exchange.*

SYNONYMS: *There is also a Pale Leaf Strain of Mullens' Mortgage Lifter.*

NY: *Nee & Goldman 54624*

A big round pink giant that tastes divinely sweet, with a lemon tingle. Grows almost as heavy as Radiator Charlie's Mortgage Lifter (see page 116), from which it may be derived.

HALLADAY'S MORTGAGE LIFTER

page 119, fig. 85c; page 120, fig. 86b

SIZE: *3½" long by 6½" wide*

WEIGHT: *2 pounds, 5 ounces*

SHAPE: *Beefsteak*

EXTERIOR COLOR(S): *Tomato pink*

FLESH COLOR(S): *Tomato pink*

SOLUBLE SOLIDS: *5½ degrees Brix*

FLAVOR: *Good; sweet and savory*

TEXTURE: *Soft; solid and succulent*

BEST USE(S): *Fresh eating; juicing*

PLANT HABIT, LEAF TYPE, AND YIELD: *Indeterminate habit; regular leaf; high yield*

MATURITY: *Late crop*

ORIGIN: *A Kentucky family heirloom. First offered in the 1985 Seed Savers Exchange yearbook as Mortgage Lifter by James Halladay of Fairview, Pennsylvania. Grown in eastern Kentucky by three generations of his family (dates to the 1930s).*

SYNONYMS: *Mortgage Lifter; Seed Savers Tomato No. 4703. Very similar to Radiator Charlie's Mortgage Lifter (see page 116).*

NY: *Nee & Goldman 54557*

Produces a huge crop of lunkers with surprisingly good flavor. Halladay's is a dead ringer for Radiator Charlie's Mortgage Lifter (see page 116).

RIEGER'S MORTGAGE LIFTER fig. 86c

SIZE: *3⅝" long by 6" wide*

WEIGHT: *1 pound, 13 ounces*

SHAPE: *Beefsteak*

EXTERIOR COLOR(S): *Tomato pink*

FLESH COLOR(S): *Tomato pink*

SOLUBLE SOLIDS: *4½ degrees Brix*

FLAVOR: *Good; acidic*

TEXTURE: *Soft to reasonably firm; meaty, sometimes mealy*

BEST USE(S): *Fresh eating; juicing*

PLANT HABIT, LEAF TYPE, AND YIELD: *Indeterminate habit; regular leaf; good yield*

MATURITY: *Late crop*

ORIGIN: *Offered in the Seed Savers Exchange 1984 yearbook as Mortgage Lifter by Rich Rieger of Weston, West Virginia, who said, "I think Mortgage Lifter was developed in Frazier's Bottom, West Virginia, on the Statler Farm." Commercialized circa 2004 by Heirloom Tomatoes of Rosedale, Maryland.*

SYNONYMS: *Mortgage Lifter; Mortgage Lifter #4; Mortgage Lifter, Rieger; SSE Tomato No. 1688*

Rieger's Mortgage Lifter, whose hefty trusses produce tomatoes in triplicate or quadruplicate, is the spitting image of German Johnson, one of the parents of Radiator Charlie's Mortgage Lifter (see page 116). Try Rieger's in a Virgin Mary.

MORTGAGE LIFTER VFN fig. 86d

SIZE: *3⅛" long by 5½" wide*

WEIGHT: *2 pounds, 5 ounces*

SHAPE: *Beefsteak*

EXTERIOR COLOR(S): *Cherry red*

FLESH COLOR(S): *Cherry red with tomato pink flecks*

SOLUBLE SOLIDS: *5 degrees Brix*

FLAVOR: *Good*

TEXTURE: *Soft to reasonably firm; meaty*

BEST USE(S): *Fresh eating*

PLANT HABIT, LEAF TYPE, AND YIELD: *Indeterminate habit; regular leaf; good yield*

MATURITY: *Late crop*

ORIGIN: *An "improved"—disease-resistant, smaller, more uniform—red version of Radiator Charlie's Mortgage Lifter (see page 116). Introduced by Southern Exposure Seed Exchange in their 1990–1991 catalog.*

SYNONYMS: *Red Mortgage Lifter. Same as SSE Tomato No. 4679. Not the same as O'Driscoll's Mortgage Lifter.*

NY: *Nee & Goldman 54638*

SEED SOURCES: *Ag7, Bo19, Ers, So1, Te4, Up2*

The loveliest red in a garden of predominantly pink Mortgage Lifters—and it's tasty, too.

MCGARITY'S MORTGAGE LIFTER fig. 86e

SIZE: *2½" long by 3¾" wide*

WEIGHT: *11 ounces*

SHAPE: *Beefsteak*

EXTERIOR COLOR(S): *Tomato pink*

FLESH COLOR(S): *Tomato pink*

SOLUBLE SOLIDS: *4½ degrees Brix*

FLAVOR: *Poor; tasteless, without merit*

TEXTURE: *Soft; mealy; bloody juice*

BEST USE(S): *Target practice*

PLANT HABIT, LEAF TYPE, AND YIELD: *Indeterminate habit; regular leaf; good yield*

MATURITY: *Late crop*

ORIGIN: *From M. H. McGarity of Greer, South Carolina, who obtained it in Columbia, South Carolina, around 1980. The name was changed from Mortgage Lifter to McGarity's Mortgage Lifter at the time of accession by Seed Savers Exchange. Commercialized circa 1984 by Heirloom Tomatoes of Rosedale, Maryland.*

SYNONYMS: *Mortgage Lifter; Mortgage Lifter, McGarity; Seed Savers Tomato No. 1686*

McGarity's has its partisans, but it's consistently the runt of my litter. I don't think you could pay off a car loan with it.

CARTER'S MORTGAGE LIFTER *fig. 87; page 119, fig. 85h*

SIZE: *2¾" long by 3⅞" wide*

WEIGHT: *13 ounces*

SHAPE: *Beefsteak*

EXTERIOR COLOR(S): *Tomato pink*

FLESH COLOR(S): *Tomato pink*

SOLUBLE SOLIDS: *6 degrees Brix*

FLAVOR: *Fair to good; slightly acidic*

TEXTURE: *Soft; meaty, bloody juice; no hard core*

BEST USE(S): *Fresh eating; juicing*

PLANT HABIT, LEAF TYPE, AND YIELD: *Indeterminate habit; regular leaf; good yield*

MATURITY: *Main crop*

ORIGIN: *A South Carolina family heirloom, first offered by Curtis D. Choplin of North Augusta, South Carolina, in limited quantity, to members of Seed Savers Exchange in 1984. Choplin had obtained seeds from M. E. Carter of Elliott, South Carolina, who had grown them for many years. Carter got the variety from J. W. DuBard of Cedar Creek Section near Blythewood, South Carolina, who had gotten them from his mother—and there, the trail turns cold. "Carter" was added to the variety name at the time of accession by SSE.*

SYNONYMS: *Mortgage Lifter; Mortgage Lifter #1; Seed Savers Tomato No. 1685. Resembles Estler's Mortgage Lifter (see page 118).*

Mortgage Lifters are a rough bunch of characters, but Carter's is easy on the eyes.

87

PESTA'S MORTGAGE LIFTER *fig. 88*

SIZE: *3¾" long by 6¾" wide*

WEIGHT: *2 pounds, 14 ounces*

SHAPE: *Beefsteak*

EXTERIOR COLOR(S): *Orange yellow with tomato pink at the blossom end*

FLESH COLOR(S): *Orange yellow with spots of tomato pink*

SOLUBLE SOLIDS: *5½ degrees Brix*

FLAVOR: *Fair to good; mildly sweet*

TEXTURE: *Soft; very susceptible to puffiness (air spaces in locules); waxy-smooth exterior*

BEST USE(S): *Fresh eating; juicing*

PLANT HABIT, LEAF TYPE, AND YIELD: *Indeterminate habit; regular leaf; good yield*

MATURITY: *Late to very late crop*

ORIGIN: *Originated with George Pesta of Wheeling, West Virginia, who is also known as the source of West Virginia Hillbilly and West Virginia Prison Farm (Penitentiary) tomatoes. First offered to Seed Savers Exchange members in 1987 by Edmund O. Brown II of Reeds, Missouri.*

SYNONYMS: *Mortgage Lifter, Pesta Strain; Mortgage Lifter; SSE Tomato No. 1620. Resembles West Virginia Hillbilly (although many sizes and shapes are reported, West Virginia Hillbilly is also very large—three pounds plus—and very late).*

NY: *Nee & Goldman 54623 and 54640*

Pesta's Mortgage Lifter is the biggest bicolor beefsteak I've ever seen. The sheer mass of it is cause for celebration. For the grower in the Northeast, Pesta's has the added benefit of staying reliable into September—thus prolonging the gardening pleasure.

88

(a) Cartwright's Mortgage Lifter, (b) Radiator Charlie's Mortgage Lifter, (c) Red and Yellow Mortgage Lifter, (d) Mullens' Mortgage Lifter

CARTWRIGHT'S MORTGAGE LIFTER *fig. 89a*

SIZE: *3¼" long by 4¼" wide*

WEIGHT: *1 pound, 2 ounces*

SHAPE: *Beefsteak*

EXTERIOR COLOR(S): *Tomato pink*

FLESH COLOR(S): *Tomato pink*

SOLUBLE SOLIDS: *5 degrees Brix*

FLAVOR: *Fair to good; mildly sweet*

TEXTURE: *Soft; puffy*

BEST USE(S): *Don't go there.*

PLANT HABIT, LEAF TYPE, AND YIELD: *Indeterminate habit; regular leaf; good yield*

MATURITY: *Main crop*

ORIGIN: *First offered to Seed Savers Exchange members as Mortgage Lifter by Robert E. Cartwright of Raleigh, North Carolina, in 1984. He made note* of the prominent green shoulders, which turn pink overnight. Cartwright's seeds came from Walter Johnson of Adelphi, Maryland.

SYNONYMS: *Mortgage Lifter; Mortgage Lifter #3; Seed Savers Tomato No. 1687. "Cartwright" was added to the variety name when accessioned by SSE. Curtis D. Choplin noted Cartwright's similarity to Carter's, Rieger's, and McGarity's Mortgage Lifters (see pages 121 and 122).*

Cartwright's Mortgage Lifter is ruined for me by its anemic color and flavor—and the hollow locules do nothing to redeem it. The variety name came from paying off the mortgage on a nursery.

RED AND YELLOW MORTGAGE LIFTER *fig. 89c*

SIZE: *3" long by 4½" wide*

WEIGHT: *1 pound*

SHAPE: *Beefsteak*

EXTERIOR COLOR(S): *Orange yellow with tomato pink at the blossom end*

FLESH COLOR(S): *Orange yellow with spots of tomato pink*

SOLUBLE SOLIDS: *5 degrees Brix*

FLAVOR: *Good; sweet*

TEXTURE: *Soft; meaty*

BEST USE(S): *Fresh eating; juicing*

PLANT HABIT, LEAF TYPE, AND YIELD: *Indeterminate habit; regular leaf; good yield*

MATURITY: *Main crop*

ORIGIN: *First listed in the 1990 Seed Savers Exchange yearbook by Charles E. Estep Sr. of Riverside, California, who* said it was similar to Brimmer Yellow. His seed source was George Pesta of Wheeling, West Virginia.

SYNONYMS: *Bicolor Mortgage Lifter (see page 111); Seed Savers Tomato No. 1971. Resembles many other red or pink and yellow bicolor beefsteaks. Not the same as Pesta's Mortgage Lifter (see page 122), which is much bigger and later to mature.*

NY: *Nee & Goldman 54576*

SEED SOURCES: *To9*

Small for a tomato of this name, Red and Yellow is the poor cousin to Pesta's Mortgage Lifter. For some strange reason, the hornworms go gaga over it.

90

91

DELICIOUS *fig. 90*

SIZE: *5" long by 6" wide*

WEIGHT: *2 pounds*

SHAPE: *Beefsteak*

EXTERIOR COLOR(S): *Cock's comb red*

FLESH COLOR(S): *Madder red*

SOLUBLE SOLIDS: *5 degrees Brix*

FLAVOR: *Fair to good; bland to delicious*

TEXTURE: *Soft; fleshy and occasionally mealy*

BEST USE(S): *Competitive vegetable growing*

PLANT HABIT, LEAF TYPE, AND YIELD: *Indeterminate habit; regular leaf; low yield*

MATURITY: *Main crop*

ORIGIN: *Brought to market by W. Atlee Burpee Company, in 1964, after thirteen years of intensive breeding and selection from Beefsteak (Crimson Cushion). Bred by Burpee's chief vegetable breeder Ted Torrey.*

SYNONYMS: *Burpee('s) Delicious; Red Delicious. Similar to Magnum, also known as Mega Tom, carried by Thompson and Morgan; selected from Delicious by giant vegetable showman and multi-world-record-holder Bernard Lavery. Also similar to Supersteak Hybrid VFN, a hybrid of Delicious.*

NY: *Nee & Goldman 53436*

SEED SOURCES: *Be4, Ear, Ers, Gr27, He8, He17, Jor, La1, Pe6, Ra6, Re8, Sa9, Se25, Se26, Se28, Sh9, Shu, So1, Sw9, Ter, To1, To3, To9, To10, Und, Vi4*

When I began concentrating on tomatoes rather than pumpkins, I thought giant vegetable growing and freak shows were a thing of the past. I was in error. But instead of shooting for fruits over a thousand pounds, tomato growers aim to break the five-pound barrier. The heaviest Delicious on record is the seven-pound-twelve-ounce monster grown by Gordon Graham of Edmond, Oklahoma, in 1986; this earned Graham a second Guinness World Record (the first was for growing the largest tomato plant: a 28-foot-high, 53½-foot-wide colossus from a Sweet 100 variety). As deliberate as Graham was about producing world records, the winning tomato—and still champ—was apparently a windfall: the sole fruit to form on a sizable plant felled by winds onto Graham's cantaloupe patch.

POLISH GIANT BEEFSTEAK *fig. 91*

SIZE: *4" long by 7" wide*

WEIGHT: *3 pounds, 14 ounces*

SHAPE: *Beefsteak*

EXTERIOR COLOR(S): *Tomato pink*

FLESH COLOR(S): *Tomato pink*

SOLUBLE SOLIDS: *6 degrees Brix*

FLAVOR: *Fair to good*

TEXTURE: *Soft; meaty and juicy; some hard core*

BEST USE(S): *Competitive tomato growing; exhibition*

PLANT HABIT, LEAF TYPE, AND YIELD: *Indeterminate habit; regular leaf; low yield*

MATURITY: *Late crop*

ORIGIN: *Accessioned by Seed Savers Exchange in 1995 from an unnamed donor in Denver, Colorado, who had saved the seed for forty years*

SYNONYMS: *Polish Giant. Not the same as the elongated Polish Giant Paste. I added "Beefsteak" to the name "Polish Giant" to avoid confusion.*

Polish Giant is so gargantuan that it could pass as a pumpkin. I think it has the potential to rival Gordon Graham's 1986 world-record heaviest tomato—a seven-pound-twelve-ounce Delicious (see previous entry).

92

TIDWELL GERMAN *page 11, fig. 2*

SIZE: *3½" long by 6" wide*

WEIGHT: *2 pounds, 8 ounces*

SHAPE: *Beefsteak*

EXTERIOR COLOR(S): *Tomato pink*

FLESH COLOR(S): *Tomato pink*

SOLUBLE SOLIDS: *5 degrees Brix*

FLAVOR: *Good*

TEXTURE: *Soft; meaty and juicy*

BEST USE(S): *Fresh eating; makes a good thick tomato juice*

PLANT HABIT, LEAF TYPE, AND YIELD: *Indeterminate habit; regular leaf; high yield*

MATURITY: *Main crop*

ORIGIN: *A pink beefsteak tomato handed down for close to 100 years in the Tidwell family of Tennessee. Farming the rolling hills, growing tomatoes for market, and saving seeds are Tidwell traditions. Commercialized by family member David Pendergrass, president of the New Hope Seed Company.*

SEED SOURCES: *Ma18, Sa9, To1, Vi4*

Tidwell German is as capable of producing gigundos as Delicious, Polish Giant Beefsteak, and Radiator Charlie's Mortgage Lifter (see pages 116 and 124). Many of mine get so weighty—almost four pounds apiece—that they need to be propped up with lengths of timber.

DIENER *fig. 92*

SIZE: *3⅛" long by 6⅜" wide*

WEIGHT: *2 pounds, 10 ounces*

SHAPE: *Beefsteak*

EXTERIOR COLOR(S): *Brownish red*

FLESH COLOR(S): *Crayfish red*

SOLUBLE SOLIDS: *4½ degrees Brix*

FLAVOR: *Poor; low acid and low sugar*

TEXTURE: *Soft; corky and misshapen*

BEST USE(S): *Competitive vegetable growing; used extensively 80 years ago in California for dehydrating, ketchup, and canning*

PLANT HABIT, LEAF TYPE, AND YIELD: *Indeterminate habit; regular leaf; good yield*

MATURITY: *Main crop*

ORIGIN: *Developed by Richard Diener and introduced in 1917 by Richard Diener Company, Kentfield, California. Mr. Diener reported (1932): "In 1916 I first got what I had in mind, a good, large tomato from a cross of San Jose Canner and Trophy."*

SEED SOURCES: *To9*

The first Dieners to set fruit—like Delicious and Tidwell German (see page 124 and this page)—often weigh in at a gratifyingly hefty three or four pounds each. The originator recommended flat field culture, generous spacing of six to eight feet between plants, and no pruning of vines. Thinning the fruits, discarding the most misshapen, about five weeks after transplant produces shapely four-pounders for me.

The Diener is impressively big, but the breeder himself leaves a mixed legacy. Richard Diener pulled a fast one by claiming that his piquant Pepper Tomato, developed in 1922, was a cross between the bell pepper and the tomato. This was followed swiftly by "new crossings" of the tomato with the bell pepper: Novato, Ignacio, Petaluma, Tulare, San Geronimo, and Sonoma. All were smooth, round or oval tomatoes and not like the hollow stuffers of today that resemble bell peppers. In 1929, the House of Gurney got in on the act by introducing the "Topepo," a supposed cross between the sweet pepper and the tomato.

Last time I looked, peppers and tomatoes didn't mix, except in Chicken Cacciatore. Cornell breeder Dr. Dick Robinson confirms that a cross between pepper and tomato is impossible, even with new techniques. Flavor volatiles might have been selected by Diener and Gurney that had pepper-like similarities, though. Dr. Robinson told me: "Technically, it would be possible to graft a tomato scion onto a pepper rootstock and vice versa—even a tomato and pepper scion onto the same rootstock. A sexual cross, however, would not be possible as the different chromosomes would not align."

Pear & Plum

(a) Green Sleeves, (b) Cream Sausage, (c, e) Super Italian Paste, (d) Antique Roman, (f) Tegucigalpa, (g) Pink San Marzano, (h) Doucet's Plum Producer, (i) Roman Holiday

a

b

c

d

e

f

g

h

i

93

GREEN SLEEVES *page 127, fig. 93a*

SIZE: *3½" long by 1⅜" wide*

WEIGHT: *2 ounces*

SHAPE: *Plum*

EXTERIOR COLOR(S): *Yolk yellow with olive yellow striping*

FLESH COLOR(S): *Sap green*

SOLUBLE SOLIDS: *4½ degrees Brix*

FLAVOR: *Poor; high acid, low sugar*

TEXTURE: *Very firm*

BEST USE(S): *Novelty; ornamental plant and fruit. A must for collectors.*

PLANT HABIT, LEAF TYPE, AND YIELD: *Determinate, prostrate habit; regular leaf; high yield*

MATURITY: *Early crop*

ORIGIN: *Bred by Thomas P. Wagner in the course of his researches on dwarf determinates. One of the parents was Green Nails, a Green Sleeves look-alike borne late on indeterminate vines. Green Nails was first offered as part of a mixture in the 1983 issue of Tom's Tater Mater Seeds. Other parents include hanging basket lines. Cataloged as Green Sausage in 2002 by Thompson and Morgan.*

SYNONYMS: *Green Sausage; Lady Green Sleeves. Similar to Green Nails.*

SEED SOURCES: *Ag7, Ba8, Hi13, La1, Ra6, Se16, Tho, To3, To9*

Green Sleeves is a "weeping tomato" whose prostrate habit and concentrated set of novelties are shown to best advantage in pots or hanging baskets. Prune off excess fruit if the load gets too heavy, or if you'd like larger tomatoes. Tomato container growing is a time-honored tradition: Swiss botanist Konrad Gessner noted in 1561 that tomatoes were easy to grow in pots or flower borders if given rich soil and plenty of water (McCue, 1952).

CREAM SAUSAGE *page 127, fig. 93b*

SIZE: *4½" long by 2" wide*

WEIGHT: *5 ounces*

SHAPE: *Plum, beaked*

EXTERIOR COLOR(S): *Yellow*

FLESH COLOR(S): *Light yellow*

SOLUBLE SOLIDS: *5¼ degrees Brix*

FLAVOR: *Fair to good; pleasantly mild*

TEXTURE: *Reasonably firm; meaty and juicy*

BEST USE(S): *Fresh eating; show and tell*

PLANT HABIT, LEAF TYPE, AND YIELD: *Determinate habit; droopy leaves; high yield*

MATURITY: *Early crop*

ORIGIN: *Bred by Thomas P. Wagner and named Banana Cream. Worked its way through the ranks at Seed Savers Exchange. Introduced as Cream Sausage in 2004 by Baker Creek Heirloom Seeds.*

SYNONYMS: *Banana Cream. Not the same as Banana Legs (see page 163).*

SEED SOURCES: *Ba8, Hi13, La1, Ra6, Se16, To9, To10*

This is the only white elongated plum I know. It makes a ghostly spectacle in the garden, and it would probably do wonderfully in a container, given its compact habit and concentrated fruit set. Use the tomatoes for white salsas or salads, but don't let the shape fool you into making sauce: Cream Sausage is metallic when cooked.

ANTIQUE ROMAN *page 127, fig. 93d*

SIZE: *5¼" long by 3" wide*

WEIGHT: *11½ ounces*

SHAPE: *Blocky plum (what the French would call* parallélépipédique*)*

EXTERIOR COLOR(S): *Blood red*

FLESH COLOR(S): *Cherry red*

SOLUBLE SOLIDS: *6 degrees Brix*

FLAVOR: *Excellent; beefy, savory*

TEXTURE: *Reasonably firm; meaty*

BEST USE(S): *Cooking; pair it with garlic*

PLANT HABIT, LEAF TYPE, AND YIELD: *Indeterminate habit; droopy leaves; high yield*

MATURITY: *Main crop*

ORIGIN: *Introduced to Seed Savers Exchange in 1991 by John F. Swenson of Glencoe, Illinois. (See Speckled Roman and Roman Holiday, pages 170 and 129.)*

Another great plum tomato from Italy. The conduit was Renaissance man John F. Swenson, who nurtures a sweet obsession for tomatoes and garlic—not to mention his passion for unusual place names, like Chicago and Sheboygan. This Roman tomato was given to John in 1990 by Ann Salomon of Tweefontein Farm, in New Paltz, New York; her seed had come from an elderly Italian neighbor.

SUPER ITALIAN PASTE *page 127, fig. 93c, e*

SIZE: *5¼" long by 2⅞" wide*

WEIGHT: *10 ounces*

SHAPE: *Giant plum; shape varies*

EXTERIOR COLOR(S): *Blood red*

FLESH COLOR(S): *Cherry red*

SOLUBLE SOLIDS: *6½ degrees Brix*

FLAVOR: *Excellent*

TEXTURE: *Firm; meaty and juicy*

BEST USE(S): *Sauce. "A huge, meaty paste tomato with a very full flavor for sauce that could make you famous," according to Jan Blum. "Fruits are a good 6 inches long and 3 inches in diameter; four times larger" than any other (Blüm, 1984).*

PLANT HABIT, LEAF TYPE, AND YIELD: *Indeterminate habit; droopy leaves; high yield*

MATURITY: *Main crop*

ORIGIN: *Introduced in 1984 by Seeds Blüm, of Boise, Idaho, as Super Italian Paste. Jan Blum, who made seed saving fun and educated heirloom gardeners in the 1980s and '90s with her quirky and whimsical catalogs, held the banner high for this superduper tomato, one of the varieties that spurred her to start a seed company.*

SYNONYMS: *Large Italian Paste; and Long Italian (the name Jan Blum gave this tomato when she listed it in the 1981 annual Seed Savers Exchange yearbook). Similar to Big Ray's Argentina Paste, which was introduced by Seeds Blüm in 1993 as the archrival for Jan's affections. Not the same as the Super Italian Plum from Mary Ann Billera's great-great-grandmother (which is narrow and tapers to a distinct point), listed in the 1978 SSE yearbook.*

NY: *Nee & Goldman 53455 and 54613*

SEED SOURCES: *Ga1, He8, Hi13, To1*

Jan Blum's growing season in Idaho was so short that she could reap only one third of the potential harvest from Super Italian Paste. I'm luckier, with 120 frost-free days. These plants keep me well provisioned with sweet-as-sugar and savory tomato sauce from one year to the next—and the fruits are great for fresh eating, too.

TEGUCIGALPA *page 127, fig. 93f*

SIZE: *4" long by 1" wide*

WEIGHT: *3½ ounces*

SHAPE: *Plum, "bullet" shape; sometimes has a constricted neck*

EXTERIOR COLOR(S): *Blood red*

FLESH COLOR(S): *Blood red*

SOLUBLE SOLIDS: *5 degrees Brix*

FLAVOR: *Fair to good; pleasing; like most plum tomatoes, this one has a more pronounced flavor when cooked*

TEXTURE: *Firm; juicy and meaty*

BEST USE(S): *Multipurpose*

PLANT HABIT, LEAF TYPE, AND YIELD: *Indeterminate habit; regular leaf; high yield*

MATURITY: *Early crop*

ORIGIN: *Obtained in 1999 by Ulrike Paradine of Kent, England, from a friend of a friend: Manfred Hahm-Hartmann of Germany. Paradine listed the variety a year later in the annual yearbook of Seed Savers Exchange.*

SYNONYMS: *Similar to the Long John illustrated by Tanksley (2004). SSE tomato 5595.*

I made a beeline for Tomato No. 5595 while strolling the gardens at Heritage Farm in Decorah, Iowa, four years ago. I couldn't leave without owning the sveltest plum tomato in the Seed Savers Exchange collection. Tegucigalpa litters the ground late in the season with ripe fruits, which the plant can apparently bear to part with. I pocketed some.

This tomato comes from Tegucigalpa, a mining town founded by the Spanish in 1578, that is now the capital city of Honduras. The word *Tegucigalpa* derives from the Nahuatl *Teguz-galpa*, meaning "silver hills." In the Aztec document known as the *Florentine Codex*, dated 1540–1585, one section describes a "thin tomato" sold by Aztec *tomanamacacs* (tomato sellers). The "Tegus" tomato emanating from those hills seems to be the best candidate.

PINK SAN MARZANO *page 127, fig. 93g*

SIZE: *2¼" long by 1¾" wide*

WEIGHT: *2 ounces*

SHAPE: *Plum*

EXTERIOR COLOR(S): *Tomato pink*

FLESH COLOR(S): *Tomato pink*

SOLUBLE SOLIDS: *5 degrees Brix*

FLAVOR: *Good; sweet*

TEXTURE: *Reasonably firm; juicy. Cracks come rain or come shine.*

BEST USE(S): *Not recommended*

PLANT HABIT, LEAF TYPE, AND YIELD: *Indeterminate habit; droopy foliage; low yield*

MATURITY: *Main crop*

ORIGIN: *Cataloged in 1954 by Glecklers Seedmen of Metamora, Ohio, and described as "a new pink San Marzano type of tomato, the most delicate tomato plant we have ever tested. Very large extended indeterminate growth but having extremely small dainty leaves and thin branches. Fruits about one third the size of the common red strain, mild and fine for salads."*

SYNONYMS: *San Marzano Pink. Assigned PI # 303775 by the USDA in 1965; their seed originated with Glecklers but was donated by L. Alexander of the Ohio Agricultural Experiment Station, who noted severe cracking. Not the same as San Marzano (see page 137)—and totally undeserving of that exalted name.*

If Pink San Marzano didn't fall apart, it would be a good tomato—right?—just like if my grandmother had wheels, she'd be a wagon. (My mother might say, "Make that your *paternal* grandmother.") This tomato provides a textbook example of radial cracking; it's for pathology collectors only.

DOUCET'S PLUM PRODUCER *page 127, fig. 93h*

SIZE: *2¾" long by 2¼" wide*

WEIGHT: *4½ ounces*

SHAPE: *Plum*

EXTERIOR COLOR(S): *Crayfish red*

FLESH COLOR(S): *Coral red*

SOLUBLE SOLIDS: *4 degrees Brix*

FLAVOR: *Good when processed*

TEXTURE: *Very firm; dry and meaty*

BEST USE(S): *Cooking; canning*

PLANT HABIT, LEAF TYPE, AND YIELD: *Determinate habit; regular leaf; high yield*

MATURITY: *Main crop*

ORIGIN: *Bred by Roger Doucet at Station Provinciale de Recherches Agricoles, Saint-Hyacinthe, Québec, and released in 1978. Cataloged by W. H. Perron Company, Laval, Québec, in 1983. Ken Ettlinger says that: "PI 263726 from Puerto Rico, a tomato brought back by Charlie Rick of the University of California at Davis, contributed germplasm to Québec 1121" as well as to eight other "Bec" tomatoes bred by Doucet.*

SYNONYMS: *Carré; Québec 1121; Q-1121*

SEED SOURCES: *Pr3, Sa9*

This tomato's proper name is Québec 1121, but it's hard to embrace a number, so Doucet's Plum Producer it shall be. The fruit is blocky and squat, pithy and hard-skinned—in other words, just right for Oven-Roasted Tomatoes (see page 237). I agree with Glenn Drowns of Sand Hill Preservation Center: This tomato is an outstanding paste for short-season areas. Maybe it should have been called Prodigious Producer.

ROMAN HOLIDAY *page 127, fig. 93i*

SIZE: *5¼" long by 2⅝" wide*

WEIGHT: *10½ ounces*

SHAPE: *Plum, nipple-tipped*

EXTERIOR COLOR(S): *Yellow with signal yellow zigzags (difficult to discern at maturity)*

FLESH COLOR(S): *Light yellow; can be streaked with pink inside, top to toe*

SOLUBLE SOLIDS: *5¼ degrees Brix*

FLAVOR: *Poor to fair; acidic*

TEXTURE: *Firm*

BEST USE(S): *Novelty; decorative*

PLANT HABIT, LEAF TYPE, AND YIELD: *Indeterminate habit; droopy foliage; high yield*

MATURITY: *Early crop*

ORIGIN: *Another tomato under the influence of Tom Wagner's Banana Legs (see page 163), Roman Holiday is a sport of Speckled Roman (Antique Roman x Banana Legs; see pages 128 and 163) that was discovered at Heritage Farm in Decorah, Iowa, in 2003 and sent to me by Aaron Whaley.*

SYNONYMS: *Speckled Roman, Yellow*

NY: *Nee & Goldman 53419*

I named this tomato in honor of its Speckled Roman and Antique Roman lineage, and because "holiday" connotes "sport." Plus it's a fun reference to the delightful 1953 movie starring Gregory Peck and Audrey Hepburn. I wish it tasted sweeter.

94

HUNGARIAN ITALIAN *fig. 94*

SIZE: *3⅛" long by 2⅜" wide*

WEIGHT: *4½ ounces*

SHAPE: *Pear or fig*

EXTERIOR COLOR(S): *Brownish red*

FLESH COLOR(S): *Crayfish red*

SOLUBLE SOLIDS: *4½ degrees Brix*

FLAVOR: *Fair to good*

TEXTURE: *Firm; mealy and dry*

BEST USE(S): *Cooking; preserving and canning*

PLANT HABIT, LEAF TYPE, AND YIELD: *Determinate habit; regular leaf; high yield*

MATURITY: *Late crop*

ORIGIN: *An Italian plum tomato, presumably named for its resemblance to Hungarian peppers. Paul M. Griepentrog of Dalton, Wisconsin, introduced Hungarian Italian (and Jim's Italian Tomato) to Seed Savers Exchange members in the 1983 yearbook. Both varieties, he says, come from Mrs. Marvin Polfuss, "an incredible woman who operates a greenhouse and produce business, and one of the few sorghum-producing mills left in this state." Commercialized in 1987 by Jan Blum, of Seeds Blüm, who described Hungarian Italian as incredibly prolific in the Corn Belt.*

SYNONYMS: *Hungarian Italian Paste; Hungarian Italian Tomato*

SEED SOURCES: *Sa9, So1, To1*

The most prolific plum tomato and the latest to mature, borne on lush compact plants. Savvy and industrious gardeners like Will Bonsall of Industry, Maine, prefer the late-ripening dry-fleshed pastes, even when faced with a short season. In a practice borrowed from Italian farmers, Will pulls "the whole vines and hangs them from the cellar beams until they ripen; thus the lateness— combined with bigger yields and drier flesh—is an advantage … when first frost finds us too busy to do a big canning. And, anyway, who needs to can water?"

GOLDMAN'S ITALIAN AMERICAN
fig. 95; page 15; page 132, fig 96c

SIZE: *4" long by 5⅛" wide*

WEIGHT: *1 pound*

SHAPE: *Fig; comes in wide and extra-wide*

EXTERIOR COLOR(S): *Blood red*

FLESH COLOR(S): *Blood red*

SOLUBLE SOLIDS: *7 degrees Brix*

FLAVOR: *Excellent; sweet and luscious. Joan Dye Gussow, author of* This Organic Life, *wrote to me one summer: "Goldman's Italian American tomato is a stunner. They taste lovely to say nothing of how they LOOK. One plant in an urn is setting absolutely gigantic tomatoes."*

TEXTURE: *Reasonably firm; meaty, juicy, with beautiful veins*

BEST USE(S): *Multipurpose. Makes the creamiest tomato sauce.*

PLANT HABIT, LEAF TYPE, AND YIELD: *Indeterminate habit; regular leaf; high yield*

MATURITY: *Main crop*

ORIGIN: *First listed by yours truly in the 2006 Seed Savers Exchange yearbook*

SYNONYMS: *Similar to Franchi's Red Pear; Gransasso; Giant Pear Piriform; and Piriform*

I have an inexplicable urge to spread the seeds of this tomato near and far. Goldman's Italian American—voluptuous, red-ribbed, and very heavy in the hips—makes sauce as thick and rich as any tomato I've ever grown. Seed saved from a Costoluto Genovese (see page 48) look-alike found by me at a roadside grocery store near the Villa d'Este in Cernobbio, Italy, in 1999 yielded this *Poma amoris fructu rubro.* I named Goldman's Italian American for my father's grocery store in Brooklyn.

(a) Jersey Devil, (b) Old Ivory Egg, (c) Goldman's Italian American, (d, h) King Humbert, (e) Black Plum, (f) Opalka, (g) Orange Banana

JERSEY DEVIL *fig. 96a*

SIZE: *5¾" long by 3¼" wide*

WEIGHT: *13 ounces*

SHAPE: *Plum, tapered and pointy; comes in a wide range of shapes and sizes*

EXTERIOR COLOR(S): *Brownish red*

FLESH COLOR(S): *Brownish red*

SOLUBLE SOLIDS: *5½ degrees Brix*

FLAVOR: *Good; sweet and rich*

TEXTURE: *Firm; meaty, well marbled, and juicy*

BEST USE(S): *Sauce. Green fruits are said to make excellent pickles.*

PLANT HABIT, LEAF TYPE, AND YIELD: *Indeterminate habit; droopy leaves; high yield*

MATURITY: *Late crop*

ORIGIN: *Introduced as a novelty circa 1986 by the Tomato Seed Company, Metuchen, New Jersey. Presumably named for the legendary flying terror of the New Jersey Pine Barrens. The tomato was dropped from commercial production when the company closed its doors, then was reintroduced in 2000 by Tomato Growers Supply Company.*

SYNONYMS: *New Jersey Red Devil. Probably the same as Jersey Giant, which was reportedly wider, larger, and irregular in shape.*

SEED SOURCES: *Ap6, To1, To10*

The first "devilish" (pointed plum) tomato I know of was the Laketa, introduced by Glecklers Seedmen in 1957; the most beautiful is the slender Carrot (Blüm's). Jersey Devil is a more voluminous paste; the one I chose for the group shot is relatively small. I've had double-whammies weighing up to 1½ pounds; just a few of those will fill up a pot of sauce. Seedswoman Jan Blum might as well have been comparing Jersey Devil to San Marzano (see page 137) in 1988 when she said: "When this super-big sauce tomato is available, why do we mess around with these little dinky-dorf things?"

OLD IVORY EGG *fig. 96b; page 161, fig. 114g*

SIZE: *2½" long by 2" wide*

WEIGHT: *2½ ounces*

SHAPE: *Fig or plum*

EXTERIOR COLOR(S): *Yellow*

FLESH COLOR(S): *Yellow*

SOLUBLE SOLIDS: *7 degrees Brix*

FLAVOR: *Excellent; sweet and lemony*

TEXTURE: *Firm; meaty and juicy*

BEST USE(S): *Fresh eating; becomes watery and nondescript when cooked or canned. Well suited to cold greenhouses.*

PLANT HABIT, LEAF TYPE, AND YIELD: *Indeterminate habit; regular leaf; high yield*

MATURITY: *Early crop*

ORIGIN: *John M. Hartman of Hartman Daughters Seed Company, Indianapolis, was the first Seed Savers Exchange member to list Old Ivory Egg, in the 1985 yearbook. His seed came from Margaret Adkins in Australia via Donna and Paul Kline of Brooklyn Park, Minnesota. Cataloged as early as 1992 by Long Island Seed and Plant, Flanders, New York.*

SYNONYMS: *Australian Yellow Plum; Ivory Egg; Yellow Plum*

SEED SOURCES: *Ba8, Sa5, To1, To9*

A favorite yellow plum, about the size of a pullet's egg. When I included Old Ivory Egg in a Slow Food taste test at my home some years ago, the experts raved about the pear overtones and bright sweet flavor. It's the most fitting tomato for Open-Faced Tomato and Sunny-Side-Up Egg Sandwiches (see page 227).

BLACK PLUM *fig. 96e*

SIZE: *2" long by 1½" wide*

WEIGHT: *1½ ounces*

SHAPE: *Mini plum*

EXTERIOR COLOR(S): *Brownish violet*

FLESH COLOR(S): *Garnet red*

SOLUBLE SOLIDS: *7 degrees Brix*

FLAVOR: *Fair; bland, low acid; not a sugar plum*

TEXTURE: *Reasonably firm; well marbled for a small tomato; juicy*

BEST USE(S): *Fresh eating; decorative*

PLANT HABIT, LEAF TYPE, AND YIELD: *Indeterminate habit; regular leaf; high yield*

MATURITY: *Early crop*

ORIGIN: *From Russia, via Moscow seedswoman Marina Danilenko. Introduced in 1994 by Seed Savers International.*

SYNONYMS: *Plum Black*

SEED SOURCES: *Ag7, Bou, Co32, Ga22, Go8, Hi13, Ma18, Pr3, Ra6, Sa9, Se7, Se16, Se17, Sk2, So1, So9, So25, St18, Sw9, Syn, Ter, Te4, To1, To3, To9, To10, Und*

I always use Black Plums to gussy up my tomato gift baskets. They add an appealing touch of color, and their shape helps fill in some of the gaps in the jigsaw puzzle of beefsteaks, stuffers, and globes. Chef Paul Bertolli (formerly of Oliveto and Chez Panisse) makes Black Plum preserves—by simmering the tomatoes with water, brown and white sugars, and sliced lemons—as a topping for vanilla ice cream.

OPALKA *fig. 96f*

SIZE: *4½" long by 2½" wide*

WEIGHT: *7½ ounces*

SHAPE: *Plum, pointy and crooked*

EXTERIOR COLOR(S): *Blood red*

FLESH COLOR(S): *Cherry red*

SOLUBLE SOLIDS: *4 degrees Brix*

FLAVOR: *Excellent. "Very different when it initially hits the palate. That's how tomatoes taste in Romania," said Chef Mona Talbott in a blind taste test in my kitchen.*

TEXTURE: *Firm; fleshy*

BEST USE(S): *Makes savory sauce, soup, and purée*

PLANT HABIT, LEAF TYPE, AND YIELD: *Indeterminate habit; droopy foliage; high yield*

MATURITY: *Late crop*

ORIGIN: *First mentioned by Carolyn Male in the 1991 Seed Savers Exchange yearbook. Opalka was given to her by co-worker Carl Swidorski, who said the seed originated in Poland circa 1900.* Cataloged in 1994 by Terra Edibles, Thomasburg, Ontario. Became part of SSE's 1997 Polish Collection.

SYNONYMS: *Opalka Paste; Opalska; and Polish Torpedo*

SEED SOURCES: *Co32, He8, Jun, He17, Pin, Sa9, Se16, Sw9, Te4, To1, To3, To9, Up2*

An extraordinary cooking tomato with an intense, concentrated flavor. Makes one of the thickest dark-red sauces. Quite similar to Jersey Devil (see page 132) although somewhat smaller and juicier. Use it for the sauce for stuffed peppers and season with Polish heirloom Ambrozja Dill, or try it on Ricotta Ravioli with Tomato Sauce (see page 205).

ORANGE BANANA *fig. 96g*

SIZE: *3¼" long by 2" wide*

WEIGHT: *4½ ounces*

SHAPE: *Plum with nipple tip*

EXTERIOR COLOR(S): *Deep orange*

FLESH COLOR(S): *Deep orange*

SOLUBLE SOLIDS: *6 degrees Brix*

FLAVOR: *Excellent; a worthy rival of Flamme (see page 83)*

TEXTURE: *Reasonably firm; meaty*

BEST USE(S): *Cooking*

PLANT HABIT, LEAF TYPE, AND YIELD: *Indeterminate habit; droopy foliage; high yield*

MATURITY: *Early crop*

ORIGIN: *The original source was Moscow seedswoman Marina Danilenko. Introduced in 1996 by Seed Savers Exchange. Offered as part of SSE's Russian Collection in 1997. Orange Banana was the first orange banana-shaped tomato in SSE's collection.*

SYNONYMS: *Banana; Banantchik; Liane Orange*

SEED SOURCES: *Ag7, Ba8, Co32, Fe5, Go8, La1, Roh, Se16, Se17, So25, Ter, To1, To3, To9, Vi4*

Orange Bananas will make you swoon. I'd always admired them for their good looks, and they're serviceable in salad, but I never suspected how fruity and rich they'd be when oven roasted (see page 237), puréed, or made into Quick Tomato and Garlic Sauce (see page 239). CR Lawn of Fedco Seeds was also taken by surprise: "The proof is in the eating … [Orange Banana's] amazing sprightly sweet flavor, reminiscent of Sungold but with more depth and diverse tones, makes an ambrosial sauce."

KING HUMBERT *fig. 97; page 132, fig. 96d, h*

SIZE: *2¼" long by 1⅞" wide*

WEIGHT: *1¾ ounces*

SHAPE: *Varies from fig to pear, with slight longitudinal furrows. Has a constricted neck. Also described as fiaschetto or bottle-shaped.*

EXTERIOR COLOR(S): *Blood red*

FLESH COLOR(S): *Cherry red*

SOLUBLE SOLIDS: *5 degrees Brix*

FLAVOR: *Fair; bland*

TEXTURE: *Very firm; thick walls, dry and mealy*

BEST USE(S): *Winter storage. A synonymous variety, Wonder of Italy, cataloged by Sutton and Sons in 1901, was used in winter by Neapolitans: "The large clusters may always be seen hanging in shop windows." Used also for canned peeled tomatoes, purée, sauce, oven roasting, and as a topping for Pizza Margherita.*

PLANT HABIT, LEAF TYPE, AND YIELD: *Indeterminate habit; regular leaf; good yield*

MATURITY: *Main crop*

ORIGIN: *This tomato was named in honor of Umberto I, King of Italy, circa 1878. Umberto's consort, Queen Margherita, was the inspiration for the famous pizza (see the recipe for Pizza Margherita, page 207). The King Humbert tomato was introduced to the United States in 1884 by W. Atlee Burpee and Company: "This new Tomato, which we secured the past summer from an Italian grower, will prove of value to family gardens. It is pear-shaped, 2 to 2½ inches long, by 1¼ to 1½ inches wide, and of a beautiful rich red color, with very few seeds; they grow 6 to 8 fruits in a cluster. The plant is quite dwarf and compact, and is very prolific, being literally covered with fruits. The tomatoes have no hard cores and are of delicious flavor. The flavor is quite distinct—being a rich, fruity, apple flavor—and the originator tells us they make 'good apple sauce.'" Two years into distribution, Burpee's summed up the response: "liked by many, while by others it is considered 'of no account.'"*

On November 8, 1884, the Rural New-Yorker, *evidently among its fans, offered free seeds of the King Humbert tomato to every subscriber who applied, with this enticement: "Sometimes resembles a pear, sometimes a red pepper; never the ordinary tomato. The flavor is nearly free of acid. It grows in clusters of from three to eight, and is remarkably productive. For preserving, or for pickles, there is probably no other tomato that will prove more popular. Our seeds were imported from France."*

Presumably Elbert S. Carman, editor of the Rural New-Yorker, *imported his seeds from Vilmorin-Andrieux in Paris. Vilmorin said in 1883: "In southern Europe, especially near Naples, a great number of pear-shaped tomatoes are grown." Two years later, the English editor of Vilmorin's* Vegetable Garden *provided a full description of King Humbert: "This variety, which is very probably derived from the Pear-shaped Tomato, is distinguished by its rather peculiar form and appearance. The fruit, which grows in clusters of from five to ten, is of a pretty regular ovoid shape, but is frequently flattened on four sides, so that a section of it, especially near the end, presents a nearly square outline."*

SYNONYMS: *Chiswick Red; Fiascone; Fiascone di Napoli; König Humbert; Koenig Humbert; Königs Humbert Scharlachrote Tomate; Re Umberto; Roi Humbert; Tomate de Malte à grappes; Tomate Éclipse; Tomate Merveille d'Italie; Tomate Roi Humbert; Umberto; Wonder of Italy. Similar to the longer and more pyriform Di Nocera; Fiascetta; Fiaschetta di Nocera; Fiaschella di Nocera. Also similar to Barese or Prugna. Shares certain features with Principe Borghese. Not the same as Sempre Fruttifero (Semper Fructifera or Pomodoro di tutto l'anno), a red pear-shaped tomato, which was also used as a winter preserving tomato (Zago, 1913). Not the same as San Marzano.*

Debbie Crowe's pink Umberto Pear, described in the Seed Savers Exchange 1990 yearbook, is not the same as Re Umberto. As Crowe says, it was "brought to America over fifty years ago by David Umberto from Italy who gave seed to his mailman, the late Keith Roberts, of Greencastle, Indiana. The seeds were passed to Jim Black, who has kept them twenty-five years and says he and his friends eat them like popcorn. Indescribably delicious and may be a long-lost heirloom."

NY: *Nee & Goldman 54641*

SEED SOURCES: *Sa5, Sa9, Sk2*

The King Humbert or Re Umberto tomato derives its importance less from its association with royalty than from of its pivotal role in the development of the San Marzano (see page 137). Its distinctive oblong shape—longer than it is broad, and more squared and flattened than rounded—is a short remove from the fig or pear tomato (see Red Pear, page 144). The coincidentally named Filippo Re described three varieties of Italian "Pomidoro" in 1811: Schiacciato, Peretto, and Globoso (McCue, 1952). Tomato historian David Gentilcore, at Leicester University in England, told me that Re's description of *peretto* tomatoes (small, thin-skinned, prolific, and more yellow than red) is probably the earliest reference to the pear or pyriform shape in Italian tomatoes.

King Humbert is an "interregnal" (that is, transitional) form between the Red Pear and the rectilinear San Marzano. It can, therefore, be regarded as ancestral to most modern plum tomatoes developed for industry. Like any landrace or primitive variety developed through serendipitous crossing and selection by amateurs, Re Umberto reflects the people and culture of the times—in this case, nineteenth-century Italy. The rustic *frutto a fiaschetto*—small flask- or bottle-shaped fruit—is ideal as a storage tomato. The smooth elongated shape allows for easy peeling: after steaming or scalding, grasp the tomato with two hands and the skin will slip right off. In addition, its small size and extra-firm, dry flesh, along with the vivid color of its pulp, make it well suited for canning and preserving. Come autumn, Neapolitans harvested entire plants or late-maturing vines covered with immature tomatoes to suspend them, sheltered from the rain, for slow ripening. The tomatoes often lasted until the beginning of the following spring (Vilmorin, 1891, 1925), keeping the home cook well supplied with an essential ingredient. San Marzano has all of King Humbert's fine qualities in spades—without some of its flaws, such as variability in shape (reversion to the pear) and uneven ripening (green shoulders). Re Umberto has another fine quality: adaptability. It produces well over a wide geographical range, is often grown without support and, further, succeeds on some of the poor soils and marginal areas of southern Italy—where San Marzano fails. I'd say that makes our *vecchia varietà*, King Humbert, a valuable genetic resource for plant breeders. As Cary Fowler said in his seminal work *Shattering* (1990), "Without the landraces and wild relatives, our modern crop varieties would be incapable of changing, of evolving, of adapting to new conditions, or stronger pests. Like so many things in this world, the new depends on the old. Without the old varieties, the new varieties could not continue. They simply could not survive. And herein lies the irony. In the long run, the future of agriculture and the very survival of crops depend not so much on the fancy hybrids we see in the fields, but on the wild species growing along the fence rows, and the primitive types tended by the world's peasant farmers in the centers of diversity."

Although King Humbert was superceded by San Marzano in the commercial production of *pelati* by 1940, it is still cultivated in Italy by home gardeners as a storage variety—and in upstate New York by me, both for nostalgia value and for sauce.

SAN MARZANO *fig. 98*

SIZE: *3¼" long by 1¾" wide*

WEIGHT: *2 ounces*

SHAPE: *Rectangular plum with some constriction at the neck (stem end)*

EXTERIOR COLOR(S): *Blood red*

FLESH COLOR(S): *Cherry red*

SOLUBLE SOLIDS: *5¼ degrees Brix*

FLAVOR: *Too bland for fresh eating but excellent in a can. Do the geometry: two-loculed elongated fruits fit better than round fruits and leave less empty space. Takes garlic like a dream.*

TEXTURE: *The flesh or pulp is extra firm, dry, and meaty, with high solids and good viscosity. Withstands scalding and is easy to peel.*

BEST USE(S): *Canning. Pelati. San Marzano ripens completely and uniformly to a beautiful red color, holds well on and off the vine and, although it requires some TLC in the form of staking and irrigation, it's almost impervious to cracking and produces well. Can be mixed with more watery tomatoes to improve the quality of canned products and increase the total solids. Makes a good Marinara Sauce or Oven-Roasted Tomatoes (see pages 238 and 237). For canning and processing, there's almost nothing it can't do.*

PLANT HABIT, LEAF TYPE, AND YIELD: *Indeterminate habit; regular leaf foliage; high yield*

MATURITY: *Main crop*

ORIGIN: *San Marzano reportedly originated in the Fiano region of southern Italy between Sarno and lower Nocera (Baldoni, 1940), but it was later named for a particular town where it flourished. This tomato was introduced commercially circa 1926. Fratelli Sgaravatti, of Saonara, Italy, offered San Marzano in their autumn 1926 catalog; and Fratelli Ingegnoli, of Milan, Italy, cataloged it in 1927. By 1930, the tomato had reached the American heartland: De-Giorgi Brothers of Council Bluffs, Iowa, cataloged the San Marzano as "medium sized, lemon shaped, red tomato, extremely meaty and superior for canning, peeling, drying, preserving, for tomato paste and catsup. Immensely productive, growing in clusters of 15 to 30 tomatoes. Medium early." (The fratelli DeGiorgi were no strangers to San Marzano: In 1930 they also offered the Goose Egg tomato, their own unfixed hybrid between Marglobe (see page 66) and San Marzano; the Goose Egg looked remarkably like Roma (1955), which also has San Marzano in its parentage.)*

SYNONYMS: *Italian Canner; Italian Paste Tomato; Italian Pear Tomato; Pomodoro; S. Marzano; San Marzana; Sammarzano; Sanmarzano; Tomate San Marzano. Shares certain features with Fiascone, Fiaschetta, Lampadina, Vesuvius (Vesuvio), and Patanara (considered inferior to San Marzano by Baldoni in 1940). There are many strains of San Marzano including San Marzano, Large Fruited Strain (1937); San Marzano Thick Type; San Marzano Nano; Super Marzano; Scatalone; San Marzano Redorta; Marzano Big Red, and many F₁ hybrids too numerous to mention. Resembles Dix Doigts de Naples (Ten Fingers of Naples), Hungarian Italian (see page 130), and others. Parent to scores of others including its most famous offspring: Roma (Pan America x San Marzano x Red Top). Not the same as King Humbert (Re Umberto).*

SEED SOURCES: *Abu, Ag7, Bo17, Bo19, But, Coo, Ha26, He8, He17, Hi6, Hi13, Hum, Mo20, Na6, Pe2, Ra6, Re8, Roh, Sa5, Sa9, Se7, Se25, Sh9, Sto, So25, Sw9, Te4, To1, To3, To9, To10, Tu6, Up2*

San Marzano has "great bones"; it's rectilinear yet curvaceous, with hallmark furrows along the locule walls and a neck that is tapered or somewhat constricted. It looks like King Humbert (see page 134) all grown up. Vilmorin said something similar of San Marzano in 1946, except in French: "Related to King Humbert, fruits parallelepipedic [rectangular] with rounded corners." Remigio Baldoni (1940) concluded that San Marzano was probably the result of a recent cross or spontaneous hybridization of Fiascone (King Humbert) and Fiaschetta (a furrowless rounded cylindrical tomato). The scientific evidence is consistent with the idea that the neck-constricted King Humbert was a parent of San Marzano: Acciarri and others in Italy have discovered that the original lines of San Marzano "carry the ovate gene in its mutated form which confers neck constriction, while most modern F₁ hybrids resembling San Marzano do not."

In my view, San Marzano is not only a bigger and better Fiascone; it is the most important industrial tomato of the twentieth century. Beginning in the 1920s, it was the pomodoro perfetto in Italy for the manufacture and export of peeled whole canned tomatoes.

And it was the tomato that took the California canning industry by storm—thanks to my cousin Tillie Lewis and her partner Florindo Del Gaizo. San Marzano's influence is still huge, although the original open-pollinated standard San Marzano, which you see here, has been supplanted by similar varieties such as the Lampedina, larger-fruited and more straight-necked selections, and hybrid forms that are smoother or more uniformly cylindrical. Tomato breeder Dick Robinson tells me that San Marzano is probably in the parentage of most if not all plum-shaped tomatoes bred in the United States.

By the beginning of the twentieth century in Italy, with the development of small family-owned canneries, tax breaks for canners, and new methods of production, the tomato had assumed a new role as an industrial crop (Zago, 1913). But it was always exports that fueled the fire. Historian David Gentilcore finds it ironic that the San Marzano, developed primarily for export to Anglo-Saxon countries and northern Europe, is now fervently embraced by Italians as an essential component of their traditional Italian cuisine. The San Marzano is the object of a preservation campaign by Slow Food Italy and, furthermore, the San Marzano "type" (including F₁ hybrids) is protected by a special appellation from the European Union: D. O. P. or *Denominazione di Origine Protetta*. San Marzano is *oro rosso*—and it deserves every one of the honors heaped on it in recent years.

99

ANNA RUSSIAN *fig. 99*

SIZE: *3¾" long by 3¾" wide*

WEIGHT: *1 pound*

SHAPE: *Plum*

EXTERIOR COLOR(S): *Tomato pink*

FLESH COLOR(S): *Tomato pink*

SOLUBLE SOLIDS: *5¼ degrees Brix*

FLAVOR: *Excellent; nice tang, mildly sweet and savory*

TEXTURE: *Soft; meaty*

BEST USE(S): *Cooking*

PLANT HABIT, LEAF TYPE, AND YIELD: *Indeterminate habit; droopy leaves; fair yield*

MATURITY: *Very early crop*

ORIGIN: *Brenda Getty Hillenius of Corvallis, Oregon, introduced Anna Russian to members of Seed Savers Exchange in 1990, after vetting it with North Carolina tomatoman Craig LeHouillier. Brenda's grandfather, Kenneth Wilcox, got his seed from a Russian immigrant who had acquired it from relatives back home. Anna Russian was brought to market in 1996 by Southern Exposure Seed Exchange.*

SYNONYMS: *Anna; Anna's Russian; and Anna Russian Paste*

SEED SOURCES: *Ap6, Ers, He8, Ma18, Re8, Sa9, Se28, So25, To1, To3, To9, To10, Vi4*

Seeing Anna Russian in my garden is like greeting an old friend. I'd know her anywhere—even before fruits have formed—by the foliage, which is finely cut and droopy. Later in the season, as the leaves turn to brown, Anna yields tomatoes that are perfectly suited to heartwarming soups and sauces.

PURPLE RUSSIAN *fig. 100*

SIZE: *3" long by 2½" wide*

WEIGHT: *6 ounces*

SHAPE: *Plum*

EXTERIOR COLOR(S): *Violet brown*

FLESH COLOR(S): *Violet brown, cardinal red, and blood red*

SOLUBLE SOLIDS: *5 degrees Brix*

FLAVOR: *Excellent*

TEXTURE: *Reasonably firm*

BEST USE(S): *Multipurpose*

PLANT HABIT, LEAF TYPE, AND YIELD: *Indeterminate habit; droopy foliage; high yield*

MATURITY: *Early crop*

ORIGIN: *Dr. Frederick Ineman, a biologist from Ravenna, Ohio, introduced this variety to the Seed Savers Exchange in 1999. Ineman's wife, Monika, and her mother, Vera Jermolenko, had come to the United States in 1950 from a displaced-persons camp in Ukraine. The seed was sent to them from the old country in 1980 by Aunt Irma Henkel, whom Dr. Ineman identifies as his mother-in-law's sister-in-law.*

NY: *Nee & Goldman 53393*

SEED SOURCES: *Ba8, Co32, He8, Ma18, Ra6, Roh, Se16, Se17, So25, Te4, To1, To9, Up2, Vi5*

A tomato worth living for.

100

POLISH LINGUISA *fig. 101f*

SIZE: *5¾″ long by 2¾″ wide*

WEIGHT: *12 ounces*

SHAPE: *Plum, pointed*

EXTERIOR COLOR(S): *Cherry red*

FLESH COLOR(S): *Cherry red*

SOLUBLE SOLIDS: *6½ degrees Brix*

FLAVOR: *Good; sweet and savory*

TEXTURE: *Firm; meaty*

BEST USE(S): *Cooking; excels in sauces, soups, and stews; tastes grassy when roasted*

PLANT HABIT, LEAF TYPE, AND YIELD: *Indeterminate habit; droopy foliage; high yield*

MATURITY: *Main crop*

ORIGIN: *A fellow in Rochester, New York, hoping to keep his 100-year-old family heirloom alive, sent "Polish" to tomato breeder Jim Waltrip at Petoseed Company in Saticoy, California, whence it was distributed. Waltrip, now semiretired and living in Des Moines, Iowa, told me the tomato was renamed in a Petoseed office contest by a young woman who equated it with a Portuguese* linguiça *sausage. Cataloged in 2002 by Nichols Garden Nursery.*

SYNONYMS: *Polish; Polish Sausage. Not the same as Polish Paste.*

NY: *Nee & Goldman 53409*

SEED SOURCES: *Coo, Ers, Go8, Ni1, Pin, Ra6, Sh9, Shu, Sk2, To1, To3*

"Tastes so good you may not care to add salt," says Rose Marie Nichols McGee, whose family seed company has been serving home gardeners for more than fifty years. I'm in total accord. Polish Linguisa makes a top-notch sauce and is ideal in Curried Meatballs with Tomatoes (see page 196)—with or without the salt.

UKRAINIAN PEAR *fig. 101c*

SIZE: *2½″ long by 2½″ wide*

WEIGHT: *4 ounces*

SHAPE: *Fig*

EXTERIOR COLOR(S): *Tomato pink*

FLESH COLOR(S): *Tomato pink*

SOLUBLE SOLIDS: *5½ degrees Brix*

FLAVOR: *Good*

TEXTURE: *Reasonably firm; thick-walled and meaty*

BEST USE(S): *Multipurpose*

PLANT HABIT, LEAF TYPE, AND YIELD: *Indeterminate habit; regular leaf; good yield*

MATURITY: *Early crop*

ORIGIN: *Dr. James A. Wolfe of Rogersville, Tennessee, was responsible for bringing this Ukrainian tomato (and many others) into the Seed Savers Exchange. The seed had been given to Dr. Wolfe in 1995 by his "wife's sister's boy," Scott Smith. Scott met and married a Ukrainian woman named Yana while serving in the Peace Corps in Yalta; the seed came from Yana's plant-breeding stepfather. Commercialized in 2002 by Tomato Growers Supply Company.*

NY: *Nee & Goldman 53396*

SEED SOURCES: *To1, To9*

A variety favored by many—including James Wolfe, who says it's probably his best all-around tomato. Gourmands gobbled it up at one of my Rhinebeck Farmers' Market taste tests. A typical comment: "It has the perfect sweet flavor with a texture to match."

AMISH PASTE *fig. 101i*

SIZE: *3¼″ long by 3½″ wide*

WEIGHT: *12 ounces*

SHAPE: *Plump plum; shape varies, sometimes grouped with the oxhearts*

EXTERIOR COLOR(S): *Cherry red*

FLESH COLOR(S): *Cherry red*

SOLUBLE SOLIDS: *6½ degrees Brix*

FLAVOR: *Excellent*

TEXTURE: *Firm; meaty and juicy*

BEST USE(S): *Anything goes. Makes a delicious tomato sauce, on the light red side.*

PLANT HABIT, LEAF TYPE, AND YIELD: *Indeterminate habit; droopy foliage; good yield*

MATURITY: *Early crop*

ORIGIN: *Thane Earle of Whitewater, Wisconsin, first listed it in the 1987 Seed Savers Exchange yearbook. Amish Paste was scooped up and commercialized by the man best known for reintroducing Red Brandywine (see page 106), Tom Hauch of Heirloom Seeds. Tom acquired this tomato from the Amish near Lancaster, Pennsylvania; his informant said the variety came from Amish farmers in Medford, Wisconsin. Landis Valley Museum in Lancaster, Pennsylvania, was an early adopter; their seed came from Tom Hauch.*

SEED SOURCES: *Ag7, Ap6, Ba8, Be4, Bou, Coo, Co32, Ers, Fe5, Ga1, Go8, Gr27, He8, He17, Hi6, Hud, Jun, Lan, Mo13, Pe2, Pe6, Ra6, Ri2, Roh, Sa9, Se7, Se16, Se17, Se28, Shu, Sk2, So1, So25, Te4, To1, To3, To10, Und, Up2, We19, Yu2*

Amish Paste's rich, sweet flavor, meaty texture, and versatility in the kitchen have made it a favorite for me, and for just about every other member of Seed Savers Exchange, for the past twenty years. Slow Food USA, whose mission is to save cherished foods, agrees that this tomato is worth preserving: Amish Paste was recently boarded on their Ark of Taste, where I know it's headed for stardom.

ROMAN CANDLE *fig. 101a; page 161, fig. 114j*

SIZE: *4″ long by 1¾″ wide*

WEIGHT: *4½ ounces*

SHAPE: *Plum, candle-shaped, with a beak or "wick" at the distal end*

EXTERIOR COLOR(S): *Signal yellow*

FLESH COLOR(S): *Light yellow*

SOLUBLE SOLIDS: *6¼ degrees Brix*

FLAVOR: *Good to excellent*

TEXTURE: *Very firm; waxy on the outside, meaty on the inside*

BEST USE(S): *Cooking*

PLANT HABIT, LEAF TYPE, AND YIELD: *Indeterminate habit; droopy foliage; good yield*

MATURITY: *Main crop*

ORIGIN: *Roman Candle was derived from John Swenson's Speckled Roman (a fortuitous cross between Antique Roman and Banana Legs, see pages 128 and 163), then selected and stabilized by Jeff Nekola and Sue Gronholtz. The new variety was initially offered to Seed Savers Exchange members in the 2000 annual yearbook; two years later, Roman Candle was commercialized in SSE's public catalog.*

SYNONYMS: *Not the same as the Christmas Candle or Yellow Candle developed by Long Island Seed and Plant Company; Roman Candle is bright yellow and tapered like a candle flame, too, but the fruit, only 1½ inches long, is borne on 10-inch-high dwarf rugose mounds.*

NY: *Nee & Goldman 53418*

SEED SOURCES: *Ag7, Ba8, Go8, La1, Ra6, Sa9, Se16, So25, To3, To9, Vi5*

I'm as enthusiastic about this tomato as is environmental biologist Jeff Nekola, who wrote in the 2000 yearbook about these "spectacular, 2 x 4", smooth, sausage shaped fruits with screaming yellow skin." The color, unique among paste tomatoes, is signal yellow—like yellow traffic lights—which is the "psychological mean" between signal green and signal red. Even if there are no fireworks, Roman Candle definitely stops traffic. I'm not usually one for yellow tomato sauces, but Roman Candle sauce (see Tomato Sauce, page 238) is exquisite on squid-ink pasta.

(a) Roman Candle, (b) Black Pear, (c) Ukrainian Pear, (d) Grandma Mary's, (e) Yellow Bell, (f) Polish Linguisa, (g) Long Tom, (h) Vilms, (i) Amish Paste

BLACK PEAR *page 140, fig. 101b*

SIZE: *3" long by 3½" wide*

WEIGHT: *8 ounces*

SHAPE: *Fig*

EXTERIOR COLOR(S): *Reddish brown and garnet brown*

FLESH COLOR(S): *Reddish brown and brownish red*

SOLUBLE SOLIDS: *6 degrees Brix*

FLAVOR: *Fair; high acid*

TEXTURE: *Relatively firm*

BEST USE(S): *Fresh eating*

PLANT HABIT, LEAF TYPE, AND YIELD: *Indeterminate habit; potato leaf; good yield*

MATURITY: *Main crop*

ORIGIN: *Introduced commercially in 1998 by Glenn Drowns of Sand Hill Preservation Center. Black Pear was part of the loot Glenn received several years earlier from Moldova via* Seed to Seed *author Suzanne Ashworth.*

NY: *Nee & Goldman 53449*

SEED SOURCES: *He17, Ma18, Sa9, To1, To10*

Black Pear has remarkable nuances of red and brown. It's shaped like Ukrainian Pear except smoother; both are more fig than pear. When cooked on the stovetop, the outer walls of Black Pear become greener, and like most blacks, this tomato smacks of green bell pepper in looks and piquancy. This is cause for indigestion for me—but perhaps rejoicing for you.

GRANDMA MARY'S *page 140, fig. 101d*

SIZE: *4⅝" long by 2¼" wide*

WEIGHT: *6 ounces*

SHAPE: *Plum*

EXTERIOR COLOR(S): *Scarlet*

FLESH COLOR(S): *Crayfish red*

SOLUBLE SOLIDS: *4 degrees Brix*

FLAVOR: *Fair to good; low acid and low sugar*

TEXTURE: *Firm; meaty, dry*

BEST USE(S): *Cooking and canning*

PLANT HABIT, LEAF TYPE, AND YIELD: *Indeterminate habit; regular leaf; good yield*

MATURITY: *Main crop*

ORIGIN: *Introduced in 1992 by Fedco Seeds*

SYNONYMS: *Grandma Mary's Paste. Not the same as High Mowing's Aunt Mary's Paste (a determinate oblong plum) or Gail's Sweet Plum Tomato (a mini plum named for the late seed saver Gail*

Cunningham Bailey; it was mislabeled as Grandma Mary's Italian Paste in 2005 by Sand Hill Preservation Center).

NY: *Nee & Goldman 53411*

SEED SOURCES: *Fe5, To1*

Grandma Mary's is similar to Roma and many other small oblong plums derived from San Marzano (see page 137), the quintessential Italian canner. She's well suited for canning or as the base for sauces, soups, and salsas; what she lacks in richness of flavor is easily corrected with a little salt, sugar, and oregano or parsley.

VILMS *page 140, fig. 101h*

SIZE: *2½" long by 2½" wide*

WEIGHT: *4 ounces*

SHAPE: *Miniature plum*

EXTERIOR COLOR(S): *Blood red*

FLESH COLOR(S): *Blood red*

SOLUBLE SOLIDS: *6 degrees Brix*

FLAVOR: *Excellent*

TEXTURE: *Firm*

BEST USE(S): *Multipurpose*

PLANT HABIT, LEAF TYPE, AND YIELD: *Indeterminate habit; regular leaf; high yield*

MATURITY: *Early crop*

ORIGIN: *The initial listing was made in 1986 by Glenn Drowns in the Seed Savers Exchange yearbook. His seed source was Lars Olov Rosenstrom of Bromma, Sweden. Vilms has been carried almost singlehandedly by Glenn's Sand Hill Preservation Center for the last dozen years.*

SYNONYMS: *Similar to the Red Plum described 150 years ago by Fearing Burr (1863)*

SEED SOURCES: *Sa9*

A sweet, fruity, and well-marbled plum, made even more delicious by the application of heat: oven roast it (see recipe, page 237).

YELLOW BELL *page 140, fig. 101e; page 161, fig. 114i*

SIZE: *3½" long by 2¼" wide*

WEIGHT: *4½ ounces*

SHAPE: *Plum*

EXTERIOR COLOR(S): *Yellow*

FLESH COLOR(S): *Light yellow*

SOLUBLE SOLIDS: *6 degrees Brix*

FLAVOR: *Good; mildly sweet*

TEXTURE: *Very firm; meaty*

BEST USE(S): *Multipurpose. Introducer Jeff McCormack said in 1986 that the variety is good for tomato paste, juice, preserves, and yellow ketchup. Adapted to cool and wet conditions.*

PLANT HABIT, LEAF TYPE, AND YIELD: *Indeterminate habit; regular leaf; high yield*

MATURITY: *Main crop*

ORIGIN: *Said to be an old-time Tennessee family heirloom. Introduced in 1986 by Southern Exposure Seed Exchange.*

SYNONYMS: *May be the same as Peace Yellow Paste (Yellow Gold) described by Ken Ettlinger in 1992 as "a yellow version of San Marzano."*

SEED SOURCES: *Sa9, So1, So25, Te4, To1, Up2*

Yellow Bell closely resembles a thoroughly modern yellow San Marzano.

ELFIN *page 25, fig. 6r*

SIZE: *1½" long by 1⅛" wide*

WEIGHT: *19.31 grams*

SHAPE: *Mini plum*

EXTERIOR COLOR(S): *Brownish red*

FLESH COLOR(S): *Brownish red*

SOLUBLE SOLIDS: *8½ degrees Brix*

FLAVOR: *Excellent; fruity and sweet*

TEXTURE: *Very firm*

BEST USE(S): *Multipurpose*

PLANT HABIT, LEAF TYPE, AND YIELD: *Determinate habit; regular leaf; high yield*

MATURITY: *Very early crop*

ORIGIN: *Cataloged in 2001 by Tomato Growers Supply Company*

SYNONYMS: *Similar to many other grape tomatoes on the market*

NY: *Nee & Goldman 53410*

SEED SOURCES: *To1, To9*

The Elfin plant is a tomato machine, generating masses of "grapes" or mini-plum tomatoes. Fruits are even sweeter when grown in containers, but productivity falls way off. Resembles the mini plums of yore, which were not nearly as sweet. The first modern grape tomato in commerce, Santa F_1 (with an indeterminate growth habit; bred by Known-You Seed Company in Taiwan), was slow to gain acceptance. Rob Johnston Jr., proprietor of Johnny's Selected Seeds, flipped over these from the start. Now grape tomatoes are favored by many over cherries. I find them tough and unyielding; peel me a grape tomato.

LONG TOM *page 140, fig. 101g*

SIZE: *6" long by 2" wide*

WEIGHT: *6½ ounces*

SHAPE: *Plum, tapered and pointy; some "deformed" (double-width)*

EXTERIOR COLOR(S): *Cherry red*

FLESH COLOR(S): *Cherry red*

SOLUBLE SOLIDS: *5½ degrees Brix*

FLAVOR: *Good*

TEXTURE: *Firm; meaty, little juice*

BEST USE(S): *Multipurpose. Breeder Elwyn Meader loved this shape. Talking about a similar tomato named 1 x 6 in a 1983 interview, he told Kent Whealy: "Take a knife and cut it into four pieces lengthwise. It's just the right size to keep on a slice of bread. Put whatever else you want, another piece of bread on top, and you've got a sandwich for Sunday night supper."*

PLANT HABIT, LEAF TYPE, AND YIELD: *Indeterminate habit; droopy leaves; good yield*

MATURITY: *Main crop*

ORIGIN: *Cataloged in 1976 by Ben Quisenberry: "Unique and rare. 5 inches long, 2 inches across. Very few seeds and little acid." Ben acquired the seed from an unnamed friend in Pennsylvania.*

SYNONYMS: *Similar to many other long Italian plums (sometimes called "banana" or "pepper" tomatoes) but rare in the United States until introduced by Quisenberry in 1976.*

NY: *Nee & Goldman 53428*

SEED SOURCES: *Ag7, Coo, Sa9, Se16, So1*

I have a wonderful taped interview, recorded in 1981, in which seedsman Ben Quisenberry tells "Mr. Tomato," John Gorman of Texas, how much he prized this "dandy salad tomata." His customers were mad for it, too. Of the dozen or so varieties he offered each year, Ben said he had "the most call" for Long Tom. Try Long Tom in Fattoush, a dandy Middle Eastern salad (see page 198).

RED PEAR page 4, fig. 1f; page 25, fig. 6b

SIZE: *1½" long by 1" wide*

WEIGHT: *17.03 grams*

SHAPE: *Pear*

EXTERIOR COLOR(S): *Blood red*

FLESH COLOR(S): *Blood red*

SOLUBLE SOLIDS: *7 degrees Brix*

FLAVOR: *Fair; high acid. What you might call "good old-fashioned flavor."*

TEXTURE: *Firm; seedy*

BEST USE(S): *Multipurpose; for pickles when green and preserves when ripe. Use for balance with sweet or bland fruits in a mixed cherry tomato salad.*

PLANT HABIT, LEAF TYPE, AND YIELD: *Indeterminate habit; regular leaf; high yield*

MATURITY: *Very early crop*

ORIGIN: *The earliest color illustration I've found is Vilmorin's 1857 plate No. 8 of Tomate poire or Love apple pear Shaped, although red pear-shaped tomatoes were noted by Filippo Re in Itay in 1811. Fearing Burr Jr. described a Fig-Tomato or Red Pear-shaped Tomato thus in 1863: "A small, red, pyriform or pear-shaped sort, measuring from an inch and a quarter to an inch and a half in length, and nearly an inch in its broadest diameter. Flesh pale-red, or pink, very solid and compact, and generally completely filling the centre of the fruit. Like the Plum-tomato, it is remarkably uniform in size, and also in shape; but it is little used except for preserving, other larger varieties being considered more economical for stewing, making catchup [sic], and like purposes."*

SYNONYMS: *The same as or similar to Austin's Red Pear; Birnförmige rothe Tomate; Fig; Fig-Shaped; Fig-Tomato; Love apple pear Shaped; Pear; Pear Red; Pear-shaped Red; Poire rouge; Red Fig; Red Pear-shaped; Tomate Poire. New Hampshire Red Pickling Tomato, early and determinate, is a cross of Red Pear with Fargo Yellow Pear: "One can pick a thousand tomatoes of pickling size per plant at one time," reported the New Hampshire Agricultural Experiment Station in 1957.*

NY: *Nee & Goldman 53479 (Red Fig) and 53501*

SEED SOURCES: *Ag7, Bo19, Co32, Coo, Ers, Ha26, He8, He17, Hi6, Hi13, Ho12, La1, Mi12, Or10, Pin, Ra6, Roh, Sa9, Se24, Se26, Sk2, So25, Te4, To1, To3, To10, Up2, Vi4, Yu2*

The Red Pear and Yellow Pear (see next entry) are in a class of their own, distinguished by their elegant elongated shape and long slender neck. These are more or less similar in shape to Burr's fig tomato. The traditional Fig-Tomato was defined by its usage more than its shape, which was variable.

For those with a sweet tooth, here's the recipe for "tomato-figs" from Mrs. Eliza Marsh, which Burr cited in *The Field and Garden Vegetables of America*: "Pour boiling water over the tomatoes, in order to remove the skin; after which, weigh, and place in a stone jar, with as much sugar as tomatoes, and let them stand two days; then pour off the sirup, and boil and skim it till no scum rises; pour it over the tomatoes, and let them stand two days as before; then boil, and skim again. After the third time, they are fit to dry, if the weather is good; if not, let them stand in the sirup until drying weather. Then place them on large earthen plates, or dishes, and put them in the sun to dry, which will take about a week; after which, pack them down in small wooden boxes, with fine, white sugar between every layer. Tomatoes prepared in this manner will keep for years."

For those with less of a sweet tooth, Slow Food USA recommends that the similar Red Fig be eaten either solo or in contemporary jams and chutneys. Red Fig was recently boarded onto Slow Food's Ark of Taste in recognition of its cultural and culinary importance.

YELLOW PEAR page 25, fig. 6i; page 27, fig. 7a; page 161, fig. 114b

SIZE: *1¾" long by 1" wide*

WEIGHT: *15.55 grams*

SHAPE: *Pear*

EXTERIOR COLOR(S): *Signal yellow*

FLESH COLOR(S): *Light yellow*

SOLUBLE SOLIDS: *6½ degrees Brix*

FLAVOR: *Fair; mild*

TEXTURE: *Firm; waxy skin*

BEST USE(S): *Multipurpose. Henry Fields said in his 1923 catalog that "of all the small tomatoes for preserving or for sweet pickles, probably the best one is the Yellow Pear." Seedswoman Jan Blum said in 1986 that Yellow Pear was "the life of the salad."*

PLANT HABIT, LEAF TYPE, AND YIELD: *Indeterminate habit; regular leaf; high yield*

MATURITY: *Very early crop*

ORIGIN: *May be the same as the yellow peretto documented by Filippo Re in Italy in 1811. This was described as small, thin-skinned, and prolific; più giallo che rosso (more yellow than red) which probably signifies that yellow pears were more common than red. Cataloged by James J. H. Gregory of Marblehead, Massachusetts, in 1863 as Yellow Fig and described as pear-shaped and used for preserves. Fearing Burr Jr described the Yellow Pear-Shaped Tomato or Yellow Fig that same year as "a sub-variety of the Red Pear-shaped, with a clear, semi-transparent, yellow skin and yellow flesh … it is little used except for preserving and pickling." Vilmorin noted in 1883 that there were various strains of Yellow Pear differing in size and maturity.*

SYNONYMS: *Similar to or the same as Fig; Pear-shaped Yellow; Poire jaune; Yellow Fig; Yellow Fig-tomato; Yellow Pear-Shaped. Not the same as Yellow Plum. Similar to Fargo Yellow Pear introduced in 1934 by Oscar H. Will and Company of Bismarck, North Dakota. Will wrote: "In this new sort Professor A. F. Yeager has combined the earliness and self-pruning habit of his Bison Tomato [see page 80] with typical Yellow Pear fruit to produce a much earlier and heavier yield on a given area of ground [determinate habit]."*

SEED SOURCES: *All, Be4, Bo17, Bo19, Bou, Bu2, Bu8, Co32, Com, Coo, Ers, Fis, Ga1, Ga22, Gr27, He8, He17, Hi6, Hi13, Hum, Jo1, Jor, Jun, La1, Mo13, Na6, Ni1, Or10, Pin, Pla, Pr3, Ra6, Roh, Sa9, Se7, Se17, Se26, Shu, Sk2, So1, So9, So25, Sw9, Syn, Te4, Ter, To1, To3, To9, To10, Vi4, We19, Wi2, Yu2*

Yellow Pear is a favorite of Kent Whealy, the cofounder of the Seed Savers Exchange. In 1975, he offered the variety to others in the inaugural yearbook, which consisted of seven typewritten pages with queries and seed offers from charter members. In retrospect, that first year's typescript seems both folksy and poignant, like an old homemade quilt. In it, Kent wrote: "The 'True Seed Exchange' is a reality. A small one, but at least it's off the ground … I personally find that gardening is one of the most rewarding things I've ever done. Good healthful food for my family is invaluable … Seeds have always seemed really magical to me. They are so little, but they contain such energy … I want the idea to grow because I believe in it … This year I'll have the following seeds to trade. Okra (gumbo), Yellow Pear Tomatoes, Radishes (red and white), Zucchini Squash, Banana Muskmelon, Yucca seed and Grandpa Ott's Morning Glories (small purple with red star in center)." Talk about seed power: In 1975 the organization had twenty-nine members and today there are more than seven thousand.

CHILE VERDE *fig. 102*

SIZE: *4½″ long by 2¼″ wide*

WEIGHT: *6½ ounces*

SHAPE: *Plum; comes in long, pointy and short, squat forms*

EXTERIOR COLOR(S): *Yellowish green and brown amber*

FLESH COLOR(S): *Yellowish green*

SOLUBLE SOLIDS: *7¼ degrees Brix*

FLAVOR: *Excellent; finely balanced*

TEXTURE: *Reasonably firm; juicy. The skin is easily peeled.*

BEST USE(S): *Fresh eating; juice, salsa verde*

PLANT HABIT, LEAF TYPE, AND YIELD: *Indeterminate habit; regular leaf; good yield*

MATURITY: *Main crop*

ORIGIN: *Bred by Thomas P. Wagner. Tom told me in 2007, "My breeding and selection work culminating with Chile Verde was an attempt to get a tomato that had a hot pepper shape and was green. I don't know if anyone likes it or not, but I put away some fresh seed of it a year ago."*

Tom, I like it; this one's begging to be more widely grown. Chile Verde has a distinctive rich flavor but none of the capsaicin bite of its namesake pepper. Makes a spectacular apple-green juice that can be spiced to taste. Hot stuff!

102

103

THAI PINK *fig. 104; page 248*

SIZE: *1½" long by 1⅜" wide*

WEIGHT: *1 ounce*

SHAPE: *Miniature plum*

EXTERIOR COLOR(S): *Grayish rose*

FLESH COLOR(S): *Grayish rose*

SOLUBLE SOLIDS: *5 degrees Brix*

FLAVOR: *Poor; too acidic for most American palates*

TEXTURE: *Very firm; tough skin; seedy*

BEST USE(S): *Flower arrangements; show and tell; Thai cookery*

PLANT HABIT, LEAF TYPE, AND YIELD: *Determinate habit; regular leaf; high yield*

MATURITY: *Main crop*

ORIGIN: *Introduced in 1997 by Nichols Garden Nursery. Rose Marie Nichols McGee bought some Thai Pinks from local market gardeners Homer and Meg Campbell; immediately taken with their unique color, she worked out a deal to harvest the end of their substantial crop for seed.*

SYNONYMS: *Kanchanaburi (a province in Thailand); Kachanaburu; Thailand Pink; Thai Pink Egg. There seem to be several favored strains of similar tomatoes in Thailand.*

SEED SOURCES: *Ap6, Ba8, Ni1, So25*

Several years ago, Maine man Will Bonsall—a lover of oddballs and offbeats—delivered to me a tomato that was truly surprising. Immature Thai Pinks look like little Egg Tree eggplants: whiter than unripe Cream Sausage (see page 128) tomatoes. They turn a shocking grayish rose at maturity, making them perfect for floral displays.

AULD SOD *fig. 103*

SIZE: *1½" long by 1¼" wide*

WEIGHT: *1 ounce*

SHAPE: *Mini plum*

EXTERIOR COLOR(S): *Cherry red*

FLESH COLOR(S): *Cherry red*

SOLUBLE SOLIDS: *4 degrees Brix*

FLAVOR: *Poor; tart*

TEXTURE: *Reasonably firm; seedy*

BEST USE(S): *Garnish*

PLANT HABIT, LEAF TYPE, AND YIELD: *Determinate habit; regular leaf; good yield*

MATURITY: *Main crop*

ORIGIN: *Evidently Irish in origin. Transported to the United States in 1991 by a farm woman.*

No one knows better than the Irish the value of preserving crop diversity. Genetically uniform potatoes felled by blight led to the Great Hunger of the 1840s. The admirable mission of the Irish Seed Saver Association is to conserve Irish biodiversity—the mediocre-at-best Auld Sod tomato included. I suspect some of their other holdings, native to Ireland, would be more successful as garden plants: Gortahork Cabbage, Balbriggan Brussels Sprouts, and Tipperary Turnip.

Bell Pepper

(a) Schimmeig Stoo, (b) Burgess Stuffing, (c) Novogogoshary,
(d) Brown Flesh, (e) Gezahnte Tomate, (f) Brown Derby, (g) Yellow Stuffer

a

b

c

d

e

f

g

105

BROWN FLESH *page 149, fig. 105d*

SIZE: *3¼" long by 3½" wide*

WEIGHT: *8½ ounces*

SHAPE: *Bell pepper*

EXTERIOR COLOR(S): *Reddish brown with grayish green stripes*

FLESH COLOR(S): *Brownish red*

SOLUBLE SOLIDS: *4½ degrees Brix*

FLAVOR: *Fair to good; mild-mannered*

TEXTURE: *Very firm; hollow locules, dry meaty walls*

BEST USE(S): *Novelty; multipurpose; for stuffing raw or cooked*

PLANT HABIT, LEAF TYPE, AND YIELD: *Indeterminate habit; regular leaf; high yield*

MATURITY: *Main crop*

ORIGIN: *Bred by Thomas P. Wagner. Introduced in 1983 by Tater Mater Seeds, St. Joseph, Missouri, in a brown-flesh-when-ripe tomato mixture. Reintroduced twenty years later by several seed firms.*

SYNONYMS: *Brown Stripe*

With its lobed brown body and mysterious green stripes, this stuffing tomato looks like something out of a fairy tale. Yet, chop it up and cook it, press it through a strainer, and you've got a thoroughly down-to-earth pleasure: thick brownish-red gravy or juice that's a world-beater. Brown Flesh bears the signature of the Tater Mater pater, Thomas P. Wagner.

YELLOW STUFFER *page 149, fig. 105g*

SIZE: *3¼" long by 3½" wide*

WEIGHT: *8 ounces*

SHAPE: *Bell pepper*

EXTERIOR COLOR(S): *Deep yellow*

FLESH COLOR(S): *Butter yellow*

SOLUBLE SOLIDS: *4½ degrees Brix*

FLAVOR: *Poor*

TEXTURE: *Very firm, with thick walls like cardboard; hollow*

BEST USE(S): *Multipurpose; novelty*

PLANT HABIT, LEAF TYPE, AND YIELD: *Indeterminate habit; regular leaf; high yield*

MATURITY: *Late crop*

ORIGIN: *Bred by Colen Wyatt of Petoseed circa 1988, according to Jim Waltrip. My first sighting of Ken Ettlinger's synonymous Yellow Cup (Long Island Seed and Plant Company) was in 1990; by 1991, twenty-three commercial sources were carrying it.*

SYNONYMS: *Gourmet Yellow Stuffer; Yellow Cup; and Yellow Stuffing. Similar to Burpee's Yellow Magic. Not the same as Gold Stuffer; or Yellow Bell (see page 142).*

SEED SOURCES: *Bo19, Ers, Go8, He17, Ma18, Pe2, Ra6, Se16, Sh9, Sk2, Te4, To1, To3, To10, Vi4*

Yellow Stuffer tastes like sawdust, but it makes a colorful vessel for dip or salsa.

NOVOGOGOSHARY *page 149, fig. 105c*

SIZE: *3" long by 3" wide*

WEIGHT: *8 ounces*

SHAPE: *Bell pepper*

EXTERIOR COLOR(S): *Cherry red*

FLESH COLOR(S): *Grayish red*

SOLUBLE SOLIDS: *4½ degrees Brix*

FLAVOR: *Fair; bland*

TEXTURE: *Very firm; thick walls, hollow*

BEST USE(S): *Comes to life when stuffed— even with leftovers*

PLANT HABIT, LEAF TYPE, AND YIELD: *Determinate habit; regular leaf; high yield*

MATURITY: *Early crop*

ORIGIN: *From Moldova via Seed to Seed author Suzanne Ashworth. "Gogoshary" is a type of sweet pepper and the name of a Moldovan village. Introduced in 1998 by Glenn and Linda Drowns of Sand Hill Preservation Center.*

SYNONYMS: *Similar to Burgess Stuffing and Liberty Bell (see next entry and page 153)*

NY: *Nee & Goldman 53457*

SEED SOURCES: *Sa9*

Novogogoshary is a dynamo. Who would guess that a tiny, waist-high plant could generate so many stuffing tomatoes? You must be nimble when extracting them; they can easily bruise or rip. Get intimate with the plant by harvesting on your back; look sky high and cut with a scissors, but be mindful of your fingers.

Seasoned home cook Linda Drowns says: "Basically, we just use them raw. There are all kinds of things you can do with Novogogoshary if you let your imagination run wild. We stuff them with chicken, tuna, crab, or fancy pasta salad. And they're great filled with a cream cheese dip on a crudité platter. Might be worth a try to serve cold soup in them—tomato, of course."

BURGESS STUFFING *page 149, fig. 105b*

SIZE: *2¾" long by 4¼" wide*

WEIGHT: *9½ ounces*

SHAPE: *Bell pepper*

EXTERIOR COLOR(S): *Vivid red*

FLESH COLOR(S): *Grayish red*

SOLUBLE SOLIDS: *7 degrees Brix*

FLAVOR: *Fair to good; mildly sweet*

TEXTURE: *Very firm; hollow with thick dry walls*

BEST USE(S): *Novelty; stuffing; attractive when sliced in rings for salads*

PLANT HABIT, LEAF TYPE, AND YIELD: *Determinate habit; regular leaf; high yield*

MATURITY: *Main crop*

ORIGIN: *Introduced in 1971 by Burgess Seed and Plant Company*

SYNONYMS: *Clover, Stuffing, Trèfle. Resembles Liberty Bell and Novogoshary (see previous entry and page 153).*

NY: *Nee & Goldman 53407*

SEED SOURCES: *To1*

Burgess Stuffing is a classic bell-pepper-shaped tomato. The self-topping plant, with gorgeous green leaves, is loaded with bunches of red stuffers. If I were a horticultural judge—maybe in my next life—I'd give this variety a blue ribbon for all-around excellence.

Disregard the fact that their flesh is like cardboard. These tomatoes were born to stuff with cold salads. As soon as you pick them, they're ready: Line up the shrimp, chicken, tuna, or cottage cheese. As pointed out by the Burgess Company in 1971, this tomato is equally delicious stuffed and baked with a meat or fish and rice recipe, macaroni and cheese, or eggplant. But they never dreamed of Roasted Tomato Crunch Sicilian Style (see page 242).

BROWN DERBY *fig. 106; page 149, fig. 105f*

SIZE: *3½" long by 3¼" wide*

WEIGHT: *9 ounces*

SHAPE: *Bell pepper*

EXTERIOR COLOR(S): *Brownish red*

FLESH COLOR(S): *Brownish red*

SOLUBLE SOLIDS: *5¼ degrees Brix*

FLAVOR: *Fair to good*

TEXTURE: *Firm; thick-walled and hollow*

BEST USE(S): *Multipurpose; stuffer*

PLANT HABIT, LEAF TYPE, AND YIELD: *Indeterminate habit; regular leaf; high yield*

MATURITY: *Main crop*

ORIGIN: *Bred by Thomas P. Wagner. Introduced in 1983 by Tater Mater Seeds, St. Joseph, Missouri, in a mixture of brown-flesh-when-ripe tomatoes named (in the 1984 catalog) "Brown Derby Mix." Some of the other variations continue and include Brown Flesh (see page 150).*

SYNONYMS: *Brown Derby Mix*

NY: *Nee & Goldman 53481*

It's hard to believe this is a "tomato tomato" and not a tomato-shaped pepper. Brown Derby is newfangled yet handy: "It may take guts to eat them raw, but cooked they make great chutney, sauce, and barbecue fixings," says Tom Wagner, the breeder. They also make a savory brownish-red gravy for pot roast. Try Brown Derby with some of Tom's brown bell peppers, if you can get them.

106

SCHIMMEIG STOO *fig. 107; page 149; fig. 105a; page 170, fig. 117a*

SIZE: *3½" long by 3⅛" wide*

WEIGHT: *8 ounces*

SHAPE: *Bell pepper*

EXTERIOR COLOR(S): *Crayfish red with carrot-red stripes*

FLESH COLOR(S): *Coral red*

SOLUBLE SOLIDS: *5 degrees Brix*

FLAVOR: *Fair; sometimes acidic*

TEXTURE: *Very firm; thick walls, mealy and dry; hollow*

BEST USE(S): *Stuffing; grilling; "a useful novelty" according to the breeder, who once recommended cutting the tops off, stuffing the tomatoes with cottage cheese or other favorite fillings, and then replacing the tops to surprise guests*

PLANT HABIT, LEAF TYPE, AND YIELD: *Indeterminate habit; regular leaf; high yield*

MATURITY: *Early crop*

ORIGIN: *Bred by Thomas P. Wagner of Tater Mater Seeds. Cataloged by him under the heading of "Lot T-1" in 1983, and as Schimmeig Stoo (Manx for "Striped Cavern") in 1985, with these words: "This year's seed is an F_{14} line meaning that I have saved seed for 14 years from the original cross." Tom recently told me: "I find it rather magical that my Schimmeig Stoo, which has four parents in the pedigree, has a prettier cousin—New Schimmeig Stoo—that has over one hundred different varieties in the pedigree. The pedigree looks like something out of the Seed Savers Exchange catalog!"*

SYNONYMS: *Lobed and Striped; Orange Striped Cavern; Schimmeig Stoo Striped Hollow; Schimmeig Striped Hollow; Striped and Lobed; Striped Cavern; Striped Stuffer. Not the same as Schimmeig Creg (Manx for "Striped Rock"; see page 171).*

SEED SOURCES: *Fe5, Hi13, Ma18, Ra6, So25, Ter*

In 1992, Craig Thomas of Skipping Stone Organics in Eugene, Oregon, sent me a generous packet of Schimmeig Stoo seed, and thus began my infatuation with a tomato only Tom Wagner could dream up. Fifteen years later, I'm still dipping happily into that one seed packet.

There are some who claim Schimmeig Stoo is synonymous with the old German Striped (Gestreifte), but this isn't so. The Japanische Gestreifte (cataloged by Benary in 1879) and the Gestreifte (from seedsman Robert Newman in Erfurt, Germany, described by Liberty Hyde Bailey in 1887) were red, round, and ribbed tomatoes with orange stripes (and sometimes, noted Bailey, orange with red stripes)—not bell-pepper-shaped.

108

LIBERTY BELL *fig. 108*

SIZE: *2⅝" long by 3⅞" wide*

WEIGHT: *8 ounces*

SHAPE: *Bell pepper*

EXTERIOR COLOR(S): *Cherry red*

FLESH COLOR(S): *Coral red*

SOLUBLE SOLIDS: *4½ degrees Brix*

FLAVOR: *Fair; can be acidic*

TEXTURE: *Very firm; thick-walled, hollow and dry interior*

BEST USE(S): *Stuffing*

PLANT HABIT, LEAF TYPE, AND YIELD: *Indeterminate habit; regular leaf; high yield*

MATURITY: *Late crop*

ORIGIN: *An unusual seed specialty introduced by Glecklers Seedmen in 1976 to celebrate America's bicentennial. Not the same as The Liberty Bell (Tomato No. 75), a red globe, introduced by Johnson and Stokes of Philadelphia in 1894 in honor of the old bell "whose tones one hundred and seventeen years ago rang out the creation of a nation and the independence of a continent."*

SYNONYMS: *Similar to Burgess Stuffing and Novogogoshary (see page 150)*

NY: *Nee & Goldman 54596*

SEED SOURCES: *Ma18, Ra6, Re8, To9*

This tomato sometimes gets so distorted that it could pass for an Edward Weston pepper. Merlin W. Gleckler, a grower, breeder, and importer who introduced many "unusualties," including this one, had a very personal relationship with language—a trait that endeared him to many. His Liberty Bell tomato was no mere stuffer but something larger than life: "A Freedom of stuffing imagination, unlimited."

Oxheart

(a) Orange Russian 117, (b) Dinner Plate

ORANGE RUSSIAN 117 *page 155, fig. 109a*

SIZE: *3¾" long by 5½" wide*

WEIGHT: *1 pound, 13 ounces*

SHAPE: *Oxheart*

EXTERIOR COLOR(S): *Yolk yellow with more or less prominent cheeks of tomato pink*

FLESH COLOR(S): *Banana*

SOLUBLE SOLIDS: *6 degrees Brix*

FLAVOR: *Excellent; honey-sweet, finely balanced, endowed with rich flavor*

TEXTURE: *Soft; meaty. All usable (no hard core like some oxhearts).*

BEST USE(S): *Fresh eating; pumpkin-y when cooked*

PLANT HABIT, LEAF TYPE, AND YIELD: *Indeterminate habit; regular leaf; high yield*

MATURITY: *Early crop*

ORIGIN: *A deliberate cross of Russian 117 and Georgia Streak made by Jeff Dawson of Grandview Farms Tomato Seeds, Sebastopol, California, and cataloged in 1998 by Jeff and his wife, Sharon. The original Russian 117 was named "Russian" when first listed by Marie Kodama of Hawaii in 1991, evidently because her original source was a Russian sailor (and not Kent Whealy, as has been erroneously reported); others who got it from her added the "accession number" 117, no doubt to keep it separate from another tomato of the same name.*

SYNONYMS: *Synonymous with Dawson's Russian Oxheart. Pink Russian 117 is a sport of Russian 117.*

NY: *Nee & Goldman 53389*

SEED SOURCES: *To1, To9*

Oxhearts make my heart sing, and none more so than Orange Russian 117. The flavor is unparalleled; the shapely yellow variety, with a broad prominent obtuse nipple, earns the French name Téton de Vénus (also given to an evocatively shaped peach). I never knew an oxheart could also be so early, easy, and prolific. When I presented a photo of this beauty to Jim Myers, Baggett-Frazier Professor at Oregon State University, he surmised that foliage covering the fruit affects color expression, with the red lycopene being slower to accumulate in shaded areas.

Whatever the effects of shading on Orange Russian 117 fruits, the table quality is always sublime. I eat mine like a peach.

DINNER PLATE *page 155, fig. 109b*

SIZE: *5" long by 4½" wide*

WEIGHT: *1 pound, 3 ounces*

SHAPE: *Oxheart*

EXTERIOR COLOR(S): *Tomato pink with occasionally prominent yolk-yellow shoulders*

FLESH COLOR(S): *Tomato pink*

SOLUBLE SOLIDS: *5 degrees Brix*

FLAVOR: *Good to excellent*

TEXTURE: *Soft; melting and juicy*

BEST USE(S): *Eat a Dinner Plate tomato as you would an artichoke: Scrape the sweet flesh off the skin with your teeth, and savor*

PLANT HABIT, LEAF TYPE, AND YIELD: *Indeterminate habit; droopy leaves; good yield*

MATURITY: *Early crop*

ORIGIN: *Introduced to members of Seed Savers Exchange in 1982 by Dorothy Beiswenger of Crookston, Minnesota. Her seed came from James Stokes. Brought to market by the Tomato Seed Company, Metuchen, New Jersey, and others, circa 1991.*

SYNONYMS: *Dinnerplate; Dinner plate; "A" and "B" versions.*

NY: *Nee & Goldman 53400*

SEED SOURCES: *Ma18, Ra6, Sa9, Se28, To1, To3, To9*

Two versions of the original Dinner Plate have been disseminated by Seed Savers Exchange: one is red and rounder; the other, featured here, is a pink oblate oxheart with a more or less prominent yellow color at the stem end. Young and MacArthur reported this unusual color patterning in oxheart in 1947. Jim Myers at Oregon State University recently explained to me that Dinner Plate has an especially large green shoulder area on the upper portion of the fruit. It also has the normal complement of carotenoids with lycopene (red) being the fully ripe state. The shoulder area on green shoulder types is slower to ripen—a trait that has been bred out of many modern types because delayed ripening is undesirable for supplying the fresh market and for processing. Still, I wouldn't trade Dinner Plate's shoulders for the world; they're dazzling.

STERLING OLD NORWAY *fig. 110*

SIZE: *3¼" long by 5¼" wide*

WEIGHT: *1 pound, 4 ounces*

SHAPE: *Oxheart; can produce beautiful heart-shapes and huge double-oxhearts*

EXTERIOR COLOR(S): *Tomato pink*

FLESH COLOR(S): *Tomato pink*

SOLUBLE SOLIDS: *4½ degrees Brix*

FLAVOR: *Fair; mildly pleasing and refreshing*

TEXTURE: *Soft; solid and meaty*

BEST USE(S): *Fresh eating; specimen tomato*

PLANT HABIT, LEAF TYPE, AND YIELD: *Indeterminate habit; regular leaf; high yield*

MATURITY: *Main crop*

ORIGIN: *Initially listed in the 1994 Seed Savers Exchange yearbook by Merlyn Niedens. The tomato was given to Merlyn by his friend Bill Schwitzer, who was also the source of the Sterling Old German tomato. Bill's seed came from a Norwegian family in Sterling, Illinois, who might have brought it from Norway.*

SYNONYMS: *Not the same as Sterling Castle or Sterling Old German.*

NY: *Nee & Goldman 54614*

Sterling Old Norway has won my heart—and some others', too. I cradled this valentine, pictured in the photo, in a wooden box to give to my friends Sven Huseby and Barbara Ettinger (Sven is Norwegian by birth, and Barbara by association). The note read, "with love from Amy—save the seeds."

ORANGE STRAWBERRY *fig. 111*

SIZE: *4½" long by 4¼" wide*

WEIGHT: *1 pound, 7 ounces*

SHAPE: *Oxheart, with a very prominent nipple tip*

EXTERIOR COLOR(S): *Orange*

FLESH COLOR(S): *Melon yellow*

SOLUBLE SOLIDS: *6 degrees Brix*

FLAVOR: *Good to excellent; can be exquisite. Subtle leafy perfume.*

TEXTURE: *Very firm, like a ripe strawberry. Has a thick woody stem, no hard core.*

BEST USE(S): *Anything is possible.*

PLANT HABIT, LEAF TYPE, AND YIELD: *Indeterminate habit; regular leaf; good yield*

MATURITY: *Late crop*

ORIGIN: *Orange Strawberry appeared, apparently as a chance seedling from bicolored Pineapple, in the 1993 garden of Marjorie A. Morris of Paoli, Indiana. Commercialized as early as 1998 by several seed houses, including Seeds by Design.*

SYNONYMS: *Appears to be the same as German Orange Strawberry*

NY: *Nee & Goldman 53505*

SEED SOURCES: *Ma18, Sa9, So25, Sw9, To1, To3, To9, Vi4*

Miraculously, astonishingly graceful, like a dancer en pointe.

111

HUNGARIAN HEART *fig. 112; page 176, fig. 122d*

SIZE: *4¾″ long by 3¼″ wide*

WEIGHT: *1 pound*

SHAPE: *Oxheart*

EXTERIOR COLOR(S): *Tomato pink*

FLESH COLOR(S): *Tomato pink*

SOLUBLE SOLIDS: *7 degrees Brix*

FLAVOR: *Excellent; savory*

TEXTURE: *Soft; meaty and juicy*

BEST USE(S): *Fresh eating*

PLANT HABIT, LEAF TYPE, AND YIELD: *Indeterminate habit; droopy leaves; low yield*

MATURITY: *Main crop*

ORIGIN: *Said to have originated in a village twenty miles from Budapest circa 1900. The first Seed Savers Exchange member to offer this variety was Jerry Muller (formerly of Tennessee; now of Alabama), who in 1988 listed his source as Ed Simon of Pennsylvania. Introduced commercially in 1999 by Seed Savers Heirloom Seeds and Gifts.*

SYNONYMS: *Heart-Shaped Hungarian; Hungarian Heart Shaped. Not the same as Kalman's Hungarian Pink.*

NY: *Nee & Goldman 53425*

SEED SOURCES: *Co32, He8, Ma18, Roh, Se16, To1*

I love Hungarian Heart—and not just because my grandmother Rose also came from a village near Budapest in the early twentieth century. These are big and irregular and come few and far between, but, like Nana, they are such sweethearts.

113

JAPANESE OXHEART *fig. 113; page 176, fig. 122b*

SIZE: *6″ long by 4¾″ wide*

WEIGHT: *1 pound, 15 ounces*

SHAPE: *Oxheart*

EXTERIOR COLOR(S): *Tomato pink*

FLESH COLOR(S): *Tomato pink*

SOLUBLE SOLIDS: *5 degrees Brix*

FLAVOR: *Excellent; winey, sweet, nice fruit acid*

TEXTURE: *Soft; meaty*

BEST USE(S): *Multipurpose*

PLANT HABIT, LEAF TYPE, AND YIELD: *Indeterminate habit; droopy leaves; high yield*

MATURITY: *Early crop*

ORIGIN: *The first Seed Savers Exchange member to list Japanese Oxheart was Ake Truedsson of Klagshamm, Sweden, in the 1993 yearbook. Brought to market by Tomato Growers Supply Company in 1998.*

SYNONYMS: *Japanese*

NY: *Nee & Goldman 53391*

SEED SOURCES: *So25, To1, To9*

An oxheart without peer. Huge and hugely prolific, meaty, mouthfilling, and well-marbled like a prime cut of ox. So big you would need only one fruit to make Spanish Tomato Bread for ten (see recipe, page 212).

Color Groups

(a, n) Galina's, (b) Sun Belle, (c) Yellow Ruffled, (d) Banana Legs, (e) Broad Ripple Yellow Currant,
(f) Golden Ponderosa, (g) Old Ivory Egg, (h) Manyel, (i) Yellow Bell, (j) Roman Candle, (k) Sun and Snow,
(l) Plum Lemon, (m, o) Blondkopfchen, (p) Yellow Pear, (q) Yellow Peach

114

SUN AND SNOW *page 161, fig. 114k*

SIZE: *2¼" long by 2½" wide*

WEIGHT: *5 ounces*

SHAPE: *Round, smooth*

EXTERIOR COLOR(S): *Light yellow*

FLESH COLOR(S): *Light yellow*

SOLUBLE SOLIDS: *6 degrees Brix*

FLAVOR: *Good*

TEXTURE: *Soft; juicy*

BEST USE(S): *Multipurpose*

PLANT HABIT, LEAF TYPE, AND YIELD: *Indeterminate habit; regular leaf; good yield*

MATURITY: *Main crop*

ORIGIN: *Bred by Tim Peters; released circa 1994 by Peters Seed and Research. Tim's mantra is, "Learn how to save seed; if you find a garden gem, propagate it and pass it on."*

NY: *Nee & Goldman 53443*

SEED SOURCES: *Pe6*

Mouthwateringly good. Harvest young, when the flesh is snowy white (light yellow in tomato speak). The breeder suggests dipping the tomato in hot water and slipping the skins off before use. Beautiful when contrasted with red, orange, and green varieties on a salad platter.

SUN BELLE *page 161, fig. 114b*

SIZE: *1¾" long by 1" wide*

WEIGHT: *15.20 grams*

SHAPE: *Miniature plum or fig*

EXTERIOR COLOR(S): *Yellow*

FLESH COLOR(S): *Light yellow*

SOLUBLE SOLIDS: *7 degrees Brix*

FLAVOR: *Good; well balanced*

TEXTURE: *Firm*

BEST USE(S): *Multipurpose*

PLANT HABIT, LEAF TYPE, AND YIELD: *Indeterminate habit; regular leaf; good yield*

MATURITY: *Early crop*

ORIGIN: *Similar in some respects to the common Yellow Plum described by Fearing Burr (1863) and Hovey and Company, Boston, back in 1849. Cataloged as Sun Belle in 1998 by Vesey's Seeds Limited. Available as early as 1996 from a commercial source in England, as well as from dedicated English seed saver John Wyncoll.*

SYNONYMS: *Resembles Small Yellow Plum and Yellow Plum*

Looks like a truncated version of Yellow Bell (see page 142) with its grooved surface. Not spectacularly beautiful—but try it in pickles and preserves, as a garnish, or in Lobster and Tomato Salad with Herbed Mayonnaise (see page 199).

PLUM LEMON *page 4, fig. 1d; page 161, fig. 114l*

SIZE: *2¾" long by 2" wide*

WEIGHT: *3 ounces*

SHAPE: *Fig, with a small beak at the distal end*

EXTERIOR COLOR(S): *Deep yellow*

FLESH COLOR(S): *Light yellow*

SOLUBLE SOLIDS: *5 degrees Brix*

FLAVOR: *Fair; lemony*

TEXTURE: *Very firm*

BEST USE(S): *Vegetable soup; not for sauce or fresh eating*

PLANT HABIT, LEAF TYPE, AND YIELD: *Indeterminate habit; regular leaf; high yield*

MATURITY: *Early crop*

ORIGIN: *Collected by Kent Whealy from an elderly seedsman at the Bird Market in Moscow during the August 1991 coup. The variety originated in the Saint Petersburg area. Cataloged in the 1995 Seed Savers International brochure.*

SYNONYMS: *Sleevuhvidnaya or Sleewuhvidneyeh (means "plum-shaped" in Russian). Not the same as Plum Yellow (a small oval heirloom tomato). Similar to, but not the same as, Wonder Light, which was introduced in 1996 by Rob Johnston Jr. of Johnny's Selected Seeds. Kate Rogers Gessert of Albany, Oregon,* had given the seed to Rob; Kate's seed came from a gardener in Irkutsk who called them "Chouda-Svyeta" (also known as Chooda Sveta, Wonder of Light, Limon-Liana, or Miracle of the World). Bred by Russian gardener A. Porozov from Ryazan, Russia, according to Andrey Baranovski of Belarus.

NY: *Nee & Goldman 53417*

SEED SOURCES: *Ba8 Bo19, Co32, Com, Go8, He8, Ma18, Ra6, Re8, Sa9, Se16, So25, To1, To9, Vi4, Yu2*

Oddly enough, Plum Lemon is shaped more like a fig than a plum or a lemon; it has a constricted neck and rough grooves over the locule walls; and the blossom end is blunted. It succeeds in short-season or cold areas where less hardy stock fails. Hide it in borscht or vegetable soup, where the beets will lend color and the cabbage, flavor.

GOLDEN PONDEROSA *page 161, fig. 114f*

SIZE: *4½" long by 5¼" wide*

WEIGHT: *1 pound, 9 ounces*

SHAPE: *Beefsteak*

EXTERIOR COLOR(S): *Light yellow*

FLESH COLOR(S): *Pastel yellow*

SOLUBLE SOLIDS: *6 degrees Brix*

FLAVOR: *Good; subacid. I want it on my plate.*

TEXTURE: *Soft; meaty*

BEST USE(S): *Fresh eating; reported to make excellent preserves. Serve it with finely sliced lemons as recommended by Aggeler and Musser Seed Company, Los Angeles, California, in 1923.*

PLANT HABIT, LEAF TYPE, AND YIELD: *Indeterminate habit; regular leaf; good yield*

MATURITY: *Early crop*

ORIGIN: *A sport of Red Ponderosa. Introduced as Henderson's Golden Ponderosa, a flavorful novelty, in 1914 by Peter Henderson and Company, New York, New York.*

SYNONYMS: *Golden Ponderosa, Super Strain; Golden Yellow Ponderosa; Henderson's Golden Ponderosa; Ponderosa Gold; Ponderosa Yellow, Yellow Whopper*

SEED SOURCES: *Re8, Shu, So1, Te4, To3*

Golden Ponderosa reigns, whether paired with her parent Red Ponderosa as "the grandest tomatoes on earth"—as one catalog described it—or all alone as "queen of the yellows." I adore this supercolossal light-yellow, waxy-smooth beefsteak, good as gold but not colored like it. Nowadays there are at least two color variations in circulation: one light yellow like the original; the other darker yellow. Neither is "real, deep orange" like Henderson's Orange Tomato (introduced in 1933).

Golden Ponderosa often has an attractive pink blush at the blossom end. As noted by Henderson from the start, "some parti-colored fruits may be expected. These but add interest to it." Yellow tomatoes like (Yellow) Ponderosa, explained Young and MacArthur (1947), tend to exhibit pink at the blossom end, especially in hot weather.

BANANA LEGS *page 161, fig. 114d*

SIZE: *4" long by 1¾" wide*

WEIGHT: *4 ounces*

SHAPE: *Plum, nipple-tipped*

EXTERIOR COLOR(S): *Yolk yellow with zigzag stripes of pastel yellow*

FLESH COLOR(S): *Pastel yellow*

SOLUBLE SOLIDS: *5 degrees Brix*

FLAVOR: *Fair; low acid*

TEXTURE: *Very firm*

BEST USE(S): *Multipurpose; novelty, whole canning, lengthwise slices*

PLANT HABIT, LEAF TYPE, AND YIELD: *Determinate habit; droopy leaves; high yield*

MATURITY: *Early crop*

ORIGIN: *Bred by Thomas P. Wagner; first offered commercially in a Tater Mater Seeds mixture in 1985. Picked up by other commercial sources a decade later under the name Banana Legs.*

SYNONYMS: *Banana Fingers. Not the same as Tom Wagner's Banana Cream (Cream Sausage, see page 128).*

SEED SOURCES: *Bo19, Ga1, He8, He17, Hi13, Ki4, Ra6, Ri2, Se17, Se28, So25, To1, To3, To10, Vi4, Vi5*

Like all of Thomas P. Wagner's creations, Banana Legs is a joy to behold: eye-filling from the top-to-toe wavy veins of light yellow to its nipple tip. With thousands of tomato varieties already to his credit in the 1980s, and never enough time and space for all the "nicknamed clones" or small experimental seed lots, Wagner encouraged his customers to have fun making selections and learning the basics of genetics.

Following Tom's lead, Mark Reusser of Ailsa Craig, Ontario, planted an experimental plot of the Mixed Long Toms (including Banana Fingers, Zebra Legs, String Bean, and Tomato Nails) featured in Wagner's 1985 commercial seed catalog. Reusser was beguiled enough by Banana Legs to single it out and perpetuate it in the 1988 Seed Savers Exchange yearbook.

The oddball name and the quirky good looks of Banana Legs make it especially lovable. A hot name, a hot item, and a lesson in naming opportunities: Rebecca Millard-Redfield of Soldier's Grove, Wisconsin, selected a tomato, synonymous with Banana Legs, from one of Tom Wagner's mixes; if she'd chosen a jazzier name than Yellow Paste, then it, too, might have been a star.

a

b

c

d

e

f

g

h

i

j

k

115

DJENA LEE'S GOLDEN GIRL *fig. 115g*

SIZE: *3¾" long by 3¾" wide*

WEIGHT: *12 ounces*

SHAPE: *Round, smooth*

EXTERIOR COLOR(S): *Deep orange*

FLESH COLOR(S): *Cadmium orange*

SOLUBLE SOLIDS: *5 degrees Brix*

FLAVOR: *Fair to good; sometimes sweet and nutty*

TEXTURE: *Soft; refreshing*

BEST USE(S): *Multipurpose*

PLANT HABIT, LEAF TYPE, AND YIELD: *Indeterminate habit; regular leaf; good yield*

MATURITY: *Main crop*

ORIGIN: *Reverend and Mrs. C. Frank Morrow of St. Paul, Minnesota, introduced Djena Lee's Golden Girl to the Seed Savers Exchange in 1981. Jeff McCormack of Southern Exposure Seed Exchange commercialized it in 1987. Boarded on to Slow Food USA's Ark of Taste in 2007.*

SYNONYMS: *Djeena Lee's Golden Girl; D. Jena Lee's; D. Jena Lee's Golden Girl; not the same as Golden Girl Hybrid.*

NY: *Nee & Goldman 54570*

SEED SOURCES: *Bou, Ers, Ga21, Go8, So1, Te4, To9, Tu6*

This tomato is the living legacy of Djena Lee, part–Native American granddaughter of Minnesota financier Jim Lee. She gave plants to fifteen-year-old Frank Morrow in 1929 when she moved to Illinois. Morrow reportedly took top honors with the tomato at a Chicago fair ten times in a row.

Djena Lee has soft, glorious, glistening orange flesh that is bland but refreshing. Comes in about the same time I pick my first sweet Orangeglo watermelon. I like to mix the two together with ricotta salata and drizzle the salad with light vinaigrette.

DAD'S SUNSET *fig. 115e*

SIZE: *3¼" long by 4½" wide*

WEIGHT: *1 pound*

SHAPE: *Beefsteak*

EXTERIOR COLOR(S): *Deep orange*

FLESH COLOR(S): *Orange*

SOLUBLE SOLIDS: *6 degrees Brix*

FLAVOR: *Good; rich and finely balanced*

TEXTURE: *Reasonably firm; meaty and juicy*

BEST USE(S): *Multipurpose*

PLANT HABIT, LEAF TYPE, AND YIELD: *Indeterminate habit; regular leaf; good yield*

MATURITY: *Early crop*

ORIGIN: *Cataloged circa 1992 by Buttercup Seed Gardens and by Seeds Blüm, Boise, Idaho*

SYNONYMS: *Not the same as Dad's Mug*

NY: *Nee & Goldman 54631*

SEED SOURCES: *Ba8, Se17, So1, To9*

The color is electric, and so is the flavor. When I gave petite Tovah Martin a gift basket of tomatoes in 2006—which a fullback couldn't've finished—she was drawn to the orange ones first. Dad's Sunset emerged as her absolute favorite. This variety has lots of other fans; it even won the contest for "Best Tasting Tomato" at Baker Creek Heirloom Seeds' 2004 Garden Show in Mansfield, Missouri. Dad's Sunset is a must for gazpacho because of its high juice viscosity (see Colorful Gazpacho, page 183).

NEBRASKA WEDDING *fig. 115i*

SIZE: *2¾" long by 4" wide*

WEIGHT: *1 pound*

SHAPE: *Round, smooth*

EXTERIOR COLOR(S): *Cadmium orange*

FLESH COLOR(S): *Melon yellow*

SOLUBLE SOLIDS: *5 degrees Brix*

FLAVOR: *Good; well balanced*

TEXTURE: *Reasonably firm; meaty and juicy*

BEST USE(S): *Fresh eating; seeds for gift-giving to brides*

PLANT HABIT, LEAF TYPE, AND YIELD: *Determinate habit; regular leaf; good yield*

MATURITY: *Early crop*

ORIGIN: *Seeds were sent to Mrs. Ed (Dorothy) Beiswenger of Crookston, Minnesota, in 1980 by seventy-year-old Mrs. Ted (Betsy) Englert of Sandpoint, Idaho, who said Nebraskan brides were given seeds of this tomato as a wedding gift. Dorothy recently found an old letter in which Betsy explains that the seed was brought from Minnesota by pioneers in the late 1800s via covered wagon. And it thrived in cold, windy Nebraska. Dorothy duly listed the tomato in the 1983 Seed Savers Exchange yearbook. Nebraska Wedding was commercialized circa 1995 by Seed Savers International and by Seeds by Design.*

NY: *Nee & Goldman 53435*

SEED SOURCES: *Ers, Go8, Ha26, He8, He17, Hud, La1, Ma18, Me7, Ra6, Sa9, Se16, Sk2, To3, To9, To10, Und, Up2*

This tomato is the ultimate love apple—at least in Nebraska, where seeds are reportedly still given to a bride as part of her trousseau. I can't think of anything more hopeful for the hope chest. Every prospective bride, be she from Colorado, Connecticut, or Delaware, should be eligible to register for Nebraska Wedding, or be the fortunate recipient.

Dorothy Beiswenger—chrysanthemum grower, certified horticultural judge, master gardener, and farmer—knew nothing about tomato seeds as wedding gifts until Nebraska Wedding fell in her lap twenty-five years ago. But she did know it was common practice for farm people, with little cash to spend, to give new couples something from the farm as a wedding gift. Seeds such as beans and lettuce were usually among the household gifts given to the bride, whereas cows, tractors, and even a place to live were gifts for the groom. Barter was also common practice: Dorothy remembers her parents trading bushels of tomatoes for groceries. If there was any credit due, it was paid in candy for Dorothy.

(a) Caro-Rich, (b) Persimmon, (c) Goldie, (d) Yellow Jumbo, (e) Dad's Sunset, (f) Dixie Golden Giant, (g) Djena Lee's Golden Girl, (h) Gold Rush Currant, (i) Nebraska Wedding, (j) Mini Orange, (k) Tangella

PERSIMMON *page 164, fig. 115b*

SIZE: *3¼" long by 4½" wide*

WEIGHT: *1 pound, 2 ounces*

SHAPE: *Beefsteak*

EXTERIOR COLOR(S): *Cadmium orange*

FLESH COLOR(S): *Orange*

SOLUBLE SOLIDS: *5 degrees Brix*

FLAVOR: *Fair to good; mildly sweet*

TEXTURE: *Soft; meaty and juicy; sometimes mealy*

BEST USE(S): *Multipurpose*

PLANT HABIT, LEAF TYPE, AND YIELD: *Indeterminate habit; regular leaf; good yield*

MATURITY: *Main crop*

ORIGIN: *Apparently introduced in 1981 by Garden Gem Seeds, Quincy, Illinois, and carried forward in 1982 by its successor, Seeds Blüm, Boise, Idaho*

SYNONYMS: *Persimmon Orange. Similar to Dixie Golden Giant, Goldie, Kaki Ronde, and others. Not the same as Russian Persimmon (with determinate plants and smaller fruits) from Seed Savers International's 1994 Russian Collection.*

NY: *Nee & Goldman 53505*

SEED SOURCES: *Be4, Coo, Co32, Ers, Ga1, He17, Hud, Ki4, Ma18, Mi12, Na6, Re8, Sa9, Se7, Se17, Sk2, So1, So25, St18, Sw9, Syn, Te4, Ter, Te4, To1, To3, To9, To10, Tu6, Up2*

A vibrant orange that would infuse any dish with color. Try it with Ricotta Ravioli with Tomato Sauce (see page 205).

DIXIE GOLDEN GIANT *page 164, fig. 115f*

SIZE: *4½" long by 5" wide*

WEIGHT: *1 pound, 4 ounces*

SHAPE: *Beefsteak*

EXTERIOR COLOR(S): *Deep orange*

FLESH COLOR(S): *Cadmium orange*

SOLUBLE SOLIDS: *6 degrees Brix*

FLAVOR: *Excellent; sweet and pleasing*

TEXTURE: *Reasonably firm to firm; meaty and juicy*

BEST USE(S): *Multipurpose; perfect for salads and sandwiches*

PLANT HABIT, LEAF TYPE, AND YIELD: *Indeterminate habit; regular leaf; high yield*

MATURITY: *Early crop*

ORIGIN: *Evidently an old Southern favorite. Synonymous with Goldie (see page 167), which was introduced by Glecklers Seedmen in 1977, and reported to be a 150-year-old family heirloom.*

SYNONYMS: *Goldie (Gleckler's). Not the same as Goldie F₁.*

SEED SOURCES: *Ra6, Re8, To1, To3, To9, To10*

Dixie Golden Giant was a crowd pleaser at one of my Rhinebeck Farmers' Market tastings. It's solid and well saturated with deep orange color, and because the flesh is firmer than most in its class, it makes a terrific slicer. No wonder Dixie has been passed down for generations.

MINI ORANGE *page 164, fig. 115j*

SIZE: *1¼" long by 1⅜" wide*

WEIGHT: *21.56 grams (some are not so "mini"—up to 3 ounces)*

SHAPE: *Cherry*

EXTERIOR COLOR(S): *Deep orange*

FLESH COLOR(S): *Cadmium orange*

SOLUBLE SOLIDS: *5½ degrees Brix*

FLAVOR: *Fair; mildly sweet, somewhat acidic*

TEXTURE: *Reasonably firm*

BEST USE(S): *Multipurpose*

PLANT HABIT, LEAF TYPE, AND YIELD: *Indeterminate habit; regular leaf; high yield*

MATURITY: *Early crop*

ORIGIN: *Introduced in 1988 by Glecklers Seedmen*

SYNONYMS: *Mini-Orange; Miniature Orange. Resembles Burpee's Sundrop (circa 1987), Tangella (circa 1970; see next entry), and Orange Bourgoin*

NY: *Nee & Goldman 54577*

SEED SOURCES: *Ga1, He8, Ma18, Sa9, So1*

Mini Orange has excellent color and crack resistance but isn't as sweet as that *other* orange cherry, Sungold Hybrid (bred by Tokita Seeds in Japan and introduced in the United States in 1991 by Johnny's Selected Seeds). But until the appearance of Sungold Select, the dehybridized version of Sungold, Mini Orange was one of the open-pollinated (heirloom) contenders. It performs well in the South or where night temperatures exceed seventy degrees. Adds brilliance to salads everywhere.

TANGELLA *page 164, fig. 115k*

SIZE: *1¾" long by 2" wide (sometimes larger)*

WEIGHT: *2½ ounces*

SHAPE: *Cherry*

EXTERIOR COLOR(S): *Reddish orange*

FLESH COLOR(S): *Tangerine*

SOLUBLE SOLIDS: *5 degrees Brix*

FLAVOR: *Good; acidic, fruity*

TEXTURE: *Firm; juicy*

BEST USE(S): *Multipurpose*

PLANT HABIT, LEAF TYPE, AND YIELD: *Indeterminate habit; regular leaf; high yield*

MATURITY: *Early crop*

ORIGIN: *Bred by Dr. L. A. Darby circa 1970 at the Glasshouse Crops Research Institute in Sussex, England. According to Dr. Richard W. Robinson, breeder of the New Yorker tomato (see page 79), Darby backcrossed the fruit stripe gene (fs) into the heritage variety Ailsa Craig (see page 70) to breed Tigerella (Tiger Tom, see page 169). Tangella and Craigella emanated from that same cross. Colin Randel at Thompson and Morgan says these varieties were bred for that "unique difference," although, in those days, prejudice against striped and non-red tomatoes was immense. Many other GCRI varieties (named for Sussex towns and villages) lasted only a few years commercially before being superceded. Tangella has been embraced in very recent years, winning an Award of Garden Merit (AGM) in 2006.*

SYNONYMS: *Sister to Tigerella and Craigella. Parent of Sungella, which resulted from a cross of Tangella with Sungold F₁ made by a dedicated Thompson and Morgan customer in East Anglia, who selected and stabilized it for eight years. Resembles Mini Orange (see previous entry) and Orange Bourgoin.*

SEED SOURCES: *Sa9, So25, To1, To9*

An adorable little orange tomato, smaller than Victory (see page 62), another English favorite. Comes closest to Caro-Rich (see page 167) in color. Tangella earns one of my highest accolades: it tastes like apricots. Use this to make a tangerine-colored dreamboat of a Thai Tomato Cocktail (see page 247).

GOLDIE *page 164, fig. 115c*

SIZE: *4" long by 5½" wide*

WEIGHT: *1 pound, 12 ounces*

SHAPE: *Beefsteak*

EXTERIOR COLOR(S): *Deep orange*

FLESH COLOR(S): *Cadmium orange*

SOLUBLE SOLIDS: *5½ degrees Brix*

FLAVOR: *Good; refreshing*

TEXTURE: *Soft; meaty and juicy*

BEST USE(S): *Multipurpose*

PLANT HABIT, LEAF TYPE, AND YIELD: *Indeterminate habit; regular leaf; good yield*

MATURITY: *Early crop*

ORIGIN: *Introduced in 1977 by Merlin W. Gleckler of Glecklers Seedmen, in an addendum to the main seed listing. Said to be more than 150 years old: "Cultured and handed down by related ancestral families … A real taste thrill and true quality giant tomato." Merlin's son George was unable to provide anything further about Goldie's family of origin when questioned by Craig LeHouillier, co-editor of* Off the Vine, *in 1996.*

Nonetheless, Goldie is considered to be synonymous with Dixie Golden Giant.

SYNONYMS: *Dixie Golden Giant (see page 166); Goldie Yellow. Not the same as Goldie F₁.*

NY: *Nee & Goldman 53405*

SEED SOURCES: *Ers, Fe5, Jo1, Sa9, Se17, So25, Syn, Te4, To1, To3, To9, Vi4*

I can't help being swayed by the neon orange and huge proportions of this tomato. Cutting one from the vine and weighing it in my hand is almost reward enough. Layer Goldie and Evergreen (see page 174) with fresh mozzarella, drizzle with olive oil, and garnish with basil chiffonade to make an Insalata Caprese that the introducer of both tomatoes, Merlin W. Gleckler, would have loved.

CARO-RICH *page 164, fig. 115a*

SIZE: *2½" long by 3½" wide*

WEIGHT: *11½ ounces*

SHAPE: *Round, smooth*

EXTERIOR COLOR(S): *Orange red*

FLESH COLOR(S): *Orange red*

SOLUBLE SOLIDS: *5 degrees Brix*

FLAVOR: *Fair; nondescript*

TEXTURE: *Soft*

BEST USE(S): *Novelty; multipurpose. Color is retained and sweetness enhanced when cooked.*

PLANT HABIT, LEAF TYPE, AND YIELD: *Indeterminate habit; regular leaf; low yield*

MATURITY: *Main crop*

ORIGIN: *An improved version of Caro Red (1958) for the home gardener. Developed at Purdue University. Breeders: E. C. Tigchelaar and M. L. Tomes. Released in 1973. According to the breeders (1974): "Caro-Rich is an F₉ generation bulk developed by pedigree selection from a cross of Summer Sunrise and a high beta-carotene Fusarium wilt-resistant breeding line of complex parentage." The parents include tomato relative* Lycopersicon hirsutum *(PI 126445), Indiana Baltimore, Rutgers (see page 67), and Ontario.*

SEED SOURCES: *Caro Rich. Side by side, cannot be distinguished from Caro Red.*

SEED SOURCES: *Bou, Ma18, Ra6, Se7, Se17, Te4, To3, To10, Up2*

Caro-Rich is a magnificent, unhoped-for, and elusive orange—just like the red-orange-colored stalks in Rainbow Chard. This tomato is rich in pro-Vitamin A, yet it is probably not as nutritious as some believe. Jim Myers, most widely known as the breeder of the first true purple tomato, explains: "Caro-Rich, with the beta gene, may have a three- to eight-fold increase in beta-carotene, but the boost comes with reduced lycopene content. It's like a garden hose with a Y. If more carotenoid precursor flows through the beta-carotene side, then less is available for the lycopene branch." Still, Caro-Rich is eye candy; and when cut in wedges or sliced, all it needs is a sprinkle of sugar.

a

b

c

d

e

f

116

BIG ZEBRA *fig. 115a*

SIZE: *4" long by 6" wide*

WEIGHT: *1 pound, 5 ounces*

SHAPE: *Beefsteak*

EXTERIOR COLOR(S): *Deep green with vivid red*

FLESH COLOR(S): *Yellowish green with vivid red*

SOLUBLE SOLIDS: *5 degrees Brix*

FLAVOR: *Fair; mild, scarcely acid*

TEXTURE: *Soft; meaty and juicy*

BEST USE(S): *Novelty*

PLANT HABIT, LEAF TYPE, AND YIELD: *Indeterminate habit; regular leaf; good yield*

MATURITY: *Early crop*

ORIGIN: *Introduced in 2005 by Linda and Vince Sapp of Tomato Growers Supply Company: "The appearance is so striking and different that we couldn't help noticing it growing in a patch of Copia [see entry below] tomatoes."*

NY: *Nee & Goldman 53413*

Big Zebra can be "groovy" and "retro," for sure, as Jeremiath Gettle of Baker Creek Heirloom Seeds puts it. But it appears to be genetically unstable, and I find that the tomato sometimes grows ugly, distorted, and discolored. Big Zebra is similar in certain respects to Ananas Noire (see page 88) and Berkeley Tie Die but has the distinctive penciled striping of Copia—and of Copia's parent, Green Zebra (see page 172).

RED ZEBRA *fig. 116d*

SIZE: *2½" long by 2¾" wide*

WEIGHT: *6 ounces*

SHAPE: *Round, smooth*

EXTERIOR COLOR(S): *Blood red with carrot-red stripes*

FLESH COLOR(S): *Reddish orange and cherry red*

SOLUBLE SOLIDS: *5 degrees Brix*

FLAVOR: *Poor; disagreeable, strongly acid, not sweet*

TEXTURE: *Very firm; tough, waxy skin. Attractive solid bicolor flesh but mealy.*

BEST USE(S): *Novelty; decorative*

PLANT HABIT, LEAF TYPE, AND YIELD: *Indeterminate habit; regular leaf; good yield*

MATURITY: *Early crop*

ORIGIN: *A natural cross between Tom Wagner's Green Zebra (see page 172) and an unknown parent. Discovered by Jeff Dawson in his California fields and shared with Seed Savers Exchange members in the 2003 annual yearbook. Introduced commercially by Totally Tomatoes in 2004. Three other tomato varieties "created exclusively at [Jeff's] Grandview Farms" (with Tom Wagner tomatoes in their ancestry) and released in 2000 were Mr. Brown (see page 53), Marz Yellow-Red Stripe, and Black Zebra*

SYNONYMS: *F₁ hybrid forms of Red Zebra introduced in 2006 include Red Lightning (Burpee's) and Red Zebra F₁ (Seeds by Design)*

SEED SOURCES: *Ba8 Co32, Ga7, He8, La1, Ra6, Se16, Se17, Sk2, To9, To3, To10, Vi5*

Look—but don't eat.

TIGER TOM *fig. 116e*

SIZE: *2⅛" long by 2⅜" wide*

WEIGHT: *5 ounces*

SHAPE: *Round, smooth*

EXTERIOR COLOR(S): *Cherry red with carrot-red tiger stripes, which are not as stable or prominent as the zebra stripes of Casady's Folly or Speckled Roman (see page 170).*

FLESH COLOR(S): *Madder red*

SOLUBLE SOLIDS: *6 degrees Brix*

FLAVOR: *Varies widely (poor to good)*

TEXTURE: *Reasonably firm*

BEST USE(S): *Multipurpose; novelty*

PLANT HABIT, LEAF TYPE, AND YIELD: *Indeterminate habit; regular leaf; high yield*

MATURITY: *Early crop*

ORIGIN: *Tiger Tom or Tigerella is an English variety bred by Dr. L. A. Darby, head of the Plant Breeding Department at the Glasshouse Crops Research Institute in Sussex circa 1970. (Unfortunately, the GCRI was closed when Margaret Thatcher privatized plant breeding in England.) Darby created Tigerella by backcrossing the fruit stripe gene (fs) into old faithful Ailsa Craig (see page 70). Tigerella possesses an Award of Garden Merit (AGM) from the Royal Horticultural Society.*

SYNONYMS: *Tigerella. Dick Robinson told me that Darby used the name "Tiger Tom" when he gave a seminar at Cornell many years ago; he may have changed the name when he introduced the variety. Also known as Mr. Stripey (not the bicolor beefsteak of the same name). Tangella (see page 166) and Craigella are apparently "sister lines," resulting from the same cross that yielded Tigerella.*

NY: *Nee & Goldman 53415*

SEED SOURCES: *Ag7, Ba8, Bo19, Ers,*

Go8, He8, He17, Hi13, Hud, La1, Mo13, Pr3, Ra6, Re8, Sa9, Se7, Se17, Shu, So25, Te4, To1, To3, To10, Vi4

Tiger-striped tomatoes have been a novelty for about 150 years—or at least since Briggs and Brothers of Rochester, New York, listed Golden Striped ("large, good quality, yellow and red striped") in their 1870 *Illustrated Catalogue of Flower and Vegetable Seeds.* Liberty Hyde Bailey's curiosity was piqued in 1887 by the Gestreifte or "Striped" from Prussia (described as a red tomato "streaked and splashed with irregular lines of orange, or sometimes, even, the orange is predominant, the red assuming the position of stripes"). About a dozen years later, James J. H. Gregory of Marblehead, Massachusetts, introduced the Diadem (1900), which he found a most novel attraction, "the deep ruby red … color of the skin being broken with stripes and spots of old gold."

The Briggs brothers, Bailey and Gregory, would get weak in the knees at the sight of today's flamboyant stripes. We're lucky to be living in such interesting tomato times.

COPIA *fig. 116b, f*

SIZE: *4½" long by 5½" wide*

WEIGHT: *1 pound, 10 ounces*

SHAPE: *Beefsteak*

EXTERIOR COLOR(S): *Orange with scarlet stripes*

FLESH COLOR(S): *Orange and scarlet*

SOLUBLE SOLIDS: *4½ degrees Brix*

FLAVOR: *Fair*

TEXTURE: *Soft; juicy*

BEST USE(S): *Novelty*

PLANT HABIT, LEAF TYPE, AND YIELD: *Indeterminate habit; regular leaf; good yield*

MATURITY: *Early crop*

ORIGIN: *The result of an accidental cross between Green Zebra and Marvel Striped (see pages 172 and 112); discovered by Jeff Dawson, then curator of gardens at* the American Center for Wine, Food and the Arts (COPIA), and named for his place of employment. Gary Ibsen featured Copia at the 2003 Carmel TomatoFest and started selling seeds that same year.

SYNONYMS: *Not the same as Kopiah (1953), which is a plain-Jane red tomato from the Mississippi Agricultural Experiment Station*

NY: *Nee & Goldman 53439*

SEED SOURCES: *Ba8, Na6, To1, To9*

An astounding-looking tomato —orange with explosive fiery red and penciled stripes—but less marvelous in the kitchen than its parents.

(a) Big Zebra, (b,f) Copia, (c) Black Zebra, (d) Red Zebra, (e) Tiger Tom

(a) Schimmeig Stoo, (b) Green Zebra, (c) Casady's Folly

CASADY'S FOLLY *fig. 117c*

SIZE: *4" long by 1¾" wide*

WEIGHT: *5 ounces*

SHAPE: *Plum, often with a small nipple tip*

EXTERIOR COLOR(S): *Cherry red with carrot-red zigzags*

FLESH COLOR(S): *Blood red*

SOLUBLE SOLIDS: *5½ degrees Brix*

FLAVOR: *Excellent; fruity*

TEXTURE: *Very firm; solid and meaty*

BEST USE(S): *Novelty; multipurpose*

PLANT HABIT, LEAF TYPE, AND YIELD: *Determinate habit; regular leaf; good yield*

MATURITY: *Main crop*

ORIGIN: *The result of one of Tom Wagner's deliberate crosses with his Banana Legs (see page 163). Named in memory of Tom's friend Mark Casady.*

SYNONYMS: *A longer, more slender version of Speckled Roman (which it predates; see next entry), with more pronounced striations.*

On the outside, this tomato is psychedelic—like a vegetable Jimi Hendrix poster. Inside, it's both fun and nourishing: Casady's Folly makes a tempting dark-red sauce and is a fine slicer.

SPECKLED ROMAN *fig. 118*

SIZE: *4½" long by 2¼" wide*

WEIGHT: *8 ounces*

SHAPE: *Plum, pointed or blunted*

EXTERIOR COLOR(S): *Cherry red with carrot-red stripes*

FLESH COLOR(S): *Blood red*

SOLUBLE SOLIDS: *5½ degrees Brix*

FLAVOR: *Excellent; sweet and savory*

TEXTURE: *Firm; meaty*

BEST USE(S): *Multipurpose; novelty*

PLANT HABIT, LEAF TYPE, AND YIELD: *Indeterminate habit; droopy foliage; high yield*

MATURITY: *Main crop*

ORIGIN: *Speckled Roman resulted from a chance cross of Tom Wagner's Banana Legs (see page 163) with Antique Roman (see page 128) in the garden of John F. Swenson of Glenview, Illinois; John listed it in the 1998 Seed Savers Exchange yearbook. Jeff Nekola and Sue Gronholtz improved the variety by selecting for more "tiger stripes" and fewer speckles. Speckled Roman was quickly picked up by the seed industry; Seed Savers listed it in their 2002 public catalog, and by 2004, eleven sources had listed it. Throws an occasional yellow-striped fruit; see Roman Holiday and Roman Candle (pages 129 and 141).*

SYNONYMS: *Striped Roman. Similar to Tom Wagner's previously developed Casady's Folly, but longer and wider, with less pronounced striping. Also similar to the striped Opalka that made the rounds some years ago.*

SEED SOURCES: *Ba8, Bo17, Fe5, He17, Hi13, La1, Pe6, Pin, Ra6, Sa5, Sa9, Se16, So1, So25, Te4, Ter, To3, To9, Und, Up2*

This looks like a novelty but it offers more than just good looks. Striped Roman should have a welcome place in every kitchen garden. I can't think of a dish it wouldn't grace. Makes an exceedingly rich and fruity dark-red sauce for curried meatballs (see recipe, page 196).

BLACK ZEBRA page 168, fig. 116c

SIZE: *2¼" long by 2⅞" wide*

WEIGHT: *6½ ounces*

SHAPE: *Round, smooth*

EXTERIOR COLOR(S): *Garnet brown with olive stripes*

FLESH COLOR(S): *Garnet brown*

SOLUBLE SOLIDS: *4½ degrees Brix*

FLAVOR: *Poor*

TEXTURE: *Reasonably firm; mealy*

BEST USE(S): *Decorative; novelty*

PLANT HABIT, LEAF TYPE, AND YIELD: *Indeterminate habit; regular leaf; fair yield*

MATURITY: *Early crop*

ORIGIN: *A natural cross derived from Tom Wagner's Green Zebra (see page 172), and stabilized by Jeff Dawson. Offered in 2000 by Jeff's commercial outfit, Grandview Farms Tomato Seeds, of Sebastopol, California.*

NY: *Nee & Goldman 53471*

SEED SOURCES: *Hi13, Ma18, So25, St18, To9, To10*

This red and green striped fruit is so ornamental that it could adorn a Christmas tree—if Christmas fell in tomato time. Black Zebra strongly resembles Tom Wagner's Christmas tomato, which predates it. I usually find Black Zebra tasteless, but, on occasion, it's so harsh that it burns the tongue like cinnamon.

SCHIMMEIG CREG fig. 119

SIZE: *2½" long by 3⅛" wide*

WEIGHT: *8 ounces*

SHAPE: *High round, smooth*

EXTERIOR COLOR(S): *Blood red with mandarin orange stripes*

FLESH COLOR(S): *Cherry red*

SOLUBLE SOLIDS: *6 degrees Brix*

FLAVOR: *Nonexistent*

TEXTURE: *Very firm; hardball. Mealy, chalky, cottony mouthfeel*

BEST USE(S): *Breeding material; canning; chunky fresh sauce*

PLANT HABIT, LEAF TYPE, AND YIELD: *Determinate habit; regular leaf; good yield*

MATURITY: *Main crop*

ORIGIN: *Created by Thomas P. Wagner and introduced in his 1983 Tater Mater Seeds catalog under the heading "T-2": "red and yellow striped fruit with solid very firm medium size tomatoes. Large determinate vine. Medium to late maturity." Tom wrote to me that he named the variety in 1985 with a little family assistance. "I asked my maternal grandfather, Joe Kaighin, what the Manx words for 'Striped Rock' were. With little hesitation he said, 'Schimmeig Creg.' I asked him to spell it, but he didn't know as Manx was only a spoken language in his day. I went to the dictionary on Manx/English to get the spelling. The name was assigned to the tomato I had given him."*

SYNONYMS: *Striped Rock. Not the same as Schimmeig Stoo (see page 153), which is a hollow striped stuffer.*

SEED SOURCES: *Se17, To10*

Ever since Tom Wagner was a farm boy in Kansas—when he had to pick bushels of soft tomatoes that fell apart at the seams—he's had designs on hard tomatoes. Schimmeig Creg counts among its ancestors Red Rock, the same tomato that Jim Hightower railed against in *Hard Tomatoes, Hard Times*. Tom obtained the Red Rock from the USDA. He wrote me: "Red Rock was a rock-hard tomato that was brilliantly red, had a concentrated set, and yielded great tomatoes for our canning at home. It has some disease resistance from a wild tomato species (*Solanum hirsutum*) and even my dad, Gene Wagner, thought it was a great tomato. My mom and others in the family would can this variety whole in glass jars as it was hard enough to hold together and make the most beautiful dark red tomato pack. Whatever it lacked in flavor was met with other benefits."

David Cavagnaro, former garden manager at Heritage Farm in Decorah, Iowa, pointed out in 1989 how important it is to preserve oddities: "Beauty is more than skin deep when it comes to genetics. Even a vegetable that no one would want to eat may carry valuable and irreplaceable genetic traits. For example, Tom Wagner used Red Rock to breed some of his tomatoes, even though he describes it as 'the worst variety ever bred.' Absolutely rock hard, it was the perfect plant to contribute firmness to other lines that had overly soft flesh. Similarly, other types of unmarketable tomatoes carry such valuable traits as resistance to nematodes and various wilt diseases. We have no way of knowing which traits we will need in the future."

GREEN ZEBRA

page 4, fig. 1h; page 170, fig. 117b; page 175, fig. 121c

SIZE: *2¼" long by 2⅜" wide*

WEIGHT: *3 ounces*

SHAPE: *Round, smooth*

EXTERIOR COLOR(S): *Olive yellow with deep green zebra stripes*

FLESH COLOR(S): *Yellowish green*

SOLUBLE SOLIDS: *5 degrees Brix*

FLAVOR: *On the acidic side. Described by others as "zingy" and "zippy," with an "invigorating lemon-lime" or "scrumptious sweet rich flavor."*

TEXTURE: *Reasonably firm. One reviewer notes, "They have the texture of a kiwi." And the color, too, I might add.*

BEST USE(S): *Novelty. In 1989, photographer David Cavagnaro said it was "gloriously decorative." Good for slicing and salads.*

PLANT HABIT, LEAF TYPE, AND YIELD: *Indeterminate habit; regular leaf; good yield*

MATURITY: *Early crop*

ORIGIN: *Bred by Thomas P. Wagner. Tom cataloged Green Zebra in his inaugural 1983 issue of Tater Mater Seeds in an apparent mix labeled "P-4" of "Green-when-ripe fruits with solid flesh and interiors. Unique in that the dark green stripes cover 50% or more of the surface skin. Large vines are indeterminate in growth." In 1985, the variety was listed separately by name and touted as "a good slicer" and "productive."*

At the 2007 Annual Convention of the Seed Savers Exchange, Tom Wagner revealed how he developed Green Zebra: "I bred that up when I was a kid back in the fifties. I was getting seeds from Glecklers, and I got the Evergreen [see page 174] and thought it was a crazy-looking tomato. It was late-maturing and I couldn't get the thing to ripen; I didn't know when it was ripe. It was cracking, and by the time I picked it I had to almost carry it in both hands to get to the house before it would either crack more or fall apart in my hands. I thought it was the perfect tomato for throwing at people; they would be all green and nobody would know what hit them. Well, Evergreen cracked, so I went down to Atchison, Kansas [nine miles away], because there was a fellow there growing some old tomatoes, and he said they were the best tomatoes he had, and they didn't crack. So I thought, 'I'm going to make my Green Zebra a noncracking tomato.' So I crossed those two tomatoes. The Kansas fellow's hybrid was red. I didn't know what the results would be, but the Evergreen crossed with a red tomato is a red tomato. So I saved the seed again, thinking maybe I could do better than that. I finally got a good green tomato that didn't crack, and I called that Glamour Evergreen.

"But I didn't stop there. I wanted something different, and I was crossing some striped tomatoes—not the Tigerella [see Tiger Tom, page 169] but one from the Plant Introduction Station in Ames, Iowa, or in Davis, California. I picked

up varieties that had a little striping on them—it wasn't very much. I crossed this striped tomato in with another variety that didn't crack, and I was trying to get more stripes on it. I was working on different levels of stripe—10, 20, 40, 60 percent—I wanted different levels of striping on it to make it more beautiful. So when I crossed this improvement with my Glamour Evergreen, once again, I got a red tomato. It was worthless. I could hardly see the stripes on it. So I saved the seed, put the plants out in the garden, saved seed from those, put them in the greenhouse that I had built, saved the seed, put the plants out in the garden, doubling up the seeds. And finally I realized that I wasn't getting the flavor I wanted in the greenhouse. I was looking for something that had more zing to it. So as I was going through my Green Zebra look-alikes at that time, I found one that had 80 percent stripes, some 90, 60, 20 percent. I settled on one with about 60 percent stripes. I liked the flavor and I thought that had to be it: It has stripes and it's green and I know when it's ripe and it doesn't crack. I had to show it to my dad and mom and all my relatives. Their response was, 'We'll see you in the funny papers. You're not going anywhere with that!' So then I thought Green Zebra was going to be a total loser and nobody would want it at that time. But I started offering it in my Tater Mater Seeds catalog." The rest is tomato history.*

SYNONYMS: *There are many sister lines of Green Zebra in all shapes and sizes, including Green and Yellow Bell (Green Cup), and Tom reports he has made improved selections for flavor. Chance and deliberate crosses of Green Zebra include Copia, Black Zebra, and Red Zebra (see pages 169 and 171).*

SEED SOURCES: *Ag7, Ba8, Bo17, Co32, Coo, Fe5, Ga1, Ga21, Ga22, Go8, Ha26, He8, He17, Hi13, Jo1, Ki4, La1, Ma18, Na6, Ni1, Pe2, Pep, Ra6, Roh, Sa5, Sa9, Se16, Se7, Se17, So1, So25, Sw9, Te4, To1, To3, To9, To10, Tu6, Up2, Vi4*

Tom Wagner's tomato creations are dazzling—and it amazes me to think he was only a ten-year-old kid (born 1946) when he began breeding Green Zebra, on the family farm near Lancaster, Kansas. This tomato may not have been his folks' cup of tea, but Tom received plenty of encouragement for his efforts from his maternal grandfather, Joseph Kaighin. An immigrant from the Isle of Man and a breeder of mules, Grandfather Kaighin taught the keen-eyed youth the art of growing potatoes,

some Manx—a nearly extinct Gaelic language that Tom later used to name tomatoes—and animal (if not vegetable) husbandry. It was his grandfather's lessons that Tom heeded when he told his mother and father what he intended to do about some cracked tomatoes: "Time to bring in a new bull!" Tom figured out how to "mate maters" by transferring pollen. And what's a kid to do but use his sister's pigtail ribbons to tag blossoms?

Now in his early sixties, Tom no longer uses pigtail ribbons for breeding projects, but he retains his youthful zest and vision. Despite early predictions, he's "gone somewhere" with that kooky Green Zebra. And he's still inspired by his grandfather; Tom charmed me by speaking in Manx-accented English during a recent phone call. "Tommy Tomatoseed," as he's affectionately known, makes hundreds and sometimes thousands of crosses every year. He has alternate breeding lines of many of his older varieties—including Green Zebra—so he could potentially release Mini Zebra, Maxi Zebra, Brandy Zebra, Tangerine Zebra, Roma Zebra, and others.

Tom wrote to me, "As a private breeder, I have created many tomatoes that are considered 'Heirloom' and this has amused me over the years to no end. How does one become an 'Heirloom Breeder' and still be alive? Is it because I have been doing this work for over 50 years? Or is it more likely that my creations naturally fall into this esteemed category? I have so many new candidates for the future heirloom varieties in my collections." Stripes of different colors, high-flavored, cold-tolerant, and disease-resistant tomatoes—I look forward to oohing and aahing over whatever's next.

(a, b) Black from Tula, (c) Black Prince, (d) Purple Calabash, (e) Black Cherry

BLACK FROM TULA *fig. 120a, b*

SIZE: *2¾" long by 3⅛" wide*

WEIGHT: *14 ounces*

SHAPE: *Beefsteak*

EXTERIOR COLOR(S): *Brownish red*

FLESH COLOR(S): *Garnet brown*

SOLUBLE SOLIDS: *5 degrees Brix*

FLAVOR: *Fair*

TEXTURE: *Soft; mealy, some hard corky areas*

BEST USE(S): *Multipurpose*

PLANT HABIT, LEAF TYPE, AND YIELD: *Indeterminate habit; regular leaf; good yield*

MATURITY: *Early crop*

ORIGIN: *Imported by Seed Savers Exchange from Russia and offered to members in 1996. Black from Tula became part of the Russian Collection made available commercially by SSE in 1998.*

SEED SOURCES: *Ba8, Co32, Ga1, Go8, He8, He17, Hi13, Hud, La1, Ma18, Pe2, Sa9, Se16, So25, To1, To3, To9, To10, Und*

Not outstanding in my taste tests but others rave about it: "magnificent," "rich," "creamy," and "delectable." *Chacun à son goût.*

BLACK PRINCE *fig. 120c*

SIZE: *2¼" long by 3⅛" wide*

WEIGHT: *7 ounces*

SHAPE: *Round, smooth (sometimes high-round)*

EXTERIOR COLOR(S): *Burnt sienna and olive*

FLESH COLOR(S): *Titian red*

SOLUBLE SOLIDS: *5 degrees Brix*

FLAVOR: *Poor to excellent*

TEXTURE: *Soft; juicy*

BEST USE(S): *Fresh eating; peel the skin if cooking*

PLANT HABIT, LEAF TYPE, AND YIELD: *Indeterminate habit; regular leaf; high yield*

MATURITY: *Early crop*

ORIGIN: *From Irkutsk, Siberia. Introduced circa 1995 by early adopter Rose Marie Nichols McGee of Nichols Garden Nursery. Kate Rogers Gessert of Eugene, Oregon, gave the original seed to Rose Marie in the early 1990s. Kate had found it in Eugene's sister city, Irkutsk, where black tomatoes are sometimes preserved with salt.*

SEED SOURCES: *Ap6, Ba8, Co32, Ga1, He8, He17, Hi13, Jo1, Ni1, Pe2, Ra6, Re8, Sa5, Sa9, Se17, Se26, Se28, So1, So25, Sw9, To1, To3, To9, Up2*

Princely in appearance, finicky to grow, iffy on the table, Black Prince has been described as bronzy, brassy, and greenish-brownish-reddish; the color almost defies description. It's more Brown Prince than Black. Adapted to Siberia and the Pacific Northwest.

AUNT RUBY'S GERMAN GREEN *fig. 121a; page vi; page 59, fig. 33a*

SIZE: *3¼" long by 5½" wide*

WEIGHT: *1 pound, 5 ounces*

SHAPE: *Beefsteak*

EXTERIOR COLOR(S): *Olive yellow*

FLESH COLOR(S): *Olive yellow*

SOLUBLE SOLIDS: *5¼ degrees Brix*

FLAVOR: *Excellent; a perfect balance of acid and sugar*

TEXTURE: *Soft; melting*

BEST USE(S): *Fresh eating*

PLANT HABIT, LEAF TYPE, AND YIELD: *Indeterminate habit; regular leaf; low yield*

MATURITY: *Early crop*

ORIGIN: *Introduced to members of Seed Savers Exchange in 1993 by Bill Minkey, of Darien, Wisconsin*

SYNONYMS: *Aunt Ruby's. Shares certain features with Grandma Oliver's Green, a tomato that apparently belonged to Jacob Hardman in Indiana during the 1920s.*

SEED SOURCES: *Abu, Ap6, Ba8, Bo17, Co32, Fe5, Ga1, Go8, He8, He17, Hi13, Hud, Jun, Ma18, Pe2, Pin, Ra6, Re8, Roh, Sa9, Se16, Se28, So25, Sw9, Te4, To1, To3, To9, To10, Und, Up2, Vi4, Yu2*

The most popular green-when-ripe (amber-when-overripe) beefsteak tomato. "Fruity," "grapey," and "spicy" are adjectives that begin to describe the taste of Aunt Ruby's German Green. Can be demure and oblate, or outrageously shaped like a coxcomb.

Aunt Ruby's is one of Bill Minkey's finest acts in a long life of fine acts. (I'll always remember the bouquet of oriental lilies he sent me "just because" from his garden one summer, carefully wrapped with damp towels inside a turkey crate.) Bill obtained seed from Ruby Arnold of Greeneville, Tennessee, via Ruby's niece Nita Hofstrom (who lived in Bill's hometown of Clinton, Wisconsin). Ruby called it German Green—the seed had been handed down from her German immigrant grandfather—but granted Bill permission to rename it. So the tomato bears Miss Arnold's name and, in many examples, her mark: a star ruby at the blossom end. This remarkable variety was recently and deservedly boarded onto Slow Food USA's Ark of Taste.

EVERGREEN *fig. 121b, d*

SIZE: *2½" long by 3¾" wide*

WEIGHT: *11 ounces*

SHAPE: *Beefsteak*

EXTERIOR COLOR(S): *Grapefruit and yolk yellow when fully ripe*

FLESH COLOR(S): *Grayish green*

SOLUBLE SOLIDS: *4½ degrees Brix*

FLAVOR: *Fair; high acid, lemony, not sweet*

TEXTURE: *Soft; meaty and juicy, sometimes mealy*

BEST USE(S): *Multipurpose. Very easily peeled without a dip in hot water. Chef Paul Bertolli says that Evergreen, "with a wonderful leaf and mineral taste, seems most naturally suited to dessert; because it is very high in acid and nearly devoid of sweetness, I … enhance it with sugar and spice."*

PLANT HABIT, LEAF TYPE, AND YIELD: *Indeterminate habit; regular leaf; good yield*

MATURITY: *Early crop*

ORIGIN: *Introduced in 1956 by Glecklers Seedmen, Metamora, Ohio. Obtained by Mr. Gleckler from a horticulturist who died before disclosing the origin.*

SYNONYMS: *Emerald Evergreen; Tasty Evergreen*

NY: *Nee & Goldman 54602*

SEED SOURCES: *Ba8, Ers, Ga1, Gr27, Ha26, He17, Ma18, Pe2, Ra6, Sa9, Se16, Se28, Sk2, Sw9, So25, Te4, To1, To3, To9, Up2, Vi5*

A green-when-ripe tomato that's still a novelty more than fifty years after its introduction. Evergreen caught the imagination of the legendary Benjamin F. Quisenberry of Syracuse, Ohio, and set him on his path as a tomato seedsman: "That's the one that got me started. I started out with Evergreen and Ruby Gold," he said in 1981. "Then good people just kept sending me their favorites."

Here's Merlin W. Gleckler's recipe for Evergreen Tomato Conserve: Peel and cut 6 cups of Evergreen. Add 6 cups of white sugar and ½ cup water. Cook for about 15 minutes, then add one can (1 pint) diced pineapple. Cook until clear, then turn into jars and seal.

(a) Aunt Ruby's German Green,
(b, d) Evergreen, (c) Green Zebra

a

b

c

d

a

b

c

d

e

f

g

h

i

j

122

PINK SALAD *fig. 122f*

SIZE: *1¾" long by 1¼" wide*

WEIGHT: *1½ ounces*

SHAPE: *Mini plum*

EXTERIOR COLOR(S): *Tomato pink*

FLESH COLOR(S): *Tomato pink*

SOLUBLE SOLIDS: *6½ degrees Brix*

FLAVOR: *Excellent; mouth-watering in the same way as Sugary (an F₁ hybrid miniature pink plum tomato, winner of a 2005 All America Selections Award)*

TEXTURE: *Firm; meaty*

BEST USE(S): *Fresh eating; pickling and preserving*

PLANT HABIT, LEAF TYPE, AND YIELD: *Indeterminate habit; regular leaf; good yield*

MATURITY: *Early crop*

ORIGIN: *Pink Salad reportedly originated as a sport of a red salad tomato circa 1973; it was first listed by Thomas J. Bailey of Harrin, Illinois, in the 1985 Seed Savers Exchange yearbook.*

SYNONYMS: *Similar to a little rose-colored Cuban beauty named Pink Plum that Ken Ettlinger (of Long Island Seed and Plant Company) obtained in 1991 from the world's foremost authority on tomato genetics, Dr. Charles M. Rick, of the University of California at Davis. Rick told Ettlinger that he made a very sweet pink tomato sauce with it.*

Miniature plum tomatoes have been in circulation since at least the time of Fearing Burr, who noted in 1863 that the red mixed with the yellow make a fine garnish, and both are excellent for salad. Pink Salad makes a comely addition; and it tastes great.

ABE HALL *fig. 122h*

SIZE: *3½" long by 6¼" wide*

WEIGHT: *2 pounds, 6 ounces*

SHAPE: *Beefsteak*

EXTERIOR COLOR(S): *Tomato pink*

FLESH COLOR(S): *Blood red*

SOLUBLE SOLIDS: *7 degrees Brix*

FLAVOR: *Good; sweet and tart—everything you'd want in a big tomato*

TEXTURE: *Reasonably firm; meaty and juicy*

BEST USE(S): *Fresh eating*

PLANT HABIT, LEAF TYPE, AND YIELD: *Indeterminate habit; regular leaf; good yield*

MATURITY: *Main crop*

ORIGIN: *Given to Jerry Moomaw of Glouster, Ohio, by Fred Hutchison, a descendent of Abe Hall. Moomaw initially listed the tomato in the Seed Savers Exchange 1997 yearbook.*

A testament to the derring-do of boater Abe Hall, who singlehandedly plucked the floating tomato from a raging Ohio River. This maritime rescue puts me in mind of another tomato saved from drowning, though with fewer acrobatics: Eighteen-Eighty-Four, a pink beefsteak found in a heap of debris after the flood of 1884 near Friendly, West Virginia, by a Mr. Williamson. Abe Hall is the better variety—at least in my Hudson River Valley garden, where it keeps me swimming in toothsome tomatoes until frost.

GIANT BELGIUM *fig. 122g*

SIZE: *4" long by 5½" wide*

WEIGHT: *1 pound, 10 ounces (In my garden it's a wee Belgium, but the variety reportedly grows five-pounders in the South)*

SHAPE: *Beefsteak*

EXTERIOR COLOR(S): *Tomato pink*

FLESH COLOR(S): *Tomato pink*

SOLUBLE SOLIDS: *6 degrees Brix*

FLAVOR: *Fair; bland*

TEXTURE: *Soft; meaty and juicy; some hard core*

BEST USE(S): *Fresh eating; reportedly makes a fine sweet dessert or cocktail wine*

PLANT HABIT, LEAF TYPE, AND YIELD: *Indeterminate habit; regular leaf; good yield*

MATURITY: *Early crop*

ORIGIN: *The history of Giant Belgium is confounded with several similar tomatoes. Ohio, Maryland, Pennsylvania, Tennessee, and Texas have laid claim to it. Belgium, anyone?*

SYNONYMS: *Belgian Giant; Belgium Giant; Giant Belgium Pink*

NY: *Nee & Goldman 53390*

SEED SOURCES: *Ba8, Bu2, Ba8, Com, He8, He17, Hi13, Hud, Ma18, Ra6, Sa9, Se28, Shu, Sk2, Sw9, To1, To3, To9, To10, Vi4, Vi5*

Give a kid a tomato to grow, and she'll become a lifelong tomato lover. Eight-year-old Jeanette "Nettie" Crumpler grew her first Giant Belgiums in Wichita Falls, Texas, in 1941, and nicknamed her three plants Peg Leg Pete, Clarabelle, and Minnie. Only Pete survived the onslaught of spider mites and blight. More than fifty years later, in the *Tomato Club* newsletter, Nettie recounted the rapture of the harvest on an early morning toward the end of that hot July: "I went out to check on

Pete and there were actually four ripe and three ripening tomatoes, huge in size and lovely in color. I triumphantly carried them into the house and announced to all that I was having one for breakfast. Dad and my grandma sat down with me and we each had a slice from the biggest one. Although there was a greenish core, the juicy slice was worth the wait. It was sweet, yet wine-y, and the pinkish red color was so pretty. I drew a picture of my Giant Belgium and tried to color it exactly right to capture its beauty. Peg Leg Pete produced only two more before blight swept over him, and Dad finally pronounced him gone."

(a) Zapotec, (b) Japanese Oxheart, (c) Peach Blow Sutton, (d) Hungarian Heart, (e) Radiator Charlie's Mortgage Lifter, (f) Pink Salad, (g) Giant Belgium, (h) Abe Hall, (i) Dr. Carolyn Pink, (j) Eva Purple Ball

recipes

When I think about cooking with tomatoes, I envision a photograph of my father: He's standing at the kitchen table, looking happy, with tomato-sauce stains on his shirt. He's been leaning over a big pot, tasting my mother's long-simmering marinara sauce, made with *pomodori pelati*. The whole house smells delicious, and the windows are steamy; we're glad to be inside as night falls on a short winter day. Just after the photograph is taken, my sisters and my niece—still half-clad in her snowsuit—join my father and me at the table. My mother puts down an enormous bowl of pasta with the tomato sauce on top, a platter of steamed broccoli *aglio e olio*, and a basket of garlic bread, and we all dig in. Thoughts of those family dinners fill me with love and delight. Twenty years later, I'm at my stove in upstate New York stirring a pot of my mother's marinara sauce, and my daughter, Sara—the same age now that my niece Robin was way back then—is asking for a taste. I almost named Sara "Solanée"—the French botanical word for the tomato family—in memory of my father, Sol. She's glad I didn't burden her with such an unusual name—and, in any case, "Solanée's Galapagos" doesn't resonate nearly as well as "Sara's Galapagos," the tomato I named after her (see page 35).

I love cooking for my family and friends. One night last August, I invited five neighbors to an all-tomato dinner. First we strolled through the tomato patch, Thai Tomato Cocktails in hand, as I gave a guided tour. Feeling stimulated, we came in for dinner at my kitchen table, which was adorned with a basket filled with homegrown tomatoes and floral sprays of Riesentraube (see page 45). Guests helped themselves to a banquet, set up on the sideboard, of Colorful Gazpacho with all the trimmings. Tomato great Ben Quisenberry (whom you've gotten to know in the Portraits) would've said the atmosphere was "very congenial." For the main dish, I served Spaghetti with Cherry Tomatoes and Toasted Crumbs. None of us was vegetarian, but the tomatoes at that time of year were so lush and perfect, we didn't miss the meat course one bit. By the time I had brought out the warm Galette of White Peaches and Tomatoes with a side of vanilla ice cream, everyone was in a state of bliss, including me.

I wish I could invite all my readers over to eat, but that's impractical; my table only accommodates twelve. So, instead, I'm going to share my recipes, which can be easily prepared in your own kitchen. I wanted to offer some things that aren't in my usual repertoire, too, so I asked Eve Felder, Associate Dean for Culinary Arts at the Culinary Institute of America, to help out. You'll find here a range of recipes, from hors d'oeuvres such as Spanish Tomato Bread to desserts such as Roasted Tomato Crunch Sicilian Style. If you use homegrown tomatoes rather than store-bought in any of these, your satisfaction quotient will go way up, as you might expect. Some dishes, such as Fattoush and Pan Bagnat, are best enjoyed in summer with just-picked tomatoes; others, such as Cream of Tomato Soup and Curried Meatballs with Tomatoes, are designed to serve on short winter days. I include a Marinara Sauce my parents would have approved of—guaranteed to steam your windows and warm your heart.

Soups

CHERRY TOMATO AND GARLIC BREAD SOUP

YIELD: *8 portions*

1 loaf levain bread, sliced ¼ inch thick
¼ cup pure olive oil, plus more for oiling
    the pan and brushing the toast
1 garlic clove, peeled and halved, plus
    ½ cup thinly sliced garlic cloves
4 cups thinly sliced onions
2½ quarts chicken stock
Salt to taste
Fresh-ground black pepper to taste
2 pints cherry, grape, and currant tomatoes
¼ pound Parmesan cheese, grated
¾ cup coarsely chopped basil leaves
Basil chiffonade, for garnish
Chopped flat-leaf parsley, for garnish

When Caterina de' Medici arrived at the royal court of France in the sixteenth century, she introduced homely Italian bread soup, thereby elevating it from peasant fare to the menu of kings. For the rest of us, this *panade* is a treat when spiked with novelty cherry and currant tomatoes.

1. Preheat the oven to 350 degrees.

2. Brush the slices of bread with olive oil on both sides. Toast on a baking sheet in the oven until golden brown on the top and bottom. Be sure to flip the slices over halfway through toasting. When toasted, brush the cut sides of the garlic gently across all surfaces of the toast. Maintain the oven temperature.

3. In the meantime, heat the ¼ cup olive oil in a large sauté pan and cook the onions until slightly caramelized, about 15 minutes. Add the garlic and cook until it is tender. Reserve.

4. Season the chicken stock with salt and pepper. Set aside 1 quart (4 cups) of the stock; the remaining 1½ quarts (6 cups) will be used to cook the panade.

5. In a lightly oiled 2½-quart ovenproof glass or pottery baking dish, layer half of the toast. Spoon or spread half of the onion mixture over the toast, add half of the tomatoes, and sprinkle one third of the Parmesan cheese and all of the basil on top. Repeat layer with remaining half of toast, onion mixture, and tomatoes, and half of the remaining cheese. Add 3 cups of the stock. Wait for about 5 minutes for the bread to absorb the stock, then add 1 cup more. Repeat until the bread looks like a wrung-out sponge. Finally, sprinkle the top of the bread with the remaining Parmesan cheese.

6. Cover with aluminum foil and bake for 45 minutes. Gently remove the aluminum foil (it may have stuck to the cheese, so be careful). Increase the heat to 400 degrees and continue baking the panade until the top is golden brown. Remove from the oven and cool.

7. Cut into 8 servings.

8. Reheat the reserved chicken stock in a pot.

9. To serve, place a portion of panade in each bowl. Ladle a few ounces of stock around (not over) the panade. Garnish with the chopped basil and parsley.

COLORFUL GAZPACHO

YIELD: *12 portions*

GAZPACHO

2½ pounds tomatoes, red and pink
2½ pounds tomatoes, green when ripe
2½ pounds tomatoes, yellow and orange
3 teaspoons salt
9 basil leaves, slightly bruised
3 teaspoons coarsely chopped garlic
Fresh-ground black pepper to taste

GARNISH

½ pound cucumbers, peeled, seeded, and
 cut into small dice
1½ pounds assorted tomatoes, cut into
 small dice
½ bunch green onions (both green and
 white parts), sliced
2 Hass avocados, cut into small dice
1 red bell pepper, peeled, seeded, and cut
 into very small dice
1 yellow bell pepper, peeled, seeded, and
 cut into very small dice
3 jalapeño peppers, seeded and cut into
 very small dice
Salt to taste
Crunchy Croutons (page 237)
Extra-virgin olive oil to taste
Opal basil, chiffonade, as needed
Italian parsley, chiffonade, as needed

Gazpacho is even more delightful when tricolored with green, red, and yellow tomatoes. Serve the soup in glass goblets and allow guests to choose from an array of garnishes on the banquet table. Place a pitcher of olive oil on the table to accentuate the positives.

1. Make the gazpacho: Coarsely chop the tomatoes, one color at a time; keep separated in three bowls. Add 1 teaspoon of the salt, 3 of the basil leaves, and 1 teaspoon of the chopped garlic to each bowl. Let sit for 2 hours.

2. In the meantime, prepare the garnishes and place each in a separate smaller bowl. Combine the bell and jalapeño peppers; season with salt and set aside. Cover each garnish with plastic wrap and refrigerate if preparing in advance.

3. Remove the basil leaves from the bowls of tomatoes. Starting with the yellow and orange tomatoes, pass the macerated mixture through a food mill to purée. Do the same for the green and red tomatoes. Rinse the food mill when changing colors. Keep the three colors in separate bowls. Taste, add black pepper, and adjust the salt. Refrigerate until ready to serve.

4. You will need some assistance to serve this soup, so ask a friend to lend a hand. (Only one hand will be needed.) Fill three 2-ounce ladles or glass measuring cups with the tomato purées; on the count of three, acting in concert, slowly add all three purées to a glass goblet. Repeat with other goblets. (If you don't have goblets, soup plates will work fine.)

5. Place a teaspoon or so of each garnish over the soup or allow guests to serve themselves.

SAVORY TOMATO CUSTARD

YIELD: *8 portions*

1 tablespoon canola oil
2 teaspoons finely minced garlic
2 teaspoons peeled and finely minced
    fresh ginger

8 large eggs
5 cups chicken stock
2 teaspoons salt
1 pound tomatoes, peeled, seeded, diced,
    and drained. Use a dry tomato like
    Doucet's Plum Producer

2½ tablespoons soy sauce
1 tablespoon hot sesame oil
3 tablespoons sliced scallions

This is not some sweet eggy thing but instead a heavenly variation on the Japanese soup *chawan-mushi*, a savory custard with chicken, shrimp, and vegetables. In this version, tomatoes complement the taste of the stock-enriched custard and yield a tomato soup like you've never had before. Can be served hot or chilled in lidded or heat-proof cups. Eat with a spoon and chopsticks.

1. Preheat the oven to 400 degrees.

2. Heat the oil slightly in a sauté pan, add the garlic and ginger, and cook over moderate heat until aromatic, about 5 minutes. Reserve and cool.

3. Whisk the eggs in a large bowl just to combine (don't create a lot of foam). Stir in the chicken stock and 1 teaspoon of the salt.

4. Combine the tomatoes with the reserved garlic and ginger and season with the remaining teaspoon of salt. Divide the tomato mixture evenly among eight 8-ounce ovenproof cups or ramekins. Pour the egg and chicken-stock mixture over the tomatoes.

5. Cover each cup loosely with foil. Place them in a baking dish and fill the dish halfway up with boiling water to create a hot-water bath in the preheated oven, or use a steamer. Cook for 25 minutes or until the eggs are set (when the cup is shaken the egg should tremble slightly).

6. Garnish each with 1 teaspoon of soy sauce, ½ teaspoon of sesame oil, and a sprinkle of scallions.

CREAM OF TOMATO SOUP

YIELD: *2 quarts*

4 tablespoons (½ stick) butter
1 cup sliced onions
½ cup thinly sliced carrots
2 tablespoons minced garlic
½ cup all-purpose flour
1 quart chicken stock, at room temperature
1 bay leaf
4 cups peeled, seeded, and diced tomatoes
1 tablespoon salt
2 teaspoons fresh-ground black pepper
2 cups heavy cream
Crunchy Croutons (page 237)

Served in a mug with warm vapors wafting, attended by a tuna fish sandwich on toast, this soup is the living end. The food hoarder in me stockpiles mega-batches of the stuff in the freezer (I wait until I defrost it to add the cream) and canned tuna by the gross in the pantry—in case of urgency.

1. Melt the butter in a 3-quart heavy-bottomed pot over moderate heat. Add the onions and carrots. Cover and cook until the onions are translucent and the carrots are tender. Add the minced garlic and cook just until it becomes fragrant, about a minute or two. Add the flour and stir until the mixture is light brown.

2. Whisk in the stock. Add the bay leaf. Bring to a boil and immediately reduce the heat to a gentle simmer, stirring occasionally. Cook for 20 minutes.

3. Add the tomatoes, salt, and pepper. Cook until the tomatoes are soft, about 10 minutes. Remove the bay leaf.

4. Purée in a blender. Return to the pan and add the cream. Cook over moderate heat until the soup is hot.

5. Serve with the croutons.

SMOKED TOMATO SOUP

YIELD: *2 quarts*

½ cup pure olive oil
2 cups diced onions
1 tablespoon plus 2 teaspoons salt
3 tablespoons sliced garlic
5 pounds firm tomatoes, quartered
2 teaspoons fresh-ground black pepper
3 basil sprigs
5 thyme sprigs
Crunchy Croutons (page 237)

Take comfort in this soup, which combines homey tomato flavor and the smokiness of a wood fire. Onions, rather than sugar, sweeten the brew.

1. Prepare a grill with charcoal. When the coals or briquettes are white-hot, add pieces of a hardwood such as oak, hickory, or apple wood. Bank the coals and wood to one side.

2. Warm ¼ cup of the olive oil in a pot. Add the onions and 2 teaspoons of the salt. Sweat over medium-low heat until the onions are translucent, about 5 minutes. Add the garlic and cook until tender.

3. Toss the quartered tomatoes with the remaining ¼ cup of olive oil, the remaining tablespoon of salt, the pepper, and the herbs. Place in a metal roasting pan.

4. Using oven mitts, carefully place the pan into the hot grill, opposite the banked coals. Cover the grill and open the air vents. Cook until the tomatoes are charred and tender, approximately 30 to 45 minutes. Cool.

5. Pass the roasted tomatoes through a food mill into the onion mixture. Stir well to combine. Add salt to taste.

6. Reheat and serve with the croutons.

Main Dishes

GRILLED SNAPPER WITH CORN AND GREEN TOMATO SALAD

YIELD: *8 portions*

FISH

3 pounds snapper fillets

1 tablespoon salt

1 jalapeño pepper

2 tablespoons pure olive oil

Zest of 2 limes

10 cilantro stems

CORN AND GREEN TOMATO SALAD

4 ears corn

2 teaspoons salt

½ cup small-diced red onions

2 tablespoons fresh lime juice

6 small green (unripe) tomatoes

1 cup medium-diced red bell pepper

3 tablespoons seeded and minced
   jalapeño peppers (if you want the salad
   spicier, leave some seeds in)

½ cup chopped cilantro

¼ cup extra-virgin olive oil

2 teaspoons fresh-ground black pepper

GARNISH

16 slices Hass avocado

8 lime wedges

8 cilantro sprigs

A glorious *agrodolce* (sweet and sour) dish for the end of summer, when the garden is full-blown or just starting to wane. The crisp and sharp acid of mature green (unripe) tomatoes perfectly complements the sweetness of grilled corn. Any firm fish such as tuna or swordfish can be substituted for snapper. Garnish with more green: slices of avocado, a wedge of lime, and sprigs of cilantro.

1. To prepare the fish: Score the fish's skin at 1-inch intervals. Season with salt. Combine the jalapeño with the oil, lime zest, and cilantro to make a marinade. Put half the marinade into a glass or pottery casserole before adding the fish; top with the remainder of the marinade. Cover and refrigerate for 4 hours.

2. In the meantime, prepare the corn and green tomato salad: Preheat a grill to a moderate temperature. Pull the husks back from the corn, leaving them attached at the base. Remove the silks. Season the corn with 1 teaspoon of the salt, then pull the husks back up to cover the corn. Grill for 10 to 15 minutes, turning periodically. Husk the corn and, with a sharp knife, remove the kernels.

3. Pace the red onions in a small bowl, add the lime juice and ½ teaspoon of the salt, and soak for 20 minutes.

4. Cut the green tomatoes into small dice. Combine the corn kernels, red onions (with soaking liquid), green tomatoes, red bell pepper, jalapeños, cilantro, and oil. The ratio of corn to green tomatoes should be about 3 to 1. Taste and add the pepper, ½ teaspoon or more salt, and more lime juice, if desired. (The salad can be made ahead to this point and refrigerated.)

5. Grill the fish skin side down until just done, about 8 minutes per inch of thickness.

6. Garnish and serve the snapper with the corn and green tomato salad.

BAKED BLACK COD WITH TOMATO BUTTER

YIELD: *8 portions*

BOILED POTATOES

3 pounds small potatoes

Water to cover potatoes

2 tablespoons salt

6 tablespoons (¾ stick) butter, sliced

TOMATO BUTTER

½ cup minced shallots

2 cups dry white wine

1 tablespoon white wine vinegar

½ cup tomato juice

1 cup heavy cream

2 cups (4 sticks) butter, cut into ½-inch
   squares

1 pound slightly unripe black tomatoes,
   peeled, seeded, and diced

2 teaspoons salt

ROASTED BLACK COD

2 tablespoons butter

2 cups white wine

3 pounds black cod (or other firm white
   fish such as sea bass or halibut), cut into
   eight 6-ounce portions

1 tablespoon salt

2 teaspoons coarsely ground black pepper

WILTED SPINACH

2 tablespoons butter

⅓ cup finely chopped shallots

2 pounds spinach, stems removed

1½ teaspoons salt

½ teaspoon fresh-ground black pepper

A gorgeous meal, especially when the black cod is paired with black tomatoes, such as Black Krim or Russian Black.

1. Peel the potatoes, if you prefer them without peels. Place them in a 4-quart pot, cover them with cold water, add the salt, and bring to a boil. Reduce the heat to a simmer and cook the potatoes until tender, approximately 20 to 30 minutes, and drain.

2. While the potatoes are draining, add the sliced butter to the potato pot and melt over low heat. Return the drained and still hot potatoes to the pot and, with a wooden spoon, roll them in the butter over very low heat. Remove from heat, cover and keep warm.

3. To prepare the tomato butter: In a 1-quart pan, combine the shallots, wine, vinegar, and tomato juice. Reduce over medium heat until almost dry, about 8 minutes.

4. Add in the heavy cream and cook, stirring frequently, until reduced by half.

5. Over moderate heat, whisk in the butter one third at a time. Do not add the next batch until the previous batch is melted.

6. Keep the butter sauce in a double boiler over low heat while preparing the tomatoes, other vegetables, and fish. If the sauce appears to be separating around the edges, it's too hot; just decrease heat and whisk in a couple more teaspoons of cold butter.

7. Season the diced tomatoes with the salt. Reserve.

8. Preheat the oven to 375 degrees.

9. To prepare the cod: Butter a large skillet with 1-inch sides. Add the white wine. Season the fish on both sides with the salt and pepper. Place in the pan with the white wine.

10. Bake the fish until opaque and firm, about 8 minutes per inch of thickness.

11. While the fish is baking, prepare the shallots for the wilted spinach: Melt the butter over moderate heat in a large sauté pan or sauce pot. Add the shallots and "sweat" over low heat, covered, until they turn translucent (but not brown) and release their natural juices. Set aside.

12. When the fish is done, remove with a spatula to drain off excess liquid. Place on a warm baking sheet and reserve in a warm place.

13. Final preparation of the tomato butter: Add the drained diced tomatoes to the butter sauce. Use the liquid that has accumulated from salting the tomatoes to thin the sauce if necessary.

14. Final preparation of the wilted spinach: Add the spinach, salt, and pepper to the reserved shallots. Wilt the spinach over moderate heat for 3 to 4 minutes, tossing with tongs to assure even cooking, then cover the pan.

15. Place the spinach in the center of the plate, top with fish, and serve three potatoes with each portion. Cover each portion of fish with a generous spoonful of sauce.

SHRIMP CREOLE

YIELD: *8 portions*

¼ cup canola oil

4 cups diced onions

2 cups diced celery

2 cups small-diced green bell pepper

¼ cup slivered garlic

2 teaspoons salt

2 pounds plum, pear, or fig tomatoes, peeled and diced

1 teaspoon hot paprika

¼ teaspoon cayenne pepper

2 teaspoons Old Bay seasoning

1 teaspoon salt

1½ teaspoons fresh-ground black pepper

¼ cup all-purpose flour

2½ pounds large shrimp, peeled and deveined

4 cups long-grain white rice

6 cups water

1 tablespoon salt

6 tablespoons (¾ stick) butter

1 bunch of scallions, chopped or cut into curls

Briny, savory, and delicious, this exceptional concoction should never be degraded by store-bought tomatoes. Try Burpee's Globe or Burbank instead. What sends me over the edge is the subtle fragrance of boiled rice.

1. Heat the oil in a large sauté pan. Add the onions, celery, bell peppers, garlic, and salt. Cook until the onions are translucent.

2. Add the tomatoes and cook for 30 minutes, or until the sauce is medium thick, about the consistency of chunky applesauce.

3. In the meantime, combine the spices, salt, pepper, and flour in a large bowl. Toss the shrimp with the seasoned flour.

4. Combine the rice, water, and salt in a 4-quart sauce pot. Bring to a boil; cover, and reduce the heat to a simmer. Cook for 15 minutes. Remove from the heat and let rest for 5 minutes before fluffing with a fork.

5. When the sauce is done, melt the butter in a large sauté pan and cook the shrimp quickly over high heat until slightly browned. (If you don't have a large enough pan to accommodate all of the shrimp, divide the butter in half and cook the shrimp in two batches.) Remove the shrimp and deglaze the sauté pan with some of the tomato sauce to capture the essence of the shrimp; add the deglazing liquid back to the tomato sauce. Reserve.

6. Add the shrimp to the tomato sauce and bring back to a simmer.

7. Serve the shrimp over the rice. Garnish with the scallions.

ROASTED COD WITH TOMATOES

YIELD: *8 portions*

3 pounds cod or salmon fillets
4½ tablespoons kosher salt
5 bay leaves
5 thyme sprigs

2 pounds tomatoes (any variety works)
2 pounds potatoes
¼ cup pure olive oil
4 cups cleaned and diced leeks
4 tablespoons slivered garlic
2 teaspoons salt
1 teaspoon fresh-ground black pepper
¼ cup extra-virgin olive oil

Salt cod with tomatoes, garlic, and onions is a Spanish specialty that dates as far back as 1745. This updated version, with a short-cured fish, is delicate and delicious. Serve with pieces of good bread brushed with olive oil and garlic and toasted, and accompany with a dollop of Aioli (page 234).

1. One day before serving, place the fish in a covered container large enough to accommodate all the fish in one layer. Sprinkle liberally with the salt, taking care to put more salt on thicker areas. Scatter the bay leaves and thyme on top of and underneath the fish. Cover and refrigerate.

2. Peel, core, and chop the tomatoes. Reserve.

3. Peel and slice the potatoes ⅛" inch thick (preferably on a mandoline); submerge in cold water. Reserve.

4. In a sauté pan with a cover, heat the olive oil over medium heat and add the leeks, garlic, and salt. Cover and cook over moderate heat until very tender, 15 to 20 minutes. If necessary add a bit of water to hasten cooking and minimize browning. Add the pepper. Reserve.

5. Preheat the oven to 350 degrees.

6. Remove the fish from the refrigerator. Gently and quickly rinse the salt from the fish with cold water. Pat dry. Cut the fish into eight 6-ounce portions.

7. Pour the leek mixture into an 8-by-12-inch baking pan and spread evenly. Layer the potatoes over the leeks and top with the tomatoes.

8. Crown with the fish and anoint with the olive oil.

9. Roast, uncovered, for 25 to 30 minutes, until the fish is flaky and the potatoes tender. Serve at once.

GRILLED BEEF WITH STUFFED TOMATOES

YIELD: *8 portions*

3 tablespoons pure olive oil

8 6-ounce portions sirloin, rib-eye, or
   porterhouse steaks, 1½ inches thick

1 tablespoon salt

1 tablespoon coarse-ground black pepper

8 thyme sprigs

3 lovage sprigs (optional)

4 garlic cloves, sliced in half

ROASTED POTATOES

2 pounds new potatoes, washed

¼ cup pure olive oil

1 head garlic, separated into cloves

4 thyme sprigs

2 bay leaves

1 tablespoon salt

2 teaspoons fresh-ground black pepper

STUFFED TOMATOES

1 pound bread, levain or other rustic type

½ cup pure olive oil

½ teaspoon salt

½ teaspoon fresh-ground black pepper

1 cup small-diced onions

2 tablespoons minced garlic

2 tablespoons finely chopped thyme

3 tablespoons finely chopped flat-leaf parsley

1 tablespoon chopped anchovies

8 medium bell pepper–type tomatoes
   (see head note)

GREEN BEANS

1 pound green beans, trimmed

3 tablespoons pure olive oil

2 tablespoons minced garlic

1½ teaspoons salt

1 cup water

2 tablespoons minced fresh marjoram

The thought of this meal makes me ravenous. Hollow bell-pepper-shaped tomatoes, such as Novogogoshary and Schimmeig Stoo—the best kept secret in tomatoland—enliven meat and potatoes and never fall flat in the oven, even when stuffed to the gills. Serve the steak with a smidgen of Aioli (page 234) or with a parsley, shallot, and anchovy sauce.

1. Pour the oil over the steaks, season them with the salt and pepper, and scatter the thyme sprigs, lovage (if using), and garlic over the top. Marinate for 8 hours or overnight prior to grilling.

2. Preheat the oven to 400 degrees.

3. Make the roasted potatoes: Toss the potatoes in a large bowl with the olive oil, garlic, thyme, and bay leaves; season with the salt and pepper. Evenly distribute the ingredients in a casserole dish in one layer. If necessary, separate the potatoes by size and roast in two pans. Tightly cover the pan with aluminum foil and roast until fork tender, about 30 minutes. Shake the pan occasionally so that the potatoes roast evenly. Remove from the oven and reserve; if necessary, reheat before serving. Lower the oven temperature to 350.

4. To make the stuffing for the tomatoes: Remove the crust from the bread; grind the bread to a coarse texture in a food processor. Place the bread crumbs in a bowl and toss with ¼ cup of the olive oil, the salt, and pepper. Spread the bread crumbs onto a rimmed baking sheet in a single layer and toast in the oven until golden, approximately 15 minutes. Toss the crumbs periodically so that they brown evenly. Maintain the oven temperature at 350 degrees.

5. In the meantime, heat the remaining ¼ cup of olive oil in a sauté pan and caramelize the onions. Add the garlic and cook until it smells divine. Remove the mixture from the heat and incorporate the herbs. Place the onion mixture and anchovies in a bowl and add the crumbs when they are done. Reserve the stuffing while preparing the tomatoes.

6. Remove the top of the hollow stuffing tomatoes (as you would for a bell pepper) and the seeds. If you have solid round tomatoes, create a cavity for the stuffing by cutting and scooping out some of the central core; stuff the tomatoes with the bread mixture.

7. Put the tomatoes in a single layer in a casserole dish. Bake for 25 minutes.

8. For the green beans: While the tomatoes are baking, cut the beans into thirds or quarters, depending on their size. In a large sauté pan, heat the olive oil over moderate heat. Add the garlic. When the garlic has a distinct aroma, add the beans and salt. Toss together. Add the water. Cook, uncovered, until the beans are tender. If the water boils off before the beans are finished, add ½ cup or so more. Add the marjoram and toss. Taste and add additional salt if desired.

9. To grill the steak: Heat a grill. Take the meat from the marinade and let it sit at room temperature for 30 minutes. Sear the meat on the hot zone of the grill until caramelized on one side, about 5 minutes; flip to the other side and sear until medium rare, about 6 to 8 minutes more. Move the meat to the moderate zone and continue cooking to desired doneness. Let the steak rest for 5 minutes, then cut into thin slices. Serve with the roasted potatoes, the green beans, and the stuffed tomatoes.

CURRIED MEATBALLS WITH TOMATO SAUCE

YIELD: *8 portions*

SAUCE

1 teaspoon coriander seeds

1 teaspoon cumin seeds

⅓ cup (5½ tablespoons) butter

2 cups sliced onions

¼ cup sliced garlic

3 tablespoons peeled and finely chopped
    fresh ginger

8 pods green cardamom

2 quarts plum tomatoes, canned or fresh

2 teaspoons salt

1 teaspoon fresh-ground black pepper

1½ cups heavy cream

MEATBALLS

½ cup dry bread crumbs or panko

⅓ cup heavy cream

1 tablespoon garam masala or curry
    powder

2 tablespoons butter

3 tablespoons peeled and finely chopped
    fresh ginger

3 tablespoons finely chopped garlic

2 pounds ground beef or lamb

1 tablespoon salt

2 teaspoons fresh-ground black pepper

½ teaspoon ground cayenne pepper

RAITA

3 cups whole-milk yogurt

1½ cups seeded, peeled, and finely diced
    cucumber

1½ teaspoons salt

½ teaspoon black pepper

A better meatball—served not on top of spaghetti, all covered with cheese, but with basmati rice and cucumber raita. These ravishing morsels should be made with savory, mouth-filling plum or sausage tomatoes, laden with umami-rich glutamic acid. Try Amish Paste, Super Italian Paste, or Opalka.

1. To make the sauce: Heat a small sauté pan over moderate heat; add the coriander and cumin. While gently shaking the pan, toast until you can begin to smell the spices and the cumin takes on a bit of color. Remove from the pan and reserve.

2. In a 3-quart heavy-bottomed pot, melt the butter over moderate heat. Add the onions and cook until translucent. Add the garlic and ginger. Cook until you can smell both of these ingredients.

3. Add the toasted coriander and cumin seeds, the cardamom, tomatoes (with the juice, if they're canned), salt, and pepper. Cook the sauce over low heat for about 30 minutes.

4. Pass the sauce through a food mill and return it to the cooking pot. Add the cream and bring to a boil, then reduce the heat and cook for 10 minutes. Taste and adjust the salt and pepper.

5. To make the meatballs: Place the bread crumbs or panko in a bowl, add the cream, and let soak for 20 minutes.

6. Heat a small pan and add the garam masala or curry powder. Shake the pan and cook until you can smell the spices. Reserve.

7. In a sauté pan, melt the butter over moderate heat. Add the ginger and garlic and cook until soft, about 5 minutes. Cool.

8. Preheat the oven to 400 degrees.

9. Combine the meat, soaked bread crumbs, ginger, garlic, salt, garam masala and curry powder, and both peppers. Mix thoroughly. Form the meat mixture into 2-inch balls and place on a baking rack set atop a rimmed sheet pan. Bake until browned, about 20 minutes.

10. Add the meatballs to the tomato sauce. Bring to a boil. Reduce to a simmer and cook for 5 minutes.

11. To make the raita: Combine the yogurt, cucumbers, and salt. Adjust salt, and add pepper to taste.

12. Serve the meatballs over basmati rice, topped with a spoonful of raita.

FRESH CORN POLENTA WITH TOMATO SAUCE

YIELD: *8 portions*

POLENTA

2 quarts water

2 tablespoons salt

2 cups cornmeal, coarse ground

3 tablespoons butter

1/2 teaspoon fresh-ground black pepper

TOMATO AND GARLIC SAUCE

2 1/2 pounds tomatoes, peeled

1/4 cup extra-virgin olive oil

1/4 cup thinly sliced garlic

1 teaspoon salt

1/2 teaspoon fresh-ground black pepper

3 ears corn

3 tablespoons butter

3 tablespoons water

1 teaspoon salt

1/2 teaspoon fresh-ground black pepper

GARNISH

4 tablespoons basil leaves

2 ounces Parmesan cheese

Conspicuously segmented tomatoes yield excellent purée and fresh chunky sauce. Use Costoluto Genovese, Rosso Sicilian, or Ceylon for this delectable meal. These sorts of tomatoes, valued by Italians for hundreds of years, appear ugly to some Americans but are popular in Europe and Asia. The Burmese grow them in carefully cultivated floating gardens.

1. To prepare the polenta: In a heavy bottomed pot, bring the water and salt to a boil. Add the cornmeal in a steady stream, whisking as you pour. When the mixture has come back to a boil, reduce the heat to a simmer and cover. Cook for 40 to 45 minutes, stirring frequently. Add the butter and pepper and adjust the salt.

2. While the polenta cooks, prepare the tomato and garlic sauce: Cut the tomatoes in quarters and remove some but not all of the seeds. Coarsely chop the tomato quarters into about 1-inch pieces. Gently warm the olive oil and garlic in a sauté pan over low heat. When the garlic begins to take on slight golden color, add the tomatoes, salt, and pepper. Raise the heat and simmer for about 10 minutes until the tomatoes are cooked but the sauce is still very fresh. Taste and adjust the seasonings. Reserve.

3. While the sauce is cooking, shuck the corn and rub with a dry paper towel to take off the silks. Remove the kernels by holding the corn vertically over a large bowl and slicing downward with a knife.

4. Place the butter and water in a sauté pan and bring to a boil. Add the corn, salt, and pepper. Cook until the corn is tender but still has a slight crunch, about 5 minutes.

5. When the polenta is done, and just before serving, stir the corn into the polenta. (If the polenta is finished before you're ready for this step, just stir in a little more water and keep at the lowest simmer until you're ready to add the corn; polenta is very forgiving.) Bring back to a simmer.

6. Chiffonade the basil.

7. To serve, place the polenta in the center of the plate and ladle the sauce around the perimeter. Garnish with shaved Parmesan (about 3 shavings made with a peeler per plate) and the basil.

FATTOUSH

YIELD: *8 portions*

GARLIC OIL

1 cup pure olive oil

1½ tablespoons finely chopped garlic

1 pound pita bread

1 teaspoon salt

GARLIC VINAIGRETTE

2 teaspoons garlic paste (store bought
   or made fresh, as in the Aioli recipe on
   page 234)

¼ cup fresh lemon juice

2 tablespoons white wine vinegar

½ teaspoon salt

¼ teaspoon fresh-ground black pepper

¾ cup extra-virgin olive oil

VEGETABLES

3 cups tomatoes, diced

1 cup cucumbers, peeled and cut into
   small dice

2 cups romaine lettuce, chopped

⅔ cup torn mint leaves

½ cup coarsely chopped flat-leaf parsley

¼ cup thinly sliced red onion

2 teaspoons salt

1 teaspoon fresh-ground black pepper

I first feasted on this Lebanese-style salad in London. It's great—if you make sure you have the right tomato. In a 1981 interview, fabled tomato-seed seller Benjamin Franklin Quisenberry, then ninety-five years old, advocated for Long Tom: "It's a dandy salad tomato, Long Tom is." Ben knew his business; long tomatoes have an evolutionary advantage as slicers.

1. Make the garlic oil: Heat the oil in a small saucepan, remove from the heat, and add the garlic. Let steep for several hours.

2. Preheat the oven to 350 degrees.

3. Split the pita in half. Brush one side of each half with the garlic oil. Sprinkle with salt. Cut each half into eighths and place in a single layer (oil side up) on a sheet pan. Bake until golden and crispy. Reserve.

4. Make the garlic vinaigrette: Combine the garlic paste, lemon juice, vinegar, salt, and pepper, then whisk in the olive oil.

5. Combine all of the vegetables and toss with half the vinaigrette; salt and pepper to taste.

6. Combine the pita, vegetables, and more vinaigrette. Toss. Add more vinaigrette to taste.

LOBSTER AND TOMATO SALAD WITH HERBED MAYONNAISE

YIELD: *6 portions*

3 lobsters, 1½ pounds apiece
2 gallons water
1 cup salt
½ cup Sherry Shallot Vinaigrette
  (page 234)

FOR THE LEMON SHALLOT VINAIGRETTE
2 tablespoons minced shallots
½ teaspoon salt
3 tablespoons fresh lemon juice
1 tablespoon white wine vinegar
¼ cup pure olive oil
¼ cup extra-virgin olive oil

2 quarts water
3 tablespoons salt
30 small, thin green beans
2 teaspoons finely chopped summer savory

1 pint assorted cherry and currant tomatoes
½ teaspoon salt
fresh-ground black pepper to taste
3 tablespoons basil chiffonade

2 cucumbers, peeled, seeded, and diced
¼ teaspoon salt

3 tablespoons finely chopped chervil
3 tablespoons finely snipped chives
1 tablespoon chopped flat-leaf parsley
¾ cup mayonnaise

In this simple, elegant meal, the mayo elevates the lobster from leanness to silken majesty (and plays a similar role with the green beans and cukes). Tomatoes and vinaigrettes perform a counterbalancing act. Serve with a warm crusty baguette and sweet butter.

1. Bring the water and salt to a boil. Plunge the lobsters into the water and return to a boil. Cook the lobsters for 12 minutes from the time they enter the water.

2. Prepare an ice-water bath. As the lobsters are done, remove them from the water and quickly plunge them into the ice-water bath. Remove from the bath within 5 minutes.

3. Separate the tail and claws from the head. Remove the shells from the tail, crack the claws, and cut the shells with poultry shears. Remove all the meat from the shells and place it in the refrigerator.

4. Meanwhile, prepare the vinaigrettes. For the lemon vinaigrette, macerate the shallots in the salt, fresh lemon juice, and white wine vinegar for 30 minutes. Whisk together with the olive oils. Reserve.

5. In a medium saucepan, bring the 2 quarts of water and the salt to a boil. Cut the beans into bite-sized pieces and cook them until tender, approximately 5 minutes. Drain and quickly spread them out in a single layer on a chilled plate or drop into very cold salted water to stop the cooking.

6. Toss the green beans with 2 tablespoons of the lemon shallot vinaigrette and the chopped savory.

7. Cut the cherry and currant tomatoes in half. Combine with the sherry shallot vinaigrette, salt, pepper, and basil.

8. Cut the cucumbers into medium dice. Combine them with the salt and toss with 2 tablespoons of the lemon shallot vinaigrette.

9. Add the chopped herbs to the mayonnaise.

10. Slice each lobster tail into 6 even slices. (Each lobster will serve 2 people.)

11. Arrange the tomatoes, cucumbers, and green beans neatly in the center of the plates. Lay the whole lobster claw on top and mound half of the knuckle meat at the bottom of the claw; then lay the 3 even slices of tail meat on top of the knuckle meat to add height to the plate. Drizzle a bit of the lemon shallot vinaigrette over the lobster meat and add about 2 tablespoons of herb mayonnaise to each plate.

PENNE WITH ROASTED EGGPLANT, TOMATO SAUCE, AND RICOTTA SALATA

YIELD:: *10 portions*

2 quarts Tomato Sauce (page 238)
Salt and fresh-ground black pepper
1 gallon water
2 eggplants, peeled
¾ cup pure olive oil
½ pound ricotta salata cheese
2 onions, sliced ⅛ inch thick
¼ teaspoon red pepper flakes
4 garlic cloves, slivered
1 tablespoon sherry vinegar
2 pounds penne
3 basil sprigs
¼ cup coarsely chopped flat-leaf parsley

Old World meets New World in this exquisite dish. Eggplant and tomato, both members of the Solanaceae family, have been paired in Neapolitan cookery from as early as the 1690s, when Naples was under Spanish dominion. The ricotta salata (dried ricotta) adds a crumbly texture and salty flavor.

1. Prepare the tomato sauce.

2. Preheat the oven to 400 degrees. Cut the peeled eggplant into 1-inch cubes and toss them lightly in ½ cup of the olive oil. Season with salt and pepper. Spread the eggplant in a single layer on a parchment-lined rimmed sheet pan and roast until the eggplant is brown and tender, about 25 minutes. Turn often with a spatula but be careful not to stir too roughly or the eggplant will turn to mush. Reserve.

3. Crumble the ricotta salata into small chunks. Set aside.

4. Sauté the onions in the remaining ¼ cup of olive oil, sprinkling on the red pepper flakes and salt and pepper to taste; continue until the onions are lightly caramelized. Add the garlic and cook until aromatic. Add the sherry vinegar and stir to deglaze the pan.

5. Combine the onion mixture with the tomato sauce. Reduce the consistency so that it will cling to the pasta. Gently add the eggplant.

6. Bring the water to a boil and add the ¼ cup salt. Cook the pasta until al dente, approximately 12 minutes.

7. When the pasta is done, drain, return to the pot, and toss with the sauce. Plate and garnish with the cheese, basil, and parsley.

PASTA PUTTANESCA

YIELD *8 portions*

1 quart Tomato Sauce (page 238)
¼ cup extra-virgin olive oil
2 tablespoons minced garlic
½ teaspoon red pepper flakes
8 anchovy fillets, chopped
3 tablespoons capers, rinsed, drained, and
  coarsely chopped
¼ cup Niçoise olives, pitted
½ teaspoon salt
½ teaspoon coarse-ground black pepper
1 gallon water
¼ cup salt
1½ pounds spaghetti

3 basil sprigs, coarsely chopped
¼ cup minced flat-leaf parsley

This "lady of the night" pasta is bliss. The sauce of tomatoes with anchovies, capers, garlic, olives, and dried red pepper flakes embodies the cuisine of Naples, so use tomatoes with a southern Italian twang: San Marzano, King Humbert, or Rosso Sicilian.

1. Prepare the tomato sauce.

2. Gently heat the olive oil in a large sauce pot. Add the garlic, red pepper flakes, anchovies, salt, and black pepper. Stir and mash until the anchovies have melted in the olive oil and you can smell the garlic. Add the tomato sauce, capers, and olives.

3. Bring the water to a boil and add the ¼ cup of salt. Cook the pasta for approximately 10 minutes, until al dente.

4. When the pasta is done, toss with the sauce. Plate and garnish with the basil and parsley.

SPAGHETTI WITH CHERRY TOMATOES AND TOASTED CRUMBS

YIELD: *10 portions*

TOASTED CRUMBS
1 loaf rustic bread
½ cup pure olive oil
Salt and fresh-ground back pepper to taste

CHERRY TOMATO SALAD
1 pint Sherry Shallot Vinaigrette (page 234)
2 pints cherry and currant tomatoes, mixed

1 gallon water
¼ cup salt
2 pounds spaghetti

3 green basil sprigs
3 purple basil sprigs
½ cup grated Parmesan cheese

The cherry tomato salad is the heart of this matter; a one-hour waiting period after assembly allows the salt, and the acid from the vinegar, to pull out the natural juices and flavor of the tomatoes. Toasted crumbs make a fine topping. I could eat this every day.

1. To make the toasted crumbs: Preheat the oven to 350 degrees. Remove the crust from the loaf of bread and cut the bread into large dice. Pulse in the food processor until the pieces are small. In a large bowl, toss the bread crumbs with the olive oil, salt, and pepper. Spread the crumbs evenly on rimmed baking sheets and bake, turning frequently, until browned. Cool and reserve.

2. To make the cherry tomato salad: Slice the cherry and currant tomatoes in half. Combine in a medium bowl with the sherry shallot vinaigrette and let rest for 1 hour prior to serving.

3. Bring the water to a boil and add the ¼ cup of salt. Cook the pasta until al dente, approximately 7 minutes. Drain.

4. Chiffonade the basils.

5. In a large bowl, toss the pasta with the cherry tomato salad.

6. Plate the pasta and garnish with the Parmesan, basil, and toasted crumbs. Serve right away so the crumbs remain crispy.

RICOTTA RAVIOLI WITH TOMATO SAUCE

YIELD: *8 portions*

PASTA DOUGH

2 cups all-purpose flour

1 teaspoon fine sea salt

2 large eggs

1 tablespoon water

2 teaspoons pure olive oil

RICOTTA FILLING

1 pound whole-milk ricotta cheese

½ cup grated Parmesan cheese

2 eggs

1 teaspoon salt

1 teaspoon fresh-ground black pepper

TOMATO SAUCE

2 tablespoons extra-virgin olive oil

1 tablespoon butter

1 teaspoon minced garlic

1 pound red tomatoes, peeled and diced

1 pound yellow tomatoes, peeled and diced

2 teaspoons salt

½ teaspoon fresh-ground black pepper

1 gallon water

2 tablespoons salt

2 green basil sprigs

3 purple basil sprigs

Coarse-ground black pepper to taste

An impressive and impressively delicious meal for special occasions. Jersey Devil and Dixie Golden Giant tomatoes give it extra flair.

1. To make the pasta dough: Combine the flour and salt in a bowl. With your hand, create a well in the center of the flour. In a separate bowl whisk the eggs, water, and olive oil. Pour into the well. Use a fork to gently incorporate the flour from the sides of the bowl into the egg mixture until all is combined. Dump the dough onto a lightly floured surface and knead into a smooth mass. Cover completely with plastic wrap. Let sit for a minimum of 1 hour or up to 4 hours at room temperature.

2. Once the dough has rested, divide into fourths. With a hand-operated pasta machine, crank the pasta through the widest setting. Switch to the next setting down and run the sheet of pasta through twice more. Repeat, working your way down to the second-thinnest setting. Cover the rolled-out pasta dough with plastic until you are ready to stuff the ravioli.

3. Combine the ricotta filling ingredients in a medium bowl. Taste for seasoning.

4. Lay out a sheet of pasta on a lightly floured work surface. With a pastry bag or a spoon, drop 1½ tablespoons of the mixture onto the dough at 2-inch intervals. With a pastry brush, brush water around the filling on the bottom dough. Place another piece of dough on top and with your fingers or the dull side of a circle cutter, or a small glass, form a tight seal around each circle of filling. Use a pasta cutter, pizza wheel, or knife to cut each section into a square.

5. To make the tomato sauce: In a large sauté pan, heat the olive oil and butter, and sauté the garlic over medium heat until aromatic. Add the tomatoes, salt, and pepper, and cook until warm.

6. Add the water and salt to a wide-surfaced pot and bring to a boil. Add the ravioli in a single layer to the water, reduce the heat to a simmer, and cook for approximately 5 minutes; the ravioli is done when it floats to the surface.

7. Chiffonade the basils.

8. Place the ravioli (4 per person) into a pasta bowl. Spoon the sauce over and around the pasta and garnish with the basil and a pinch of black pepper.

PIZZA DOUGH

YIELD: *enough for 5 12-inch pizzas*

2 teaspoons dry yeast
¾ cup lukewarm water, 110–115 degrees
⅔ cup bread flour
4 cups all-purpose white flour
¼ cup whole-wheat flour
1 cup room-temperature water
2 teaspoons salt
⅓ cup pure olive oil

A great foundation for pizza, calzones, and even crackers when rolled very thin.

1. In a small bowl, sprinkle the dry yeast over the lukewarm water. Let sit for 5 minutes, then stir. Allow it to sit until yeast becomes bubbly, about another 5 minutes.

2. Add the bread flour to the yeast mixture to make the "sponge." Rest it for 30 minutes.

3. In a large bowl, mix the white and whole-wheat flours and salt.

4. Make a well in the mixed flour and add the sponge, the remaining cup of water, and the oil. Mix until shaggy. This can be done in a mixer with the paddle.

5. Dump the shaggy mass out of the bowl onto a lightly floured work surface and knead until smooth. Place in a lightly oiled bowl and cover with plastic wrap. Let it rise in a warm place until doubled in volume.

6. Form the dough into "pizza balls," about 4 ounces apiece for 6-inch pizzas and 8 ounces apiece for 12-inch ones. Wrap each ball loosely in plastic.

7. Let the balls you'll be using rest at room temperature for about 45 minutes. Extra dough balls may be frozen.

8. To shape the pizza: On a well-floured surface, form the dough into a disk by pushing it down with the tips of your fingers, working from the center to within about ¼ inch of the edge of the dough.

9. Lift the pizza up and, working with your knuckles (palm out) on the underside of the dough, gently pull it into a round shape, alternately stretching and turning the dough until it's 12 inches in diameter and very thin, almost translucent.

PIZZA MARGHERITA

YIELD: *one 12-inch pizza*

1 8-ounce ball Pizza Dough (see page 206, or use store-bought dough)

Flour for dusting surfaces

2 tablespoons Garlic Oil (page 239)

2 teaspoons extra-virgin olive oil

½ cup grated mozzarella cheese

2 pounds tomatoes, cut in ¼-inch slices

1 teaspoon salt

½ teaspoon fresh-ground black pepper

5 basil leaves, torn

Named in 1889 for Queen Margherita of Italy, consort of Umberto I. If you're so inclined, you can honor both royals by making this pizza with Umberto's eponymous Re Umberto (King Humbert). That marvelous tomato is the forefather of the San Marzano (Sammarzano).

1. Prepare the pizza dough and garlic oil.

2. Preheat the oven to 500 degrees. Place a pizza stone—or, alternately, a baking sheet lined with unglazed quarry tiles—in the oven. (If you don't have either stone or tiles, simply use a baking sheet turned upside down.) Heat for at least 30 minutes.

3. Shape the pizza: On a well-floured surface, form the dough into a disk by pushing it down with the tips of your fingers, working from the center to within about ¼ inch of the edge of the dough. To ensure a fluffy and crunchy crust, do not press the edges. Continue with the tips of your fingers and make a ¼-inch rim.

4. Lift the pizza up and, working with your knuckles (palms out) on the underside of the dough, gently pull it into a round shape, alternately stretching and turning the dough until it's 12 inches in diameter.

5. Place the dough on a well-floured peel. Gently brush the dough with oil.

6. Sprinkle the mozzarella over the surface of the dough. Gently lay down the slices of tomato. Season with salt and pepper.

7. Place the pizza in the oven on top of the stone, quarry tiles, or baking sheet. Cook until the edges begin to brown. When the pizza is done, remove it from the oven. Brush the rim with olive oil. Sprinkle the remaining oil over the tomatoes and garnish with the torn basil.

PIZZA WITH ROASTED EGGPLANT AND GREMOLATA

YIELD: *one 12-inch pizza*

½ cup Tomato Sauce (page 238)

1 8-ounce ball Pizza Dough (page 206, or
    use store-bought dough)

2 tablespoons Garlic Oil (page 239)

Flour for dusting surfaces

2 eggplants

½ cup pure olive oil

1 teaspoon salt

1 teaspoon fresh-ground black pepper

FOR THE GREMOLATA

1 tablespoon coarsely chopped flat-leaf
    parsley

2 tablespoons finely minced garlic

1 teaspoon finely minced lemon zest

1 red onion, cut in ⅛-inch slices

1½ ounces mozzarella cheese, grated

¼ teaspoon red pepper flakes

3 ounces Parmesan cheese, grated

Eggplant and tomato are an enticing pair that once shared a name: *Poma amoris*, or love apple. The unusual element in this recipe is gremolata, a mix of parsley, lemon zest, and garlic more commonly used for grilled tuna and steak.

1. Prepare the tomato sauce, pizza dough, and garlic oil.

2. Preheat the oven to 400 degrees. Slice the eggplants into ⅓-inch-thick slices. Brush with olive oil on both sides. Place on a parchment-lined cookie sheet and season with the salt and pepper. Roast for 15 to 20 minutes, or until the eggplant is brown and tender. Reserve.

3. Make the gremolata by combining the parsley, garlic, and lemon zest in a small bowl. Reserve.

4. Place a pizza stone (or a cookie sheet lined with unglazed quarry tiles) in the oven. Turn the oven to 500 degrees and allow the stone or tiles to heat for at least 30 minutes. If you don't have quarry tiles, just preheat the oven to 500 at this stage.

5. On a well-floured surface, form the dough into a round shape by pushing it down with the tips of your fingers, working from the center to within about ¼ inch of the edge of the dough. To make sure the rim is fluffy and crunchy, do not press the edges of the pizza.

6. Lift the pizza up and, working with your knuckles (palm out) on the underside of the dough, gently pull it into a round shape, alternately stretching and turning the dough.

7. Place the dough on a well-floured peel. Brush the center but not the rim with garlic oil.

8. With the back of a ladle, spread the tomato sauce to within ¼ inch of the rim. Scatter the red onions, mozzarella cheese, and red pepper flakes over the sauce. Lay the eggplant down from the center to the edges.

9. Place the pizza in the oven on top of the quarry tiles or cookie sheet. Cook until the edges begin to brown, 25 to 30 minutes. When the pizza is done, remove from the oven and garnish with Parmesan and then the gremolata. Cut into eighths and serve.

Snacks & Sandwiches

CHERRY TOMATO SALAD AND BAKED RICOTTA CHEESE WITH TAPENADE CROUTONS

YIELD: *10 portions*

BAKED RICOTTA CHEESE
1½ pounds whole-milk ricotta cheese
¼ cup extra-virgin olive oil
Coarse-ground black pepper as needed

SHERRY SHALLOT VINAIGRETTE
1 tablespoon sherry vinegar
2 teaspoons red wine vinegar
2 teaspoons balsamic vinegar
Salt to taste
3 tablespoons finely diced shallots
½ cup pure olive oil
¼ cup extra-virgin olive oil

CHERRY TOMATO SALAD
2 pints assorted cherry and currant
    tomatoes
Salt to taste
Fresh-ground black pepper to taste
¼ cup basil leaves

TAPENADE
1 cup Niçoise olives
1 garlic clove
Salt as needed
4 oil-packed anchovies
1½ tablespoons capers, rinsed and coarsely
    chopped
¼ cup extra-virgin olive oil
2 teaspoons fresh lemon juice

8 ¼-inch-thick slices rustic or levain bread
Pure olive oil as needed

An eating experience that verges on perfection. This partnership of Italian and French cuisines combines rich, succulent ricotta, powerful tomato salad (full of sour, sweet, and salty tastes), bitter tapenade, and crisp bread.

1. Preheat the oven to 450 degrees. In a bowl, combine the ricotta cheese with 2 tablespoons of the olive oil. Place the mixture into an oval gratin dish that has been greased with olive oil. Smooth the top and drizzle with the remaining olive oil. Grind black pepper over the top. Bake on a foil-lined sheet pan until the cheese is heated through and a golden-brown crust forms on top. (If the cheese is heated before the crust starts to form, you can finish it under the broiler.) Cool at room temperature, about 25 minutes.

2. In the interim, prepare the sherry shallot vinaigrette: Mix the vinegars and salt; add the shallots and soak for 30 minutes. Whisk in the olive oils. Taste and adjust with additional vinegar, oil, or salt. Reserve.

3. For the cherry tomato salad: Slice the cherry and currant tomatoes in half and mix with the vinaigrette one hour before serving. Season with salt and pepper. Combine in a bowl with a wooden spoon, working gently so as not to bruise the tomatoes.

4. Prepare the tapenade: Remove the pits from the olives. Make a garlic paste by slicing the garlic clove thin, sprinkling with salt, and using the flat of your knife to mash the garlic into a fine paste. Place the anchovies, garlic paste, and capers in the bowl of a food processor. Process until almost smooth. Add the olives and pulse until finely chopped and spreadable but not pasty. Transfer the mixture to another bowl and stir in the olive oil and fresh lemon juice. Taste and adjust the seasoning. Set aside.

5. Brush the bread slices lightly with olive oil. Cut each slice into three triangular pieces with two diagonal cuts. Grill the slices over low heat on a grill, griddle, or grill pan until crispy; or toast them in a 400-degree oven, flipping once, until browned. When they're cool enough to handle, spread the tapenade on the croutons.

6. Just before serving, chiffonade the basil, and use it to garnish the salad. Serve with the baked ricotta and the tapenade croutons.

SPANISH TOMATO BREAD

YIELD: *10 slices*

10 slices baguette, sliced on bias,
 ½ inch thick
¼ cup extra-virgin olive oil
2 garlic cloves, peeled
2 medium-size ripe tomatoes, sliced in half
 at the equator
1 teaspoon coarse salt

GARNISH
Oil-packed anchovies
Marcona almonds
Manchego cheese, sliced

This tapa, common to Catalonia and other regions of Spain, calls for a ripe oxheart or beefsteak tomato so soft and meaty inside that it can be scraped across a crouton without breaking the crouton. Garnish with anchovies, toasted Marcona almonds, and Manchego cheese.

1. Preheat the oven to 400 degrees.

2. Lay the baguette slices on a baking sheet and brush each side with the olive oil.

3. Toast in the oven for approximately 10 minutes, turning once.

4. Remove from the oven. While the toasted bread is warm, gently scrape the garlic clove across its surface. Do the same with the tomato, being sure to leave a substantial amount of pulp on the bread. Lightly salt the tomato pulp, then garnish with anchovies, toasted almonds, and cheese.

TOMATO FRITTATA

YIELD: *8 portions*

3 tablespoons extra-virgin olive oil
½ cup small-diced onion
1 tablespoon minced garlic
2 teaspoons salt
1 teaspoon fresh-ground black pepper
2 cups peeled, seeded, and diced tomatoes
6 large eggs
2 tablespoons basil chiffonade

A mix of eggs and tomatoes so soigné it makes a fabulous midnight supper as well as a satisfying brunch.

1. Preheat the broiler.

2. Heat the olive oil in a 10-inch nonstick ovenproof skillet over moderate heat. Add the onions and cook until translucent. Add the garlic, salt, and pepper. When the garlic begins to give up its aroma, add the tomatoes. Cook until heated through.

3. Whisk the eggs together in a medium bowl. Add the eggs to the tomato mixture in the skillet. Briefly mix together so that all of the ingredients are incorporated. Then do not disturb.

4. Cook until the eggs are almost set, 8 to 10 minutes.

5. Place the skillet briefly under the broiler to set the top, about 2 minutes.

6. Put a serving plate on top of the skillet and, holding the two firmly together, flip them over so the frittata lands bottom-side-up on the plate. Garnish with the basil. Cut into 8 wedges, pie-style, and serve.

CHERRY TOMATO FOCACCIA

YIELD: *Serves 8*

FOCACCIA DOUGH

2 teaspoons active dry yeast

1 teaspoon honey or sugar

¾ cup lukewarm water, between 110 and 115 degrees

1 cup room-temperature water

⅔ cup bread flour

4 cups all-purpose white flour

¼ cup whole-wheat flour

2 teaspoons salt

1 cup plus 2 tablespoons pure olive oil

¼ cup sliced garlic

1 pint assorted cherry and currant tomatoes

¼ cup grated Parmesan cheese (optional)

GARNISH

3 tablespoons basil leaves

1 teaspoon kosher or coarse salt

In this unusual focaccia, sweet-as-candy cherry and currant tomatoes, such as Sara's Galapagos, Green Grape, Blondköpfchen, and Black Cherry, give a boost to savory bread. This makes a stunning presentation as an hors d'oeuvre or as part of a meal.

1. Make the focaccia dough: Sprinkle the dry yeast over the lukewarm water. Let it sit for 5 minutes, then stir in the honey or sugar. Allow it to sit about another 5 minutes until bubbly. Add the bread flour and combine to form the "sponge." Rest it for 30 minutes. Combine the white and whole-wheat flours and the salt. Make a well in the flour and add the sponge, ¾ cup of the oil, and the remaining cup of water. Mix until shaggy (this can be done in a mixer with the paddle). Once it becomes a shaggy mass, dump the dough out of the bowl onto a lightly floured work surface and knead until smooth. Place in a lightly oiled bowl and cover with plastic wrap. Let it rise in a warm spot, about 80 degrees, until it doubles in volume; this should take about 1½ hours.

2. While waiting for the dough to double, warm ¼ cup of the olive oil in a small saucepan, add the garlic, and cook until tender. Reserve both the oil and the garlic.

3. Preheat the oven to 350 degrees.

4. Brush a cookie sheet (or half sheet pan) with the remaining 2 tablespoons of olive oil. Place the dough in the center. Gently spread the dough out until it is about 8 inches by 12 inches.

5. When the dough has just begun to rise, scatter the cooled garlic and olive oil over the top. Place the whole tomatoes on the surface of the dough, pushing slightly to fix them in place. Allow the dough to rise again to double its volume, surrounding the tomatoes.

6. Bake until browned, about 30 minutes. Sprinkle with the Parmesan cheese and continue baking for 10 minutes.

7. Chiffonade the basil. Sprinkle the salt and basil on the focaccia.

TOMATO, EGGPLANT, AND MINT SALSA WITH PITA CHIPS

YIELD: *1 quart*

¾ cup plus 2 tablespoons pure olive oil

4 garlic cloves, coarsely chopped

1 cup small-diced red onion

2 teaspoons minced garlic

2 teaspoons salt, plus more for sprinkling
  on the pita

¼ teaspoon fresh-ground black pepper

4 cups medium-diced eggplant

6 pieces pita bread

4 pounds tomatoes, peeled, seeded, and
  cut into small dice

2 teaspoons aleppo pepper or smoked
  paprika

¼ cup red wine vinegar

½ cup finely chopped mint

Ketchup may not qualify as a "vegetable"—as the Reagan administration learned to its chagrin—but this tangy tomato and eggplant salsa certainly does. Salty pita chips wear the salsa well.

1. To make the garlic oil: Combine ½ cup of the oil with the chopped garlic and gently warm in a sauté pan until the oil just starts to ripple slightly, no higher than 140 degrees. Turn off the heat and allow the garlic to infuse the oil for about 1 hour. Remove the garlic.

2. In the meantime, warm 2 tablespoons of the oil in a sauté pan. Add the onions and cook until tender and slightly caramelized. Add the minced garlic and cook until fragrant. Season with ½ teaspoon of the salt and the pepper.

3. Preheat the oven to 450 degrees. Toss the eggplant with the remaining ¼ cup of oil and 1½ teaspoons of the salt. Spread onto a parchment-lined rimmed baking sheet in a single layer and place in the oven. Gently and occasionally turn the eggplant with a spatula. Roast until tender, about 20 minutes.

4. Reduce the oven temperature to 350 degrees. Separate the pita breads into round halves, then cut them into wedges. Brush one side of each piece of pita with the garlic oil and sprinkle with salt. Put the pieces on a baking sheet, oiled side up, and bake for about 15 minutes until crispy and golden brown.

5. Combine the onions, eggplant, tomatoes, aleppo pepper, red wine vinegar, and mint in a large bowl. Taste and add salt and pepper, if desired.

6. Transfer to a serving bowl and surround with the pita chips.

INDIAN TOMATO SALSA

YIELD: *1 quart*

¼ cup plus 1 tablespoon vegetable oil

2 tablespoons minced garlic

2 tablespoons peeled and minced fresh
ginger

2 pounds plum tomatoes, peeled, seeded,
and chopped

2 teaspoons salt

2 teaspoons fresh-ground black pepper

2 teaspoons black mustard seeds

2 teaspoons black onion seeds

2 teaspoons cumin seeds

40 mini pappadams

This salsa is so captivating that you need not worry about throwing the flavor away when you peel, cut, seed, and furiously rough-chop the plum tomatoes. Serve with pappadams, thin flatbreads from India made with lentil flour that bubble when heated.

1. Heat the ¼ cup of oil in a sauce pot over moderate heat. Add the garlic and ginger and cook until fragrant. Add the tomatoes, salt, and pepper. Cook until the mixture thickens, about 30 minutes.

2. Meanwhile, heat the remaining tablespoon of oil in a sauté pan. Add the mustard seeds, black onion seeds, and cumin seeds. Cook until they begin to pop. Add to the tomato mixture.

3. To heat the pappadams: Place on a hot griddle or cast-iron skillet. Cook until blistered. If microwaving, brush pappadams lightly with oil, place on paper towels, and zap one at a time on high for 40 to 60 seconds.

4. Serve the salsa as a dip and the pappadams as the chips.

SPICY TOMATO SALSA

YIELD: *1 quart*

1 cup small-diced red onions

2 tablespoons fresh lime juice

2 teaspoons salt

½ teaspoon fresh-ground black pepper

4 pounds tomatoes, peeled, seeded, and cut into small dice

1 teaspoon minced or pressed garlic

2 tablespoons minced and seeded jalapeño peppers

½ cup finely chopped cilantro

The key to a well-balanced salsa—apart from picking the right tomatoes—is pickling the onions in lime juice. This recipe can be combined with mashed avocados to make an outstanding guacamole. Serve as a dip for chips or spoon as salsa over grilled fish or fowl.

1. Combine the red onions with the lime juice, salt, and pepper in a medium, nonreactive bowl. Cover and set aside for 20 minutes while preparing the other ingredients.

2. Combine the tomatoes, garlic, jalapeños, and cilantro in a medium bowl. Add to the onions and serve immediately.

FRIED GREEN TOMATOES

YIELD: *8 portions*

4 pounds green (unripe) tomatoes
Salt and fresh-ground black pepper
5 eggs
½ cup milk
3 cups all-purpose flour
4 cups panko
½ cup fine-ground cornmeal
1 quart oil (canola, peanut, or corn)

Fried green tomatoes are the darlings of the South. North Carolinian Eve Felder has a fond childhood memory of eating fried green tomatoes in the fall, after the weather turned cooler (and no more tomatoes could ripen on the vine). Her family soaked their green tomato slices in buttermilk, dredged them in flour, and fried them in bacon fat, producing a crispy covering and a soft, tangy interior. Fried green tomatoes are heavenly with creamy grits and butter.

1. Cut ½ inch from the stem and blossom ends of the tomatoes and discard. Slice the tomatoes ¼ inch thick.

2. Spread the tomatoes out on trays or paper towels and sprinkle with 2 teaspoons salt and 1 teaspoon pepper.

3. Whisk the eggs together in a shallow bowl. Add the milk and whisk to combine. Reserve.

4. Combine the flour, ½ teaspoon salt, and ¼ teaspoon pepper in a shallow bowl. Set aside.

5. Combine the panko with the cornmeal in a shallow bowl. Season with salt and pepper.

6. Dip the sliced tomatoes into the flour mixture. Shake off excess. Dredge in the egg mixture. Shake off the liquid and dip in the bread crumb and cornmeal mixture to coat.

7. Reserve on a wire rack until all tomatoes have been coated.

8. Heat half of the oil in a 10-inch skillet until hot. To test, dip a piece of the tomato into the oil: It should sizzle immediately.

9. Add as many tomatoes as the skillet will hold in a single layer. Fry until golden about 3 minutes, then turn and fry the other side.

10. Repeat with all of the tomatoes. Replace the oil midway through.

11. Drain on paper towels. Salt to taste while still hot.

TOMATO CHIPS

YIELD: *1 pound*

1 cup pure olive oil
2 tablespoons finely minced garlic

3 pounds assorted tomatoes, sliced
  ¼ inch thick

2 tablespoons salt
2 teaspoons fresh-ground black pepper
¼ cup finely chopped thyme

A beautiful sight. Tomato chips of many colors and sizes are fun as a garnish.

1. In a sauté pan, warm the olive oil over medium-low heat until it begins to ripple slightly at the bottom of the pan, no higher than 140 degrees. Add the garlic and remove from the heat. Infuse the olive oil for 2 hours. Strain out the garlic and reserve the oil.

2. Preheat the oven to 250 degrees. (If using a dehydrator, follow the manufacturer's instructions.)

3. Line 2 rimmed baking sheets with Silpat mats.

4. Brush the sliced tomatoes with the garlic oil. Season with the salt, pepper, and thyme. Place in the pans in a singe layer and bake for 1 hour, then lower the temperature to 200 degrees. Continue baking for 3 to 5 hours (or longer, depending on the moisture content of the tomatoes) until the chips are dehydrated and crisp. If not eaten immediately, the chips should be stored in an airtight container.

PAN BAGNAT

YIELD: *4 sandwiches*

2 6-ounce cans oil-packed tuna, drained
1 teaspoon minced garlic
2 tablespoons capers, rinsed and drained
¼ cup pitted Niçoise olives
3 tablespoons extra-virgin olive oil
2 tablespoons red wine vinegar
2 tablespoons chopped flat-leaf parsley
4 sandwich-sized rosemary potato rolls
  (or use ciabatta rolls, or any other with
  a soft interior)
1 large tomato, sliced thin
1 small cucumber, peeled and sliced thin
½ small red onion, sliced thin
4 leaves green leaf lettuce, washed and torn
2 hard-boiled eggs, sliced in eighths
  lengthwise
Salt and fresh-ground pepper to taste

This portable meal is available at any train station in the south of France. As long as you're making a juicy and toothsome sandwich, you might as well use the most luscious and melting slicing tomatoes you can find; some of my favorites are Red Brandywine and White Beauty. Rosemary potato rolls upgrade this sandwich and serve as a delicious sop.

1. Combine the tuna, garlic, capers, olives, vinegar, parsley, and oil in a medium-sized bowl and mix.

2. Slice the rolls horizontally and place the bottom halves on a sheet pan.

3. Place a layer of thinly sliced cucumbers on the bottom half of each roll. Repeat with the onions, tuna mixture, tomatoes, and lettuce, and finish with the hard-boiled eggs.

4. Sprinkle each sandwich with a little salt and a bit of pepper.

5. Place the tops of the rolls on the sandwiches. Leaving the sandwiches on the sheet pan, cover them with another sheet pan and weigh it down with a couple of cans or a pan. Set them in the refrigerator for 30 minutes. Remove and serve.

PITA SANDWICH WITH TOMATOES AND FALAFEL

YIELD: *8 sandwiches*

FALAFEL MIXTURE

2 cups raw chickpeas
6 cups water

1 cup chopped onions
2 teaspoons chopped garlic
1 teaspoon ground cumin
½ teaspoon ground coriander
2 teaspoons salt
1 teaspoon fresh-ground black pepper
½ cup finely chopped flat-leaf parsley

Canola oil (for frying) as needed

TAHINI SAUCE

½ cup sesame paste (tahini)
1 teaspoon minced garlic
¼ cup fresh lemon juice
⅓ cup water or more as needed
½ teaspoon salt

4 cups diced tomatoes
¼ cup thinly sliced red onion
2 teaspoons salt
1 teaspoon fresh-ground black pepper

8 pita breads

SPICY SAUCE (OPTIONAL)

1 jalapeño pepper, roasted
1 red bell pepper, roasted
1 teaspoon ground cumin
½ teaspoon minced garlic
½ teaspoon hot paprika
¼ teaspoon cayenne pepper
2 tablespoons extra-virgin olive oil
1 teaspoon fresh lemon juice
½ teaspoon salt

A gift from the Middle East, falafel offers the entire spectrum of tastes and textures: crunchy, smooth, hot, and tangy. Smother them with sweet love apples.

1. To make the falafel: Combine the chickpeas and water in a large bowl. Cover and refrigerate for 12 hours.

2. Drain the chickpeas and mix them in a clean bowl with the onions, garlic, cumin, coriander, salt, and pepper.

3. Grind half of the mixture in a food processor until smooth. Do the same with the remaining half. Mix both halves together and stir in the parsley. Let the mixture rest for 30 minutes.

4. Form the mixture into balls, using two tablespoons for each one. Flatten into 1-inch-thick patties. Place on a sheet tray and reserve. Extra falafel patties can be frozen.

5. To make the tahini sauce: Combine the sesame paste, garlic, fresh lemon juice, water, and salt in a food processor and process until smooth and thick (not pourable). Add more water if needed. This sauce may be made several days in advance and kept in the refrigerator.

6. For the spicy sauce, if using: Cool the roasted jalapeño and bell pepper in a bowl covered with plastic wrap. Peel and remove the seeds. Coarsely chop. Combine the jalapeños, bell peppers, cumin, garlic, paprika, and cayenne in a blender. Grind until smooth, then remove the paste to a bowl. Gradually whisk in the olive oil. Add the lemon juice and salt. Taste and adjust the seasonings. This sauce can be made a day or two in advance and refrigerated.

7. Combine the tomatoes, red onions, salt, and pepper in a large bowl.

8. Preheat the oven to 350 degrees. Wrap the pita breads in foil and warm in the oven while frying the falafel patties.

9. Put about 1½ inches of oil into a large frying pan. Heat the oil over moderate heat until it sizzles when a piece of the falafel patty is placed in the oil. Cook the patties in batches until they are browned on one side, then flip them and continue cooking until they are cooked through, another 2 to 4 minutes. Drain on paper towels and place in the oven until all of the patties are cooked.

10. To assemble the sandwich: Remove the pita breads from the oven. Cut into half-moons. Open up the bread and place a tablespoon of tahini sauce in the bottom; add about a teaspoon of the spicy sauce, if desired. Place several spoonfuls of the tomato mixture in the pita, add 2 falafel patties, top with more tomatoes, and drizzle with tahini and spicy sauce. Serve immediately.

STEAK, TOMATO, AND ONION SANDWICH

YIELD: *8 sandwiches*

START THIS RECIPE AT LEAST
8 HOURS IN ADVANCE.

¼ cup pure olive oil
1 tablespoon sliced garlic
2 pounds rib-eye steak
2 teaspoons salt
2 teaspoons coarse-ground black pepper

CHIPOTLE MAYONNAISE
1 canned chipotle pepper in adobo sauce
2 teaspoons adobo sauce
¼ cup mayonnaise to taste

1 pound red onions, peeled and sliced
  ½ inch thick
2 pounds beefsteak tomatoes, sliced
  ½ inch thick
¼ cup pure olive oil
1 teaspoon salt
½ teaspoon fresh-ground black pepper
2 tablespoons balsamic vinegar
2 or 3 baguettes, or 8 flour tortillas
4 ounces baby arugula

This hearty sandwich with a Mexican flair is substantial enough to serve as supper. It would work just as well with a tortilla as with a baguette. Lay on a big meaty slab of well-marbled beefsteak or oxheart tomato.

1. Sprinkle the olive oil and garlic over the steaks. Generously season each side of the steaks with salt and pepper. Cover and refrigerate for 8 hours or overnight.

2. To make the chipotle mayonnaise: Split the chipotle pepper in half; remove the seeds. Purée with the 2 teaspoons of adobo sauce in a food processor or chop very fine. Stir the purée into the mayonnaise. Reserve.

3. Thirty minutes prior to cooking, remove the steaks from the refrigerator so that they come to room temperature. Heat the grill to medium high.

4. Brush the onions and tomatoes with the oil and season with the salt and pepper. Grill the onions over moderate heat until done, about 8 minutes per side. Put in a bowl and toss with the balsamic vinegar. Reserve and keep warm.

5. Grill the steaks. This should take about 5 minutes per side for medium rare. Remove from the grill and let rest for 6 to 8 minutes. Cut on the diagonal into ¼-inch slices.

6. Cut the baguettes into four 5-inch pieces. Split each in half and brush lightly with olive oil. Grill crumb side down until warm. If you're using tortillas, wrap them in barely moistened paper towels and microwave them on high for 15 to 20 seconds.

7. To assemble each sandwich: Spread chipotle mayonnaise on a piece of baguette. Cut the tomato halves into half-moons, and put slices on the bread with the steak, onions, and arugula. Cover with the top of the baguette and serve.

TOMATO AND FONTINA PANINI

YIELD: *4 sandwiches*

8 slices Italian bread
4 tablespoons (½ stick) butter, softened

8 tablespoons mayonnaise
8 slices fontina, thinly sliced (Gruyère
   or other Swiss can be substituted)
8 tomato slices
¼ teaspoon salt
⅛ teaspoon coarse-ground black pepper
4 tablespoons chopped basil

A glorious grilled cheese and tomato sandwich.

1. Butter one side of each slice of bread. Put the slices, buttered side down, on a cutting board.

2. To assemble the sandwich: Spread the mayonnaise on the exposed side of each piece of bread. Lay a slice of fontina on one side of the sandwich. Put 2 slices of tomato on top of the cheese. Season with salt and pepper, sprinkle with the basil, and place the other slice of cheese and bread on top of the tomatoes. The buttered sides should be on the outside.

3. Preheat a panini press, griddle, or cast-iron pan. If using a panini press, follow the manufacturer's directions; otherwise, place the sandwich on a griddle or cast-iron pan, gently press with a spatula, and cook until toasted on one side and the cheese is melted. Flip and do the same for the other side. Cut on the diagonal and serve.

TOMATO, AVOCADO, AND SPROUTS SANDWICH

YIELD: *8 sandwiches*

Mayonnaise to taste
16 slices multigrain bread
2 pounds tomatoes, sliced
2 Hass avocados, peeled, pitted, and sliced
2 teaspoons salt
1 teaspoon fresh-ground black pepper
4 ounces alfalfa sprouts

A sandwich popular during the "natural foods movement" of the 1970s and still going strong in health food stores. It can be toasted and pressed or dressed in vinaigrette; the sprouts can be changed to spicy radish or arugula; and cheese may be added. But the tomato is sacred.

1. Spread the mayonnaise on each slice of bread and top 8 of the bread slices with several slices of tomato.

2. Place 3 to 4 slices of avocado (about one quarter of an avocado) on top of the tomatoes on each sandwich. Season with salt and pepper.

3. Top with sprouts and the remaining slices of bread. Cut in half and serve.

OPEN-FACED TOMATO AND SUNNY-SIDE-UP EGG SANDWICH

YIELD: *8 sandwiches*

4 tablespoons (½ stick) butter

8 eggs

8 slices toasted bread

Mayonnaise to taste (or substitute butter)

2 pounds beefsteak tomatoes, cut in ½-inch slices

2 teaspoons salt

1 teaspoon fresh-ground black pepper

No need to go to the drive-through when a superior breakfast sandwich can be so easily constructed. This is something even a little one could love; so create childhood taste memories. There are countless renditions of this recipe. George Washington Carver floured his tomatoes and fried them in bacon fat (and served the sandwich with bacon on the side).

1. In a sauté pan, melt the butter over moderate heat. Crack the eggs into the butter. Lower the heat so that the whites cook through and the yolk is warm.

2. Toast the bread, and spread a light coating of the mayonnaise on one face of each piece. Place a thick slice of tomato on top of the mayonnaise. Place an egg on top and sprinkle with salt and pepper.

Accompaniments

TOMATO BREAD PUDDING

YIELD: *8 portions*

1 pound brioche or hearty white bread

¼ cup pure olive oil

2 cups small-diced onions

2 tablespoons finely chopped garlic

2 pounds tomatoes, peeled, seeded, diced

2 teaspoons salt

2 teaspoons finely chopped thyme

½ teaspoon finely chopped rosemary

1 tablespoon coarsely chopped flat-leaf
   parsley

7 eggs

2 cups milk

2 cups heavy cream

½ cup grated Gruyère cheese

½ cup grated Parmesan cheese

A soothing dish for breakfast, lunch, or dinner. Eating it is like wrapping yourself in a soft, warm blanket on a chilly day. Make it even more soothing by following the advice for Dry Tomato Soup from *The Jewish Manual; or, Practical Information in Jewish and Modern Cookery with a Collection of Valuable Recipes and Hints Relating to the Toilette* (1846): strew crumbs of bread and a little warmed butter over the top.

1. Preheat the oven to 350 degrees.

2. Cut the bread into ½-inch cubes. Spread in a single layer on a rimmed baking sheet. Place in the oven and toast the bread, turning as needed, until golden brown, about 15 minutes.

3. Heat the oil in a sauté pan. Add the onions and cook until translucent. Add the garlic and cook until aromatic. Combine with the tomatoes and herbs in a large bowl. Reserve.

4. Whisk the eggs in a large bowl just to combine. Add the milk, cream, and salt and stir lightly.

5. Toss the Gruyère with the bread and tomato mixture. Butter eight 8-ounce ramekins and divide the mixture among them.

6. Pour the egg and milk mixture over the bread mixture, dividing it equally among the ramekins. Let it rest, stirring occasionally, until the custard has been absorbed.

7. Top the ramekins with the Parmesan cheese.

8. Place the ramekins in a baking dish and fill the dish halfway up with boiling water to create a hot-water bath.

9. Bake for 25 minutes. Put under the broiler until the top is crispy and browned.

GREEN TOMATO CHOW CHOW

YIELD: *8 pints*

6 pounds green (unripe) tomatoes

2 cups seeded and chopped green
  bell peppers

2 cups seeded and chopped red bell
  peppers

2 cups finely chopped onions

2 red chili peppers, seeded

2 cups finely chopped green cabbage

5 tablespoons kosher salt

1 quart cider vinegar

3 cups sugar

½ cup mustard seeds

1 tablespoon celery seeds

1 tablespoon whole allspice

1 teaspoon ground turmeric

There are three basic kinds of green tomatoes in the world: soft and spicy green-when-ripes for fresh eating (like Green Giant and Aunt Ruby's German Green); hard and sour green-when-unripes for pickles and preserves (pick a tomato—any mature green tomato—just before it colors up); and tomatoes with the ripening inhibitor gene (rin) that won't ripen even when you walk seven times widdershins around the vines (such as Tom Wagner's aptly named Never Will, and Tim Peters' Green Thumb and Forever Green). Choose tomatoes from the last two groups for chow chow (or even unripe green-when-ripes for a lark).

1. Remove a thin slice from the stem and blossom ends of the tomatoes and discard. Chop the tomatoes very fine. Combine with all of the vegetables and the salt and toss. Place in a stainless-steel or glass bowl. Press plastic wrap on the surface and put a plate on top to weight the vegetables and help bring out their juice. Place in the refrigerator overnight.

2. The next day, strain the solids, pressing the liquid out. Discard the liquid.

3. Combine the vinegar, sugar, and remaining spices in a large nonreactive saucepan. Bring to a simmer. Add the vegetables and cook for 10 minutes. Cool.

4. Chow chow can be refrigerated for 1 month. If you wish to can the chow chow, place into sterilized jars, follow the manufacturer's directions, and process in a boiling water bath for 15 minutes. Chow chow served with cornbread, sweet potatoes, long-cooked greens, and roast turkey is the way to celebrate the bounty of the garden come winter in the Deep South or in the North.

GREEN TOMATO AND CURRANT CHUTNEY

YIELD: *4 quarts.*

6 pounds green (unripe) tomatoes, cut into small dice

2 cups small-diced onions

3 tablespoons slivered garlic

3 tablespoons peeled and slivered fresh ginger

2 cups dried currants

3 cups light brown sugar

3 cups cider vinegar

1 tablespoon salt

2 tablespoons finely chopped fresh cayenne (or other hot red) pepper

1 cinnamon stick

1 teaspoon ground cloves

If, according to tomato guru Jan Blum, "paste tomatoes specialize in sauces," then green tomatoes specialize in chutneys, chow chows, and pickles. This sweet and spicy chutney is an appetizing aside.

1. In a large pot, combine all ingredients and stew uncovered at a gentle simmer for 30 minutes. If liquid remains, strain the solids, reduce the liquid to a syrupy consistency, and stir the liquid back into the chutney. Discard the cinnamon stick and pour the chutney into jars.

2. Reserve in the refrigerator for up to a month until ready to use.

GREEN TOMATO PICKLES

YIELD: *8 pints*

2 cups pickling lime (calcium hydroxide)

1 gallon water

7 pounds green (unripe) tomatoes

2 quarts cider vinegar

5 pounds sugar

1 teaspoon celery seed

1 teaspoon ground ginger

1 teaspoon ground allspice

1 tablespoon mustard seeds

1 teaspoon ground cinnamon

1 drop green food coloring (optional)

Eve Felder remembers green tomato pickles made emerald with a drop of green food coloring and served in a silver pickle platter against a white pressed-linen tablecloth. The food coloring is optional in this recipe; the pickling lime, a crisping agent for the tomatoes, is not.

1. Dissolve the pickling lime in the water in a glass crock or jar. Remove a thin slice from the stem and blossom ends of the tomatoes and discard. Slice the tomatoes ¼ inch thick. Place them in the crock and soak for 24 hours. The next day, rinse the tomatoes in cold water four times. Then soak in fresh water for two hours.

2. Bring the remaining ingredients to a boil over moderate heat in a large nonreactive pot; reduce to a simmer, and cook for 5 minutes.

3. Drain the tomatoes, place in heat-proof bowl, and pour the hot pickling mixture over the top. Let sit for 6 hours.

4. Return the tomatoes and liquid to a medium-heat burner and simmer for 45 minutes or until tender. If you want very green pickles, add a drop of green food coloring to the liquid.

5. Place in sterilized jars, following the manufacturer's directions. Process in a boiling water bath for 15 minutes.

TOMATO AND SHELLY BEAN SALAD

YIELD: *8 portions*

SHELLY BEANS

3 cups fresh beans, shelled

½ onion, sliced

1 small carrot, peeled

1 thyme sprig

6 cups water

1 ½ tablespoons salt

RED WINE VINAIGRETTE FOR THE BEANS

1 shallot, finely diced

½ cup red wine vinegar

1 teaspoon salt

½ cup pure olive oil

¼ cup extra-virgin olive oil

2 tablespoons minced summer savory

2 tablespoons coarsely chopped
   flat-leaf parsley

SHERRY VINAIGRETTE FOR THE TOMATOES

1 shallot, finely diced

3 tablespoons sherry vinegar

1 tablespoon red wine vinegar

2 teaspoons balsamic vinegar

1 teaspoon salt

½ cup pure olive oil

¼ cup extra-virgin olive oil

1 pint cherry and currant tomatoes
   (mixed)

Salt and fresh-ground black pepper
   to taste

1 cup Aioli (page 234)

This is the grown-up version of one of Eve Felder's childhood favorites: warm "sieve beans"—the tiniest lima beans you can imagine—combined with cool tomatoes and mayonnaise. Feast on this seasonal dish at the end of July, or whenever your first cherry tomatoes ripen and beans are swollen in their pods and can be shelled out.

1. To make the shelly beans: In a 2-quart pot, combine the shelled beans with the onion, carrot, thyme, water, and salt. Bring to a boil. Reduce to a simmer and cook until the vegetables are tender, 30 to 45 minutes. Remove from the heat and reserve in the liquid until just warm.

2. In the meantime, make the red wine vinaigrette for the beans and the sherry vinaigrette for the cherry tomatoes. Use the same method for the two vinaigrettes but keep them separate. Combine the shallots with the vinegar and salt in a medium, nonreactive bowl. Let the shallots soak for 30 minutes. Whisk in the olive oils. Reserve the vinaigrettes.

3. When the beans are still warm but no longer hot, drain them and remove the onion and carrot. Place the beans in a bowl and toss with the red wine vinaigrette. Add the summer savory and parsley. Taste and adjust the salt.

4. Slice the cherry and currant tomatoes in half and toss with the sherry vinaigrette. Season with salt and pepper. Reserve.

5. To assemble, use a slotted spoon to place the shelly bean salad in the center of the plate; scatter the tomato salad over and around the shelly beans. Garnish with the aioli.

AIOLI

YIELD: *2 cups*

2 egg yolks
1 ¾ cups peanut oil
¼ cup extra-virgin olive oil
1 garlic clove, peeled
1 ½ teaspoons salt
½ teaspoon red wine vinegar
½ teaspoon fresh lemon juice
Fresh-ground black pepper to taste

Dab this classic sauce from Mediterranean France on Tomato and Shelly Bean Salad (page 233), grilled steak, and any other dish that could use a bit of spark.

1. Place the yolks in a bowl and whisk in the oils, adding a little at a time, until the mixture achieves the consistency of mayonnaise. If it becomes too thick, adjust with a few drops of water.

2. Slice the garlic thin and sprinkle it with the salt. Use the flat of your knife to mash the garlic into a fine paste, or pound the garlic and salt in a mortar with a pestle.

3. Add half of the garlic paste to the bowl, along with the vinegar and fresh lemon juice. Taste and add more garlic, if desired. Season with black pepper. The aioli will keep for about a week in the fridge.

SHERRY SHALLOT VINAIGRETTE

YIELD: *1 pint*

2 shallots, cut into fine dice
¼ cup sherry vinegar
2 tablespoons red wine vinegar
1 tablespoon balsamic vinegar
Salt to taste

1 cup pure olive oil
½ cup extra-virgin olive oil

The sweet, complex taste of this vinaigrette brings out the best in tomatoes, particularly those that are sweet and low in acid. Pickle the shallots by soaking them in vinegar and salt for 30 minutes, while you make a round trip to the garden. Whisk in the olive oils, and you've got it made.

1. In a medium bowl, soak the shallots in the vinegars and salt for 30 minutes.

2. Whisk in the olive oils. Taste and adjust with additional vinegar, oil, or salt as needed. Store in a tightly closed jar in the refrigerator. The vinaigrette will keep for 4 or 5 days.

KETCHUP

YIELD: *2–3 quarts*

2 tablespoons peppercorns
1 tablespoon cumin seeds
1 tablespoon coriander seeds
1 tablespoon whole allspice

½ cup canola oil
3 pounds onions, sliced
1 pound red bell peppers, sliced
4 tablespoons minced garlic
15 pounds plum tomatoes, coarsely
    chopped
3 tablespoons salt

3 cups light Karo syrup
3 cups cider vinegar

One of the best uses for a bumper crop of plum tomatoes or commercial heirlooms (such as Marglobe or Rutgers) with high juice viscosity and plenty of solids. This homemade ketchup is distinctly different from the bright red kid stuff—more tangy and less sweet—but you can always sweeten to taste if desired.

1. Place all of the spices in a cheesecloth bag.

2. Heat the oil in a large pot. Add the onions, bell peppers, and salt and cook over moderate heat until the vegetables are tender. Add the garlic and cook until it becomes fragrant. Add the spice bag and the tomatoes; cook until the tomatoes have blended.

3. Place the Karo syrup in a nonreactive saucepan and cook over medium heat until it begins to caramelize and turn golden. Slowly and carefully stir the vinegar into the syrup. It will seize up. Continue to stir while adding the vinegar slowly. After the vinegar is incorporated into the syrup, add the mixture to the tomatoes.

4. Cook the tomato mixture, uncovered, until it thickens, about 1½ hours.

5. Pass the ketchup through a food mill and pour into a clean pot.

6. Reheat the ketchup and put into canning jars and seal.

OVEN-ROASTED TOMATOES

YIELD: *20 tomato halves*

10 San Marzano tomatoes (or other
    small- to medium-size dry red plum
    or pear tomatoes)
2 tablespoons Garlic Oil (page 239)
1 teaspoon salt
1 teaspoon fresh-ground black pepper
2 tablespoons chopped thyme

These are celestial and a cinch to make. Oven-roasted tomatoes are the next best thing to the Tomaisin, a tomato that—"Look, Ma, no hands!"—dries on the vine, developed by Dr. Arthur Schaffer of the Volcani Center in Israel. Orange Banana and Speckled Roman tomatoes are as sweet as apricots when oven-roasted and are perfect for sandwiches or with mozzarella. Larger plum tomatoes require longer roasting.

1. Preheat the oven to 300 degrees.

2. Cut the tomatoes in half and put them skin side down on a rimmed baking sheet. Drizzle with the garlic oil and season with the salt and pepper. Sprinkle the thyme over the top.

3. Roast until they have wilted and shrunk by half. This should take 2 to 3 hours.

CRUNCHY CROUTONS

YIELD: *2 quarts*

1 loaf levain or Tuscan-style bread
½ cup pure olive oil
1 teaspoon salt
½ teaspoon fresh-ground black pepper

More than 150 years ago, in her book *The Good Housekeeper, or The Way to Live Well, and to Be Well While We Live*, self-declared good housekeeper Sarah Josepha Hale dressed up her soups with toasted breads or crackers. The bad housekeeper, according to Mrs. Hale, served boiled doughy dumplings, "libels on civilized cookery," as hard to digest as bricks "from the ruins of Babylon." Crunchy croutons are delicate and digestive; the crunchiest croutons with soft innards are made with fresh bread and toasted in a hot oven.

1. Preheat the oven to 400 degrees.

2. Tear the bread into small chunks. Toss with the olive oil, salt, and pepper. Spread in a single layer on a cookie sheet and toast. Toss occasionally with a spatula so the croutons brown evenly. Reserve.

MARINARA SAUCE

YIELD *2 quarts*

⅓ cup pure olive oil

¼ cup finely chopped garlic

¼ cup finely chopped anchovies

2 quarts canned San Marzano tomatoes, drained

1 cup chicken stock

2 teaspoons salt

1 teaspoon fresh-ground black pepper

½ cup grated Parmesan cheese (optional)

I asked Eve Felder to duplicate the marinara sauce served at my favorite Italian restaurant in New York. She went them one step better. This rendition truly considers the marine aspect of a classic sauce: the secret ingredient is salty little fish. The not-so-secret ingredient is canned tomatoes—whole and peeled—known in Italy as *pomodoro pelati*. The foremost pelati are San Marzano.

1. Add the oil to a 3-quart pot with a heavy bottom and warm over gentle heat. Add the garlic and cook until it just begins to sizzle. Add the anchovies, increase the heat slightly, and stir until the anchovies have dissolved into a paste.

2. Add the tomatoes, chicken stock, salt, and pepper. With the back of a spoon or a potato masher, press the tomatoes to break them up into small pieces. Cover and cook over low heat for about 45 minutes.

3. Add the Parmesan cheese, if using, and taste. Adjust the seasoning.

TOMATO SAUCE

YIELD *2 quarts*

5 pounds plum tomatoes, cored and quartered

1 small head of garlic, cut across the equator

3 basil sprigs

2 oregano sprigs

3 thyme sprigs

¼ cup pure olive oil

1 tablespoon salt

1 teaspoon fresh-ground black pepper

3 tablespoons butter

1 pound onions, cut into large dice

1 cup large-diced celery

1 cup large-diced carrots

I like this sauce so much that at harvest time, when the plum tomatoes are perfectly ripe, I pack my freezers full of quart jars, assisted by capable students from the nearby Culinary Institute of America.

1. Preheat the oven to 400 degrees.

2. In a 4-quart casserole dish or roasting pan, combine the tomatoes, garlic, basil, oregano, thyme, olive oil, salt, and pepper. Roast in the oven for 30 minutes.

3. While the tomatoes are roasting, melt the butter in a large pot and gently cook the vegetables in the butter until translucent.

4. Add the roasted tomato mixture to the vegetables and cook together on a low simmer for 30 minutes. Cool until manageable and purée through a food mill. (The sauce will be thin at this point.)

5. Reduce the sauce in a wide sauce pot to the desired consistency.

QUICK TOMATO AND GARLIC SAUCE

YIELD: *1 quart*

⅓ cup extra-virgin olive oil
3 garlic cloves, sliced thin
4 cups peeled and chopped tomatoes
½ teaspoon salt
½ teaspoon coarse-ground black pepper

Fully ripe tomatoes with dry, firm flesh—especially the ones shaped like bananas, bell peppers, tomato peppers (round angular or ribbed), sausages, or giant plums—dissolve quickly into thick, flavorful pan sauce when paired with garlic. Toss with pasta or position in the middle of soft, creamy polenta.

1. In a 12-inch sauté pan, warm the oil over gentle heat. Add the garlic, stir to evenly distribute, and cook until it just begins to sizzle and the aroma is apparent.

2. Add the chopped tomatoes, salt, and pepper. Increase the heat slightly. Cook until the tomatoes have just begun to release some of their juices into the olive oil and a slight emulsion is formed, about 5 minutes.

3. Taste and adjust for salt and pepper.

GARLIC OIL

YIELD *1 cup*

5 garlic cloves, peeled
1 cup pure olive oil

Garlic oil gives zip to tomatoes and their close associates, such as pizza dough, pasta, and croutons.

1. Finely mince the garlic in a food processor.

2. Heat the oil in a small saucepan to about 140 degrees. Add the garlic, remove the oil from the heat, and cool. Strain and discard solids, and place the oil into a jar.

3. Refrigerate for up to 1 week.

Desserts

GALETTE OF WHITE PEACHES AND TOMATOES

YIELD: *8 portions*

CRUST

1 cup all-purpose flour

2 teaspoons sugar

½ teaspoon salt

8 tablespoons (1 stick) cold butter,
    cut into ¼-inch cubes

4 tablespoons ice water

FILLING

4 medium-size white (or yellow) peaches,
    peeled

6 small white peach (or light yellow)
    tomatoes

2 tablespoons all-purpose flour

2 teaspoons sugar

4 ½ tablespoons sugar

2 tablespoons melted butter

When newly introduced in sixteenth-century Europe, the tomato was mistaken for the "wolf peach" or *Lycopersicon* that Galen had identified more than a thousand years earlier. The name stuck in one form or another (now *Solanum lycopersicum*) even after botanists realized the tomato was strictly New World in origin; and I can't help equating the peach and the tomato. White peaches and white peach tomatoes are more equal than others. This galette is filled with succulent and delicious surprises. Serve with vanilla ice cream.

1. To make the crust: Place the flour, sugar, and salt in the work bowl of a food processor. Pulse to combine. Add 4 tablespoons of the butter (½ stick). Pulse until the pieces are the size of pennies. Add the remaining butter and pulse for 2 seconds. Remove the mass to a lightly floured work surface.

2. Press the mass together gently with your hands. With the palm of your hand, smear a quarter of the mass in short, quick movements away from you; continue with the remaining dough, smearing it a quarter at a time until all the dough has rejoined the first quarter. (Work quickly, so the dough doesn't get tough.) Gather the dough together in a ball and repeat one more time. Cover in plastic wrap and press into a flat round disk. Refrigerate for at least 30 minutes or up to 2 days. (The dough can also be frozen for 1 month.)

3. After resting the dough, use a pastry mat and a rolling pin wrapped in a pastry cloth to roll it into a ⅛-inch-thick circle. Place the dough on a Silpat-lined pan. Refrigerate while preparing the peaches and tomatoes.

4. Slice the peaches into ¼-inch slices. Using a sharp serrated knife, do the same with the tomatoes.

5. Preheat the oven to 400 degrees.

6. Mix the flour and sugar together and scatter on the dough, leaving a 1-inch border free of flour.

7. Lay the peaches in concentric circles around the dough, still leaving a 1-inch border. For every three slices of peaches, set down one tomato slice. Sprinkle with 4 tablespoons of the sugar.

8. Fold the 1-inch border over the fruit in a scalloped edge. Brush with the melted butter and sprinkle with the remaining ½ tablespoon of sugar.

9. Bake until the crust is golden and the fruit is tender, about 35 minutes. If juices have run over, brush the fruit with them. Slide the tart to a rack to cool. Then slide on a plate to cut.

ROASTED TOMATO CRUNCH SICILIAN STYLE

YIELD: *8 portions*

STUFFING

2 cups water

½ cup sugar

1 bay leaf

1 strip of lemon zest

½ cinnamon stick

1 teaspoon black peppercorns

1 cup dried currants

1 cup finely chopped golden raisins

1 cup finely chopped dried apricots

CRUNCHY TOPPING

¾ cup pine nuts, raw

1 large egg

1 cup all-purpose flour

1 cup brown sugar

8 tablespoons (1 stick) butter

8 medium-size stuffing tomatoes (hollow tomatoes), or any firm, round tomatoes

1 teaspoon salt

CARAMEL SAUCE

1½ cups sugar

2 tablespoons dark rum

¾ cup heavy cream

This is the first sweet tomato dessert Eve Felder ever created. Her very discriminating recipe testers—her young daughters—absolutely loved it. Your daughters and sons will, too. This is best made with bell-pepper-shaped tomatoes, such as Burgess Stuffing or Schimmeig Stoo, which hold their own under fire.

Serve with vanilla ice cream.

1. Preheat the oven to 350 degrees.

2. To make the stuffing: Combine the water, sugar, bay leaf, lemon zest, and cinnamon in a 1-quart pot. Tie the peppercorns in a little cheesecloth bag and add to the mixture. Bring to a boil over high heat and reduce to a simmer. Cook for about 5 minutes, stirring, until the sugar is completely dissolved. Remove the pot from the heat. Add the dried fruit to the spiced water and cover the pot. Allow the fruit to plump for 15 minutes.

3. Strain and reserve the fruit from the spiced water. Discard the water and spices.

4. To make the crunchy topping: Spread the pine nuts in a single layer in a small saucepan. Toast on low heat for about 6 minutes or until very lightly browned, stirring occasionally to prevent burning. Cool.

5. Whisk the egg in a large bowl and add the flour, brown sugar, and toasted pine nuts. Combine well. Reserve.

6. Melt the butter and cool slightly.

7. Remove the top of the hollow stuffing tomatoes (as you would for a bell pepper) and discard the seeds. If you have solid round tomatoes, create a two-inch cavity for the stuffing by cutting and scooping out about a third of the pulp. Sprinkle the cavity of the tomatoes with the salt.

8. Place the tomatoes on a foil-lined rimmed baking sheet. Stuff the cavity of each tomato with about ½ cup of the fruit mixture, or until nearly filled. Add about 4 tablespoons of the crunchy topping. Spoon the melted butter over the top.

9. Roast the tomatoes for 25 minutes, until their skin gets a little wrinkly.

10. In the meantime, make the caramel sauce: Pour the sugar into a stainless-steel pan, and shake the pan so that the sugar spreads evenly. Over moderate heat, melt the sugar until it has a deep, rich golden color. Carefully add the rum and cream. Melt the sugar again, stirring with a wooden spoon, until a thick sauce has formed.

11. Remove the tomatoes from the oven. Put 2 tablespoons of the sauce in the center of each plate, top with a tomato, and add a scoop of vanilla ice cream on the side.

Drinks

TOMATO WATER

YIELD: *2 quarts*

5 pounds tomatoes, chopped fine
3 tablespoons salt
1 tablespoon fresh-ground black pepper
2 small basil sprigs
2 thyme sprigs
2 garlic cloves, crushed

A distilled tomato juice, best made with white or yellow tomatoes, whose juices run clear. This can be gelatinized into tomato aspic, served as an aperitif with a sprig of basil, or used as the base for cold tomato soups and not-so-bloody Bloody Marys.

1. Combine all ingredients in a large bowl. Stir and crush the tomatoes with a wooden spoon.

2. Place a large double thickness of cheesecloth, big enough to accommodate all of the tomatoes, into another bowl. Pour the tomato mixture into the cheesecloth and tie the cloth into a bag with a long sturdy string. Place the bowl in the refrigerator and tie the sack above the bowl so that the liquid drips freely; the bag should be high enough so that the liquid never touches the bottom.

3. Hang the bag for at least 8 hours. Do not squeeze the bag to extract liquid; this will make the tomato water cloudy. Discard the tomato bag and its contents after it has drained, and reserve the water.

SUMMER VEGETABLE AND TOMATO BLOODY MARYS

YIELD: *8 servings*

1 tablespoon salt
4 pounds red tomatoes, chopped

2 cups finely chopped cucumber
1 cup finely chopped carrots
1 cup finely chopped celery with leaves
1 jalapeño pepper, halved and seeded
1 tablespoon fresh lemon juice
2 thyme sprigs, chopped
¼ cup chopped basil
½ garlic clove, crushed
Fresh-ground black pepper to taste

Pepper vodka to taste (optional)

GARNISH
8 cucumber or celery sticks

The élan vital of tomato, to be taken with or without vodka. Pass the tomatoes through a food mill rather than using a blender, which makes too many bubbles and ruins the red color and texture of the juice. Serve to bloodthirsty guests.

1. Salt the tomatoes, then, in a mixer fitted with a paddle, crush them until they are well broken down. Let sit in a large, nonreactive bowl for 2 hours to allow for the greatest extraction of juice.

2. In the meantime, in a food processor combine the cucumber, carrots, celery, jalapeño, lemon juice, thyme, basil, and garlic and purée until smooth and almost liquid. Season with black pepper and add to the macerating tomatoes.

3. Pass the tomato mixture through a food mill or sieve. Taste and adjust the seasonings. Refrigerate until ready to serve.

4. Serve over ice in tall chilled highball glasses. Add vodka, if desired. Stir, garnish with a stick of cucumber or celery, and serve.

THAI TOMATO COCKTAIL

YIELD: *8 servings*

4 pounds tomatoes, coarsely chopped
1 tablespoon salt
2 teaspoons sugar

4 strips of lime zest
3 tablespoons husked and finely chopped
    lemongrass
2 tablespoons fresh lime juice
2 teaspoons fish sauce
2 tablespoons peeled and finely grated fresh
    ginger
½ Thai Hot chili
1 tablespoon coarsely chopped Thai basil
1 garlic clove, crushed
Fresh-ground black pepper to taste

Vodka to taste (optional)

GARNISH
8 stalks lemongrass, peeled

I like my Thai tomato cocktails to resemble saffron, or else the peel of the ripe mandarin orange—an effect achieved with tomatoes such as Caro Rich and Aunt Gertie's Gold. This zesty drink will transport you and your guests to Thailand—or to some other altered state.

1. In a mixer fitted with a paddle, combine the tomatoes, salt, and sugar. Crush the tomatoes. Let sit in a large, nonreactive bowl for 2 hours for maximum juice extraction.

2. In the meantime, blanch the lime zest in boiling water until tender, approximately 5 minutes. In a blender, combine the blanched lime zest and chopped lemongrass with the lime juice, fish sauce, ginger, chili, basil, and garlic and purée until smooth and almost liquid. Season with black pepper and add to the macerating tomatoes.

3. Pass the tomato mixture through a sieve. Taste and adjust the seasonings. Refrigerate until ready to serve.

4. Serve over ice in tall chilled highball glasses. Add vodka, if desired. Garnish each glass with a stalk of lemongrass.

Thai Pink bouquet

seed sources

Abu
ABUNDANT LIFE SEEDS
P.O. Box 157
Saginaw, OR 97472
541-767-9606
www.abundantlifeseeds.com
Offers only organically certified seed.

All
ALLEN, STERLING AND LOTHROP
191 U.S. Route 1
Falmouth, ME 04105
www.allensterlinglothrop.com
Specializes in vegetable seeds adapted
to northern New England. Company
founded in 1911.

Ag7
AGRESTAL ORGANIC HERITAGE
SEED CO.
P.O. Box 646
Gormley, Ontario
Canada L0H 1G0
farmerbob@agrestalseeds.com
www.agrestalseeds.com
Offers certified-organic, open-polli-
nated varieties of heirloom vegetables,
herbs, fruits, and flowers. No print
catalog for 2008; online only.

Ap6
APPALACHIAN SEEDS
99 Treehouse Lane
Burnsville, NC 28714
seeds@appalachianseeds.com
www.appalachianseeds.com
Online catalog. Carries organically
grown heirloom tomatoes.

Ba8
BAKER CREEK HEIRLOOM SEEDS
2278 Baker Creek Road
Mansfield, MO 65704
417-924-8917
seeds@rareseeds.com
www.rareseeds.com
Free catalog. Sells only nonhybrid rare
heirloom seeds, Asian and European
varieties.

Bo17
BOTANICAL INTERESTS, INC.
P.O. Box 271107
Littleton, CO 80127
www.gardentrails.com
Family-operated business offering a
full line of untreated flower, vegetable,
and herb seeds. No seed products
shipped out of the continental United
States.

Bo19
BOTANIKKA SEEDS
P.O. Box 182
Iron Ridge, WI 53035
mark@botanikka.com
www.botanikka.com
Online catalog. Sells heirloom and
rare specialty seeds with an empha-
sis on herbs and vegetables. Grows,
imports, and packages garden seeds
for sale through retail stores, farm
markets, and Web site. Retail sales;
bulk prices on request.

Bou
BOUNTIFUL GARDENS
18001 Shafer Ranch Road
Willits, CA 95490
Phone: 707-459-6410
Fax: 707-459-1925
bountiful@sonic.net
www.bountifulgardens.org
Free catalog. Offers open-pollinated,
untreated heirloom seeds adapted to
varied conditions.

Bu2
W. ATLEE BURPEE AND CO.
300 Park Ave.
Warminster, PA 18974
800-333-5808
www.burpee.com
Free catalog. Extensive selection,
including many original introductions.
Retail and wholesale.

Bu8
BUNTON SEED CO.
939 East Jefferson Street
Louisville, KY 40206
info@buntonseed.com
www.buntonseed.com
Online catalog. Offers vegetable, herb,
and flower seeds.

Co32
THE COTTAGE GARDENER
4199 Gilmore Road, R.R. 1
Newtonville, Ontario
Canada L0A 1J0
www.cottagegardener.com
Carries heirloom perennials, annuals,
herbs, and vegetables. Sales within
Canada only.

Com
COMSTOCK, FERRE & CO.
263 Main Street
Wethersfield CT 06109
860-571-6590
www.comstockferre.com
Free catalog. Established in 1820,
incorporated in 1853. "From packets
to pounds": sells vegetable varieties,
numerous heirlooms, annuals, herbs,
and perennials. Retail and wholesale
prices listed in same catalog.

Coo
THE COOKS' GARDEN
P.O. Box C5030
Warminster, PA 18974
800-457-9703
www.cooksgarden.com
Free catalog. Heirloom organic veg-
etable seeds from around the world.

Ers
E & R SEED LLC
1356 E 200 S
Monroe, IN 46772
Phone/Fax: 260-692-6827
Free catalog. Over 1,000 varieties of
vegetable and flower seeds, including
many organically grown, open-pollinated, and heirloom varieties. Retail
and wholesale.

Fe5
FEDCO SEEDS
P.O. Box 520
Waterville, ME 04903
207-873-7333
www.fedcoseeds.com
Selections for cold climates and
short-growing-season areas. Offers
untreated vegetable, herb, flower,
cover-crop, and green-manure seeds.
Retail and wholesale.

Ga1
IRISH EYES AND GARDEN CITY
SEEDS
5045 Robinson Canyon Road
Ellensburg, WA 98926
509-964-7000
www.gardencityseeds.net
Free catalog. Vegetables are trialed
and taste-tested to ensure good quality.
Retail and wholesale.

Ga21
GARDEN MEDICINALS AND CU-
LINARIES
P.O. Box 320
Earlysville, VA 22936
434-964-9113
www.gardenmedicinals.com
Online catalog only. Sells open-pollinated seeds and plants, including
medicinal and culinary herbs, select
ethnic and heirloom vegetables, and
flower varieties. Retail and wholesale.

Ga22
THE GARDEN PATH NURSERY
395 Conway Road
Victoria, British Columbia V9E 2B9
thegardenpath@shaw.ca
www.earthfuture.com/gardenpath
Handles Seeds of Victoria vegetable
and flower seeds. Organically grown
and locally harvested open-pollinated
seeds.

Go8

GOLDEN HARVEST
ORGANICS LLC
404 North Impala Drive
Fort Collins, CO 80521
www.ghorganics.com
Online catalog. Supplies organically
grown tomato seeds.

Goo

GOOD SEED CO.
195 Bolster Road
Oroville, WA 98844
www.goodseedco.net
Online catalog. Deals in open-pollinated, heirloom, and homestead
seeds adapted to northern gardens.
Retail only.

Gr27

GREEN THUMB SEEDS
17011 West 280th Street
Bethany, MO 64424
Free catalog. Heirloom seeds for the
home gardener. Retail and wholesale.

Ha5

HARRIS SEEDS
355 Paul Road
Rochester, NY 14624-0966
Phone: 800-514-4441
Fax: 877-892-9197
www.harrisseeds.com
Free catalog. Sells treated, untreated,
and organic seeds. Separate retail and
wholesale catalogs.

Ha26

HARVEST MOON FARMS &
SEED CO.
HC 12, Box 510
Tatum, NM 88267-9700
Small family-owned seed company
dealing in heirloom and gourmet
seeds from several countries around
the world. Retail and wholesale.

He17

HEIRLOOM ACRES
2529 CR 338
New Bloomfield, MO 65063
www.heirloomacresseeds.com
Online catalog. Family-owned and
-operated business offering the finest
in heirloom, open-pollinated, and
other selected vegetable, herb, and
flower seeds.

He8

HEIRLOOM SEEDS
P.O. Box 245
West Elizabeth, PA 15088-0245
412-384-0852
www.heirloomseeds.com or
www.heirloomtomatoes.com
Small family-run seed house selling
only open-pollinated vegetable and
flower seeds, many first introduced in
the 1700s and 1800s. Catalog costs $1
(refundable with order).

Hi13

HIRT'S GARDENS
4943 Ridge Road (Rt. 94)
Medina (Granger Township), OH
44281
www.hirts.com
Online catalog. One of Ohio's oldest
horticultural establishments, special-
izing in unusual vegetables, perennials,
flowers, houseplants, and bulbs.

Hi6

HIGH MOWING SEEDS
76 Quarry Road
Wolcott, VT 05680
802-472-6174
www.highmowingseeds.com
Free catalog. Formerly the Good Seed
Company of Vermont. Deals in rare
locally adapted New England heirlooms, certified organically grown by
a network of growers in the Vermont
area. Separate retail and wholesale
catalogs.

Hig

SEEDS TRUST/HIGH ALTITUDE
GARDENS
P.O. Box 596
Cornville, AZ 86325
208-788-4363
www.seedstrust.com
Catalog available for a nominal fee.
Small regional seed company special-
izing in short-season, open-pollinated,
hardy seeds adapted to cold mountain
climates. Separate retail and wholesale
catalogs.

Hud

J. L. HUDSON, SEEDSMAN
P.O. Box 337
LaHonda, CA 94020
www.jlhudsonseeds.net
Free catalog. Provides seeds of rare
and unusual plants, Zapotec varieties,
and useful wild and cultivated plants.
Established in 1911. Has endorsed
open-pollinated unpatented nonhybrid seeds and preservation of biological and cultural diversity since 1973.

Hum

ED HUME SEEDS
P.O. Box 73160
Puyallup, WA 98373
www.humeseeds.com
Sells seeds for cool and short-season
climates, with special selections for
Alaska and for autumn planting.
Retail catalog; wholesale rack sales in
Pacific Northwest.

Jo1

JOHNNY'S SELECTED SEEDS
955 Benton Avenue
Winslow, ME 04901
877-564-6697
www.johnnyseeds.com
Free catalog. Vegetable, flower, herb,
and farm seeds and garden acces-
sories. Many heirlooms and new
introductions. Extensive trial grounds
throughout North America. Retail
and wholesale.

Jor

JORDAN SEEDS INC.
6400 Upper Afton Road
Woodbury, MN 55125-1146
651-738-3422
www.jordanseeds.com
Free catalog. Untreated seed for organic growers. Retail and wholesale.

Jun

J. W. JUNG SEED COMPANY
335 South High Street
Randolph, WI 53956
800-297-3123
www.jungseed.com
Free retail catalog. Quality seeds since
1907. Seeds and nursery stock suitable
for northern climates.

Ki4

JOHN SCHEEPERS KITCHEN
GARDEN SEEDS
23 Tulip Drive/P.O. Box 638
Bantam, CT 06750
860-567-6086
www.kitchengardenseeds.com
Free catalog. One of the oldest and
most prestigious seed importers, offering the finest heirlooms, cottage-
garden flowers, gourmet vegetables,
and aromatic herbs from around the
world. Retail only.

La1

D. LANDRETH SEED CO.
60 East High Street, Building #4
New Freedom, Pennsylvania 17349
800-654-2407
www.landrethseeds.com
Founded in 1784, making it the oldest seedhouse in the United States.
Specializes in rare and heirloom
vegetable and flower seeds. Retail and
wholesale.

Lan

LANDIS VALLEY HEIRLOOM
SEED PROJECT
Landis Valley Museum
2451 Kissel Hill Road
Lancaster, PA 17601
Phone: 717-569-0401
Fax: 717-560-2147
www.landisvalleymuseum.org
Carries open-pollinated vegetable varieties of Pennsylvania German origin, dating from 1740 to 1940. Retail and wholesale catalogs.

Ma18

MARIANNA'S HEIRLOOM SEEDS
1955 CCC Road
Dickson, TN 37055
615-446-9191
www.mariseeds.com
Online catalog. Offers Italian cooking tomatoes, peppers, and eggplants. Retail only. Formerly known as Pomodori di Marianna.

Mo13

MORGAN COUNTY SEEDS
18761 Kelsay Road
Barnett, MO 65011-3009
Phone: 573-378-2655
Fax: 573-378-5401
www.morgancountyseeds.com
Free catalog. Supplies a full line of vegetable seeds, with a large selection of untreated and open-pollinated varieties. Retail and wholesale.

Na6

NATURAL GARDENING COMPANY
P.O. Box 750776
Petaluma, CA 94975-0776
www.naturalgardening.com
Free catalog. Started the nation's first certified organic nursery. Deals in untreated and organic vegetable seeds and certified-organic seedlings.

Ni1

NICHOLS GARDEN NURSERY
1190 Old Salem Road NE
Albany, OR 97321-4580
Phone: 800-422-3985
Fax: 800-231-5306
www.nicholsgardennursery.com
Free catalog. Unusual varieties for the gardener-cook, including Asian and European specialties, as well as quality herbs and elephant garlic. Separate retail and wholesale catalogs.

Or10

ORGANICA SEED CO.
P.O. Box 611
Wilbraham, MA 01095
413-599-0264
www.organicaseed.com
Online catalog. Offers untreated, organic vegetable, flower, and herb seeds.

Pe2

PEACEFUL VALLEY FARM SUPPLY
P.O. Box 2209
Grass Valley, CA 95945
Phone: 888-784-1722
Fax: 530-272-4794
www.groworganic.com
Free catalog; U.S. addresses only. Tools and supplies for organic gardeners and farmers since 1976. More than 2,000 items sold, including fertilizers, organic and/or open-pollinated vegetable and cover-crop seeds, weed and pest controls, beneficial insects; also, in fall, has bulbs, garlic, onions, potatoes, and fruit trees. Retail and wholesale.

Pep

PEPPER GAL
P.O. Box 23006
Ft. Lauderdale, FL 33307
Phone: 954-537-5540
Fax: 954-566-2208
peppergal@peppergal.com
www.peppergal.com
Free catalog. Supplies seed for more than 300 hot, sweet, and ornamental peppers, plus tomatoes and gourds. Retail and wholesale.

Pe6

PETERS SEED AND RESEARCH
P.O. Box 62
Riddle, OR 97469
psr@pioneer-net.com
www.psrseed.com
Online catalog. Furnishes open-pollinated, uncommon vegetables and many original introductions. Includes northern varieties and a unique tomato collection. Retail, with some wholesale on contract-grown items.

Pin

PINETREE GARDEN SEEDS
P.O. Box 300
New Gloucester, ME 04260
Phone: 207-926-3400
Fax: 888-527-3337
www.superseeds.com
Free catalog. Flavorful varieties for home gardeners and some unique material. "Smaller packets and lower prices." Over 300 gardening books plus tools and bulbs. Retail only.

Pla

PLANTS OF THE SOUTHWEST
3095 Agua Fria Street
Santa Fe, NM 87507
Phone: 505-438-8888
Fax: 505-438-8800
contact@plantsofthesouthwest.com
www.plantsofthesouthwest.com
Free catalog. Specializes in heirloom and traditional Southwestern native plants, including berry- and nut-producing trees and shrubs. Also native grasses, wildflowers, ancient drought-tolerant vegetables, and rare Native American crops.

Pr3

PRAIRIE GARDEN SEEDS
(CONTACT JIM TERNIER)
Box 2758
Humboldt, Saskatchewan
S0K 2A0 Canada
306-682-1475
prairie.seeds@sasktel.net
www.prseeds.ca
Online catalog. Carries open-pollinated vegetable and flower varieties grown without agricultural chemicals, and seeds for dry-land, short-season growing. Offers many heritage seeds with historical information. Retail only.

Ra6

RACHEL'S TOMATO SEED SUPPLY
3421 Bream Street
Gautier, MS 39553
www.rachelssupply.com
Online catalog. Vegetable varieties from around the world.

Re8

REX'S SEED CO.
5308 51st Avenue North
Crystal, MN 55429-3612
www.rexseedco.com
Online catalog. Family-owned and -operated business serving the home gardener, truck farmer, hobbyist, and greenhouse grower.

Ri2

RICHTERS
357 Highway 47
Goodwood, Ontario
L0C 1A0, Canada
Phone: 905-640-6677
Fax: 905-640-6641
OrderDesk@Richters.com
www.richters.com
Free catalog. Family-owned company carrying more than 800 types of herbs, plus unusual gourmet vegetables. Retail and wholesale.

Roh

P. L. ROHRER AND BRO. INC.
P.O. Box 250
Smoketown, PA 17576
Phone: 717-299-2571
Fax: 800-468-4944
info@rohrerseeds.com
www.rohrerseeds.com
Quality farm and garden seeds locally grown by Amish and Mennonite gardeners. Established in 1918. Retail and wholesale catalogs for $2.

Sa5

SALT SPRING SEEDS
Box 444, Ganges P.O.
Salt Spring Island, British Columbia
V8K 2W1 Canada
www.saltspringseeds.com
Canada only. Open-pollinated, organically grown seeds, all adapted to northern climates. Retail only. Catalog $2.

Sa9

SAND HILL PRESERVATION
CENTER
Heirloom Seeds and Poultry
1878 230th Street
Calamus, IA 52729
563-246-2299
sandhill@fbcom.net
www.sandhillpreservation.com
Free catalog. Vast selection of rare and unusual tomatoes. All varieties are open-pollinated and grown on site. Retail only.

Se7

SEEDS OF CHANGE
P.O. Box 15700
Santa Fe, NM 87592-1500
888-762-7333
www.seedsofchange.com.
Free catalog. Deals in vegetables, flowers, and herbs that are certified organic, open-pollinated, public-domain varieties. Separate retail and wholesale catalogs.

Se16

SEED SAVERS CATALOG
3094 North Winn Road
Decorah, IA 52101
Phone: 563-382-5990
Fax: 563-382-5872
www.seedsavers.org
Free 100-page catalog offering a unique selection of outstanding vegetables, flowers, and herbs. Retail catalog also contains bulk prices for specialty growers, truck gardeners, CSA growers, and other seed companies. Wholesale price list available on request.

Se17

SEED DREAMS
P.O. Box 106
Port Townsend, WA 98368
Seed preservation project maintaining rare open-pollinated heirloom seeds.

Se24

SEEDS FROM ITALY
P.O. Box 149
Winchester, MA 01890
seeds@growitalian.com
www.growitalian.com
Free catalog. Offers more than 300 varieties of traditional Italian vegetable, herb, and flower seeds, along with growing instructions and Italian recipes. Retail only.

Se26

SEEDS
410 Whaley Pond Road
Graniteville, SC 29829
orders@vegetableseedwarehouse.com
www.vegetableseedwarehouse.com
Online catalog. Small family-owned business dealing in heirloom vegetable and herb varieties, many certified organic. Retail only.

Se28

SEEDS ETC.
2616 Turk Drive
Marysville, WA 98271
info@seedsetc.com
www.seedsetc.com
Online catalog. Furnishes seed from reliable seed collectors from around the world. Retail only.

Shu

R. H. SHUMWAY, SEEDSMAN
334 West Stroud Street
Randolph, WI 53956-1274
Phone: 800-342-9461
Fax: 888-437-2733
info@rhshumway.com
www.rhshumway.com
Specializes in heirloom and open-pollinated seeds. Separate retail and wholesale catalogs. Free catalog.

So1

SOUTHERN EXPOSURE
SEED EXCHANGE
P.O. Box 460
Mineral, VA 23117
Phone: 540-894-9480
Fax: 540-894-9481
gardens@southernexposure.com
www.southernexposure.com
Sells more than 500 varieties of open-pollinated heirloom and traditional vegetables, flowers, and herbs. Catalog free to U.S. addresses.

So25

SOLANA SEEDS
17 Place Leger
Repentigny, Quebec
J6A 5N7 Canada
www.solanaseeds.netfirms.com
Online catalog. Small seed company offering a variety of rare and unusual vegetables, flowers, and heirlooms. Retail only.

So9

SOW ORGANIC
P.O. Box 527
Williams, OR 97544
888-709-7333
www.organicseed.com
Online catalog. Open-pollinated varieties grown and processed by the company and certified organic by the Oregon Tilth Certified program. Formerly "Southern Oregon Organics." Separate retail and wholesale price lists.

St18

STELLAR SEEDS
S6, C5, RR 1
Sorrento, British Columbia
V0E 2W0 Canada
www.stellarseeds.com.
Certified organic farm offering many heritage varieties along with unique cultivars. Catalog costs $2.

Sw9

SWALLOWTAIL GARDEN SEEDS
122 Calistoga Road, #178
Santa Rosa, CA 95409
www.swallowtailgardenseeds.com
Online catalog. Supplies seeds for 1,200 varieties of untreated heirloom and modern vegetables, flowers, and herbs.

Syn

SYNERGY SEEDS
Box 415
Willow Creek, CA 95573
www.synergyseeds.com
Online catalog. Specializes in experimental breeding projects and homegrown family favorites. Retail and wholesale.

Te4

TERRA EDIBLES
535 Ashley Street
Foxboro, Ontario
K0K 2B0 Canada
613-961-0654
www.terraedibles.ca
Free catalog. Deals in organically grown heirlooms, edible landscaping plants, and varieties that require little space or are extra-nutritious. Retail only.

Ter

TERRITORIAL SEED COMPANY
P.O. Box 158
Cottage Grove, OR 97424-0061
541-942-9547
www.territorialseed.com
Free catalog. Varieties for maritime climates (west of the Cascades), all grown without chemical pesticides and fertilizers. Retail and wholesale.

Th3

THOMAS JEFFERSON CENTER
FOR HISTORIC PLANTS
Monticello
P.O. Box 316
Charlottesville, VA 22902
434-984-9822
www.monticello.org
Specializes in vegetables and flowers that were grown by Thomas Jefferson. Retail only.

To1

TOMATO GROWERS SUPPLY
COMPANY
P.O. Box 60015
Fort Myers, FL 33906
www.tomatogrowers.com
Free catalog to U.S. addresses. Large selection of choice heirloom and open-pollinated tomatoes and peppers. Retail only.

To3

TOTALLY TOMATOES
334 West Stroud Street
Randolph, WI 53956
Phone: 800-345-5977
Fax: 888-477-7333
www.totallytomato.com
Free catalog. Specializes in tomatoes and peppers, half of which are open-pollinated. Retail and wholesale.

To9

TOMATOFEST®
HOMEGROWN SEEDS
P.O. Box W-1
Carmel, CA 93921
www.tomatofest.com.
Online catalog. Catalogs many certified organic, open-pollinated tomato seeds with photos and information.

To10

TOMATO BOB'S
HEIRLOOM TOMATOES
Robert Price
5764 Saucony Drive
Hilliard, OH 43026
www.tomatobob.com
Online seed list. Small family-owned seed company. Offers more than 100 heirloom tomato varieties.

Tu6

TURTLE TREE SEED FARM
Camphill Village
Copake, NY 12516
Phone: 888-516-7797
Fax: 678-202-1351
turtle@turtletreeseed.org
www.turtletreeseeds.com

Und

UNDERWOOD GARDENS
1414 Zimmerman Road
Woodstock, IL 60098
www.underwoodgardens.com
Hard-to-find, untreated, open-pollinated and heirloom seeds, many of which are grown organically. Retail sales, with bulk seed available depending on harvest. Catalog costs $3.

Up2

UPPER CANADA SEEDS
8 Royal Doulton Drive
Don Mills, ON
M3A 1N4 Canada
416-447-5321
uppercanadaseeds@rogers.com
www.uppercanadaseeds.ca
Free catalog. Top quality, untreated organically grown seeds that are suitable for the climatic conditions of Eastern Canada and the Northeastern United States. All seeds are open-pollinated and many are rare heirlooms. Retail only.

Vi4

VICTORY SEED COMPANY
P.O. Box 192
Molalla, OR 97038
Phone/Fax: 503-829-3126
www.victoryseeds.com
Family-owned and -operated retail packet seed company selling only open-pollinated varieties. Catalog costs $2 (refunded with order).

Vi5

VIRTUAL SEEDS
92934 Coyote Dr.
Astoria, OR 97103
www.virtualseeds.com
Online retail catalog only. Ships within U.S. High-quality garden seeds.

We19

WEST COAST SEEDS
3925 64th Street
Delta, British Columbia
V4K 3N2 Canada
Phone: 604-952-8820
Fax: 877-482-8822
www.westcoastseeds.net
Free catalog. Sales within Canada only.
Deals in seeds for organic growers. Retail and wholesale.

Wi2

WILLHITE SEED INC.
P.O. Box 23
Poolville, TX 76487-0023
Phone: 800-828-1840
Fax: 817-599-5843
www.willhiteseed.com
Free color catalog. Family-owned seed company provides quality seed to gardeners and commercial growers.

Yu2

YUKO'S OPEN-POLLINATED
SEEDS
(contact: Yuko Horiuchi)
202 Arklan Road
Caroleton Place, Ontario
K7C 3R9 Canada
www.yuko.ca
Online catalog. Sells organically grown vegetable seeds.

advocacy groups

AMERICAN HORTICULTURAL
SOCIETY
www.ahs.org
7931 East Boulevard Drive
Alexandria, VA 22308
703-768-5700

AMERICAN SOCIETY FOR
HORTICULTURAL SCIENCE
www.ashs.org
113 South West Street, Suite 200
Alexandria, VA 22314-2851
703-836-4606

CHEF'S COLLABORATIVE
www.chefscollaborative.org
89 South Street
Boston, MA 02111
617-236-5200

ETC GROUP
www.etcgroup.org
431 Gilmour Street
Ottawa, Ontario K2P OR5 Canada
613-241-2267

GARDEN ORGANIC
www.gardenorganic.org.uk
Garden Organic Ryton'Coventry,
Warwickshire
CV8 3LG United Kingdom
+44 24 7630 3517

GLOBAL CROP DIVERSITY TRUST
www.croptrust.org
c/o FAO
Viale delle Terme di Caracalla
00153 Rome, Italy
+39 06 570 55142

GRAIN
www.grain.org
Girona 25, pral., E-08010
Barcelona, Spain
+34 933011381

INTERNATIONAL SOCIETY FOR
HORTICULTURAL SCIENCE
www.ishs.org
P. O. Box 500
3001 Leuven 1
Belgium
+32 16229427

JUST FOOD
www.justfood.org
208 East 51st Street
New York, NY 10022
212-645-9880

NATIONAL GARDENING
ASSOCIATION
www.garden.org
1100 Dorset Street
South Burlington, VT 05403
800-863-5251

NATIVE SEEDS/SEARCH
www.nativeseeds.org
526 North Fourth Avenue
Tucson, AZ 85705
520-622-5561

ORGANIC SEED ALLIANCE
www.seedalliance.org
P. O. Box 772
Port Townsend, WA 98368
360-385-7192

SEED SAVERS EXCHANGE
www.seedsavers.org
3094 North Winn Road
Decorah, IA 52101
563-382-5990

SEEDS OF DIVERSITY CANADA
www.seeds.ca
P. O. Box 36
Station Q
Toronto, Ontario
M4T 2L7 Canada
866-509-7333

SLOW FOOD USA
www.slowfoodusa.org
20 Jay Street
Brooklyn, NY 11201
718-260-8000

UNION OF CONCERNED
SCIENTISTS
www.ncsusa.org
2 Brattle Square
Cambridge, MA 02238
617-547-5552

bibliography

Album Benary: Alte Gemüsesorten. Warendorf: Manuscriptum Verlagsbuchh, 2000.

Allison, Ellyn Childs, ed. *The Besler Florilegium: Plants of the Four Seasons.* New York: Harry N. Abrams, 1989.

Amadei, Giorgio; Luciano Trentini, and Gian Piero Soressi. *Il Pomodoro/The Tomato.* Milan: Enichem Agricoltura and Agrimont, 1990.

American Horticultural Society. *Tomatoes.* Mount Vernon, Va.: American Horticultural Society, 1982.

Ashworth, Suzanne. *Seed to Seed: Seed Saving and Growing Techniques for Vegetable Gardeners.* 2d ed. Decorah, Iowa: Seed Savers Exchange, 2002.

Baggett, J. R., and D. Kean. "'Oregon Spring' and 'Santiam' Parthenocarpic Tomatoes." *HortScience* 21, no. 5 (1986): 1245–47.

———. "'Gold Nugget' tomato." *HortScience* 20, no. 5 (1985): 957–958.

Bailey, Liberty Hyde. "Notes on Tomatoes." Agricultural College of Michigan *Bulletin,* no. 19 (1886): 3–15.

———. "Notes on Tomatoes, Etc." Agricultural College of Michigan *Bulletin,* no. 31 (1887): 3–36.

Barker, Nicolas. *Hortus Eystettensis: The Bishop's Garden and Besler's Magnificent Book.* New York: Harry N. Abrams, 1994.

Boches, Peter S., and James R. Myers. "Occurrence of Anthocyanin in Cultivated Tomato." *Tomato Genetics Cooperative Report* 57 (2007): 14–19.

Baldoni, Remigio. *Il Pomodoro Industriale e da Tavola.* Rome: Ramo Editoriale Degli Agrocoltori, 1940.

Bertolli, Paul. *Cooking by Hand.* New York: Clarkson Potter, 2003.

Boswell, Victor R., et al. "Descriptions of Types of Principal American Varieties of Tomatoes." United States Department of Agriculture *Miscellaneous Publication,* no. 160 (October 1933): 1–23.

Boswell, Victor R. "Improvement and Genetics of Tomatoes, Peppers, and Eggplant." United States Department of Agriculture *Yearbook of Agriculture* (1937): 176–87.

Burr, Fearing. *The Field and Garden Vegetables of America: Containing Full Descriptions of Nearly Eleven Hundred Species and Varieties; with Directions for Propagation, Culture, and Use.* Boston: Crosby and Nichols, 1863.

Burr, Fearing. *The Field and Garden Vegetables of America: Containing Full Descriptions of Nearly Eleven Hundred Species and Varieties; with Directions for Propagation, Culture, and Use,* 1865 (2d ed). Reprint, with a preface by Kent Whealy and an introduction by Robert F. Becker. Chillicothe, Ill.: American Botanist Booksellers, 1994.

Carncross, John W., ed. "The Rutgers Tomato." *American Tomato Yearbook* (1951): 8–9.

Carver, George Washington. "How to Grow the Tomato and 115 Ways to Prepare it for the Table." 2d ed. Tuskegee Institute *Bulletin,* no. 36. Tuskegee, Ala.: Tuskegee Institute Press, 1936.

Cavagnaro, David. "Cushions, Stuffers, and Oxhearts." *Harrowsmith* (July–August 1989): 55–61.

Creasy, Rosalind. *Cooking from the Garden.* San Francisco: Sierra Club Books, 1988.

Cutler, Karan Davis, ed. *Tantalizing Tomatoes.* Brooklyn: Brooklyn Botanical Garden Publications, 1997.

Darwin, Sarah C., Sandra Knapp, and Iris E. Peralta. "Taxonomy of Tomatoes in the Galápagos Islands: Native and Introduced Species of *Solanum* section *Lycopersicon* (Solanaceae)." *Systematics and Biodiversity* 1, no. 1 (May 2003): 29–53.

Daunay, Marie-Christine; Henri Laterrot, and Jules Janick. "Iconography of the Solanaceae from Antiquity to the XVII Century: A Rich Source of Information on Genetic Diversity and Uses." In *Solanaceae VI: Genomics Meets Biodiversity, Proceedings of the Sixth International Solanaceae Conference,* edited by D. M. Spooner and others. *Acta Horticulturae* 745, June 2007.

Deppe, Carol. *Breed Your Own Vegetable Varieties: The Gardener's and Farmer's Guide to Plant Breeding and Seed Saving.* White River Junction, Vt.: Chelsea Green, 2000.

"Descriptors for Tomato (*Lycopersicon spp.*)." Rome: International Plant Genetic Resources Institute, 1996.

Dibble, C. E., and A. J. O. Anderson. *General History of the Things of New Spain,* Fray Bernardino de Sahagun, Book 10, *The People.* Translated from Aztec into English with notes and illustrations in thirteen parts. Monographs of the School of American Research and the Museum of New Mexico, part XI, 1961.

Esquinas-Alcazar, Jose T. "Genetic Resources of Tomatoes and Wild Relatives." Rome: International Board for Plant Genetic Resources, 1981.

Fowler, Cary and Pat Mooney. *Shattering: Food, Politics, and the Loss of Genetic Diversity.* Tucson: University of Arizona Press, 1990.

Gorman, John. "The Tomato Factory." Snook, Tex.: Mr. Tomato, 1978.

Grewe, Rudolf. "The Arrival of the Tomato in Spain and Italy: Early Recipes." *Journal of Gastronomy* 3, no. 2 (Summer 1987): 67–83.

"Guidelines for the Conduct of Tests for Distinctness, Homogeneity and Stability (Tomato)." Geneva: International Union for the Protection of New Varieties and Plants, 2001.

Hale, Sarah Josepha. *The Good Housekeeper.* 1841. Reprint ed., with a foreword by Janice Bluestein Langone. Mineola, N.Y.: Dover Publications, 1996.

Harlan, Jack R. *The Living Fields: Our Agricultural Heritage.* Cambridge: Cambridge University Press, 1995.

Harris, C. H. "Meigs-Made Tags Are Being Worn by Thousands of Dogs in America," *Athens (Ohio) Messenger,* January 24, 1951.

Hedrick, Ulysses P. *The Peaches of New York. Report of the New York Agricultural Experiment Station for the Year 1916.* Albany: J. B. Lyon, 1917.

Hedrick, Ulysses P. *Sturtevant's Notes on Edible Plants.* Albany: J. B. Lyon, 1919.

Heuvelink, Ep, ed. *Tomatoes.* Oxfordshire, U.K.: CABI Publishing, 2005.

Ibsen, Gary. *The Great Tomato Book.* Berkeley: Ten Speed Press, 1999.

"Italian Canners Step into the American Picture." *Western Canner and Packer,* September 1935.

Jenkins, J. A. "The Origin of the Cultivated Tomato." *Economic Botany* 2 (1948): 379–92.

Johnson, Charles. *The Seed Grower: A Practical Treatise on Growing Vegetable and Flower Seeds and Bulbs for the Market.* Marietta, Pa.: 1906.

———. *The Seedsman's Assistant: Compendium of the Growing Sources of Seeds, Vegetables, and Flowers.* Marietta, Pa.: 1904.

Jones, J. Benton. *Tomato Plant Culture: In the Field, Greenhouse, and Home Garden.* Boca Raton, Fla.: CRC Press, 1999.

Jones, J. B., et al. *Compendium of Tomato Diseases.* 2d ed. St. Paul: APS Press, forthcoming.

Jones, J. B., John Paul Jones, R. E. Stall, and Thomas A. Zitter, eds., *Compendium of Tomato Diseases.* St. Paul: APS Press, 2006.

Kornerup, A., and J. H. Wanscher. *Methuen Handbook of Colour.* 3d ed. London: Eyre Methuen, 1978. Originally published as *Farver I Farver* (Copenhagen: Politikens Forlag, 1961).

Lambeth, Victor N., E. F. Straten, and M. L. Fields. "Fruit Quality Attributes of 250 Foreign and Domestic Tomato Accessions." University of Missouri *Research Bulletin* no. 908 (May 1966): 1–53.

Livingston, A. W. *Livingston and the Tomato*. 1893. Reprint ed., with foreword and appendix by Andrew F. Smith. Columbus: Ohio State University Press, 1998.

Luckwill, Leonard C. "The Evolution of the Cultivated Tomato." *Journal of the Royal Horticultural Society* 68 (1943): 19–25.

———. "The Genus *Lycopersicon*: An Historical, Biological, and Taxonomic Survey of the Wild and Cultivated Tomatoes." Aberdeen University Studies, no. 120. Aberdeen: Aberdeen University Press, 1943.

Magelli, E. *Coltivazione del Pomodoro*. 2d ed. Florence: Vallecchi Editore, 1958.

Male, Carolyn J. *100 Heirloom Tomatoes for the American Garden*. New York: Workman Publishing, 1999.

Marra, John L. "The Mortgage Lifter: A Man and His Tomato." *Goldenseal* 20, no. 2 (1994): 9–16.

Maynard, Donald N., and George J. Hochmuth. *Knott's Handbook for Vegetable Growers*. 5th ed. Hoboken, N.J.: John Wiley and Sons, 2007.

McCormack, Jeffrey H. "Isolation Distances: Principles and Practices of Isolation Distances for Seed Crops: An Organic Seed Production Manual for Seed Growers in the Mid-Atlantic and Southern U.S." www.savingourseed.org, 2004.

———. "Tomato Seed Production: An Organic Seed Production Manual for Seed Growers in the Mid-Atlantic and Southern U. S." www.savingourseed.org, 2004.

McCue, George Allen. "The History of the Use of the Tomato: An Annotated Bibliography." *Annals of the Missouri Botanical Garden* 39, no. 4 (1952): 289–348.

McGee, Harold. *On Food and Cooking: The Science and Lore of the Kitchen*. Revised ed. New York: Scribner, 2004.

Meisner, Marvin H. *Giant Tomatoes: Giant Yields, Giant Weights*. Norton, Wash.: Annedawn, 2007.

Morrison, Gordon. "Tomato Varieties." Michigan Agricultural Experiment Station *Special Bulletin* 290 (1938): 3–68.

Muller, Cornelius H. "A Revision of the Genus *Lycopersicon*." United States Department of Agriculture *Miscellaneous Publication* no. 382 (July 1940): 1–28.

———. "The Taxonomy and Distribution of the Genus *Lycopersicon*." *National Horticultural Magazine* (July 1940): 157–60.

Nicholson, George, ed. *The Illustrated Dictionary of Gardening: A Practical and Scientific Encyclopaedia of Horticulture for Gardeners and Botanists*. Vol. IV, T to A, and Supplement. London: L. Upcott Gill, 1886, 1901.

Pacher, Sara. "A Small Seed Company Is Saving a Precious Plant Heritage." *Mother Earth News* (January–February 1988).

Pellett, Frank C., and Melvin A. Pellett. *Practical Tomato Culture*. New York: A. T. De La Mare, 1930.

Peralta, Iris Edith, and David M. Spooner. "Classification of Wild Tomatoes: A Review." *Tomo* 28, no. 1 (2000): 45–54.

Richman, Irwin. "The History of the Tomato in America." *Proceedings of the New Jersey Historical Society* 80 (1962): 151–73.

Rick, Charles M. "The Tomato." *Scientific American* 239, no. 2 (1978): 76–87.

Robinson, Richard W., and S. Shannon. "New Yorker: An Early Tomato Variety with a Bonus." *Farm Research* 32, no. 4 (January–March, 1967): 6–7.

Robinson, Richard W., S. Shannon, and W. Mishanec. "Low Temperature Influences Pollen Production and Fruit Set of Tomatoes." *Farm Research* (April–June, 1965): 13.

Rubatsky, Vincent E., and Mas Yamaguchi. *World Vegetables: Principles, Production, and Nutritive Values*. 2d ed. Gaithersburg, Md.: Aspen Publishers, 1999.

Schermerhorn, Lyman G. "Introducing 'Queens,' Early Market Tomato for New Jersey." *Horticultural News* (November 1950).

Seed Savers Exchange, various editors. *Harvest Edition*. 27 vols. Decorah, Iowa: Seed Savers Exchange, 1981–2007.

Seed Savers Exchange, various editors. *Summer Edition*. 20 vols. Decorah, Iowa: Seed Savers Exchange, 1988–2007.

Seed Savers Exchange. *Seed Savers Yearbook*. 32 vols. Decorah, Iowa, 1975–2007.

Smith, Andrew F. *Pure Ketchup: A History of America's National Condiment*. Washington, D.C.: Smithsonian Institution Press, 2001.

———. *The Tomato in America: Early History, Culture, and Cookery*. Columbia, S.C.: University of South Carolina Press, 1994.

———. *Souper Tomatoes: The Story of America's Favorite Food*. New Brunswick, N.J.: Rutgers University Press, 2000.

Stevens, M. Allen, and C. M. Rick. "Genetics and Breedings." In *The Tomato Crop: A Scientific Basis for Improvement*, edited by J. G. Atherton and J. Rudich. London: Chapman and Hall, 1986.

Tanksley, Steven D. "The Genetic, Developmental, and Molecular Bases of Fruit Size and Shape Variation in Tomato." *Plant Cell* 16, supplement (2004): 181–89.

Tracy, William W. *List of American Varieties of Vegetables for the Years 1901 and 1902*. Washington, D.C.: U.S. Department of Agriculture, Bureau of Plant Industry *Bulletin* no. 21, 1903.

———. *Tomato Culture*. Revised ed. New York: Orange Judd, 1919.

Kinet, J. M., and M. M. Peet. "Tomato." In *The Physiology of Vegetable Crops*, edited by H. C. Wien. Oxfordshire, U.K.: CABI Publishing, 1999.

Van der Knaap, Esther, and Steven D. Tanksley. "The Making of a Bell Pepper–Shaped Tomato Fruit: Identification of Loci Controlling Fruit Morphology in Yellow Stuffer Tomato." *Theor. Appl. Genet.* 107 (2003): 139–147.

Vilmorin-Andrieux. *Les Plantes Potagères: Description et Culture des Principaux Légumes des Climats Tempérés*. Paris: Vilmorin-Andrieux, 1883, 1891, 1904, 1925.

Vilmorin-Andrieux. *The Vegetable Garden: Illustrations, Descriptions, and Culture of the Garden Vegetables of Cold and Temperate Climates*, trans. W. Miller. London: John Murray, 1885.

Vilmorin-Andrieux. *Dictionnaire Vilmorin des Plantes Potagères*. Paris: Ateliers A. B. C., 1947.

Whealy, Kent, ed. *Garden Seed Inventory*. Decorah, Iowa: Seed Savers Exchange, 1985, 1988, 1992, 1995, 1999, 2004.

Lowell Wingett, "Ben F. Quisenberry, Jack of All Businesses, Retires Today from Upriver U.S. Mail Route," *Pomeroy (Ohio) Daily Sentinel*, December 11, 1959.

Work, Paul. *The Tomato*. New York: Orange Judd, 1942.

Young, P. A., and J. W. MacArthur. "Horticultural Characters of Tomatoes." Texas Agricultural Experiment Station *Bulletin*, no. 698, 1947.

Young, Robert E. "Trellis Tomatoes." Massachusetts Agricultural Experiment Station *Bulletin*, no. 419, 1944.

Zago, F. *La Coltivazione Industriale Dei Pomodoro*. Casalmonferrato: Casale, 1913.

acknowledgments

My deepest thanks to the following people and institutions: Jose Esquinas-Alcazar; Tom Andres; Teresa Arellanos; Larry Ashmead; Daniel Atha; Jacques Aubourg; Nate Auchter; Maya Baran; Andrey Baranovski; Angelo Barbetti; Bob Barnitz; Matt Barthel; Andrew Beckman; Dorothy Beiswenger; Clive Blazey; Peter Boches; Annie Bond; Will Bonsall; Matthew Bouloutian; Philippa Brathwaite; Sandra Bywater; Alex Caron; Ariella Chezar; Ethne Clarke; Larry Condon; Bryan Connolly; Shelly Coon; John Coykendall; Ros Creasy; Keith Crotz; Shannon Croutch; Rachel Crow; Marie-Christine Daunay; Sylvia Davatz; Jeff Dawson; Ludovico del Balzo; Dan DiClerico; Lou Di Palo; Glenn Drowns; Linda Drowns; Jennifer Enloe; Ken Ettlinger; Eve Felder; Sandi Fellman; Gina Fiorillo-Brady; Colin Flynn; Cary Fowler; David Gentilcore; Jeremiath Gettle; Vivian Ghazarian; Lynn Goldberg; John Gorman; LuAnn Gorman; Phillip Griffiths; Diana Gurieva; Joan Dye Gussow; Khanh Hamilton; Neil Hamilton; Tom Hauch; Arthur Heiser; Barbara Heiser; James Hill; Don Hubbard; Steph Hughes; Gary Ibsen; Frederick Ineman; Jules Janick; Kevin Jeffreys; Liza Jernow; Rob Johnston; Beth Jordan; Addie Juell; Amy King; Annik LaFarge; Henri Laterrot; CR Lawn; Dick Levine; Ellen Levine; Matt Liebman; Neil Lockhart; Gregory Long; Brent Loy; Barbara Ann Lund; Deborah Madison; Mike Madison; M. Mark; Ken Marshall; Don Maynard; Donald McClelland; Jeff McCormack; Janet McDonald; Jan Merchant; Laura Merrick; Steve Miller; Bill Minkey; George Moriarty; Aly Mostel; Fanny Moyse; Jim Myers; Gary Nabhan; Michael Nee; Jeff Nekola; Scott Newman; Merlyn Niedens; Rose Marie Nichols McGee; Eileen Pagan; Ulrike Paradine; Harry Paris; Laura Pillar; Garrett Pittenger; Roger Quisenberry; Colin Randel; Karen Rinaldi; Dick Robinson; Grace Romero; Emery Ruger; Linda Sapp; Arthur Schaffer; Victor Schrager; Burkhard Schulz; Debbie Scott; Jay Scott; Bob Sherman; David Smith; Gian Piero Soressi; David Spooner; Gary Staley; Bob Stein; Emma Sweeney; John Swenson; Mona Talbott; Jim Ternier; Kyle Tobin-Williams; Nick Trautwein; Joanne Thuente; Sherry Vance; Esther van der Knaap; Greg Villepique; Tom Wagner; Kim Watson; Jim Waltrip; Marsha Weiner; Aaron Whaley; Diane Ott Whealy; Kent Whealy; James A. Wolfe; Abbie Zabar; Tom Zitter; Ethel Zoe Bailey Horticultural Catalogue Collection, Bailey Hortorium, Cornell University; Special Collections, National Agricultural Library, Beltsville, Maryland; LuEsther T. Mertz Library, New York Botanical Garden; Perth and Kinross Council Archive (Scotland); San Joaquin County Historical Society and Museum; Robert Becker Memorial Library, Seed Savers Exchange; Humanities and Social Sciences Library, New York Public Library.

index

Published by Bloomsbury USA, New York
Distributed to the trade by Macmillan

All papers used by Bloomsbury USA are natural, recyclable products made from
wood grown in well-managed forests. The manufacturing processes conform to
the environmental regulations of the country of origin.

LIBRARY OF CONGRESS CATALOGING-IN-PUBLICATION DATA HAS BEEN APPLIED FOR.

ISBN-10 1-59691-291-X
ISBN-13 978-1-59691-291-5

First U.S. Edition 2008

10 9 8 7 6 5 4 3 2 1

Designed and typeset by Matthew Bouloutian and Vivian Ghazarian

Printed in Singapore by Tien Wah Press